Month-By-Month™

WHAT TO DO EACH MONTH TO HAVE A BEAUTIFUL GARDEN ALL YEAR

GARDENING in WASHINGTON & OREGON

Published by Cool Springs Press, a Division of Thomas Nelson, Inc., P. O. Box 141000, Nashville, Tennessee, 37214.

Cataloging in Publication Data is Available.
ISBN: 1-59186-106-3

First printing 2006

Printed in Singapore
10 9 8 7 6 5 4 3 2 1

Managing Editor: Ramona Wilkes
Designer: James Duncan, James Duncan Creative
Production Artist: S.E. Anderson
Horticulture Editor: Christina Pfeiffer

On the cover: Rhododendron 'Livonia Lindsley', photo by Jerry Pavia

Visit the Cool Springs Press website at **www.coolspringspress.net**

Month-By-Month™

WHAT TO DO EACH MONTH TO HAVE A BEAUTIFUL GARDEN ALL YEAR

GARDENING in WASHINGTON & OREGON

MARY ROBSON

WITH CHRISTINA PFEIFFER

COOL
SPRINGS
PRESS

Nashville, Tennessee
A Division of Thomas Nelson, Inc.
www.ThomasNelson.com

DEDICATION

To Washington and Oregon gardeners, hoping they experience the pleasure of a lifetime learning about plants and the partnership between plants and people. With thankful remembrance of horticulturalist Liberty Hyde Bailey, who wrote: "Sensitiveness to all life is the highest product of education." (1898)

—Mary Robson and Christina Pfeiffer

ACKNOWLEDGEMENTS

Christina Pfeiffer gave her attention, intelligence, and knowledge to shaping and forming this book, which would not exist without her participation in it. Her four chapters on Trees, Shrubs, Vines and Groundcovers, and Native Plants combine solid information and lively writing. And she made the General Introduction focused and useful. Her work as Horticulture Editor kept it accurate.

Thanks also to Pat Munts, horticulturalist from Spokane, Washington, who reviewed all chapters and zone information to keep me on track for colder inland areas. Pat knows her stuff and shares her knowledge generously. Readers of the *Spokane Spokesman-Review* can meet Pat Munts through her gardening column. She helped me to learn about cold weather roses from Heather Figg, Spokane Rose Society; Larry Parton, Northland Rosarium, and Steve Smith, Manager, Manito Rose Garden, Manito Park, Spokane.

Extension colleagues in both Washington and Oregon provided help: I appreciate the writings of Tonie Fitzgerald, Marianne Ophardt, and Dr. Tom Cook at OSU, as well as the WSU Turfgrass Science Team, led by Dr. Gwen Stahnke.

For general encouragement, my writing friend Julia Eulenberg boosted my output at a crucial time.

—Mary Robson

I am grateful to the innumerable horticultural friends, colleagues, and teachers who have enriched my life personally and professionally. The influence of their shared knowledge and pleasure in engaging with the plant world is reflected throughout my work on these pages.

I am indebted to the staff of the Miller Horticultural Library for their knowledgeable and kind assistance, for their outstanding collection, and for the haven of the library itself in which to think, write, and study.

Mary Robson has been a generous mentor and collaborator. She provided thoughtful feedback and kept me focused on what was most important to include for our readers. I am deeply appreciative of her invitation to join her on this effort.

—Christina Pfeiffer

Thanks also to the Cool Springs Press publishing team of Hank McBride and Cindy Games for their support, and especially to Ramona Wilkes, extraordinary editor, who made it work.

CONTENTS

INTRODUCTION

Welcome to Gardening in Washington and Oregon!

The long Pacific coast, Cascade Mountains, rivers, rainforest, and desert of Washington and Oregon's terrain influence the character and life cycles of the gardens and plant communities of this region. Garden tasks of one kind or another might occupy part of every day of the year in the milder western reaches, or be concentrated into a few months in hotter but shorter growing seasons found east of the Cascade Mountains. But in all areas, a garden's beauty and benefit carry throughout the year. *Month-by-Month Gardening in Washington and Oregon*, companion to *Washington and Oregon Gardener's Guide* (Cool Springs Press) is designed to help you maximize the beauty of your garden every month of the year. It focuses on the cultivation of plants selected specifically for our region. It contains a wealth of garden management tips and routines that help you get the most out of your gardening efforts. Each chapter of this book follows the progress of the garden through the months. Divided by plant groups, this book will help you build your own planned routine of garden activities matched to the rhythm of the seasons in your location.

"Rhythm of the seasons" reminds all gardeners that plants don't live by the traditional written calendar. They respond to cues of light intensity and day length, of temperature and moisture patterns. Seasonal

climate factors influence the cycles of growth and dormancy through the year. These monthly garden calendars are valuable reminders of what plants need. But stay attuned to the weather because plants grow more quickly or slowly as a result of temperature patterns and rain or snow. Looking at weather, the plants, and the monthly calendar is the right combination. As you become better acquainted with your own patch of earth and its seasonal benchmarks, you will be able to develop your own personal monthly guideposts.

KNOW WHERE YOU ARE

To garden successfully in Washington and Oregon you must first understand the geography and its effect on garden climate. The Cascade Mountains divide the region north to south, and differing climates occur within those areas. West of the Cascades, ocean air keeps winter temperatures moderate, seldom dipping below the twenties, though locations along the mountains and in the Willamette Valley regularly turn colder. The high Cascade peaks retain much of the winter clouds and precipitation to the west side. Mild, rainy winters and cool, dry summers pervade. Most of the area lies in gardening Zone 8, cooler Zone 7 along the Cascade foothills, and a spot of nearly tropical Zone 9 on the southern Oregon coast.

The Inland Northwest, lying east of the Cascades and west

of the Rocky Mountains, copes with frigid winters and sunny, hot, arid summers. It is sunnier and drier than the west side. Much of this area falls into Zones 5 or 6, but deep winter cold may plunge temperatures to below Zone 5 in eastern Oregon's high desert country.

LOW FAHRENHEIT TEMPERATURES OF WASHINGTON AND OREGON ZONES	
Zones	Temperature
Zone 5	-20 to -10
Zone 6	-10 to 0
Zone 7	0 to 10
Zone 8	10 to 15
Zone 9	15 to 25

IT WILL BE DRY HERE

The common impression that the Coastal Pacific Northwest has soggy rain year-round isn't accurate. Available rainfall is probably the most limiting factor to garden cultivation throughout the region. A few areas on and near the Olympic Peninsula in western Washington form a genuine temperate rainforest with over one hundred inches of rain per year. Certainly the thirty-five-inch average in Seattle would be ideal for plants, but most of the rain falls during winter when plant growth is least active.

For gardeners in all parts of Washington and Oregon, summer water management is a major necessity. Our driest low-rain season coincides with the active growth period for plants. East of the Cascades, the total annual rainfall can be less than twelve inches. Referring to the "high desert" country of Oregon may seem strange, but summer heat, dry winter cold, and little moisture make the

term accurate. Washington and Oregon live with the paradox that our rainy national reputation doesn't provide what plants need in summer when it's dry here.

REGIONAL GARDENING CLIMATES

Use the USDA hardiness zone map and the accompanying monthly average temperature and precipitation tables to help you determine the patterns of the growing season for your area. Tables, because they are averages, will not reflect specific seasonal conditions one year at a time. Keep your own records for your garden.

Seattle/Western Washington

Western Washington's maritime climate is moderate and welcoming to a broad palette of plants. Conifers, ferns, and broadleaf evergreens dominate much of the native forests. Summer temperatures are moderate, with the typical growing season from May through September, April to November in milder reaches. The occasional hot spell reaching into the nineties can intensify the already droughty summer conditions. People in sweltering summer climates can't comprehend that air conditioners are rare west of the Cascades. Cool temperatures mean that plants requiring heat, such as tomatoes, need special encouragement to ripen here.

The warmest and driest part of the season falls between August and September. Plants like peaches, needing bright, hot growing conditions throughout the summer, do not fare as well here as they do east of the Cascades.

First frosts come to the **Seattle** area mid-November, earlier in the month to the north and the foothills. Elevations below 1000 feet, especially near water, average winter temperatures above freezing in ordinary years. However, unexpected freezes are not uncommon in either spring or fall, damaging plants unconditioned for

the sudden cold. November and December are typically the darkest and wettest of the year. Non-irrigated soils are usually at their wettest by March and their driest by September. Nearer the Canadian border, northeast winds blowing out of the Fraser River Valley can rapidly draw temperatures down by twenty degrees in a few hours, killing plants from **Bellingham** in the south and west to parts of the **Olympic Peninsula**.

Okanogan Valley

One of the coolest corners of the state is found in the **Okanogan** river valley, where frosty nights can occur almost any time of year. Natural plant communities here are dominated by ponderosa pine and grasslands. An area with abundant summer sunshine and low precipitation, it receives about eleven inches per year, mostly in winter months with snowfall. Cold air drains from high ridges, but the many lakes moderate otherwise cooler conditions. The growing season falls between May and September, though frosts are known as late as June and can halt the growing season in early September. These sudden freezes can make growing conditions for many plants unreliable. Look to the resident native species as a guide to choosing garden plants, especially those adapted to similar conditions.

Spokane Area

The **Spokane** area climate can be harsh, reaching one hundred degrees in summer and falling below zero in winter. The growing season falls between May and early September. Summer sun is abundant, and gray winter months have freezing temperatures and snowfall. Annual precipitation averages sixteen inches, or less. Garden plants adapted to cold dormant seasons and hot summers will thrive here.

Richland, Tri-cities, Walla Walla

Closer to the Cascade Range, **Ellensburg** and **Yakima** have a greater number of frost-free days. A belt of warm eastward-flowing air comes in from the coast through the Columbia River Gorge stretching along the Yakima River through **Richland**, the **Tri-Cities** to **Walla Walla**. Winter temperatures here hover above freezing, at USDA Zone 7, and the growing season is a bit longer than the rest of eastern Washington.

Portland/Willamette Valley

The **Willamette Valley** in Oregon hosts some of the region's richest growing conditions for commercial nurseries and home gardens. The areas stretching through **Portland, Salem,** and **Eugene** share many characteristics with western Washington but are warmer and wetter throughout the year. However, the Portland area is vulnerable to the impact of cold winter winds out of the **Columbia Gorge** which can inflict serious ice damage to trees and other plants. The growing season falls between March and November.

Medford

Farther south toward the **Medford** area, the elevation is higher, temperatures cooler, and precipitation lessens to twenty inches per year. Chaparral conditions with scrubby, dry plants are found here. The vegetation becomes lush with higher precipitation nearer the coast. Average January temperatures are around thirty-eight degrees, though cold air draining off the mountains brings cooler night temperatures.

Bend/Redmond

Redmond and **Bend** in the Oregon central plateau are at a higher elevation with coarser weather conditions—high, flat country with strong winds and temperature extremes. Frost can come any time of year. Pine, juniper, and sage dominate

native plant communities here. Farther east to **Baker**, a high basin between two mountain ranges, is occupied largely by juniper forests and savannahs. Summers are dry and hot, reaching 100-degree highs. Long winters can reach down to minus twenty with scant snow cover. Annual precipitation is eleven inches.

MICROCLIMATES

Once aware of the general USDA hardiness zone, the precipitation patterns, and the growing season of their gardens, gardeners also need to be aware of the influence of microclimate conditions. Microclimates are those spots with slight variations from the greater area. You can see it on a neighborhood walk, passing a lilac bush in full sun on the west side of the street bursting with color, then half a block later find a lilac bush in the shade of a pine, facing east with no morning sun and no sign of color.

ELEMENTS OF THE MICROCLIMATE

Altitude affects temperature, and as any hiker knows, higher elevation means cooler temperatures. Fall frosts come earlier, and spring frosts stay later as elevations rise. A large body of water will moderate temperature extremes. Gardens near Puget Sound, for example, are less likely to freeze late in the season. But surprisingly these spots will remain cooler in very warm weather. Very low areas like valleys can also experience lower temperatures. Cold air flows downhill like water, and fruit growers planting hillside orchards know that very low sites have a higher risk of late spring freezes. The temperature halfway down a slope is more moderate than at the bottom. Be aware of heat radiated from pavement and buildings. A balcony garden facing west above the Pike Place Market in Seattle will have modified temperature: afternoon heat on a sunny day will radiate out of a concrete building after dark, with water moderating temperatures. A north-facing garden in North Bend that lacks these influences would stay colder as a result of exposure and the higher terrain.

Vegetation can also influence microclimate. Tall trees provide shelter from sun and wind. Humidity is greater amid groups of trees. Deciduous trees make cool shade in summer but let in warmth and light in winter. Hedges can provide windbreaks as well as shade. What are the microclimate conditions in your garden?

Temperature zone realities can be altered with microclimate conditions. For example, a tender plant in the warmest garden spot with extra winter protection, or placed against a south-facing stone wall results in the winter survival of a Zone 9 plant in Zone 8. Garden designers enjoy manipulating these zone-stretching realities.

SOIL—KNOWING WHAT IS UNDERFOOT

Soil provides the foundation for plant survival. It is the reservoir for moisture and nutrients where roots anchor and the home of insects and micro-organisms that decompose organic matter and improve tilth. Soil types vary throughout Washington and Oregon. Deep loam in the **Willamette** and **Puyallup River Valleys** drastically changes in other areas to shallow, mixed gravel, rock, and clay soils left thousands of years ago by receding glaciers. One gardener described her western Washington soil as "clay except for the rocks." With low rainfall east of the Cascades, soils in high desert country tend to be higher in pH (more alkaline) and soluble salts and have lower organic content than coastal loam soils. Urban areas are always a toss-up because of disturbance to native soils.

INTRODUCTION

Knowing the structure of your soil is one of the most important things you can do in your garden. Pick up a small damp handful of soil. Squeeze it, then force out a "ribbon" with your thumb, pressing the soil into a narrow band. Clay soil will hold together, allowing several inches of ribbon to develop, and it will also show the imprints of your fingers. Loam soil, a balance of clay and sand, will form a short but breakable ribbon. Sandy or gravelly soil won't hold together; it crumbles apart as you press. Another method is described on page 120.

CHARACTERISTICS OF SOIL TYPES

Clay soils can hold too much water. They drain slowly and are hard to dampen if they dry out. They do hold mineral nutrients well, requiring less fertilizer than sandy soils. Sandy soils allow plenty of air and oxygen to the roots, but drain too fast. They are difficult to keep moist in summer and don't hold nutrients very long. Loamy soils strike a good balance between texture and water, they remain fertile and drain well. Contrary to a common belief, clay garden soil cannot be readily improved by adding sand or gypsum! The tinier clay particles fill in the space between the much larger sand particles, causing the resulting mix to be even denser. Remember that concrete is made by mixing sand and fine-particle cement. Sometimes described as a cure-all for soil problems, gypsum is actually beneficial only to specific soil types and soil problems.

Both clay and sandy soils can be improved with a regular, modest addition of organic material such as compost, manures, biosolids (composted sewage sludge), aged sawdust, and organic mulches.

"Green manure" cover crops such as rye, buckwheat, or crimson clover can reduce weed invasions on bare ground and improve soil when they are later dug in to decompose in place. This practice is useful in vegetable and annual flower beds, which normally lie empty of plants until spring weather returns.

Maintaining organic matter for established plantings is best done with a surface application (topdressing) of amendments and mulch. Soil texture and nutrient content will be improved, and the population of decomposers—insects, earthworms, fungi, and microbes—will also increase. Choose well-composted material and add up to two inches over bare soils. Allow time for the compost to decompose into the soil before applying more, as it is possible to over-apply organic amendments. Use smaller amounts—about one inch—over ground covers and on arid soils where decomposition is much slower.

UNRAVELING THE pH MYSTERY

Most landscape plants commonly available in nurseries grow well in pH between 6.0 and 7.0, with 7.0 being neutral. Soils west of the Cascades tend to be acid, with pH from 5.0 to 6.0. Native plants such as salal and rhododendron grow well in these acidic conditions. Soils in eastern areas of Oregon and Washington are mostly alkaline, up to 7.5 or 8.0. Grasslands tend to be more alkaline and forest land more acid. Soil pH is also affected by the amount of annual rainfall, with alkaline (higher pH) soils more prevalent in arid regions.

HELPFUL HINTS

If the pH level is poor for the plant, additional fertilizer will not help. The pH will need to be lowered. Sulfur will lower pH; lime increases it. Soil tests are necessary to determine the correct amounts. Get an accurate diagnosis of the problem before choosing action, as yellowing leaves can be symptoms of several different maladies. Soil testing information comes from the Washington and Oregon Extension office. See page 288.

INTRODUCTION

Urban soils can have higher pH due to disturbance and contamination from gypsum and lime that wash into the ground from building and cement materials. A rhododendron (adapted to acidic soils) planted into a highly alkaline soil can develop yellowing, chlorotic leaves; its roots are unable to absorb needed nutrients at this pH level.

SOIL TESTING

Soil tests are essential to verify the need for fertilizers and soil amendments. Simple kits are available in garden centers to check soil pH and nutrient levels; however, for the most accurate information on what kind of soil you have, its fertility, organic matter content, and pH, you should send a sample to a soil laboratory (see Gardening Resources on the Web). Contact your local Washington State University or Oregon State University Extension Office for more information on soil testing.

NOW THAT YOU'RE READY TO GARDEN: TIPS FOR PREPARATION

Start with a soil test before you install a new landscape. Determine the soil texture, pH, fertility, organic content, and drainage patterns. This information helps you select plants naturally adapted to your resident soil type. Your local WSU or OSU Extension Office will be able to help you interpret the results or answer questions when the results come back.

Check soil drainage by digging a hole one foot deep and one foot wide. The ground should be moist—not saturated and not bone dry. To measure the drainage rate, fill the hole with water then time how long it takes recede. Water should drain out at the rate of one inch per hour. If drainage problems are severe, you may need to install subsurface drains before planting and correct the finished grade so that it has an even, gentle slope for positive surface drainage. Building berms, raised beds above the soil, is

also helpful where drainage is slow. When topsoil or a soil mix is to be added to build a berm, incorporate a layer of the new mix into the native soil to create a shallow transition zone between the two soils. Otherwise water will not drain freely where the two meet.

Spade or till the area when soil is damp. Cultivating soggy soil will cause compaction and damage. This is most serious for clay soils. Soils that have dried out completely are physically difficult to break up and do not accept additions of organic material readily. Not too wet, not too dry is the rule when handling soil.

A word of caution: Soil volume and level will shrink in subsequent years as the organics continue to decompose, often resulting in difficulties with drainage as the soil becomes more compact. With too much organic amendment, plants in these areas can sink as the soil does, which can result in roots being covered too deeply. For most soils west of the Cascades, five percent by weight (ten percent by volume) of organic materials will be adequate; arid soils east of the Cascades may need only half that amount. There is less risk of compaction if amendments are spread on the surface and organic content is maintained with yearly applications of organic mulch.

An effective, no-till method to prepare a new landscape bed is to apply a thick layer (six to eight inches) of *very coarse* organic mulch over the entire area at least a couple of months before you intend to plant. This can be done in summer for fall planting, or fall for spring planting. When available, wood chips from tree removal are an ideal material. Expose the soil surface as needed when you come back to plant.

USING FERTILIZER: OR, EVERYTHING IN MODERATION

While we casually call fertilizer "plant food," it is really more "soil food." Photosynthesis makes the

INTRODUCTION

food; nutrients from the soil combine with solar energy and water to produce carbohydrates. We apply fertilizer to supply additional nutrients to the soil.

They come packaged in different forms, from organic (derived from previously living sources) to synthetic (manufactured, generally from non-living sources). Both sources provide the same nutrients, but many gardeners choose organic fertilizers, which support the soil micro-organism population.

UNDERSTANDING N-P-K

Nitrogen (N), phosphorous (P), and potassium (K) are the nutrients found in "complete" fertilizers, with the most critical for all plants being nitrogen. Nitrogen moves down away from root zones during rainy weather and is the nutrient most frequently lacking in all soil types. Phosphorous and potassium are less likely to be deficient in landscape soils. Excess phosphorus is harmful to beneficial soil fungi (mycorrhizae), which enhance nitrogen uptake in roots of woody plants, and pollutes fresh water by causing excessive algae growth. Sensible fertilizer application can protect water resources while ensuring good plant growth and performance. Apply fertilizers only as needed and avoid times when heavy irrigation or rainfall can wash nitrates below the rooting zone into ground water.

Slow- and controlled-release fertilizers provide a flow of nutrients through the growing season. Nutrients are released from organic products such as fish emulsion, cottonseed meal, or manures through decomposition by soil fungi and bacteria when the soil is warm and moist. Synthetic products such as Nutricote or Osmocote release their nutrients slowly, and the rate of release depends upon the coating type, temperature, and moisture. In general, they release faster with wetter conditions and higher temperatures. Water must partner with all fertilizer types for the nutrients to be available to roots. Don't apply granular fertilizers to dry soil; they'll be ineffective and may burn roots. And in drought conditions, using less fertilizer reduces water needed for survival because the plants don't grow as vigorously.

APPLICATION RATES

Different types of plants have differing needs. Established trees and shrubs need little or no fertilizer if they are growing well. Actively growing plants can benefit from moderate springtime applications during the first years of establishment. Regular fertilization on a careful schedule is needed for vegetables, turf, annuals, roses, and plants in containers.

See the individual chapters on different plant types for more specific information.

Fertilizer packages list N-P-K content by percentage weight per one hundred pounds of fertilizer: a 5-10-10 contains five percent N, ten percent P, and ten percent K. Some products include some or all of the ten other "trace" nutrient elements. With so many different N-P-K ratios available, it can be confusing as to what to use and how much to apply.

A SIMPLE FERTILIZING FORMULA

The simplest approach for surface applied granular products is to calculate for the amount of actual nutrient element needed per area. For example, to apply one pound of actual nitrogen per 1000 square feet of a lawn or landscape bed with a 21-0-0 product:

1 pound nitrogen / 21 x 100 =
4.75 pounds of 21-0-0 product

This is also a helpful way to calculate the relative cost of different products. To apply 1 pound nitrogen per 1000 square feet with 10 percent nitrogen content, you would need 10 pounds of product—about twice as much as the 21 percent nitrogen formulation.

INTRODUCTION

Liquid fertilizers have label directions for mixing at different concentrations for different plant types. Check the package to find out how much nitrogen is in the formula. Too little nitrogen will result in poor growth. Too much nitrogen produces lush, leafy shoots, but the plant may not flower well. Again, use these products in moderation for the best results. Nitrogen levels of 6, 7, or 8 provide moderate fertilization. If your fertilizer formula is high in nitrogen, such as 20-20-20, use just half the concentration suggested on the package.

FERTILIZER IS NOT A CURE-ALL

In recent years, there has been less emphasis on routine fertilizing. Fertilizer cannot fix poor soil or bad drainage. Nor can it help if plants are installed in the wrong light condition: a shade loving *Skimmia* turning yellow in the sun won't green up with a fertilizer application. Nor can nutrients be absorbed when root rots or poor soil drainage are present. In fact, declining or diseased plants should not be fertilized. For best plant health, don't overfertilize. Disease and insect difficulties can intensify on plants receiving too much nitrogen. Aphids and powdery mildew are two common problems that get worse on the kind of extra succulent growth that results under high nitrogen applications. Overfertilized plants will also require more water—difficult to supply in dry summers. And in arid regions, a harmful buildup of dissolved salts in the soil can occur.

If the plants appear normal in color and produce good blossoms, leaves, and branches then fertilizer is not needed.

When should the garden be fertilized? Apply fertilizer to the garden in late winter or earliest spring, just as plants move into active growth. For trees, shrubs, and most herbaceous perennials, fertilizing once a season using a moderate nitrogen formula such as 4-2-2 is generally adequate unless a soil test reveals other needs. Spread the fertilizer *on top of the soil* over the root zone and water it in. Newly installed trees and shrubs do not usually require fertilization at planting time unless soils are known to be nutrient deficient.

Plants that grow throughout the summer season require regular fertilizer. Annuals or perennials that are being grown in containers should receive a complete fertilizer twice a month until frost to keep them growing well. Hybrid tea roses and others grown for exhibition require fertilizer monthly. Apply rose fertilizer as late as the middle or end of July, but no later.

MULCH

An annual application of coarse-textured organic mulch is one of the best things you can do to maintain good garden soil and healthy plants. Good mulching habits can lighten the work of weeding, watering, and fertilizing. It protects soil from surface erosion, it improves water penetration and holds in moisture, and it reduces weed growth. Mulch will insulate against frost heaving in cold regions. As it decays, it replenishes soil nutrients and organic content. Thicker layers of mulch can gradually help improve compacted soil on new sites.

Mulch can be put down anytime, except under very wet or saturated conditions. Use it to cover bare ground immediately after weeds are pulled. Mulch when new plants are put in the ground to reduce moisture stress. Mulch in fall to insulate against frost heaving. In winter rain regions, fall mulch will suppress winter weeds and improve soil tilth during the extended moist conditions of the dormant season.

MAKING YOUR OWN MULCH

Leaf mold (crumbled, composted leaves) is a great source of organic mulch for the garden. The fragrance of leaf mold is pleasant and mild, and it is only available as a homemade product. If your

INTRODUCTION

yard is blessed with an abundance of autumn leaves, pile them into a bin or wire enclosure, wet thoroughly, and cover the top. Another method is to compost fallen leaves inside plastic bags. Small leaves, such as Japanese maple, birch or alder, break down in about six months. Be sure they are damp or wet when filling the bag, tie it at the top, and poke some holes in the sides with a pitchfork for some air circulation. If your garden contains huge leaves, such as big leaf maple or evergreen leaves such as laurel, they will compost better if shredded or chopped before being bagged. In all cases, keep your leaves damp throughout the decomposition.

How much and when to apply? Mulch should be kept at about three to four inches for most landscape plantings. Never bury the trunks of trees and shrubs in mulch—it's damaging to the health of the trunk and an invitation to basal rots and plant stress.

Even with all this good work that mulch does for the garden, too much of it can be harmful. If mulch gets too thick, it can block vital oxygen exchange for roots and soil or cause the soil to stay too wet or cold. It's best to let mulch break down and diminish enough for the soil to start showing through before new mulch is added. When replenishing existing mulch, keep the total

MULCH FROM YOUR LOCAL FRIENDLY ARBORIST

Wood chips from tree services are becoming a popular source of mulch. Find out how large the loads are beforehand; if the resulting yardage is much more than you need, you may want to arrange to share with a neighbor. Let fresh wood chips age or compost for at least a few weeks before use. Look for a place away from large established trees to stockpile all mulch materials since the roots of large trees can be smothered by the heavy weight and heat of materials stacked over them.

depth at three to four inches for coarse material, or two to three inches for finer textured mulches.

WEEDS

Pulling weeds can be the bane of pleasure gardening. Or it can be a reasonably enjoyable routine that immerses you into the life of your garden.

Tips for weed control include:

1. Use well-adapted plants that crowd out undesirable weeds.

2. Use mulch. There will be fewer weeds and they will be easier to pull.

FIGURING OUT HOW MUCH MULCH YOU NEED

Begin by measuring the square feet of garden space that needs to be covered. Remember some of the space is occupied by plant trunks and stems. The table below provides some guidelines based on an average coverage of three inches deep, suitable to average landscape situations.

Amount of Mulch	Square Feet Covered (3 to 4 inches deep)
1.5 cubic foot bag	5 square feet or a $2^1/_2$-foot diameter circle
2 cubic foot bag	8 square feet or a 3-foot diameter circle
3 cubic foot bag	12 square feet or a 4-foot diameter circle
27 cubic feet	Approximately 100 square feet

[0.25 foot depth (3-inches) x square foot area to cover = cubic feet of mulch needed]

INTRODUCTION

3. Weed frequently to eliminate them before they complete flowering and seed production.

5. A spading fork and the hori hori weeding knife are two of the gardener's tools for getting weeds out roots and all.

Fabric or plastic weed-barriers are often seen as a quick fix for weed control, but they can cause problems over time. Some weeds, such as horsetail, have been known to penetrate fabric barriers. Other weeds often end up growing in organic material accumulating on top of the fabric. Fabric cover also prevents replenishment of organic matter in the soil.

HANDLING MONSTER WEEDS

Special tactics may be needed to subdue very dense weed growth or particularly persistent weed types. Information on identification and control methods for difficult weed species can be obtained through regional noxious weed boards as well as WSU and OSU Extension Offices. (See Resources.) Control of some noxious species that pose serious economic and/or environmental threat is required by law. Tansy ragwort on rangelands is one example; purple loosestrife in wetlands is another.

WATERING TECHNIQUES TO KEEP PLANTS GROWING

As population grows, efficient water use is crucial because water is both scarcer and more expensive. Living with limited summer water is a condition that affects every gardener in Washington and Oregon. But dry conditions don't necessarily result in a desiccated landscape.

Remember that water is taken in through the roots, not the leaves. Speedy sprinkling, even if it's fun to wave the hose on a bright summer day, doesn't reach the roots. The same rings true for our swift summer showers.

Some good garden planning helps water management.

1. Select plants that will manage dry times, although it's certainly not necessary to avoid using water-lovers.

2. Prepare soil properly, maintain organic matter, and use mulches to help with water retention.

3. Group plants according to their water needs and cultural adaptations. A gathering of thirsty ferns, hostas, and rhododendrons tucked into a shady corner can thrive with a well-placed soaker hose and regular irrigation. Group water-loving roses, perennial, and annuals for brilliant summer color in a spot where hoses or sprinkling systems will deliver sufficient moisture.

Plants lose water through their leaves in transpiration, which is normal and necessary for health. But plants can wilt when the soil is too dry. Overcast days with misty rain may not provide much measurable rainfall, but they do reduce plant water loss.

WSU soil scientist Dr. Craig Cogger, Ph.D., reminds us that "soil type or texture is a major determining factor of how much water a soil will hold, or how quickly a soil can be irrigated. For example, 1 inch of water applied to a sandy soil will penetrate 12 inches. It will move anywhere from 6 to10 inches into a good loam soil, and in a clay soil it will percolate down only 4 to 5 inches." Adjust the rate you apply water to how quickly the soil can absorb it—if water is sheeting off the surface then you need to apply it more slowly.

YOUR TARGET: THE ROOT ZONE

When irrigating, thoroughly wet the entire plant root zone with water and then let the soil dry partially before re-watering. Probe the root zone with a trowel or shovel to see how far down the water has wet the soil. Whether you use an irrigation

system, a soaker hose, or hand water with a garden hose, the objective is the same for all plants: Fill the root zone with water. The smaller the root zone, the more quickly it will dry and the more often it will require water. Seedlings just sprouting have no reserve to deal with dry soil.

Trees and shrubs, even those which will eventually reach drought tolerance, require deep watering in their first two to three summers of growth. For most newly planted trees and shrubs, irrigating to the twelve-inch root level will help them establish broad, strong root systems. If you have a drip irritation system, be sure to provide for deeper water delivery to these newer plants.

Soaker hoses and solid irrigation tubing with pressure-compensating emitters are an easily installed, efficient means of supplying water to home gardens. They can be hooked up to hose bibs, with a simple water timer added. Soaker hoses perform best in short runs (less than one hundred feet) on level ground. Pressure compensating heads will deliver water evenly over slopes and larger areas. Look for them in garden centers and from irrigation suppliers.

You can also water from a hose by filling a shallow planting basin around the plant, allowing it to sink in, and filling twice more. The objective is to get several gallons of water into the root zone at each watering. Allow soil to dry two to three inches down before watering again. This method is effective when new plants have been added to an established garden needing extra water.

The plant's location as well as the length of time it's been installed affects water needs. Shrubs and trees located in southern or western exposures require more water because they experience stronger sunlight and heat. Plants won't get much water from rainfall if they're grown next to a home's foundation, under overhangs, and under eaves. Consider re-locating plants that pose

continual problems and exhibit drought stress in these locations.

PLANTING TECHNIQUES: TREES AND SHRUBS

In the coldest areas, plant in spring. In Zones 5 to 6, fall planting can be done. In milder sections, Zones 7 to 9, planting can continue through fall, winter, and into early spring in the absence of extreme cold or wet conditions. Most trees and shrubs do not grow well in heavy, water-retentive soils. Some sensitive plants with fine surface roots, like rhododendrons and azaleas, will die in heavy soils. Check with a landscape professional about possible drainage installation for chronically wet soils. Or choose plants adapted to wet sites, such as red alder, willow, or red twig dogwood.

PLANTING LARGE INSTALLATIONS

When planting trees and shrubs it's best to prepare the entire large planting bed at once. You may be familiar with old advice to add lots of peat moss or compost to one hole before planting, but this has been discounted by research. Do not dig the hole and then fill it with organic material because plant roots tend not to grow out of the localized enriched spot into native soils.

Loosen the soil to at least eight inches throughout the planting area, remove larger rocks, and add organic materials. Add three to four inches throughout the planting area, then till or dig it in again. Rake the area smooth, and water it or allow rain to help it settle for a week or so before planting.

PLANTING AN ORNAMENTAL TREE OR SHRUB

What if you are planting only one tree or shrub? Or the terrain is difficult to cultivate? Install the plants in unamended native soil and apply

organic amendments and/or mulch to the surface.

Plants will be available in containers, or balled and burlapped, or bare root (only in earliest spring before growth starts). Proper planting means caring for the plant's roots while installing and not getting the plant too deep in the ground. Overly deep planting can cause eventual plant decline. Professional plant installers take great care to get trees and shrubs installed at, or slightly above, the soil surface. Protect all roots from drying while planting by keeping them covered with damp burlap, wet newspapers, mulch, or soil before installation.

For all trees and shrubs, no matter how they are packaged, dig a hole two to three times wider than the plant's width and as deep or slightly shallower than the plant's root depth (nine to ten inches for a plant with a ten-inch rootball). You'll want to rest the rootball on firm, undisturbed ground so the plant doesn't settle in too deep. For plants in containers, slide the plant out and check its root condition. Matted or even circling root systems often follow the outline of the pot. When tangled roots are cut off, root growth will rejuvenate when properly planted and kept moist. Make two or three vertical slices through the matted root mass to allow roots to spread properly. Gentle rinsing off of some of the container soil can help expose circling roots that need trimming and ensure that root tips are in good contact with the native soil when planted.

Balled-and-burlapped plants come wrapped in fabric, with twine securing it on the rootball. These fabrics aren't always traditional "burlap." In general, if it's plastic or other non-degradable fiber, it should be pulled off the rootball along with the twine before planting. All wrapping and ties should be removed from the top and sides of the rootball at planting, and this can be done once the plant is set into final position in the planting hole. Be sure the top of the ball rests even with the ground level, or an inch higher. Moisten the rootball thoroughly before disturbing the packing material. Remove the wrapping, cutting it loose and taking it out of the hole. Do not allow any of the material to remain above the soil surface as it will wick water out of the hole. Fill in with the native soil, lightly tamp it down, and water well.

Bare-root plants require extra care to keep roots moist before planting. They may be packed in sawdust to keep the roots damp. When you're ready to plant, soak the roots four to six hours in plain water. Soaking longer than this can damage the roots. Fill the hole gradually, holding the plant with one hand, keeping the roots spread, and placing soil carefully around the roots. Gently water as you add soil to the hole to eliminate air pockets around the roots. Bare-root plants also need extra care to plant them at the correct height, with the soil covering the roots but not the base of the trunk. This area is called the root collar and is usually visible by the change in bark texture where the trunk meets the smoother, below-ground root structure. Water thoroughly and mulch after planting.

WHAT ABOUT STAKING?

Only provide staking to those trees that are actually wobbly at planting time. Bare-root trees may be the most in need of staking and may be the least "attached" to the ground, so check them carefully. Drive stakes into the undisturbed soil outside the planting hole, and attach ties at the lowest position on the trunk that will hold the tree upright. Young tree trunks need some movement in the wind to develop strong wood. Use soft, pliable ties and avoid the use of wires that may dig into the trunk. Untie the staking periodically during the first season to see if the tree still needs support. Healthy, well-planted young trees should not normally need to be staked more than one year, and ties left on too long can cause damage as they embed into the rapidly growing trunk.

INTRODUCTION

WHAT DO WE MEAN BY "ESTABLISHED PLANTS?"

"Establishment" means that the plant's roots have penetrated the surrounding soil and that emerging root growth has replaced roots lost from transplanting. Established plants will produce healthy shoots while requiring less water. The process requires at least two to three years of attentive watering and plant observation. After establishment, drought tolerant plants may get along with relatively little or no extra summer irrigation, making a true waterwise garden. Other types of established plants such as azaleas, rhododendrons, and hydrangeas may always require supplemental water, no matter how long they have been in the ground.

Well established plants will settle into a pattern of seasonal growth with fewer requirements for water and fertilization. Their growth slows as summer progresses, settling down to ripen seeds and prepare for dormancy. Dry months of July and August often show leaves turning color early. If you look at the landscape as if you were choosing colors to paint it, you'll notice that the fresh blue green of early summer becomes khaki as deciduous tree leaves take on more brown hues at the end of the growing season. These "early autumn" symptoms are predictable in our region.

ENJOY YOUR GARDEN— MONTH BY MONTH

This chapter has presented up-to-date, basic techniques to help you care for and get the most out of your garden. You'll be coming back to this chapter as you go through the activities outlined in the following chapters. If this seems to offer a lot of guidelines to follow, the good news is that the more time you spend in the garden, the more quickly you'll become acquainted, informed, and equipped with the knowledge of your own corner of the Northwest and what your chosen landscape plants require.

As you spend time observing your garden, watching how your favorite plants respond to climate conditions and seasonal changes, you will find a flow of garden tasks and activities complementary to each season.

Learning from others adds to the pleasure. The resources offered in our reference section suggest great public gardens to visit and local experts who can inspire you.

Enjoy the journey. Whether you're a beginner or an experienced gardener, new to the Northwest or a native venturing into gardening for the first time, you'll have a splendid time discovering how rewarding it is to grow a garden here.

—Christina Pfeiffer and Mary Robson

USDA COLD HARDINESS ZONES

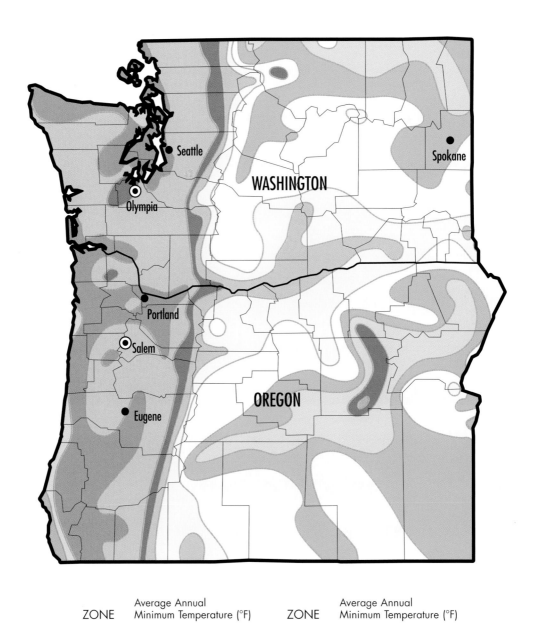

ZONE	Average Annual Minimum Temperature (°F)	ZONE	Average Annual Minimum Temperature (°F)
4A	-25 to -30	7A	5 to 0
4B	-20 to -25	7B	10 to 5
5A	-15 to -20	8A	15 to 10
5B	-10 to -15	8B	20 to 15
6A	-5 to -10	9A	25 to 20
6B	0 to -5	9B	30 to 25

WASHINGTON MONTHLY CLIMATE SUMMARIES

SEATTLE, WASHINGTON 1971-2000 Averages

	Jan	Feb	Mar	Apr	May	Jun	Jul	Aug	Sep	Oct	Nov	Dec	Annual
Average Max. Temperature (F)	43.7	47.2	51.6	57.0	64.7	66.8	75.0	76.4	67.2	56.9	48.3	43.5	58.3
Average Min. Temperature (F)	36.0	38.2	40.7	42.8	48.8	52.4	56.4	57.3	52.6	46.3	41.1	36.2	45.9
Average Total Precipitation (in.)	4.93	5.09	6.69	3.08	1.05	1.72	0.82	1.15	2.35	2.49	4.00	4.90	38.29

OLYMPIA WASHINGTON 1971-2000 Averages

	Jan	Feb	Mar	Apr	May	Jun	Jul	Aug	Sep	Oct	Nov	Dec	Annual
Average Max. Temperature (F)	45.5	49.2	54.4	59.4	65.6	70.7	76.6	77.4	71.8	61.1	48.7	44.7	60.6
Average Min. Temperature (F)	31.7	32.8	34.3	36.8	41.9	46.5	49.7	49.6	45.1	39.3	34.1	32.0	39.6
Average Total Precipitation (in.)	7.37	6.56	5.31	3.48	2.28	1.80	0.86	1.11	2.07	4.18	7.99	7.99	51.00

SPOKANE, WASHINGTON 1971-2000 Averages

	Jan	Feb	Mar	Apr	May	Jun	Jul	Aug	Sep	Oct	Nov	Dec	Annual
Average Max. Temperature (F)	33.0	39.6	48.8	57.5	66.1	73.8	82.4	82.3	72.4	58.3	40.3	33.0	57.5
Average Min. Temperature (F)	21.6	25.9	30.6	35.6	42.6	49.0	54.5	54.2	45.8	36.1	27.5	21.7	37.2
Average Total Precipitation (in.)	1.81	1.57	1.52	1.31	1.53	1.22	0.75	0.69	0.73	1.13	2.25	2.20	16.70

YAKIMA WASHINGTON 1971-2000 Averages

	Jan	Feb	Mar	Apr	May	Jun	Jul	Aug	Sep	Oct	Nov	Dec	Annual
Average Max. Temperature (F)	37.8	45.9	56.1	64.1	72.3	79.5	87.0	86.4	77.4	64.2	46.4	37.5	63.0
Average Min. Temperature (F)	22.2	26.5	30.7	35.3	42.1	48.2	52.9	51.8	43.9	34.5	26.7	21.8	36.5
Average Total Precipitation (in.)	1.20	0.84	0.69	0.54	0.55	0.54	0.26	0.36	0.41	0.53	1.10	1.30	8.31

DATA SOURCE: Western Regional Climate Center, http://www.wrcc.dri.edu/CLIMATEDATA.html

OREGON MONTHLY CLIMATE SUMMARIES

PORTLAND, OREGON 1971-2000 Averages

	Jan	Feb	Mar	Apr	May	Jun	Jul	Aug	Sep	Oct	Nov	Dec	Annual
Average Max. Temperature (F)	46.1	51.0	55.8	60.7	69.5	72.3	81.7	82.2	73.2	62.0	49.8	44.4	62.6
Average Min. Temperature (F)	36.5	38.7	41.3	42.9	49.2	53.4	58.7	59.6	53.1	46.3	39.7	35.7	46.4
Average Total Precipitation (in.)	7.46	4.74	5.33	2.89	1.58	1.48	0.44	0.99	2.87	3.00	5.43	10.20	46.39

BEND, OREGON 1971-2000 Averages

	Jan	Feb	Mar	Apr	May	Jun	Jul	Aug	Sep	Oct	Nov	Dec	Annual
Average Max. Temperature (F)	41.5	45.6	51.5	57.6	64.8	72.7	80.9	81.1	73.4	62.7	46.6	41.1	60.1
Average Min. Temperature (F)	22.6	24.8	27.1	30.0	35.4	41.0	45.9	45.3	38.5	32.3	26.6	22.6	32.8
Average Total Precipitation (in.)	1.70	1.16	0.90	0.73	0.96	0.73	0.62	0.57	0.47	0.70	1.54	1.74	11.80

EUGENE, OREGON 1971-2000 Averages

	Jan	Feb	Mar	Apr	May	Jun	Jul	Aug	Sep	Oct	Nov	Dec	Annual
Average Max. Temperature (F)	46.8	51.1	56.3	60.9	67.1	73.5	81.7	82.0	76.4	64.9	50.8	46.1	63.3
Average Min. Temperature (F)	33.6	35.6	37.5	39.7	43.4	47.7	51.5	51.6	47.6	41.6	36.5	34.0	41.8
Average Total Precipitation (in.)	7.41	6.43	5.72	3.79	2.58	1.55	0.65	1.00	1.53	3.47	8.49	8.40	51.00

MEDFORD, OREGON 1971-2000 Averages

	Jan	Feb	Mar	Apr	May	Jun	Jul	Aug	Sep	Oct	Nov	Dec	Annual
Average Max. Temperature (F)	47.3	53.6	58.9	64.6	72.7	81.3	90.1	90.1	83.0	69.7	51.2	45.2	67.5
Average Min. Temperature (F)	31.1	33.2	35.9	38.9	44.0	49.9	55.1	54.8	48.3	40.5	34.0	31.3	41.5
Average Total Precipitation (in.)	2.47	2.07	1.78	1.37	1.20	0.69	0.39	0.47	0.74	1.36	2.97	2.93	18.42

DATA SOURCE: Western Regional Climate Center, http://www.wrcc.dri.edu/CLIMATEDATA.html

ANNUALS & BIENNIALS

Annuals add beauty in containers, window boxes, hanging baskets and bedding areas. They give your garden continual blooms from spring through autumn, and even into winter in milder areas of Washington and Oregon.

WHAT ARE ANNUALS AND BIENNIALS?

What makes a plant annual? The name helps describe it: an annual germinates from seed, matures, blooms and sets new seeds in one growing season, before dying with the arrival of winter frost. Garden sunflowers (*Helianthus annuus*) fit the pattern, starting and finishing their life from spring through early autumn. The classic yellow sunflower with the brown center—the types that sprout from fallen birdseed—is grown for both flowers and seeds throughout the temperate world. But gardeners are now tempted by a vivid array of other sunflower types, which illustrates another fact about annuals. Their short life span makes breeding new hybrids easy and tempting: with sunflowers alone you'll find tall burgundy, red, and orange as well as short fuzzy-all-over-types, and graceful whites. Part of the enjoyment of choosing annuals for the garden is the amazing variety of new seeds and plants offered each year within each familiar genus.

Hardy Annuals: These can be sown or planted from containers directly into the garden in spring

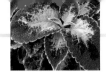

or fall. Often frost-tolerant, these include—but are not limited to—alyssum, calendulas, cosmos, snapdragons, poppies, sunflowers, pansies and violas, ornamental cabbage and kale.

Half-hardy Annuals: This is a rather strange term for a group of annuals that need warm soil to germinate. They're often started indoors, or purchased from nurseries after being grown in greenhouses. New Guinea impatiens, garden impatiens, marigolds, (*Tagetes* spp.), Cape daisy (*Osteospermum* spp.), petunias, zinnias and many others make up this group. They're generally native to warm regions, such as South Africa, Mexico, and South America. Valuable for their colors, forms, and garden interest, they need warmth to mature; in maritime western Washington, they benefit from being tucked into very warm, sunny garden corners.

Tender perennials: Tender perennials cannot survive a harsh winter and behave, in some sense like an annual. They're grouped with annuals only because they do not have a year-round outdoor garden presence. (And if many of these remind you of houseplants, that's not surprising;

many have uses as decorative indoor plants.)

Such tender plants might also include perennials—a mixture of tender bulbs like elephant ear (*Colocasia* spp.), brilliant foliage like coleus, vines such as passion flower and tender herbaceous plants like bananas (*Musa* spp.).

Sometimes plants like geraniums (*Pelargonium* spp.) are called "tender annuals" because they do not live through cold winters. In their native areas, and in mild climates, tender annuals can become perennial, returning year after year. So we have categories of plants that last only one season in the garden, but do not necessarily go to seed and complete their life span in one season.

Biennials: Biennials grow through their first season producing only leaves. After wintering over, they bloom and go to seed in their second year. Because they seed themselves, it's possible to have biennials in various stages of growth at the same time, some as foliage only, others at the flowering stage.

HOW, WHEN, AND WHY TO PLANT

Think of annuals and biennials as more than color "fillers." They can bring life to hanging baskets or be combined with perennials to make intriguing color echoes and chimes, and help with adding variety to new and established gardens.

How long will it be until those tiny green petunia—or lobelia—or impatiens sprouts fill up their garden spot and spill over container edges? Most annual starts purchased in small paks—6 or more at a time— require about 7 weeks to grow and bloom fully if cared for properly with adequate light, water, and fertilizer. As a rule of thumb with annuals, larger plants grow faster. If the plant is in a 4 inch pot, it may reach flowering in 5 weeks. With all annuals you'll see the flowers sporadically at first, and then in a flurry, covering the stems in color as the plant matures.

Because annuals offer such a range of colors—even to shade and tone—they are helpful in planning special event decoration. Allow 7 to 8 weeks from planting time to the party date for small unbudded annual plants. Just count back from the party date to the planting date.

If the party's on July 4, plant annuals in both containers and garden beds about May 10. If you use larger plants, growth time will be reduced to 5 weeks, about May 25. For a spring or summer family reunion, graduation, wedding, or anniversary celebration, rely on annuals for container plantings, table centerpieces, and fillers for existing perennial and shrub beds. Exact color availability will depend on the season and on your nursery resources.

COLOR COORDINATE

Planning annual use may be simplified by choosing only two colors—perhaps rose and pale pink—to set a tone for the plantings that can be uncomplex but effective. Petunias bloom bounteously, scent the air with fragrance, and come in dozens of elegant colors including pale blues, dark purples, reds, yellows and whites. The newer Surfinia™ series petunias (as well as Wave™ and Supertunias™) cascade over pots and hanging baskets and can rapidly add color to garden beds, often covering 3 or 4 square feet with one plant. They combine beautifully with scented annual alyssum, in white, pink or purple. (*Lobularia maritima* cultivars.) Many excel-

lent independent nurseries offer individual annuals, such as snapdragons (*Antirrhinum majus* cultivars), in a variety of colors. Snapdragon cultivars shine in nearly every color of tropical sunsets, from brilliant red through pinks and palest yellows and cream.

GETTING STARTED WITH ANNUALS

Gardeners in all zones anticipate finding annual plants in nurseries. Those green nubbins with the bright photo promises say "it's spring." Buying plants saves times and provides many choices. (Be sure to shelter tender annuals like zinnias from cold weather until planting out time, because they often appear in nurseries long before the ground is ready.)

Growing your own from seed will allow selection from the incredible variety in seed catalogs. It's necessary to have some space and equipment for true success with this. While starting seeds indoors is an early spring ritual for many gardeners, the seeds of hardy flowering annuals can often be planted directly into the soil after the date of your area's last expected frost. Some, such as sweet peas in the mildest temperature zones, will winter over and pop up in earliest spring.

Follow seed-planting directions printed on the packet. Annuals require fertile, well-drained soil, but because most annuals need only a small amount of healthy soil for their roots (about 8 inches), even the poorest soil conditions can be readied for seed. Amend sandy or clay soil by incorporating 2 inches of compost throughout the top 12 in. of the planting bed. Or, create an ideal home for annuals by building up raised bedding areas with rocks, bricks or boards. The raised beds can be filled with 8 to 12 inches of soil mix, providing a receptive medium for your seeds or plant starts.

If you have planted indoors using a seed-starting soil mix, begin moving seedlings outdoors after last frost. You will need to harden off transplants (by bringing them outside for gradually longer periods of time) for several days. Generally, this means placing flats of seedlings in a protected spot outdoors during the daytime and returning them inside at night.

GARDEN FRAGRANCE

Fragrance wafts from several different annuals and biennials. Not only the splendid sweet peas (*Lathyrus odoratus*), but sweet annual alyssum (*Lobularia* 'Sweet White'), sweet sultan (*Centaurea moschata*) in purple, pink, and white; mignonette (*Reseda odorata*) and night scented stock (*Matthiola longipetala* ssp. *bicornis*.) The easiest of these to grow from seed is annual sweet alyssum. Scatter seed anywhere after danger of frost is over. Your evening garden can be alive with fragrance, often more noticeable after dark from plants like nicotiana.

Deep watering is preferred for most annuals. It is best to moisten the root area approximately 8 in. deep applying water slowly at the base of the plant. Take care not to bruise or damage plants with strong bursts of water from a wand or spray gun. For plants in containers, summer's heat may require you to water daily (containers tend to dry out quickly, especially when situated in full sun). Irrigate plants during the early morning hours or after sunset when it's cooler and evaporation is less likely.

Annuals have rapidly growing root systems that are sensitive to water needs. Learn about your annuals by watching their performance after you irrigate. If the plants look vigorous and healthy and if the foliage is plump and green, then you've irrigated appropriately. Annuals, because they are in such active growth, do not recover well from wilting, so keep a close look at them during hottest days.

Annuals do require more frequent fertilization than woody plants or herbaceous perennials. When grown at nurseries, they receive regular fertilizing and water. Once they are settled into the ground or container, fertilize twice a month with a low nitrogen formula. A granular 6-6-6 or a liquid 9-6-6 works well. Keep the nitrogen level (the first number) the same as or lower than the next two. If annuals are combined with herbs or perennials in containers, feed with a liquid fertilizer diluted to half its strength twice a month.

When it comes to grooming your annuals or biennials, trim away or pinch off spent blooms. If a plant begins to look leggy, try cutting it back by one-third to one-half to stimulate new growth.

Annuals are typically not ranked by zones because the USDA hardiness zones designate the average minimum temperatures that a plant can tolerate. However, in very cold zones 4 to 6, the timing of installation and care will differ from that in zones 7 to 9. Find your zone map on page 20 and follow the zone-specific instructions for each month.

Choosing Annuals and Biennials

ANNUALS

Plant Name	Color	Height	Special Features
Bacopa (*Sutera cordata*)	white, lilac, blue	4 inches	spreads and trails in baskets
Calendula (*Calendula officinalis*)	yellow, orange	18 inches	fall color Zones 7-9
Coleus (*Solenostemon* sp.)	varied and brilliant	18 inches	shade loving color
Cosmos (*Cosmos bipinnatus*)	white, rose, purple	2-5 feet	grand cut flowers, reseeds
Geranium (*Pelargonium* sp,)	white, red, pink, salmon	2 feet	foliage effect, hot and dry tolerant
Heliotrope (*Heliotropium arborescens*)	lavender	8 inches	fragrance powerful, good in pots
Impatiens (*Impatiens walleriana*)	white, red, pink	2 inches	shade tolerant, bright, reliable color
Licorice Plant (*Helichrsum petiolare*)	green, gray, cream	8 inches to 4 feet	foliage "filler"
Lobelia (*Lobelia erinus*)	white, blue, pink	4 inches	sun or part shade tolerant, good blues
Love-in-a Mist (*Nigella damascena*)	blue, white, pink	18 inches	ferny foliage, soft color unusual seed pods
Marigold (*Tagetes* sp.)	white, yellow, orange, rust	6 inches to 3 feet	useful color, various bloom shapes
Nasturtium (*Tropaeolum majus*)	yellow, red, bicolor	1-8 feet	edible leaves and flowers
Nicotiana (*Nicotiana alata*)	white, red, lime-green	1-2 feet	part-shade, accent fragrant
Pansy (*Viola* x *wittrockia*)	nearly all colors	6-12 inches	fragrant, cool weather charmer
Petunia (*Petunia* x *hybrida*)	nearly all colors	1-4 feet	fragrant
Snapdragon (*Antirrhinum majus*)	nearly all colors	1-3 feet	tall accent, rebloom if trimmed
Sunflower (*Helianthus* sp)	cream, yellow, burgundy	2-12 feet	great accent, edible seeds
Sweet Pea (*Lathryus* sp)	white, lavender, rose	to 8 feet	fragrant vine
Verbena (*Verbena* x *hybrida*)	varied	8-12 inches	trails, vivid accent

BIENNIALS

Plant Name	Color	Height	Special Features
Angelica (*Angelica* sp.)	cream or purple	5-6 feet	moisture, tall accents
Canterbury Bells (*Campanula medium*)	white, blue	2-4 feet	spire of flowers
Forget-me-nots (*Mysotis sylvatica*)	white, blue, pink	6-24 inches	bulb ground cover
Money Plant (*Lunaria annua*)	rose	2 feet	papery, circular seed heads
Wallflower (*Erysimum* sp.)	yellow, rose, red	6-12 inches	perennial

JANUARY
ANNUALS & BIENNIALS

PLANNING

If this is your first year in gardening, you'll be happy to discover the wide world of annuals with many choices for quick garden color. With annuals, the time line is measured in weeks and months rather than years, and you'll enjoy trying new types with varied foliage and flower color.

Make lists of what annuals interest you. Shop when nurseries begin to stock annuals at the proper planting season. Exact varieties differ between the catalog and the nursery, but you'll be able to find great substitutes at a well stocked nursery. You'll always have fun with annuals, especially when you try mixing it up or breaking away from your usual choices. If you've always planted red **geraniums** in one container, this year maybe some salmon or **fancy-leaved scented geraniums** could be tucked into that spot.

Be sure to consider light exposure. Once you've decided which perennials or shrubs you wish to complement, note whether it's sunny or shady in the desired location. Make notes so that when you get to the nursery, intriguing new types may snatch your eyes, but you'll have a plan and know where they fit.

Think of annuals as the garden's accessories . . . as strong as a colored scarf on a neutral dress, or bold accent pillows on a sofa. They offer a big return for a small investment, and yearly changes add punch to the garden.

PLANTING

Do you have viable seeds left? Sort out those old paper seed packets tucked in drawers and check. Here's how:

1. Wet a paper towel.
2. Sow 10 to 20 seeds on the damp surface. Roll it up and lay it in a plastic bag to prevent drying.
3. Open the towel in 4 to 6 days and count how many seeds have sprouted roots.

Most gardeners choose to discard seeds that have less than 30 percent germination. If the seeds came from a precious home-gathered heirloom plant, any degree of germination is good news. Some seeds stay viable for years.

Zones 7-9: Nurseries will have **pansies** and **primroses** now, in many different colors. Both pansies and primroses manage cool temperatures well. They are most often used in containers in midwinter. Both **pansies** and **primroses** could be considered perennials, coming back year

after year, but they don't respond well to the summer season in Westside gardens unless pampered. They have been cared for in greenhouses, and when fresh from the nursery they look their best. Harden them off before setting them outside. (See March for "Hardening off".)

CARE

Zones 5-6: You'll have a quiet month in January. Temperatures are too cold for garden work.

Zones 7-9: Protect pots containing winter **pansies** or other flowers from heavy freezes Sudden weather events with temperatures below 30 degrees F. could cause damage. Tuck them into a sheltered, above freezing spot like a garage until the weather moderates. Be certain to water during this time. Plants may develop yellow leaves or other symptoms when receiving less light while in storage, but they recover when set outside again. Pick off any damaged foliage after emergency storage.

WATERING

All zones: Water any tender annuals being overwintered indoors.

USING BIENNIALS IN THE GARDEN

If biennials are started from seeds, they produce a leafy rosette close to the ground their first year. **Foxgloves**, for instance, produce soft, fuzzy leaves 6 inches long and 4 inches tall. After a summer in rosette form, they spend winter evergreen or dormant depending on your zone. During the second summer they develop a flowering stem.

If you buy biennials with buds or bloom from a nursery, they have completed their first year and will bloom buoyantly their first summer in the garden, set seeds, and die. The seeds will germinate and return as small plants the next summer, repeating the cycle. Many biennials, such as **forget-me-nots** scatter seeds prolifically and may reappear in garden paths and other random spots.

Hybrid biennials with cultivar names—such as **wallflower** (*Erysimum cheiri* 'Ruby Gem')—may not look the same when their next year's seedlings emerge. Like all hybrids, they do not necessarily come true to type from seed. But they can still be beautiful.(See September for tips on saving seeds and on plants "coming true" from seed.)

Biennials have been in gardens for centuries, and many have memorable common names: **moneyplant** (*Lunaria annua*), named for its round silver seed pods resembling 50 cent pieces; **wallflower** for its habit of emerging from snug spots in rock walls; **Canterbury bells** (*Campanula medium*), evoking the shape of a cathedral bell; and **foxgloves** (*Digitalis* spp.), whose name somewhat defies understanding unless the fox is meant to tuck a paw into the tubular flower.

FERTILIZING

No outdoor plants require fertilizer this month.

GROOMING

Zones 7-9: Fall **kale** (*Brassica oleracea* cultivars) has a tired aspect by mid-January and could be replaced by fresh **pansies** or **primroses**. The 'Peacock', and other kale cultivars, will be losing older leaves. If left ungroomed, it will eventually shoot up unto a messy flowering stem. Pull off dead leaves and tidy the plant, or remove the **kale** altogether if the winter wreckage is too severe.

Also, watch out for winter weeds that may seed themselves when blown by wind or carried by animals. They'll grow easily in mulch. Remove them before they set seed again.

All zones: Check any indoor over-wintered annual **geraniums** (*Pelargonium*) or **fuchsias** for health; prune out any blackened foliage and stems on the **geraniums**. Water lightly.

PROBLEMS

Aphids may appear on plants brought into shelter. You will see little green translucent blobs the size of a comma. Rinse them off with warm water or treat the plants with insecticidal soap. Just a few aphids can launch an indoor epidemic that affects your houseplants.

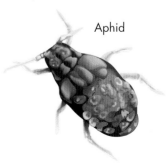

Aphid

FEBRUARY

ANNUALS & BIENNIALS

PLANNING

Throughout the spring, public garden exhibits and flower shows abound. Check your local newspaper for upcoming events and get them on your calendar. Interacting with other gardeners and seeing a vast array of ideas make flower shows essential and delightful.

PLANTING

Zones 4-6: Start **sweet peas** indoors in mid-February; they can grow in cool soils but need a good head start for your area because they do not flower well in hot summer temperatures.

If you stepped into your favorite nursery's greehouses right now, you'd find hundreds of annuals just seeded or getting ready for transplanting. Perhaps allowing the nursery to grow your seedlings works best for you, but you may want to do it yourself.

Growing from seed: Timing is important. Some types of annuals, such as **wax begonias** and seed **geraniums,** require 120 days (now until the end of May) to reach garden planting size. There's satisfaction in growing these from seed, but the time and effort needed to care for them may not fit your schedule. More difficult to work with are small seeds, such as **petunias**, with 4,000 seeds to $1/8$ teaspoon.

Start now if you want plants for May when annuals may be set out in all parts of our region. For quicker plants, such as **cosmos**, **marigolds**, and **zinnia**, start in mid- to late-March.

1. **Planning:** Analyze your layout. It's easy to have room indoors when the seedlings are babies, but more space is needed as they grow and are transplanted into the second container. It's a bit like what happens to household space when toddlers turn into teen-agers. Start the quantity of seeds you can care for until outdoor planting.

2. **Light:** In all parts of our region, winter lacks daylight strength to support seedlings. Plus, those placed next to windows may suffer from cold air. So set up some lights. Even in longer days, they usually do best with overhead fluorescent light. A simple setup uses a 48-inch shop light on chains to allow easy raising and lowering (holds true for vegetables too which are generally annuals). Check seed packets for light requirements.

3. **When to Plant:** Check the seed packet for instructions or work backward from the date they will be transplanted outside. Ideally, the seedling you start will be just the right size when weather cooperates.

4. **Material:** Use bagged seeding mix, wetting it thoroughly before filling seed containers.

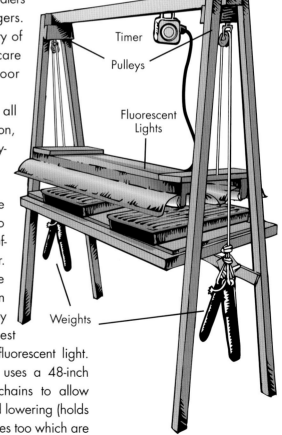

Light stand with seed starter trays.

Timer

Pulleys

Fluorescent Lights

Weights

5. How to Plant: Seeds need warmth to germinate, 68 to 75 degrees F. for summer heat lovers. If your basement is at 45 degrees F., seedlings would be slow or fail to grow, exactly as if you planted them in cold outdoor soil.

Provide warmth with a heat mat under the planting flat. Heat is concentrated where the plants need it. Some soil heating cables can be laid inside the flat before it's filled with soil. However, mats offer flexibility to use with various container sizes.

6. **Cover Seeds:** Place a plastic bag over the seeds until they germinate, removing after they grow.

Zones 7-9: Sow **sweet peas** (*Lathyrus* spp.) in compost-enriched soil outdoors. Put up a trellis for climbing types and watch them grow. 'Cupani', a descendant of the original sweet pea, with tiny flowers, is one fragrant variety.

 CARE

Adjust indoor lights with seedling growth, keeping the light 6 inches above the plants 12 to 14 hours daily.

 WATERING

Water indoor plants overwintering. Tender annuals like **bananas** or **brugmansia** cannot go dry.

Keep seedlings moist but not soggy—they will die if they dry out. Little seedlings with new roots cannot stand drought. Mist them from the top or water from the bottom (some seed trays come with watering channels.)

 FERTILIZING

Check **fuchsias, tuberous begonias**, and others in storage. Repot tender **fuchsias** in fresh, compost- enriched soil, water thoroughly, and place it in a well lit spot. Fertilize with $1/2$ strength liquid fertilizer when new green leaves appear.

 GROOMING

Fuchsias, geraniums, tuberous begonias: when bringing these out of winter storage, it's sometimes difficult to tell what the alive or dead parts are. If a section is obviously dead (like geranium's blackened twigs) prune it off. But otherwise wait until the plant produces foliage before trimming. **Fuchsia** stems, for instance, can look completely dead but then sprout new leaves.

 PROBLEMS

Watch for symptoms of etoliation, a fancy word meaning "stretched out and leaning," caused by insufficient light. Sow when the soil is warming, not heavy with frost, to prevent seeds rotting from being sown too early in cold, wet soil.

Aphids: You'll think that the world's entire aphid population wants your annuals . . . they like the succulent young foliage with its lively sap.

Look on overwintered or outdoor plants for tiny clumps of pale green aphids. If you see them, isolate the plant. Swish the new leaves carefully in water. Check it every 4 days for return aphid vistors.

Also, watch outdoor planting beds for winter weeds that may seed themselves when blown by wind or carried by animals. They'll grow easily in mulch. Remove them before they set seed again.

MARCH

ANNUALS & BIENNIALS

 PLANNING

Planning annuals for a special event? If the color is availale only from seed, you'll need to start 6 weeks ahead. For example, for a July 4 event, plant seeds in mid-March under lights.

Nurseries help guide the planning. However, annuals often arrive earlier than you can plant them. Be choosy about bringing home tender plants this month; they may have to be household residents until weather warms. If your garden includes a heated greenhouse or your basement has a light set up for plants, you'll be able to care for them appropriately.

 PLANTING

Zones 5-6: It's still too early for planting outdoors. Toward the end of March, gather supplies to start warm weather vegetables and tender flowers indoors. At month's end, set out seedlings of **sweet peas**.

Zones 7-9: Cold hardy annuals and annual seeds can land in the garden now as long as the soil is not soppy or frozen. Once sown, they can often withstand a light freeze before germinating. After emergence, they'll need a bit of frost protection. Keep a light cover available to spread over just-grown seeds in case of hard rains or hail.

 CARE

Zones 5-6: Adjust lights over seedlings to keep good light 6 inches above them as they grow. When seedlings have 2-3 sets of true leaves, they are ready to transplant. Don't allow them to grow too long and get crowded, tangled roots in their first growing flat.

Zones 7-9: Finding strong plants at the nursery: Choose short, stocky green plants with sturdy stems and buds. If they have already begun to bloom, their life in the garden will be shorter.

 WATERING

Keep indoor seedlings moist but do not over water. Spray gently with room temperature water. Probe the soil with a pencil or chopstick to determine that roots are receiving water.

 FERTILIZING

Fertilize any overwintering plants like **fuchsias** or **geranium** (*Pelargonium*) as soon as they begin to send out new green leaves. Use a liquid fertilizer with a moderate level of nitrogen, such as a 9-6-6 or a 6-8-8. If your fertilizer has a lot of nitrogen, such as a 20-20-20, dilute it to half strength. Do not fertilize any overwintering plants that are still dormant, where no new growth is visible. For new seedlings, use $1/2$ strength fertilizer when the plants have only two sets of leaves.

For nursery plants: After transplanting any annual, fertilize when you see new growth, which indicates the roots have settled into the soil.

 GROOMING

Remove any dead leaves from overwintering plants. Do not prune **fuchsias** until growth is well under way. **Fuchsias** send up entirely new stems from the base if they are healthy. Allow these new stems to grow for another month before selecting the ones that look best.

Pinch out the tips of seedlings or purchased nursery plants that begin to stretch out and appear weak and lanky. (Are they receiving enough light?)

 PROBLEMS

You'll know seedlings grown indoors or outside suffer from "damping off" when they suddenly keel over. This fungal infection is caused by crowded conditions with poor air circulation. To reduce the risk, use clean seedling mix rather than recycling soil. Do not over water or set trays in standing water. Use new seed trays or soak the old ones for an hour in a solution of 1 part household bleach and 10 parts water. Also, don't plant more than you can handle. Thin plants to give them adequate space.

Continue vigilance for aphid populations, especially indoors. Wash off infected plants with water, or spray an insecticidal soap registered for indoor use. Do not spray tender new seedlings.

Our favorite mollusk, the slug, loves March and April and will be happy to chew off the new outdoor annuals such as **pansies** and **primroses**. Handpick them, also looking closely at bulb plantings for small colonies. Slugs love to hide in beds mulched with leaves or leaf mold. Set out beer traps by using saucers filled with beer. Refresh often as rain dilutes them.

DID YOU KNOW?

Check the packets for length of time to raise plants indoors before setting outdoors:

4 weeks—**cosmos, marigold, sunflower, zinnia, sweet pea**
8 weeks—**cleome, coleus, nicotiana, petunia**
10 weeks—**impatiens, petunia, snapdragon**
16 weeks—**annual geranium** (*Pelargonium*), **wax begonia**

Even if you are new to the seed-starting game, these annuals start easily. The big seeds of **cosmos, marigolds,** and **zinnias** are easy to handle. **Petunias, begonias,** and **impatiens** have fine seed. If you want to start these types, look for seed pellets with coatings that make them simpler to handle.

Hardier annual types will sow themselves. **California poppies** and other poppies appear reliably year after year (not always where you want but always cheerful). **Bachelor's buttons, cosmos, nigella,** and others will add informality to the garden as they pop up from last year's plants.

Cosmos

APRIL
ANNUALS & BIENNIALS

PLANNING

April and May ring with plant sales as community organizations showcase garden starts, donated plants, and material from specialty nurseries. Take your garden plan along and find unusual treasures at these sales. Check newspaper calendars for dates and enjoy the "community fair" atmosphere of spring plant sales.

PLANTING

Zones 5-6: Hold off on planting until last frost date except for the hardiest of annuals such as **pansies**. Make sure they are hardened to night temperatures before setting out. Keep them indoors during night freezes, setting them out during the day.

Zones 7-9: Sow the following hardy annual seeds outdoors: **sweet alyssum**, **cosmos**, **cleome**, **marigolds**, **California poppies** and **sunflowers**. If the garden isn't cleared of weeds and generally prepared, you can seed them into flats and then transplant. If your garden is ready, sprinkle seeds and mark the edges of the planting with twigs or stones and an identifying label. This will help you'll remember to pay special attention to their watering needs as they emerge.

All zones: Toward month's end complete planting of cooler-season containers. Get creative by combining annuals with perennials, ferns, foliage plants like **hosta**, and even summer bulbs, including small **gladiolus**.

CARE

Seedlings: Harden off all seedlings before planting out whether you grew them indoors or they came from a nursery. They can't move directly from the warmth of a greenhouse or your home without a staged adjustment plan. Days out and nights in, then a full night out. Do this over about 7 to 10 days before you intend to plant them out. Halt the process if freezing temperatures threaten. Most seedlings won't appreciate being set out in temperatures below 45 degrees F.

All zones: Reserve covering materials to lay over annual plantings when the night temperatures drop. Even if the temperature is above freezing, the drop into the upper 30s can be tough on newly emerged summer flowers. Cover plants with spunbonded lightweight landscape cloth (Reemay) just as the evening air starts to cool. Place sticks to support the cloth, both to protect the plans and to allow for a layer of warm air above them.

Be mindful, however, that any system providing protection from cold at night may cause them to cook when temperatures go up during the day. Here's one solution: cut the large end out of a gallon plastic juice jug and put it over the plant. Replace the jug

Pansy 'Melody Purple'

lid at night and remove it during the day. A more complex idea is a portable plastic hoop house to set over the plants at night and on the coldest days. Once temperatures moderate at night, usually by the end of May, such protection can be removed. In coldest zones. However, sudden freezes can occur into June and return again in early September in zones 5-6.

WATERING

All zones: April starts the summer watering regimet that will repeat each month from now through September. Water plants recently moved outdoors. If you're using soaker hoses, be sure plant roots are receiving sufficient moisture.

Carefully water any seedlings still growing indoors. In April, this may be many because tender annuals like **marigold** and **petunias**, no matter how large, cannot stand cold night temperatures.

FERTILIZING

All zones: Fertilize annuals in containers once just after new growth starts from their initial planting and then again when

---

VEGETABLES CAN FILL IN TOO

No one sets the rules in your garden. And one of the loveliest and most space efficient of plantings can be vegetables combined along with annual flowers. Most vegetables are annuals; we consume them after they've given their bounty. Then we compost their remaining spent leaves. **Lettuce** as edging, **parsley** tucked in with small French **marigolds**, and frilly **carrot** tops setting off **snapdragons** can all add to the enjoyment of the garden. Choose small vegetables without heavy root systems or underground tubers, because harvesting those can affect the roots of annual flowers. Herbs such as **chives**, though perennial, make well-mannered vegetable companions, and can be sheared after flowered.

---

roots establish; you'll know this by increased leaf production.

GROOMING

Monitor your garden for seedlings of past annuals and perennials. You may wish to allow some to stay and grow, and move others to discard or transfer to pots. Check seed packets to help you identify the vagrant new plants. You can lift them gently out of the garden, and transplant them into 2-inch pots to grow larger, thus gradually increasing your stock of plants. Scoop the seedling up gently, getting the entire root. If you have to touch the plant, hold it by the leaves. The stem carries all the water and nutrients. It's

easily bruised and this can kill the seedling.

Pinch off any flowers or buds on newly purchased small annuals. They'll catch up and set new buds with a stronger established root system. Hard to do, but necessary.

PROBLEMS

Slugs will eat anything with tender new growth (they do not bother strong scented culinary herbs but they are fond of **marigolds**). Keep up all slug control methods.

MAY

ANNUALS & BIENNIALS

 PLANNING

May summons warmth, though freezing temperatures are certainly possible in coldest zones. By the end of May, night temperatures east of the Cascade Mountains begin to moderate, especially at lower elevations. In all parts of our region, spring nursery supplies peak this month and in June. Select what you want now, especially if you are planning for a special event with a particular annual color.

 PLANTING

Zones 5-6: Plant hardy annuals such as **alyssum**, **cosmos**, and **lobelia**. Hold off on installing tender annuals, such as **cleome**, **nicotiana**, and **heliotrope** until night temperatures stay steadily above 45 degrees F.

Zones 7-9: Mother's Day marks the traditional date for planting patio containers. Mix all types of summer annuals with perennials and **helichrysum**. Be prepared to cover tender **geraniums** and other half-hardy annuals if temperatures drop below 45 degrees F. at night.

Tips for successful container plantings:

1. Container size and structure: The larger the container, the easier the maintenance. Smaller pots can grow plants but daily maintenance is more demanding because the soil volume does not hold water. A 3- to 4-gallon size (10 inches x 10 inches) is the minimum. To keep larger containers lightweight, choose plastic over ceramic or wood. You can recycle black plastic nursery pots if you disguise with a non heat-absorbing material, such as an inexpensive woven basket that fits.

2. Drainage holes: Be sure that water drains well from the container. Do not add a bottom layer of pebbles, marbles, or rocks; these will not help drainage and decrease soil depth. Pots without holes are useful only for water feature plants like small floating **waterlilies**. Be sure to check for drain holes on wooden $1/2$ barrels. If they don't have them, drill 6 to 8 one-inch holes before planting the oak barrel. Barrels, after all, are designed not to leak.

3. Soil mix that drains well: The biggest danger to container plants is soggy soil. Soil scooped from the garden packs down too much and reduces oxygen to roots. Instead, in a wheelbarrow, mix $1/4$ garden soil by volume, $1/4$ perlite (a light weight soil amendment) and $1/2$ bagged potting soil. Moisten it thoroughly before adding it to the pot.

If you plan to use commercial potting soil, be sure it drains well. Ask questions, read the bags, and look for mixes containing pumice or perlite for added drainage. It's not necessary to use mixes with added fertilizer, microorganisms or water-holding polymers.

4. Fill the container: Lay a piece of window screen, or even a paper coffee filter, over the holes before filling the pot $3/4$ with potting mix. Water well again and check drainage.

5. Add plants: Plants in 1-gallon containers go about 6 inches apart, in 4-inch pots about 3 inches. Plant tiny start "paks" in groups of three. Spacing will vary with your design. Plants such as *Fatsia japonica* or **castor bean** (*Ricinus communis*) will need plenty of room to grow. Tease out any tangled roots. Water again to settle the planting.

6. Topdressing compost: Add 1 inch of screened compost or worm compost to contribute to plant health.

7. Fertilize: Every 2 weeks, fertilize with a balanced liquid fertilizer (6-6-6, 5-2-2 or 5-10-10) containing trace nutrients. If using 20-20-20, dilute it to half strength. Do not overfertilize because that will reduce or can even eliminate annual flowering by growing leaves instead.

IT'S NOT JUST ABOUT FLOWERS

Annual and biennial plants can also brighten the garden with foliage effects, in both color and texture. Some plants like **petunias** exclusively specialize in flowers—and a garden with only blooms rapidly becomes monotonous. Variety comes with foliage. Such is the case with annuals, including *Amaranthus* sp., **castor bean** (*Ricinus communis*)—be aware of its toxicity—**coleus**, **cosmos**, *Eryngium*, *Lunaria*, **red orach** (*Atriplex hortensis* var. *rubra*) annual **sages** (*Salvia* spp.), and **nasturtium**. All of these have leaf patterns to add summer-lasting interest.

Nasturtium

CARE

If your annual plant starts originate from a heated greenhouse at the nursery, they'll need careful and deliberate adjustment to the outside chill. Follow directions for "Hardening Off" in April entry.

WATERING

All zones: Establish a planned watering schedule for all summer annual plantings (and vegetable plantings). These plants do not generally adjust to dry soils and will need watering all summer. Few exceptions include **cosmos**, **portulaca**, and **sunflowers** which can endure drier conditions after the summer progresses and their roots develop. They cannot, however, go entirely without water.

FERTILIZING

Continue to fertilize annual plantings with a liquid fertilizer when you see new growth starting, about 10 days after planting.

GROOMING

Pinch off spent flowers of any annuals, perennials, or bulbous flowers that have completed their bloom. The garden will look tidier and the plant will not put extra energy into seed production.

PROBLEMS

Odd leaf color? Red, maroon, or sometimes silvery color on larger leaves of annuals, such as **geraniums** and tender **fuchsias,** can signal overexposure to cold temperatures. (As temperatures warm, this symptom will depart.) It's connected to the plant's ability to take in nutrients. A light spray of foliar fertilizer may assist the plants in developing new leaves.

The tiresome twins, slug and aphid, continue this month. Continue to patrol for slugs. If any plants—such as **marigold**—are severely attacked, cut off the worst leaves and remove all mulch. Then use slug bait, choosing a least-toxic variety, such as iron phosphate (Sluggo™).

JUNE
ANNUALS & BIENNIALS

PLANNING

Weather begins to settle into summer patterns this month. day and night temperatures stay cooler during summer in the Northwest's Zones 7 to 9 than they do in Zones 5 to 6. Many annuals (especially tender annuals) are sensitive to cool nights under 50 degrees F.

When choosing a site for annual plantings in the coastal Northwest, think warmth. Tuck them against walls or in the sunniest spots of garden beds. **Zinnias** and **sunflowers**, brilliantly easy to grow east of the Cascades, need extra light on the maritime side. East of the mountains, provide morning sun exposure and shelter from scorching dry afternoons.

PLANTING

All zones: Tender plants can march outdoors this month: **tomatoes** and **squash** started from seeds, **brugmansia, cactus, poinsettias**, and **amaryllis** that was over-wintered. Tropical or Zone 10 to 15 plants that have been wintering inside will go out now.

Add culinary herbs to outdoor containers: **basil**, the sumptuously flavored herb for Italian and Thai cooking, grows as a red-leafed form and as a dwarf ('Marseille'), in addition to the soft green standard type. Look for new forms at your nursery.

Petunias, marigolds, lobelia, snapdragons, and many other annuals planted in beds, baskets, or containers this month will fill in well and look good through August if sufficiently watered and deadheaded. Like all annuals, Surfinia™ **petunias** (and 'Wave'™ or 'Supertunias'™ series) look small at first. In 6 weeks stems reach 4 feet and cascade from baskets or act as ground cover.

CARE

Move plants into nighttime shelter or cover them if temperatures drop below 50 degrees F. Cool temperatures can stint the growth of these heat-lovers. Culinary **basil** will absolutely refuse to thrive in cold nights.

Zone 7-9: Provide more summer heat for tropicals by putting them on stone or concrete patios or against stone or brick walls that will hold heat at night.

Deadheading will improve the appearance and extend the bloom period of flowers.

FERTILIZING

Every two weeks container plants need liquid fertilizer with a low-nitrogen formula, such as a 5-10-10 or organic kelp.

Fertilize plant beds in the garden monthly. Annuals continue to produce fresh leaves and flowers throughout the summer. Liquid fertilizer in summer reaches roots better; use a low nitrogen formula like a 6-2-2 or a 5-10-10, or if you prefer an organically-based fertilizer, both kelp and fish fertilizers work well.

GROOMING

Deadheading is simply pinching off old flowers. This can become a calming summer ritual as you move from plant to plant pinching off the old flowers before they go to seed. Your job is to keep the plants producing flowers. If they begin to set seed, their biological mission is accomplished. No more flowers. **Pansies** are difficult to deadhead because the seed pods hide under leaves and sometimes remain unseen until they ripen seeds. **Petunias** benefit from deadheading regularly.

A few annuals, including **impatiens**, drop their own flowers without requiring deadheading, which may explain their popularity in national sales.

WATERING

Water thoroughly to the root zones of all annual and biennial plants in the garden. Check the roots with a trowel or small hand fork to note depth of dampness.

Keep all container plants well watered.

DID YOU KNOW

Flowering annuals suited for shade gardens: if the garden area gets 3-4 hours of sun, or filtered sun coming through trees, you'll have bright color with **impatiens** (*Impatiens walleriana*), and **wax begonias** (*Begonia Semperflorens Cultorum* Group). Both plants provide shades from white through pinks, oranges, purple, and red. With a bit more light, up to 4 hours steadily, try blue **sapphire flower** (*Browallia speciosa*), the patterned foliage of **coleus**, and fragrant **white nicotiana** (*Nicotiana alata*).

Zones 5-6: When growing **fuchsias** and fuchsia baskets, remember fuchsias of all types grow poorly in the hotter summers of zones 5-6. Keep them well watered and in shade (such as hanging from a tree branch) if trying them where summer temperatures soar above 80 degrees F. Morning light will help them thrive; many stop growing when temperatures rise in hot sun.

Zones 7-9: Nurseries sell fully grown **fuchsias** now. Before hanging the basket, immerse it in water from the bottom up. Tender fuchsias can fill their containers with roots and then do not take up water well. They require water daily, or even twice a day—morning and night—on hottest days. Overhead watering is fine, but check roots to be sure that water reaches all parts of the plant.

All zones: Every 10 days, take the **fuchsia** plant down and soak it from the bottom as you did when first hanging it. Strategies for keeping them watered also include drip irrigation where the display includes many plants and using the tubing is convenient.

PROBLEMS

Slugs: **Basil**, often grown as an ornamental as well as for its piquant herbal use, attracts slugs. Controlling these mollusks will be easier if plants are in containers rather than being set out in open ground.

JULY

ANNUALS & BIENNIALS

 PLANNING

Nurseries hold sales this month, offering fresh summer annuals, hanging basket plants, and flowering perennials. Do you have containers to fill or a garden area that needs a color spot?

Take pictures of the annual plantings, which peak this month from spring installation. Visit public and special open house gardens to get ideas, especially about combining plants.

 PLANTING

Zones 5-6: hot, dry conditions in July make this a poor month for planting.

Zones 7-9: Seeds planted now—annuals such as **cosmos** and **zinnias**—will come into bloom in mid-September and last through October. You may want to plant a different color theme for fall. Think of some autumn leaf orange or yellows for the fall season.

Cosmos, either the Sensation Mix or 'Sonata White' or yellow and orange 'Bright Lights' will survive cool autumn weather well, as will **calendula**, which often blooms all winter in milder areas. If you want a certain **pansy** to set out in September, seeds started in flats early this month will be planting size by then. **Pansies** and **violas** often stay healthy and provide color throughout the winter if set out in mid to late September.

All zones. When purchasing plants on sale, check the plant roots, which should be growing actively—not dark brown, matted, or mushy. Even when healthy, annuals that have been in their nursery paks for weeks often have roots grown thick and tangled. Water them before detaching them from containers. Set the paks in a deep tray, allow them to take up water until thoroughly dampened. Slide them out one at a time. Pull out roots gently when planting. If you see a thick, white mat of roots at the bottom of the plant, peel it off, leaving roots on the sides intact.

When planting in hot weather, work in cool morning or evening temperatures. Shade plants from hot sun for at least a week after planting. Check plants for wilting and water regularly.

 CARE

Check shading needs of annuals in the garden. Even those established since spring may need some temporary shading on the hottest days.

Continue weeding as necessary. Summer temperatures may reduce the numbers of weeds that sprout, but many continue to defy the weather and grow.

Stake any tall **sunflowers** or **cosmos** that may be vulnerable to winds or sudden thunderstorms, especially in Zones 5 to 6.

 FERTILIZING

Container plants lose nutrients whenever watered. The fertilizer

If you want to grow a more unusal variety, try starting from seed.

is washed out. Fertilize twice a month keeping the nitrogen level low.

If annuals in flower beds grow strongly, having good leaf color and normal blooms, fertilize only once toward the end of the month. Use a liquid fertilizer, applying it after watering. Even liquid fertilizers must be used over damp soil. Never fertilize dry roots.

 WATERING

Keeping all garden beds thoroughly watered is the main task for July and August. Irrigate to root depth. Poke the soil around annuals with your finger to check if it's dry at one inch. If so, water.

Because sun can hit containers and warm the sides, affecting the roots within, container plantings may need watering once or even twice a day depending on the amount of sun they receive in their garden location. Dark black plastic containers can absorb so much heat that they kill roots within the soil. Do not use this container type where sun hits the surface directly.

 GROOMING

California poppies, **red field poppies**, and **Iceland poppies**, go to seed just after bloom. Cut

---

DID YOU KNOW?

Plants can endure some insect and disease problems. Be sure that treatment is necessary before reaching for a pesticide. Identify garden problems before choosing management methods. To protect beneficial insects, care for water quality, and save money, take any garden questions to a WSU or OSU trained Master Gardener (see Resources) or to a qualified nursery specialist. Often plants will outgrow problems. Caution with garden and household chemicals helps the environment.

---

off the flowers before seed heads form unless you want the plants to seed and naturalize in the garden. California poppies can become an attractive nuisance, with gray ferny plants popping up everywhere. If you allow them to seed, they will appear next year without fail. It's a gardener's choice!

Pinching off dead flowers will prolong flowering.

If a plant has been in since April (often true in warmer zones) it may start to look tattered and "bloomed out" by mid-July. This often happens to **petunias**, **lobelia**, and **trailing bacopa**. Shear the entire plant to remove all old flowers and keep at least 6 inches of leafy foliage. This will prod the plant into setting buds again, although full attractiveness will take 6 weeks or even more. Use liquid fertilizer after pruning. In colder zones, this trimming will produce mid-September bloom.

Some gardeners remove spent annuals now rather than cutting them back. You may prefer to plant a fresh, smaller seedling—such as **alyssum**, **dusty miller**, and **zinnias**—that will grow for color in September.

 PROBLEMS

Powdery mildew: Remove any annuals with severe symptoms of silky gray substance on leaves. For a cherished or prominently sited plant, use a registered fungicide.

Aphids bother plants less in July: beneficial insects, including ladybugs, wasps, and spiders control the populations, as do birds. Even hummingbirds help, snatching gnats out of the air for necessary protein. Plants resist aphid damage better after mid-summer because of sturdier foliage growth.

AUGUST
ANNUALS & BIENNIALS

 PLANNING

August slows the garden, with heat and dry air reducing plant growth. Gardeners too tend to slow down this month, one of the quietest in all zones. Garden care this month will help plants look good in September.

Review your summer plantings, highlighting successes and noting the annuals that were less successful—the color, shape, or form didn't suit the garden. Continue to visit display gardens and note color combinations. Talking to professional gardeners this month also helps to get ideas for the difficult end of the season in flower gardens.

Check nurseries for seed sales: annuals to scatter in late fall in zones 7-9, or in spring in **Zones 5-6**, often show up reduced on seed racks.

 PLANTING

No planting is suggested this month in any zone.

 CARE

Around August 1st, loosely wrap expanding **sunflower** heads intended for harvest with cheese-cloth to prevent squirrels and birds from nibbling the seeds.

Deadhead: continue to pinch off flowers after bloom finishes. Pinch back **cosmos**, annual **sages** (*Salvia* cultivars) and remove flowering scapes on **snapdragons**. Cutting flowers for bouquets also helps keep plants—like **zinnias** and **dahlias**—blooming into September.

Weeds grow vigorously where watering systems create moist soil; keep scuffling the smallest ones or pulling the larger. By August they will germinate where they blow onto mulch or are carried in by birds and animals, or even the gardener's shoes.

 WATERING

If your garden has rain barrels, use the remaining water now, drain and scrub out the barrels—they can develop algal deposits. Keep screening and rain barrel covers tight to prevent mosquitoes from laying eggs in them. After the barrels are cleaned, rain showers in late August may fill them again.

Again this month, watering takes full attention. Check soaker hoses to be sure that water is penetrating to the root depth of annuals. In hot dry summers, the plants themselves will show where the water system fails to reach. Unfortunately, they do it by dying. If annuals turn wilt and turn brown, pull them out. They will not recover as herbaceous perennials might when allowed to go temporarily dry.

Containers and hanging baskets demand careful watching. You may wish to move hanging baskets from hot, sunny spots to more shaded areas until the weather moderates. They will need daily or twice daily watering.

Annuals that were cut back last month or now will need deep watering to support their new foliage and buds. Watch any July-planted new starts for wilting during the day, and replace shading (a bucket in the path of the sun, or wood shingles propped up) if they show stress.

 FERTILIZING

Fertilize container plants and hanging baskets every two weeks.

Fertilize any annual plants in the garden that were cut back last month—using 1/2 the strength recommended on the label.

 GROOMING

Continue to remove all spent flowers from annuals. Shear about 6 inches into **petunias**.

DID YOU KNOW?

Plants originating in zones considerably warmer than the range for this book—Zones 4 to 9—can add exotic edginess to summer gardens. These tender tropicals will look their best in August, glowing when temperatures rise, if provided with enough water through the summer and now.

If you've been inspired by a visit to a garden using zone 10 to 15 plants, check catalogs and nurseries for those suiting your style. Many can be discarded as annuals or wintered over to become somewhat perennial. Some, such as *Canna* sp., are started in spring from rhizomes, and may winter over in the ground in zone 9.

They reach peak size now and in September.

Since these tender tropicals generally require water to grow well, grouping them in one area makes sense. Growing your favorites in containers simplifies moving them indoors for winter protection. Look for the lovely climber **glory lily** (*Gloriosa superba*)—not a true lily. Once established in a container, it can climb to about 6 feet with red and yellow flowers. **Ornamental ginger**, (*Hedychium* spp.), provides towering stems of scented blooms in soft orange and red. Tropicals thrive best if purchased in late spring as small plants or started indoors.

Certain types of **petunias**, including the multiflora type and petunia-look alike *Calibrachoa* 'Million Bells'™ need less deadheading, because their flowers are somewhat self-cleaning. The most demanding of **petunias** are the large-flowered frilly grandifloras, fragrant and floriferous but requiring that all dead flowers be removed.

Geraniums look especially unkempt when their seedheads form. They will continue to set buds for fall bloom if the old flowers are snapped off where the flower stem meets the branch. Carry a bucket around the garden on a morning walk and tidy as you go.

PROBLEMS

All zones: Powdery mildew appears on many different plants this month. Trim off slight damage. Spraying plants with water may help reduce the infection. If annual plants such as **salvia** have the problem, cut them down or pull them out. In general, annuals are so transient in the garden that they do not require chemical treatment, but rather can be removed. But for valuable plants such as **trailing begonias** in hanging baskets, use a registered fungicide. Powdery mildew can be treated with fungicides after the gray fuzzy

symptoms appear on leaves. In this, it is an unusual disease—most fungal problems on plants—such as rust on **hollyhocks** or **snapdragons**—cannot be managed once the symptoms are apparent.

Spraying with a fungicide can protect your plants from mildew.

SEPTEMBER
ANNUALS & BIENNIALS

 PLANNING

Seasonal change sweeps in with September. The return of cooler nights and fresh plants into nurseries reinvigorates the gardener's enthusiasm.

September garden work combines the pleasure of cooler air with continuously warm soil. With these conditions, the garden in September will be comfortable for garden work. The difficulty is that as we approach the fall equinox, light for garden work becomes more and more scarce. In the more northern parts of Washington, light diminishment reduces both plant growth and the gardener's pleasure. Some adventurous gardeners in this region invest in head-lamps—those often used for setting up camp at night—and stretch the gardening day into evening by carrying their own light.

Review which annuals you wish to remove from the garden, perhaps planning to replace them with fresh fall color in **pansies**, **violas**, and **annual chrysanthemums**. If your perennial garden contains **asters** coming into bloom now, or beautiful leaf color in dark **dahlias** and herbs, take flowers or leaves to the nursery to find a good color echo when you select new plants.

 PLANTING

Fall and winter blooming annuals go into the ground and into pots this month.

Fall containers and fall bedding plants: **chrysanthemums** that will be treated as annuals (grown only once for their flowers) will billow into nurseries in many different colors this month. Most do best if planted in September rather than later months. **Pansies**, grown in dozens of attractive colors from white through true blues and pinks and even deep black, last well throughout winter in zones 7-9. They need to get good root systems down into warm soil now, and to set buds for winter. In zones 5-6, they offer intriguing but transient color now, because they will be killed by heavy frosts.

 CARE

Select which tender **geraniums**, **fuchsia** baskets, and **begonias** you may wish to protect for winter. They can stay outside until October, but trim off any damaged or too-long pieces now.

 WATERING

Continue to water annuals and container plantings throughout the garden; fall rains often come late in September or even hold off until October.

Cosmos can endure drier soils, and may need watering about half as often as the other annuals.

 FERTILIZING

For containers and annual basket plants still in bloom, fertilize once more this month. If you plan to remove the plants in a few weeks, fertilizer isn't needed. Stop all fertilizing, including baskets, by September 30.

 GROOMING

Deadhead any summer annuals remaining for one more month interest. You'll be noticing renewed bloom on plants cut back in July. Keep cutting garden flowers picked to encourage more buds.

 PROBLEMS

Slugs: They do less damage on older, mature annual leaves; you'll likely see fewer rasped leaves this month. (The slug does

DID YOU KNOW?

Allow annuals to form seed pods so you can collect and save them. **Hollyhock** (a biennial), **zinnias**, **marigolds**, **cleome**, **nigella** and others will set seed now when blossoms remain to ripen. Seeds of hybrids, such as *Zinnia* 'Profusion Series' or *Coleus* 'Merlot', will differ from what you saw in the garden this year. The joyous fervor of plant breeding for garden annuals brings new hybrid types each year: yellow **impatiens** for shade (*Impatiens* 'Jungle Gold'), **California poppies** with ruffles ('Apricot Chiffon'), and of course, those Supertunias™.

Marigold 'First Lady'

What is a hybrid: A hybrid plant has 2 parents—and like humans, gathers characteristics from both parents. Plant breeders select the best characteristics, choosing for garden interest, or fruit productivity, or color, or a combination of qualities. If it sets seed in the garden, the newly pollinated plants will have different qualities as a result of having pollen introduced from different relatives. The experimenting may result in your own discovery.

Standard, unhybridized plants, such as plain **cosmos**, or the species of **California poppy**, or **native columbine**, will produce usable seed year after year, and often simply drop it into the garden where it germinates in the proper season. With hardy plants like California poppy, you may decide to scatter the seed when it ripens, without storing it.

To store collected seed, pick seed capsules when they turn brown. Make labels to keep with the seeds at all stages the process. Shake or pull out the seeds. Store them on paper towels for about 10 days until fully dry. Store in paper envelopes or small jars (babyfood size), keeping them in a cool, dry spot. Some gardeners put a small amount of dried milk in a twist of paper inside the jar to reduce humidity. Heat and humidity are the enemies of seed storage. Plan to use the stored seeds in the next season.

not chew, it draws on and damages the leaves through a rasping system. You may notice the fibers of leaves uncovered by slug attack, as if yanked through a metal carpenter's rasp.)

Slugs reproduce year round but they tend to be most productive of eggs in early fall. Look for slug eggs this month and next, they deposit small piles of pearly eggs—smaller than bee-bee shot—in stacks of 40 to 120 each. Look under mulches, woodpile edges, and any wood refuse. You may come across them accidentally while weeding. Scoop these up and destroy them by dropping into soapy water, or stomping. Don't toss them into a compost pile where the eggs will settle down and hatch into new munchers, infant size.

Powdery mildew: remove and discard annuals disfigured by powdery mildew. You'll notice it on **zinnias**, and on vegetables—which are, after all, generally annuals. Trim off affected leaves on **squash** plants. The fruit will mature well and be unaffected.

OCTOBER

ANNUALS & BIENNIALS

PLANNING

Consider which plants you intend to store for winter, which will be discarded, and what seeds you wish to harvest.

PLANTING

Zones 7-9: Have annual seed packets on hand when planting bulbs this fall. **Forget-me-not, calendula, Shirley poppies** and **California poppies, larkspur, toadflax** (*Linaria*), and **annual alyssum** will bloom early in spring from seeds scattered in October or November.

Look for bright, hardy annuals related to vegetables, though not for eating.

Chard and **kale** get the attention of hybridizers and bring reds, purples, yellows, and gold to the winter garden (*Beta vulgaris* ssp. *cicla* var. *flavescens* 'Bright Lights', chard 'Bright Lights'; *Brassica oleracea*, **ornamental cabbage**; *B. oleracea* Acephala group, **kale**).

Sweet pea seeds may be planted in late October or November, or later in February. Prepare the soil by loosening it and amending with compost; plant where you'll provide a trellis or other vertical support. One of the most beautifully scented is

Toadflax

an old cultivar 'Cupani', named for the first grower of sweet peas in the 17th century. They're tiny in size and lack traditional color, being deep maroon and dark blue. Planting 'Cupani' in combination with other sweet peas provides the old-fashioned perfect fragrance, no matter what the scent characteristics of other cultivars.

Zones 5-6: Wait until spring thaw to plant sweet peas. Gather annual seeds when tidying the garden.

CARE

All zones: Pull out annuals killed by frost, composting all plants after chopping them up to speed the process (do not compost diseased ones). Scrub hanging baskets clean and store them empty for next year's planting. Starting fresh in spring will be easier with a stack of clean hanging baskets on hand.

Mulch over any areas where you've removed spent annuals. A layer of compost, or composted leaves, will keep weeds down until spring, or plant spring bulbs in the empty spots.

Storing tender plants for next season. **Begonias, geraniums** and **fuchsias**, generally purchased as plants in bud during spring, may be wintered over indoors.

Keep **geraniums** as house plants if the area has sufficient light and space. Water sparingly during winter and groom the plants. If you wish to keep several, they can be potted together about 5 plants to a 10-inch pot. Trim back both roots and foliage; rootballs should be about 4 inches in diameter and length. Foliage can be cut back to about 6 inches. Tuck them in the pots, label, and water. They can go dormant, in a 40- to 45-degree F. storage spot. Water lightly each month and check for shriveling. If you do not have room for any geranium storage, compost the plants. Nurseries will provide you with beauties again in spring.

Tender basket **fuchsias** can take light frost. As fall progresses, leaves turn yellow and drop, flowers dwindle and go to seed, and berries form. Leave plants in their baskets. In Zones 7 to 9, they may survive winter if cut back to 6 inches, buried in the ground or tucked under a porch, and mulched. For real security, and in coldest zones, store indoors in their original baskets. A basement or cold (but not freezing) garage is fine, with temperatures about 45 degrees F. They do not need much light, but will die if their roots dry. Check for renewed growth in spring.

CAN YOU REUSE— RECYCLE—POTTING SOIL?

1. Potting soil doesn't "wear out." It's easily renewed for use next season. With the money you save, you can buy more plants. (See Houseplants chapter for more detail on potting soil.) If the plants were healthy with no disease problems, use it again. Note: Do not reuse any potting soil for winter that has contained water-holding crystals, the gelatinous material that is sometimes added to commercial composts. It will make soil too damp in winter for successful bulb planting or planting of winter annuals.

If you plan to use the soil now to plant a few more winter containers, or for fall plantings of spring-blooming bulbs, do this:

2. Dump the compacted, root-filled soil onto a tarp or into a wheelbarrow. If you have a hardware cloth screen with holes big enough for the larger particles of the mix, rub it through the screen to remove roots and debris. Allow it to drop into the wheelbarrow or onto the tarp. (A wheelbarrow is easier to use.)

3. Renew the mix. Add some new "grit"—either pumice or perlite—about 1/4 by volume. Exact proportions don't matter. Also add about 1/4 by volume of compost: either your own compost put through a screen, or bagged compost, any kind. Mix thoroughly. You can store this mix in a bag for spring or use it right now.

4. If you're planting spring-flowering bulbs such as **daffodils** with flowering annuals on top of the pot, check the pot for drainage holes. Fill it with wet soil and add water to be sure it drains well.

WATERING

Watering will not be needed this month in any zone unless rains come late.

FERTILIZING

Stop fertilizing all annuals now.

GROOMING

Zones 7-9: Trimming annuals in late September or early October may produce a few new buds. Regardless, the lack of light as days shorten reduces their growth. You may decide to pull them out even if they haven't been frosted.

PROBLEMS

Look over any annuals being removed from the garden; keep any diseased or insect-infested ones out of the compost. Insects slow their lives during fall just as plants do, so you won't be seeing as many aphids on plants.

NOVEMBER

ANNUALS & BIENNIALS

PLANNING

Gather your notebooks and photographs of summer to think of what you enjoyed, or what you missed and would like to add. You'll notice that review is frequently suggested in this *Month-by-Month* guide. Since looking at the entire garden simultaneously is rather daunting, you may want to review the flower garden—bulbs, perennials, and annuals—during November and December. Look at the trees and shrubs in January and February during pruning season.

Would your garden perk up with some new, unfamiliar but stunning annual plants? Collect catalogs and dream on through December and January. Growers continue to offer seeds and plants with new looks.

Perhaps you will want to follow a color theme: Blues? **California bluebell** (*Phacelia campanularia*), started from seed in April (Zones 7-9), will form low mounds covered with clear blue flowers in mid-summer. **Larkspur** (*Delphinium* 'Gentian Blue'), hardy in all zones, is another elegant blue annual that's not used enough. **Bachelor's buttons** (*Centaurea cyanus*) traditionally blue, can be found in tall or short cultivars, and in other colors—white, soft pink, and rose. Pair these with with **meadow foam** (*Limnanthes douglasii*), a crisp yellow and white flower native to California.

PLANTING

In coldest zones, winter has landed, and no planting can be done.

Zones 7-9 can sow **sweet pea** seeds or other hardy annual seeds (see October.) Plants on sale in local nurseries may tempt you into adding just one more **ornamental kale** or **pansy** splash to the landscape. The ornamental kales look their best in sunny locations, and have been hybrid-

Ornamental kale

ized into some astonishing color combinations, such as purple on purple with white.

CARE

All zones: Plan winter shelter for any large containers remaining outdoors. In zone 5-6, wooden half barrels can winter over if the plants in them have 6 inches of soil between the plant roots and the barrel edge. For smaller containers, bring them into garage shelter in the coldest areas, or sink them in soil if convenient. Do this in early November.

Zones 7-9: Winter freezes will seldom harm any container that is 15 inches in diameter or larger. If they can be moved onto soil in a protected spot, the ground warmth also helps. Smaller ones can be temporarily brought indoors in case of hard freezes, which tend to be infrequent and relatively short west of the Cascades.

WATERING

Take a rest from watering in all zones—unless container plants on a sheltered porch have not been receiving rain.

DID YOU KNOW?

Look at the Chapter on Groundcovers and Vines for ideas on annual vines to add to your garden next year. Twiners and scramblers like **glorious cup** and **saucer vine**, with intricate blue flowers (*Cobaea scandens*) can add height to the flattest garden. **Morning glories** (*Ipomoea* spp.), often shunned because of a mistaken identification with the nasty weed called 'field bindweed' will tumble over fences beautifully, especially in warmest summer areas.

Planting in pouches? You may have noticed catalogs and nurseries offering plastic planting pouches, either to hang up and tuck plants in, or to stretch along the ground. These are popular in Europe, especially the hanging types. When you visit spring garden shows, look for some demonstrations of these. They require careful attention so they are not over-watered, and they look like—well, a plastic pouch—before the plants cover them completely. They would be handy for a short-term planting situation, such as a rental home with no garden space and no containers on hand. If the pouch will be hung where hottest sun can hit it, the roots may suffer damage; keep them in morning sun only until plants cover the plastic.

FERTILIZING

While not watering, don't fertilize. All plants are in winter dormancy.

GROOMING

Zones 7-9: Cut back bloomed-out **chrysanthemums** to about 6-8 inches. Mulch around them and wait for spring to see if they survive. It isn't always easy to tell which ones will be perennial, and the effort of mulching

is worth the chance of their returning.

PROBLEMS

Check planting areas for drainage problems; if there is a spot that holds water all winter, spring revision of drainage may be necessary.

As plants go dormant, slug problems recede.

DECEMBER
ANNUALS & BIENNIALS

PLANNING

December always goes by in a whirl, but a bit of garden reverie can be comforting during many activities.

We can continue with November's dream of new annuals. Pinks, oranges and reds? **Geranium** 'Black Velvet Series' (*Pelargonium* spp.) shows off its rose or salmon flowers against dark, nearly black leaves. For zippy red, the **Mexican hat** or **Mexican sunflower** (*Tithonia* spp.) shines with the clearest bright red-orange flowers, resembling **daisies**.

Sunflowers in vivid rusty red and deep orange light up the late summer garden. Use the winter planning time to map some garden adventure by studying magazines and catalogs.

Check nurseries and garden centers for sales on containers, seed starting equipment, and potting soil.

DID YOU KNOW?

Magazines often review the newest annuals in their January and February issues; check for articles listing the best of the newest. Also, checking the web sites of favorite catalogs can help locate the plants that will thrill you next season.

PLANTING

Annuals, by definition, complete their lives in one season. The end of the year finds the end of their garden life. In all zones, gardeners take a rest from planting annuals in December.

CARE

Some familiar annuals may appear as color spots at nurseries in December. If you bring these home as container plants, perhaps red **primroses** for a vivid centerpiece, keep them well watered and cool at night. In zones 7-9, annuals may be used as interior decoration while waiting out a cold spell before being planted to cover the surface of a pot of bulbs.

Setting small plants in the sink and spraying their leaves with water occasionally will also help their indoor survival.

FERTILIZING

No plants need fertilizer in December. If hardy annuals such as primroses stay indoors for more than a few weeks, they will begin to show yellowed leaves from lack of light. Fertilizer doesn't fix that problem. Keep them in as much light as possible.

GROOMING

Zones 7-9 Trim off faded flowers or leaves on any winter **pansies**, **calendulas**, or other hardy annuals outside in containers.

PROBLEMS

Check all plants for aphids or other insects that may have hitchhiked indoors. Rinsing leaves thoroughly with water helps, but keep up the vigilance because aphids enjoy warm temperatures and can multiply fast.

BULBS, CORMS, RHIZOMES, & TUBERS

Magicians of the garden, the family of bulb-like plants starts from unpromising brownish lumps of many sizes and shapes. They flower into some of the brightest and most vivid of all garden beauties. The earliest white snowdrop bulbs will open the season in mid-winter. Color brightens with tulips and sweeps forward through the summer to lilies, daylilies, and up with dahlias. Plants in this family range from the most winter-hardy daffodils to fragile, summer-blooming tropicals. These plants—bulbs, corms, rhizomes, and tubers—provide both fascination and garden pleasure.

Gardens in Oregon and Washington benefit nearly year-round from the beautiful colors of these plants. There's a selection for every garden in every zone. The long, cool springs and mild summers of the western region, Zones 7 through 9, suit these perfectly. The hardiness of spring bulbs makes them reliable for even the coldest areas, Zones 4 through 6.

IDENTIFYING, SELECTING, AND STORING

Bulbs, corms, rhizomes, and tubers originate in many different parts of the world and enjoy different garden conditions. They're linked by an odd but practical reality: each of them can be dug from the ground and moved around or stored without damage. Although we can't take a rooted plant like a daisy out of the ground and leave it on a shelf, we can set a tulip bulb on a workbench for weeks or leave an iris rhizome out of the ground while we find its proper garden spot. Because they store nutrients for long periods, they can live out of ground for several months while stored or shipped. Gardeners take a verbal short

cut by calling all these plants "bulbs," but they have different names in botany. Some are true bulbs, like lilies, tulips, hyacinths, and daffodils. True bulbs have distinct fleshy layers surrounding the central embryo. An onion is a true bulb; think of the layers as it is cut and the growing central stem being visible as onions or garlic stay in storage. If you were to slice a tulip, you'd see the same formation as an onion.

Corms, including cyclamen, crocosmia, crocus, and gladiolus, are firm and solid, nearly one distinct substance throughout, without layers. Blooming shoots emerge pointed from the top of the mature corm. They multiply quickly, which make them a good buy if you want more for your money. Summer corms such as gladiolus may remain in the ground during moderate winters (Zone 7) or may be dug and stored in colder zones. When digging corms, you'll find miniature new ones developing around the original.

Tubers and rhizomes, both modified roots, may be dahlias, iris, or cannas. The obvious tuber is the familiar potato, providing nutrition for us while storing carbohydrates for it. Dahlias resemble small elongated potatoes, with small pinkish growing points rather than "eyes" like a potato. Rhizomes like German iris appreciate being planted near the surface of the soil where

they can get summer warmth. They can multiply into mats of rhizomes, one on the other, and may require division.

PLANTING TIMES

Hardy bulbs, equipped to live through winter cold, bloom in spring. They form roots during fall and winter and must be planted in fall before ground freezes. Many of the flowers that say "spring is here" are hardy bulbs, including crocuses, snowdrops, hyacinths, daffodils, tulips, and allium.

Summer-blooming ("tender") bulbs, cannot survive winter and are planted in late April and May as the soil warms. Cannas, dahlias, gladiolus, and more exotic types like eucomis and acidanthera must be planted in warm soil. Some, like tuberous begonias and cannas, bloom well if planted indoors two months before summer. This allows them to get their roots started and gives them a better chance to reach full bloom.

SELECTING AND STORING

When selecting, look for the firmest and most solid, especially with the true bulbs like daffodils and tulips. Small "bargain" types often bloom poorly or fail to bloom at all. Buying large, well-developed bulbs, tubers corms and rhizomes pays off in garden excellence.

Proper storage helps these grow best. Even though they adapt to a life of storage out of soil, they should be planted during the season when purchased. For instance, tulips bought in fall should be planted in fall; if they remain out of the ground through the following spring and summer, the interior flower embryo will dry and fail to bloom. All of these plants desiccate if neglected while in storage.

Hardy bulbs require cool but not refrigerated storage for fall planting. Remove them from plastic bags if they're sold in those and store them loosely in brown paper bags. An exception will be professionally packed bulbs in plastic bags with extensive perforation that supplies enough air. A cool dark spot with good air circulation, such as a garage or basement or even an airy cupboard, will keep them healthy until planting time. Keep them out of light to prevent premature shoot extension. Hardy bulbs don't require refrigeration anywhere in our region.

Summer-blooming bulbs such as dahlia and gladiolus need darkness during their winter storage. Tuck them into slightly damp sawdust or peat moss or even compost. Check their health during winter. As the spring planting season approaches, many of them will begin to grow, sending up shoots inside

their storage boxes. Keep them misted if that happens and pot up as they grow.

SOIL PREPARATION AND PLANTING TECHNIQUE

Choose a sunny or shady spot according to the individual plant's needs. Most spring-bloomers need part sun or full sun; most summer-bloomers definitely enjoy sun. Well-drained, organically amended soil is best for most bulbs; few of them survive soggy soil or standing water. (See the General Introduction for instructions on amending soil with composted material.) Most are easily handled and planted, making them excellent plants for beginning gardeners and for youngsters.

Fall planted bulbs and corms, such as crocus, narcissus, and tulips, should be planted at three times their depth; for example, if the crocus is one inch in diameter, set it three inches down. Space them about two times their depth apart. Plant with roots pointing down and shoots facing up. All of these spring-bloomers look better in groups. You can set them one at a time in individual holes, but it's easier to dig a larger hole, set all of them, and backfill the planting.

Spring-bloomers contain their first-year flower within. Many will perennialize or naturalize. Fertilizing? Many professional growers recommend planting with fertilizer on top, then adding fertilizer in the early spring when shoots emerge and are 2 to 3 inches tall.

After planting, water well. Autumn rains may be late, and soils are often dry when it's planting time for spring-bloomers. Apply two inches of any mulch type after watering.

Keep the planting watered until rains become regular.

Summer-bloomers planted in warm, late spring soils also require systematic watering and fertilizing. Fertilize when planting and keep plants moist throughout the blooming season.

CARE AFTER BLOOM

Spring-blooming plants that will perennialize, such as daffodils, crocus, and snowdrops, must have foliage completely ripened before it's removed. After blooming, remove the flowers only, leaving the stems, but allow all leaves to die back naturally, often six to seven weeks after bloom. Don't braid or fold them because that retards ripening.

Summer-blooming bulbs slow their growth as days shorten, and foliage will brown with fall frosts. Lift the plants gently, allow the foliage to turn brown for a few days, and store the dry tubers or corms in sawdust or peat moss in darkness where temperatures stay above freezing. Replant in spring.

PEST PROBLEMS

Though generally care-free, these plants universally suffer from problems with garden slugs that chew emerging new leaves and eat buds.

CONTAINER PLANTING

Almost all bulbs, corms, tubers and rhizomes thrive in containers. Use a well-drained potting mix or add one-fourth pumice by volume if further drainage is needed. Check the container for adequate drainage holes. Plant at the same time as you would plant them in the garden, allowing spring-blooming bulbs to experience the normal outdoor winter chill. (Protect pots from freezing by sinking them in the ground or surrounding them with a mulch like sawdust or leaves.)

Fill the pot three-fourths full with potting mix, watering it thoroughly. Then install bulbs. Set bulbs and corms closer together than you would in the ground, about one to two inches apart. Cover with soil to within one inch of the container top, then water again. This method allows for plenty of root room beneath the plants as they grow.

Summer-blooming bulbs, which may grow much larger, require big containers, sufficient to plant about eight inches down and six to eight inches apart (for lilies, tall dahlias, and cannas).

JANUARY
BULBS, CORMS, RHIZOMES, & TUBERS

 PLANNING

Take a deep breath and relax. With bulbs there are few immediate tasks.

Gather catalogs for summer bulbs. Even if you order bulbs prior to planting time, shipments arrive later in spring. Coordinate summer-blooming bulbs like pink **Asiatic lilies** with shrubs, such as **lilacs**. Lilies keep color in the garden when lilacs fade.

Update your garden notebook by adding labels or photos of bulbs planted last fall. You'll want to identify new favorites when they flower.

 PLANTING

Zones 4-6: It's generally too cold to plant outside now. Pot leftover bulbs up instead. Fill containers (even nursery pots work well) with potting soil, wet it, and plant the leftover **daffodils** and **tulips**. Place them in an unheated garage or fruit cellar where temperatures stay between 32 and 45 degrees F. Don't allow them to freeze or go dry. When shoots emerge in mid- to late-March, sink the pots in soil outdoors where they'll receive necessary light.

Zones 7-9: "Can I plant now?" is one of the most commonly asked questions this time of year. Yes, you can. Although spring bulbs must go in pots in zones 4-6, they can still be planted outdoors now. Spring-bloomers like **tulips, daffodils,** and **hyacinths** are better off in the ground than languishing under the kitchen sink or in a basement drawer. Discard any that seem dried or, worse, soft and diseased. Plant anytime the ground is workable, neither squishy nor frozen. Set them at the same depth you'd use for fall planting. Cover with a loose mulch of compost, pine needles or fallen leaves.

Check stored dahlia bulbs for rot and cut off any rotted portion.

The planting delay may cost some garden quality; spring-bloomers planted now may not bloom normally—they'll be late or may come up "blind" (with leaves but no flowers). But many will recover after this year to bloom normally next season, especially **crocuses, daffodils,** and **hyacinths.**

All zones: Start **paperwhite narcissus** and **amaryllis** (*Hippeastrum*) indoors. Check nurseries and garden centers for **amaryllis** bargains during January and February. Choose firm, solid bulbs, and they'll thrive as vigorously as those potted two months ago. Blooms will emerge more rapidly than they did in November.

 CARE

Zones 4-6: East of the mountains, bulbs soil need a three- to four-inch layer of mulch to endure frozen ground. They won't be harmed if their roots began growing last fall.

Bulbs in most containers will be damaged if left outside unprotected. If potted in small containers, tuck them into the ground—perhaps where you choose to see them bloom in spring—with the pot rim level with soil. Cover with three to four inches of mulch. Bulbs in large containers, such as half-barrels, survive winter because of the soil volume. Keep these large containers out of bright sun to avoid January or February mild spells. Thawing can shock bulbs into harmful premature growth.

For smaller pots in zones 4-6: If you have an extra refrigerator that can reach 35 degrees F., bulbs can receive their chill time there. Don't store the pots with **apples** or other fruit that emits ethylene, which harms plant embryos.

Zones 7-9: Occasional frigid weather can affect bulb plantings west of the mountains. Check any pots of bulbs during extended dry or cold periods. If they desiccate once root formation has started, the bulbs will be damaged or even killed. Moisten them well before adding mulch to protect from freezing weather. Winter rains generally keep them damp, but you'll need to monitor. Bulbs placed under a porch overhang or an eave can dry out.

Group the pots, filling in spaces between with light mulch like leaf compost or screened compost. If temperatures drop to the low 20s, use a plastic bag filled with dry fallen leaves as an insulating "pillow" across the pot tops and edges.

DID YOU KNOW?

Zones 4-6: Set bulbs at the proper depth by mid-November Spring-blooming bulbs and they'll survive the toughest winters.

Zones 7-9: West of the Cascades, hardy bulbs die in winter more from drowning than freezing. Check gutter flows and divert heavy water flow away from bulbs. Otherwise, they'll rot rather than root.

 ## WATERING

Indoors: After they bloom, potted **amaryllis** (*Hippeastrum*) require weekly watering to promote new leaf growth, which promotes another year's blooms. Remove any frilly foil wrappers that impede water drainage.

Outdoors: Check ground bulb plantings for sufficient irrigation, and water thoroughly if the area is dry. Bulbs under shrubs may lack water.

 ## FERTILIZING

Zones 7-9: Late January may bring a mild spell of temperatures in the 40s when **snowdrops** (*Galanthus nivalis*) grace the garden with full bloom. Fertilize them after blooms fade using either liquid or granular bulb fertilizer, kelp or fish fertilizer. (See General Introduction for explanation of fertilizer formulas.)

 ## PROBLEMS

All zones: Snow? No problem. Snowfall protects bulb shoots and other plants from drying cold. Ice storms bring the real peril. Trees can drop branches on shoots, crushing them. Resilient bulbs often bloom even with early shoot damage from ice, which affects only the foliage.

 ## GROOMING

Indoors: After **amaryllis** drops its petals, trim the stem down to the bulb.

FEBRUARY
BULBS, CORMS, RHIZOMES, & TUBERS

PLANNING

Late February begins the growing season. Survey any emerging spring-bloomers. Would some look better in different spots? Perhaps an orange-centered **daffodil** landed under a pink **rhododendron**? Take photos to plan.

Order summer-bloomers from catalogs or buy them from nurseries. Store them in a cool, dry environment until planting time when soil warms in April or May.

PLANTING

Zones 4-6: This month is too cold for planting.

Zones 7-9: Move or divide **snowdrops** just as blooms fade early this month. Resetting immediately after digging gives the best chance of blooming next year.

Spring-bloomers: Are hardy spring-blooming bulbs still unplanted? Discard soft or hollow ones. Get the rest into soil, knowing that bloom won't be normal. Don't plant after February because warmth stunts their development.

Hardy true **lilies** (*Lilium* species) of all types go into the ground by month's end. Set them six to eight inches deep in well-drained, loose soil. Place markers with them; they will not emerge until May, and it's easy to plop another plant on top of a bare spot.

CARE

Zones 7-9: Bring "forcing" spring-blooming bulbs indoors into light and cool temperatures after their October or early November planting. They've received the necessary eleven to twelve weeks of outdoor or refrigerator temperatures at 40 degrees F. or below. When they're ready for "forcing," you'll see roots emerging below the pot's drain hole and new shoots poking out. A cool greenhouse or basement (50 to 55 degrees F) with hanging fluorescent light six inches above the plants (twelve hours a day) provide the ideal forcing conditions for emerging **tulips, daffodils,** and **hyacinths**. When buds show color, treat them as houseplants and move them into warmer temperatures and window light. Blooms last longer kept cool at night in a basement or on a cold porch, like a refrigerator used to keep cut flowers alive and fresh.

Check your stored **dahlias, gladiolus,** and **begonias**—the summer-bloomers—for water needs. Remove rotted ones, and dampen the withered ones with a spray bottle. The sawdust or peat you've stored them be slightly damp.

WATERING

Continue to water **amaryllis** after their bloom fades.

Provide supplemental water for bulbs under eaves, in window wells, or in overhangs. Check the moisture level of bulbs stored in pots or tucked under mulch outside. In Zones 7 to 9 they'll be actively growing, filling the pots with roots and beginning to shoot. In coldest zones, you will see no shoots yet.

Check the moisture level of the sawdust or peat of stored bulbs.

FERTILIZING

Small shoots of **crocus, grape hyacinth,** and earliest **daffodils** (like 'February Gold' and 'Tete á Tete') will poke up. Apply a balanced, water-soluble bulb fertilizer according to label directions when shoots extend one to two inches. Use granular types early in the season only if rain is frequent.

Fertilize bulbs that perennialize (returning from past years) before buds show, when shoots extend two to four inches. Spring fertilizer helps strengthen the bulb for next year's bloom, which is essential for **daffodils** and **crocuses**.

GROOMING

Discard **paperwhite narcissus** with spent blooms. If you wish to attempt re-bloom, cut back flowers. Then leave paperwhites in their pots, water until the leaves fade, and then tuck them in a cool, dry place throughout the summer. They may emerge again when watered in late fall at the normal planting time for paperwhites.

DID YOU KNOW?

Spring bulbs: Forced **daffodils** or **tulips** display better where temperatures stay cool. In all zones, treat these as houseplants after flowers fade. They can be reintroduced into the garden. Slide them out of their pots once soil temperatures allow outdoor planting.

Your own pots of forced blooming **crocuses, hyacinths,** or **daffodils** can be set into the garden after they bloom. Dig a hole in unfrozen ground and slide the bulbs out without breaking the roots or disturbing the leaves. Water in, and you'll often get flowers the following year. **Tulips** produce smaller flowers the following year, but others generally give a repeat performance.

Zones 4-6: If temperatures remain below freezing, water forced bulbs normally and allow them to grow as houseplants until warmer temperatures.

PROBLEMS

All zones: Squirrels, voles, and birds nibble foliage and dig out bulbs. Use a protective hardware cloth mesh for bulbs such as **crocuses** and **tulips** (see October). Gently lift mesh off to allow expansion room to accommodate growth.

Slugs threaten emerging bulb shoots and continue their attacks through spring, rasping holes in **lilies, dahlias,** and other tender early bloomers. Check under mulch and new leaves. Infant slugs, smaller than a pencil eraser, can cause nearly as much havoc as their parents. Handpick these pests or use the least-toxic slug bait. Avoid slug-attracting plants like **hostas** as a bulb companion. Perennial *Vinca minor* or low-growing *Cotoneaster* planted over **daffodils** appeal less to slugs. Unfortunately, slugs will still wander onto bulb foliage regardless.

Not happy with blooms? They may have been planted too late or too deep. **Daffodils** that do not bloom in thick clumps may need division next month. Separate them when foliage yellows and flops over. Dig carefully, disturbing the roots as little as possible, and set two inches apart. Water well and mulch with compost after separating. (This can also be a September task though it's harder when foliage has vanished. If you're waiting for fall, mark the clumps. Small **bamboo** twigs work well.)

MARCH
BULBS, CORMS, RHIZOMES, & TUBERS

PLANNING

Photograph or draw garden beds in spring bloom before summer's energy and flush of green cover their traces.

PLANTING

Tuberous begonias fill summer baskets with frilly flowers perfect for lightly shaded spots. Plant them indoors in early or mid-March and slightly later in colder zones. Lay tubers on soil, concave side up, with their quarter-inch pink shoot up. Cover the edges of the tubers with soil; cover the tops with less than 1/2 inch.

Water well in a dark but warm spot until sprouts show and roots form. Bottom heat helps them root. Move into bright light, such as fluorescents, for twelve hours a day when shoots reach 1 inch. Keep the soil consistently moist. Without sufficient indoor light you should wait until April to plant.

Zones 4-6: Move or divide **snowdrops** just as blooms fade early this month.

If your eastern Washington garden is in a warmer spot, such as Walla Walla or the Tri-Cities in Washington, prepare spots for **dahlias** if the snow has gone and the ground is drying.

Zones 7-9: Summer bulbs: Prepare planting spots in full sun with fertile, well-drained soil for **dahlias, gladiolus, crocosmia,** and **agapanthus**. If dahlias have begun to produce shoots, plant them in shallow flats under lights or in a bright window light to encourage growth.

Other tropical plants, including **caladium** and **cannas**, require considerable heat—start them on a heat mat. If you have only one or two, place them temporarily on top of the refrigerator or water heater.

CARE

Zones 7-9: Fall-blooming bulbs: **Colchicum**, sometimes called **autumn crocus** though it isn't a true crocus, will have large, ragged, green leaves now. After the leaves begin to yellow, divide crowded plantings in all zones. Dig carefully. Set them in compost-amended soil about 3 inches apart. They're fully hardy and perennialize well, coming up year after year.

Zones 4-6: As bulbs emerge, gradually remove mulch throughout the month. Late snows generally don't harm bulbs if they've grown leaves but not yet budded.

WATERING

Spring-blooming bulbs—**daffodils**, **tulips** and **hyacinths**—require regular moisture during budding and blooming. Water the plantings if rain is scarce and bulbs have emerged.

Water forced bulbs started inside. Keep soil evenly moist but not soggy. Do not allow bulbs to sit in saucers of water.

FERTILIZING

All zones: Fertilize bulbs once when shoots are 2 to 4 inches out of the ground, using either a liquid or granular formula with 5-10-10, 6-8-6, or 9-3-6 ratios. This helps strengthen and rejuvenate bulbs after flowering.

Zones 7-9: Fertilize perennial flower beds that may contain **iris, daylilies,** true **lilies,** and other bulbs, using a granular fertilizer, preferably just before a rain. The same fertilizer used for spring bulbs will also work for summer bulbs. If rain is absent, water the area thoroughly. All fertilizers need water to reach roots.

Soil pH: Dahlias, and most summer bulbs, do best where soil is about 6.5 pH. Dahlias will grow on the edge of a vegetable garden that produces good tomatoes or carrots, which also like a 6.5 pH. They make great cut flowers late in the season.

GROOMING

When the flower finishes, leave foliage in place for at least six weeks. Don't fold, braid, rubber-band, or otherwise mutilate the leaves. The leaves must be whole to carry nutrients into the bulb to form next year's flowers.

Snap off the bloom of spent flowers; leave the stem. Do not gather quantities of foliage from plants for cut flowers—the bulb needs as much "green life" as can remain. Don't allow the **daffodils** or **tulips** to go to seed.

After blooom, place container-forced bulbs outdoors in a light, sunny spot and keep them watered until the foliage ripens, at least six weeks after the flowers end.

PROBLEMS

Patrol for slugs...these icky mollusks chew off new shoots and ruin buds of all spring bulbs. They're known to shimmy up **daffodil** stems—ignoring the foliage—gnawing into the bud.

All zones: Tulip plantings can contract a nasty fungal disease called tulip botrytis (*Botyrtis tulipae*) especially west of the Cascades. Flowers crumple into

TIPS ON SELECTION

Spring-blooming bulbs show best when they have ground cover or perennial accompaniments. In sunny spots, **daylilies,** hardy perennial **geraniums,** and **campanula** cover bulb's bare knees.

For shady sites where **scilla, grape hyacinth,** and small **daffodils** go, try *Alchemilla mollis* or *Epimedium* as edgings.

Calla lilies (*Zantesdechia*) winter over in Zones 7 to 9. The hardiest and most prolific bloomer is the creamy white, although you'll also find oranges, pinks, and purples. Plant them in sites with ample water in summer. In Zones 4 to 6, they're treated as container plants or as annuals. You can grow your own Georgia O'Keeffe painting with callas.

gray wads; leaves show brown splotches and roll inward. Confirm the diagnosis with a WSU or OSU Master Gardener volunteer or take it to a nursery specialist. Remove affected **tulip** leaves, flowers, bulbs, and roots. Do not compost it. The fungal spores persist in the ground, so you cannot replant tulips in the same spot. Rotate plantings next year by choosing spring bulbs such as **daffodils, Dutch iris,** or **hyacinths** that are unaffected by tulip blight. If the problem is severe, affecting all your tulips, plant next season in pots, using clean soil.

Deer proof bulbs? **Snowdrops, grape hyacinth,** and **daffodils** escape damage in all zones. But you'll need to protect **tulips, hyacinths,** and **lilies.** Containers that can be moved to protected decks helps. The best defense is the fence (at least 8 feet tall). Dog

Scilla

owners say their pet assistants make deer scram. They aren't deterred by human activity or noise, but motivated dogs can spook them.

APRIL
BULBS, CORMS, RHIZOMES, & TUBERS

PLANNING

All zones: Choose and prepare garden areas for the hottest weather summer-bloomers, including **dahlias, gladiolus,** and **cannas**.

Select containers for summer bulbs. Small 'Mignon' **dahlias** can go in windowboxes or containers of mixed annuals. If your favorite container still contains bloomed-out spring bulbs, such as **narcissus** or **tulips**, you can tip those out and plant them, roots intact, in the garden.

Review spring bulb plantings one more time, noting changes and additions for bulb orders in fall. If you've got too many bright yellow **daffodils** and need some creamy relief, consider ordering some of the whites such as 'Mt Hood', 'Ice Follies', and 'Thalia' for next season. Walk though neighborhoods noting or photographing bulb plantings you like.

For more ideas, visit local public gardens to see spring bulb plantings. Excellent ones are Bellevue Botanical Garden in Bellevue Washington and Point Defiance Park in Tacoma. Later this month, look in Manito Park in Spokane, Washington. In Oregon, throughout the spring, hardy bulbs thrive at Berry Botanic Garden in Portland.

PLANTING

After all danger of frost has passed, **dahlias, gladiolus, crocosmias,** and **cannas** can go into ground in sheltered, warmer areas toward the end of the month. When deciduous trees begin to open their leaves, the weather is settled enough for summer bulb planting. Coldest zones need to wait until weather moderates.

Gladiolus planted every two weeks until late June will keep the color show going throughout the summer. Because each corm produces only one flower stalk, unlike **dahlias** which flower continuously from buds, the corm will not rebloom after it is finished. Many growers solve this by sequential planting. Consider selecting some of the smaller 'Nanus' gladiolus which do not require staking and bloom gracefully.

Brilliant **crocosmia**, most often seen in the tomato-red 'Lucifer', also grow in shades of yellow and orange. Look for 'Ambergate' and yellow *Crocosmia aurea*. They're vivid midsummer-bloomers hardy in Zone 6. Set them about 3 inches apart and 3 inches down. Full sun helps. Zone 5 gardeners find that 'Lucifer' has the best chance of surviving winter, with deep 4-inch mulch and planting close to a house foundation for a bit of warmth.

CARE

All zones: Weed around all emerged bulbs—weed every-

April is a good month to plant dahlias in containers.

where. The spring weeds will fill the garden if we ignore them this month.

For spring bulbs like **daffodils** and **tulips** just finishing their bloom, continue to deadhead by nipping off the faded flowers.

Zones 7-9: After last frost date, remove mulch from over-wintered **dahlias** and **gladiolus**.

 WATERING

All zones: Tulips, hyacinths, and **daffodils** need water during and just after bloom; water the plantings if rain is scarce.

Water all newly set summer-blooming bulbs . . . and do not allow them to dry once they've begun growth. True **lilies, calla lilies, dahlias,** and others require steady supplies of water up to and through their bloom time.

 FERTILIZING

All zones: Fertilize spent spring-bloomers as they finish if you did not do it last month. As they die back, hardy spring bulbs replenish themselves and set flowers for next year. They need only one spring fertilizing, in April or May. If your bulbs are set into beds containing perennial flowers, the spring fertilization of the perennials with a 5-10-10 will also feed the spring bulbs.

You won't need to do them separately.

Indoor: Continue to fertilize **amaryllis** bulbs every two weeks with a houseplant fertilizer, watering consistently as their leaves multiply.

 GROOMING

Remove spent flowers from spring-bloomers as they finish.

 PROBLEMS

All zones: Continue slug patrol—they can remove new **lily** and **dahlia** shoots immediately on emergence, almost before you realize that anything has grown. Cold winter temperatures don't deter them. Slugs can tuck themselves into soil or lay eggs that survive winter and hatch ravenous baby slugs, about $1/5$ inch long but eager to grow by chomping spring bulbs. Use beer traps, less-toxic slug baits like iron phosphate, hand-picking, and constant observation.

Keep bulb plantings free of mulch, a hiding spot slugs prefer. You can replenish mulches later in the summer in order to save water, but for earliest spring, remove slug habitat until the bulbs grow strongly.

MAY
BULBS, CORMS, RHIZOMES, & TUBERS

 PLANNING

Catalogs for bulbs planted in fall may arrive now and in June; mark your favorites. Or try something completely new! It's easiest to think of spring bulbs now. By fall purchasing time, the garden has changed, and thinking of spring becomes challenging. Give yourself some guidance by making notes now and through the end of spring bulb blooming.

Tiny **dahlias** that suit containers and windowboxes may be available at nurseries.

 PLANTING

All zones: Set spring-flowering bulbs that bloomed in containers in the ground now. Choose a sunny spot and dig a hole just as deep as the pot but wide enough to use all the roots. Disturb the roots as little as possible. Slide the bulb mass out of the pot, gently loosen the roots, and settle it in the ground a little deeper than it was in the pot. Cover with soil and water well. Keep watered until foliage ripens (or until six full weeks after bloom).

Early in the month: Set out new and stored **dahlia** tubers. Place markers identifying the bulbs. If the dahlia is a dinner-plate size on a stalk soaring six or seven feet or similar, allow 8 inches deep for planting. Set a sturdy wooden or metal stake firmly beside the tuberous root. Cover the tuber completely. Smaller dahlias can be set three to four inches down. In coldest zones, plant **dahlias** a week after the last frost date and keep covers handy to protect emerging shoots in case of sudden freeze.

True lilies: May is the last month to plant **true lilies** (*Lilium* sp.) in coldest zones; they need cool soil to get their roots started. They also need time for stalks to grow. (See February for planting instructions.) For instance, In Zone 7, Asiatic **lilies** planted in late May do not bloom until late July, instead of their usual June. The stress of late planting also caused them to be a bit dwarfed. Indulge yourself at nurseries with **lily** sales in May, but be sure they're planted promptly. They never go dormant and are stressed by being out of the ground. **Lilies** require well-drained soil and hate the competition of heavy tree roots or other established shrub root masses. Plant far enough away from shrubs to allow for sufficient sunlight and air to reach them.

 CARE

All zones: Dig and transplant spring-flowering bulbs after the foliage turns yellow and is visible. If you do not wish to do this now, wait until fall. Mark locations of spring bulb plantings with popsicle sticks, golf tees, or labels. Photos, or hand-drawn maps in your garden journal also help.

Remove and discard any spent bulbs, such as **tulips**, that are being treated as annuals.

 WATERING

All zones: Rain is sometimes sparse in May. Water all bulbs in pots. Water newly planted summer-bloomers.

Spring-blooming bulbs and corms need water until their foliage ripens. After they disappear into dormancy, they can survive the summer with no water, making them splendid additions to "waterwise" gardens.

 FERTILIZING

All zones: Lightly fertilize emerging **lily, dahlia, crocosmia**, and **canna** shoots.

Zones 7-9: Soils warm slowly west of the Cascades. Some fertilizer types that use slow-release granules (like the Osmocote™) require warm soils (70 degrees F) in order to release their nutrients. They'll be most effective on container plants in warm sheltered spots. Liquid fertilizers reach plants more effectively at this time of year west of the Cascades.

 GROOMING

All zones: Remove spent foliage from any **daffodil** that bloomed more than six weeks ago. Late bloomers such as 'Cheerfulness' and 'Actea' need more time to ripen. Remove flower stalks of early blooming **German iris** (the delicious purple ones). Allow **iris** foliage to multiply and grow naturally throughout summer.

Allium foliage often disappears before the bloom opens, which is normal. Allium leaves can appear as early as February in warmest zones. Leaves wither before flower stalks emerge. Allium bulbs burst into purple (or cream, pink, or yellow) bloom this month. The taller types with prominent golfball- or baseball-sized blooms (such as 'Purple Sensation') look lovely as flowers fade, shading to green and ripening to tan. Many gardeners leave these as accents for most of the summer.

WHERE DO THE TULIPS GO?

Tulip bulbs ripen best if kept dry during the summer. If planted where summer irrigation happens regularly, such as annual or perennial flower gardens, they won't repeat bloom as well. **Crocus** and **hyacinths** also prefer dryness when dormant.

Lilies are so well adapted to western Washington and Oregon, Zones 7 to 9, that some of the finest twentieth century **lilies**, such as Bellingham hybrids, were developed here.

Blue is a rare color in summer bulbs, but it shines in **agapanthus**. Agapanthus, **Lily of the Nile**, generally hardy in Zones 7 to 9, does well in containers. The tall stems topped with midsummer bloom in balls of blue or white make a grand garden accent. Plant the roots now, in a sunny spot, and you'll get good bloom as they settle in. Sometimes they take two to three years to reach full size in the garden. Many types winter over well in the ground in Zones 7 to 9, including the most common 'Peter Pan' (a blue only 18 inches) and 'Storm Cloud' (a smoky blue to 2 feet).

 PROBLEMS

All zones: Record the location of **tulip** plantings. If any develop "fire" (tulip botrytis), you will need to remove them completely along with the soil around them. If you have disease problems with tulips, they shouldn't be replanted in the same soil. Rotating plantings of affected spring bulbs is prudent. Eastside gardeners with lower humidity may not experience these disease problems.

The tulip fire fungus persists in soil, so mark the area and plant non-susceptible **daffodils**, **hyacinths**, or **Dutch iris**.

BULBS, CORMS, RHIZOMES, & TUBERS

PLANNING

Getting ready for fall bulb orders? Try these. If you have shady spots, fall-planted bulbs, such as **snowdrops, scillas,** and small **narcissus,** enhance a woodland edge in dappled shade.

If you love arranging flowers, you'll enjoy the **ornamental onions** in bloom this month and in May. The best ones for dried arrangements include **allium** 'Purple Sensation', *Allium christophii,* and *Allium schubertii,* which produces knock-out flowers in twelve-inch diameter spheres. Include some of these when planning for your fall-planted bulb orders.

In June, temperatures east of the Cascades exceed those on the west side, and summer-blooming flowers may grow more swiftly in Spokane than in Portland. Cool summers west of the mountains mean slower growth for all the tropical bulbs.

PLANTING

All zones: Dahlias and other summer bulbs happily go into the ground this month. If **gladiolus** or **dahlias** or **begonias** show sprouts coming out before planting, handle them carefully because they are brittle. But they will grow well after planting and watering.

Plant out **begonias, cannas,** and **caladium** started indoors. **Caladiums**—sometimes called "fancy-leaved caladium" with leaves in reds, pinks, whites, and striped green—thrive in hot east-side areas if given some afternoon shade. They do well in pots and often look better by the end of summer in Spokane or Walla Walla than they do in Seattle or Bellingham. They need steady heat, over 55 degrees F. and hot nights for best growth. In cooler west side areas, try **caladium** in glassed-in patios for heat concentration until leaves develop.

If planting **calla lilies** now, soak the tuber for up to six hours in tepid water to give it a jump start.

CARE

All zones: Nip out the growing top of tall **dahlias** (over four to six feet) when they reach about fourteen inches or when they have three pairs of true leaves. This will help them produce more blooms and stand stronger against rain and wind. The tallest sorts should be tied loosely to stakes as they grow up.

Caladium 'Candidum'

Monitor the garden for "leaners"; lack of staking can cost blossom because dahlia's brittle foliage breaks easily.

WATERING

All zones: Summer-bloomers require regular water when growth begins. Set soaker hoses around the flower garden to provide deep watering to roots. June may deceive gardeners west of the Cascades with gray skies, but heavy rain can be rare. Keep monitoring water needs by probing with a trowel.

FERTILIZING

All zones: Fertilize **dahlias** with a 5-10-10 granular fertilizer when plants are eight to twelve inches high, watering it into the roots. Some growers use liquid fertilizer. Either type is fine when plenty of water is provided. Dahlias require regular nutrients, applied monthly through August, to put on their late-summer show.

GROOMING

Allium: Avoid removing fully bloomed heads of larger **allium**. If you do wish to harvest them for arrangements, take the entire stem, standing it up with a little water in a supportive container. Allow the water to evaporate and the stem to dry.

Chives, an **allium** often included as a vital part of the herb garden, have attractive pink flowers. Buds and flowers are edible and often used as salad garnish. Cut the flowers when spent, to prolong culinary tastiness of the chive leaves. Trim back older leaves to produce a fresh herb crop.

Pacific Coast iris (*Iris douglasii*) grown in Zones 7 to 9 must keep all its foliage when the bloom is complete. Let the flowers go to seed to expand the planting. In many coastal zones, Pacific Coast iris foliage is evergreen. Allow the plants to ripen naturally. They don't succumb to the disfiguring leaf spot common to **German iris**.

PROBLEMS

All zones: Big flowered May and June bloomers, such as **German iris** (*Iris germanica*), often show signs of iris leaf spot. Oval splotches of brownish spots appear as summer progresses. Trim off the affected leaves and keep them out of compost. Fresh leaves will form, though also likely to be affected with leaf spot. Leaf spot will be more prevalent in warmer zones and coastal areas with high humidity. It can disfigure iris leaves, and the ugliness is dismaying among the fresh leaves of the June garden. Good air circulation and sun exposure also helps manage iris leaf spot.

Check with WSU or OSU Extension Offices or master gardeners for fungicides currently registered to reduce leaf spot; apply a fungicide after cleaning out old, affected leaves. **Iris** especially worth treating for leaf spot are those known as re-bloomers which will produce late summer or fall stalks of new bloom.

Slug patrol: Keep it up, especially around newly growing **dahlia** shoots and **lilies** of all types. It's not too early to start hunting for small piles of slug eggs. Slugs produce eggs most heavily in August and September, but they aren't shy about mating now. The eggs resemble small pearls, almost perfectly round. They're light tan in color and have an odd resemblance to time-release fertilizer nuggets. If you find a stack, under a log or under mulch, of forty to about one hundred and twenty eggs, scoop them up and dispose of them anywhere but in the garden.

DID YOU KNOW?

Perennial flower gardens enhance summer-blooming, bulb-type plants. **Daylilies, true lilies, gladiolus, dahlias,** and **begonias** look their best when accompanying herbaceous perennials. Keep a record of beautiful plant companions seen this month.

JULY
BULBS, CORMS, RHIZOMES, & TUBERS

PLANNING

Many catalog bulb suppliers offer discounts for early summer purchasing for the spring garden. If you've kept notes of your needs and wishes for next year's spring garden, check catalogs to see about ordering now. Bulbs arrive at the appropriate planting time in early fall. It's odd to consider **daffodils** now, but this is a fine time to order.

Photograph and document summer-blooming bulbs; choose sites for next year's **true lilies**. Continue visiting public show gardens for ideas on water-saving bulbs.

PLANTING

July 15 is traditionally the last time to plant **gladiolus** corms.

Planting every two weeks staggers the flowers for display or cutting. **Gladiolus** planted this month blooms in late August or early September when gardens are short of newly emerging flowers.

Check nursery sales this month for small, already-started plants. Patio sized **dahlias**, **begonias** like the colorful 'Nonstop' series, and even very tender bulbs like **freesias** refresh the garden in early July with new, already-budded plants. If planting in the hottest areas, plant in evening or early morning, and shade the new plants from direct sun and heat for the first week.

CARE

Deadhead **daylilies** (*Hemerocallis* sp.) to prolong their beauty. It's easy to snap off the dead flowers that bloom only one day. They'll be surrounded by buds for tomorrow and days beyond. When the entire stalk has finished blooming, cut it to the ground, leaving the foliage.

Stake taller **true lilies** very carefully, avoiding the bulb itself. If pierced, it will die. Bamboo stakes offer flexibility and strength for use with lilies. Some growers set them into the ground when planting the lilies. Shorter lilies do well with metal hoop stakes such as those for **peonies**. Staking protects from sudden summer rain and windstorms.

Zones 4-6: Large showy **German iris** (*Iris germanica*) can be dug four weeks after bloom in the coldest zones and divided. Pry the entire clump of rhizomes gently out of the ground with a spading fork, shaking soil from the rhizomes and roots. Discard any soft, damaged, or bad-smelling rhizomes, keeping only the most solid.

Separate into smaller clumps, trimming back foliage if desired. Replant in a triangle, setting three clumps about nine inches apart. Plant rhizomes shallow, just barely covered with soil to allow sun to reach them. Water in well and keep watered while new roots form. Leaves form in "fans" that are easy to see when

Large German iris can be dug and divided now in zones 4-6 or in late August in zones 7-9.

handling. New fans will develop after dividing. Complete this early in colder zones so that **iris** will be solidly rooted when ground freezes. Keep old rhizomes and diseased leaves out of compost.

Weed (of course) and add mulch to two to three inches afterwards.

WATERING

All zones: Watering is a primary concern in July because of scarce or non-existent rainfall. Thunderstorms east of the mountains can damage gardens with wind or hail but still fail to provide sufficient rainfall. Cover soaker hoses with mulch for more efficiency.

Waterwise, spring-blooming bulbs like **daffodils** and **tulips** are now fully dormant for summer and don't need moisture. Indeed, they suffer if watered in summer. Summer, for springbloomers, is like winter for other flowers; they don't grow one bit. If you accidentally dig a daffodil bulb, you'll notice the roots have turned brown and died back. New roots form with cool and damp fall weather.

Apply water to **dahlias, cannas, gladiolus,** and **begonias** with a soaker hose system, keeping the foliage and flowers dry to prevent disease. (All these

plants can be affected by powdery mildew and other fungal diseases.)

Daylilies, especially the rebloomers, produce better flowers with a regular source of water. Re-bloomers, *Hemerocallis* 'Stella d'Oro' for instance, form new stems and buds after their first bloom. Other daylilies stop blooming once they complete their first. Daylilies require less water when not blooming. Occasional moisture, however, does maintain better looking foliage.

FERTILIZING

Most summer-blooming bulbs require fertilization once per year during planting. **Dahlias**, however, need a boost of extra fertilizer in midsummer. Do not fertilize any plant in dry soil. Water first, then use either a chemical, water-soluble form, or an organic product with moderate amounts of nitrogen (7 percent or less). Kelp and fish-based fertilizers supply nutrients gradually and contain trace nutrients that plants require.

Container plants need regular fertilization. If you're growing **lilies, dahlias,** or **caladium** in pots with annuals like **impatiens** or with other perennials, fertilize every three weeks with a moderate nitrogen formula like a 6-5-5 or a 5-10-10.

GROOMING

Keep **dahlias, gladiolus,** and **daylilies** trimmed, clipping off spent flowers. Gladiolus can't be easily deadheaded since the stalk opens flowers from the bottom up to the top. Remove faded individual flowers. Many gardeners trim the whole stem when it has completed bloom.

PROBLEMS

All zones: Aphids, small sucking insects present from early spring through fall, seek well-watered plants that are producing new leaves. This, of course, describes the midsummer **dahlia**. Birds, wasps, lacewings, and ladybugs will help keep aphid populations down, but you may also use insecticidal soap for heavy infestations.

To encourage birds, provide a water source year-round. You'll notice wasps, also your garden allies, dipping into the water during summer.

Slugs subside a bit, especially if mulches are dry on top, but can spend their summer under mulch romping in your **lilies** and **hostas**. As plant leaves toughen up in late summer, slugs damage them less.

AUGUST
BULBS, CORMS, RHIZOMES, & TUBERS

 PLANNING

Order spring-blooming bulbs from catalogs this month. While most companies take orders through October for Zones 7 to 9, do it now if you're in Zones 4 to 6. Bulbs arrive on time for you to plant before the ground freezes. Yes, it's strange to consider freezes in August!

Consider adding some unusual, summer-blooming bulbs such as **Peruvian lilies** and **oxalis** next year. Study catalogs and wander the garden making notes about what might perk up an area.

 PLANTING

All zones: Divide and replant **German iris**, cutting back top foliage and resetting the divisions in soil amended with fresh compost. Set the rhizome just at soil level; don't bury it.

Special fall-blooming bulbs like **colchicum** (*Colchicum autumnale* or *Colchicum speciosum* 'The Giant' or the white form *C. speciosum* 'Album') deliver fresh energy in the fall garden, with pink or white flowers that remind of spring. Look for **colchicum** in nurseries sending pink bloom out of its bulb with no soil at all, just propped against a dish or desk edge. A fine garden plant that

DID YOU KNOW?

Lily bulbs—the Asiatic, Oriental, Trumpets, and new hybrids like Orienpets—regenerate from their entire stem. When picking lilies for bouquets, guard their health by allowing at least $2/3$ of the stem to remain on the plant. One lily specialist in western Washington says that large lilies can lose over half their weight in sending up the stem and buds. Your task is to help the bulb regenerate by keeping the stem as tall as possible.

multiplies beautifully in western areas and is hardy all the way down to Zone 4, colchicum is often nicknamed **fall crocus** though it isn't a crocus. Or it may be called **meadow saffron**. Plant it in full sun, about three inches down. **Colchicum** yields colchicine, a powerful and toxic drug present throughout the plant. It's not recommended for gardens with young children,

The **fall crocus** (*Crocus speciosus*), an actual crocus, shines clear blue and complements fallen yellow leaves. It's superb in all zones, from 4 to 8. Choose a spot with light shade or full sun, and plant immediately about two inches deep and one inch apart. Flowers pop up in late September, followed by leaves. Mulch them with two to three inches of compost.

 CARE

Occasional rain or windstorms can dislodge stakes on **lilies** and

dahlias; check carefully after any unusual weather and retie them.

 WATERING

Water all summer-bloomers. They need the sustenance. August is often our driest month.

Zones 4-6: Humidity may drop to 15 to 20 percent.

Give special attention to **tuberous begonias** in hanging baskets, and all other hanging basket plantings. These may need daily—or even twice daily—watering; hang them where they'll receive gentle morning light but be protected from hottest afternoon sun. In August, the baskets fill with plant roots, and water may scoot down the sides of the pots without supplying the rootball within. If plants appear stressed and there's no watering system, take them down once a week and immerse them to the pot rim in water—a wheelbarrow works well for this. Leave them for up to an hour. Check for water penetration into the center of the roots.

FERTILIZING

Fertilize **dahlias** after watering. Keep nitrogen applications moderate after July, using a formula like a 5-10-10. Too much nitrogen will retard or stop blooming. Dahlia experts even advise switching to a 0-10-10 in August to avoid nitrogen, or using the 5-10-10 at half the recommended rate. Dahlias start their best bloom in August and will continue until frost; this fertilization and watering supports the bloom.

Never apply fertilizer to dry soil (and indeed don't let **dahlias** or other summer-blooming bulbs dry out because they'll fail to bloom or reduce their budding).

GROOMING

Deadhead all summer-bloomers. This is a pleasant early morning task when the garden is still and cool.

Gladiolus will not produce new growing stalks once finished. Allow the bloom to finish then trim out the blooming stem but allow the tall green leaves to remain.

As **daylilies** complete bloom and turn brown, cut off browning leaves. Mulch the plants but don't cover the crowns.

PROBLEMS

Summer-blooming plants have grown large enough by August to host several problems. Before taking action, be sure you've received a good diagnosis of the problem. One spot to check for photos of difficulties is www.wsu.pep.hortsense, a pictorial website at Washington State University.

Thrips: These nearly invisible insects rasp **gladiolus** leaves and cause a stippled, even silvery, appearance. They also deform the buds. Once symptoms appear, the gladiolus can't be saved. Remove it.

Viral problems: **Lilies**, **dahlias**, **gladiolus**, and other plants including many herbaceous perennials, suffer odd viral symptoms. Leaves may be streaked (lily streak virus) or mottled and marked with color. Stunting is one of the most common and recognizable symptoms. A tall **trumpet lily**, destined to reach six feet, may stop at one foot if virally afflicted. Take an affected leaf to a nursery or to a trained WSU or OSU Extension Office or master gardener for diagnosis. If it is viral, remove the entire plant from the garden.

Viral problems are generally transmitted by aphids. Insecticidal soap or strong spurts of water help manage aphids, but won't prevent viral problems existing in the garden or neighborhood. Once virally affected plants are removed, replant **lilies** or other bulbs in the same area the following season. Viruses do not survive removal of live tissue.

Powdery mildew: **Dahlias**, **lilies**, **daylilies**, and other bulbs can succumb to this common, late-summer fungal infection. Plants in advanced stages of the problem develop gray fuzzy symptoms? and deformed leaves.

Fungal botrytis: True **lilies** planted in poor air circulation may wither and appear covered with fine black powder. Clip off the diseased part, carefully easing it into a bag after cutting to prevent dragging the fungal spores through the rest of the plant. Follow up with a registered fungicide.

DID YOU KNOW?

Shallow planting: **daylilies**, **peonies**, and **German iris** grow best with shallow soil above their roots or rhizomes. When dividing them later this fall, be certain to keep about one inch of soil above the emergent point. If planted too deeply, they will produce leaves but bloom sparsely.

SEPTEMBER
BULBS, CORMS, RHIZOMES, & TUBERS

 PLANNING

September is such a busy month! It might as well be spring.

Zones 4-6: September is a good month for planting, transplanting, and mulching. Plan to keep protective sheets, or other frost covers handy to cover summer-blooming bulbs during the first light freezes.

Zones 7-9: Warm days provide the last remnants of summer, inviting us into the garden.

Purchasing hardy bulbs: Nurseries have plenty of bulbs just after Labor Day. Even if you've prudently placed a catalog order, it's fun to meander and find new colors or forms of spring glory.

If you're shopping on a hot day, keep the bulbs as cool as if they were a carton of eggs. Don't stuff them in a hot car trunk.

Storing hardy bulbs: Bulbs hold lots of moisture, so they can mold if left in warm, enclosed environments. **Tulips** or **daffodils** left in plastic bags can develop blue mold on the surface. If you bring them home in plastic bags, take them out and store them in brown paper bags or mesh bags.

Place stored bulbs in a cool, dry spot, that's 60 degrees F. or below, such as an unheated garage, a basement, or a cool, dark cupboard. Don't put them into the refrigerator. Avoid any

Species tulip

area where fruit is stored because fruit releases ethylene, which can affect the embryonic flower.

 PLANTING

Zones 4-6: Spring bulbs—**snowdrop, crocus, daffodils, tulips, hyacinths, allium,** and **lilies**—can go in this month. Spring-blooming bulbs must initiate root formation before the ground freezes hard. Brent Heath, bulb expert, comments "Once roots are initiated, the bulb's cellular walls join in, becoming more elastic and resistant to freezing." So early, successful rooting protects the plants through winter.

Here are some instructions you should follow in all zones:

• **depth**: two to three times the length of the bulb measured from top to bottom

• **soil type**: well-drained soils are vital. Sandy, gravelly soil amended with compost is fine. If you have heavy clay, plant in pots or in a raised berm at least eighteen inches high.

• **fertilizer**: apply as a top-dressing after planting, and water in well. Use a fertilizer formulated for bulbs (with a 5-10-10 or 9-6-6 ratio). You can wait until spring when bulbs are up one to two inches, but absolutely do not skip it then.

• **mulch**: after planting, cover with two to three inches of pine needles or "pine straw." (These do not "acidify" the soil.) Other mulches include fully composted leaves or other organic mulch.

Zones 4-6: Use large plastic containers for spring bulbs—a nursery pot about 15 inches deep and 12 inches across is a good size for 8 to 10 **daffodils**

or medium **tulips**. Plant early and sink the container in soil to protect it from freezing while roots form. Mulch over the planted container.

Zones 7-9: Use large containers, over three gallons, with enough soil volume to protect roots during cold spells.

CARE

Daylilies (*Hemerocallis* spp. and cultivars like 'Stella d'Oro') begin dormancy in Zones 4 to 6; trim back foliage and mulch for winter. In Zones 7 to 9, daylilies go dormant in late October. Some cultivars are nearly evergreen, though they become progressively more scruffy.

Indoor: treated as a houseplant all summer, **amaryllis** (*Hippeastrum* hybrids) will have healthy leaves but begin to yellow slightly toward fall. Just after Labor Day, bring the amaryllis indoors. Store it in a dark, dry spot at room temperature, laying the pot on its side. Stop watering and allow the foliage to brown. Leave it for ten to twelve weeks without water or attention.

WATERING

Spring-bloomers: open a planting area, fill it with water, allow it to drain, and then set the

DID YOU KNOW?

Larger hybrid **tulips** often "run out" after one or two years. This is no reason to avoid planting them. Simply expect a shorter garden life.

The longest lasting in gardens are small species **tulips** such as *Tulip tarda*, *Tulip kaufmanniana*, and the Emporer tulips (*Tulip fosteriana*). They resent summer water. Place them where they'll be dry when dormant, such as a rockery planted with low water-use plants.

bulbs. Soils can be dried out to twelve to fourteen inches down by mid-September, and hardy bulbs will not root in dry soil. If they begin to root then dry out again, they can be damaged or even killed. Watering through September will help rooting establish well before winter. Think of the spring bulbs as shooting into growth now, though it's all happening underground.

Summer-bloomers: Keep **dahlia** and **gladiolus** plantings watered while they are still in bloom.

FERTILIZING

Zones 5-6: Fertilize over the top of underground bulbs—those from last year—sprinkling a granular formula or a liquid.

GROOMING

Keep **dahlias** picked as they bloom, leaving plenty of stem for emerging buds. They'll be knocked back soon by frost in the coldest areas but can be wonderful cut flowers during October and early November in the warmest zones.

Take care in deadheading true **lilies**. Even though their old stalks can look untidy now, complete browning renews the bulbs for next year.

PROBLEMS

Remove and discard any **dahlias** that show virus symptoms—small plants, leaf mottling, odd coloration, and patterns known as "mosaics" and "ring spots." (See August for a full description.)

OCTOBER
BULBS, CORMS, RHIZOMES, & TUBERS

PLANNING

All zones: When buying bulbs, choose the biggest possible bulb or corm for its type—it should be firm and heavy. Larger bulbs bloom better. For some plants, such as **daffodils** and **tulips**, bulbs come in various sizes depending on the ultimate height of the plant. A tiny 'Tete a Tete' daffodil may be less than the size of a quarter to grow six inches tall. An 'Unsurpassable' may be half the size of your fist and will be twenty inches tall. You're choosing the largest bulbs based on the variety itself. A little experience with looking at bulbs in nurseries will make this point clear. "Bargain bags" may disappoint, though **daffodils** and hyacinths can catch up in a few years.

Zones 5-6: Your gardening year closes all too soon. Finish spring bulb planting this month before the first heavy freeze. Snow flurries, should not deter bulb planting, though they might deter the gardener. It's the deep, heavy, soil-freezing cold that makes planting impossible.

Zones 7-9: As the light dwindles, the garden slows, and blooms reduce. Determine which container plantings, now spent, you can replace with bulbs and corms tucked in for spring.

PLANTING

All zones: Get the earliest blooming bulbs or corms in the ground first. The sequence generally goes: **snowdrops, snow crocus,** large **Dutch crocus**, small **daffodils**, larger **daffodils**, small **tulips, hyacinths**, large **tulips,** and **allium.** This advice may apply more to warmer zones; the colder zone may require simultaneous planting.

Zones 5-6: Finish planting all spring-blooming bulbs—**crocus, daffodils, tulips,** and **hyacinths**—this month before hard freezes.

Zones 7-9: Begin planting as soil cools and continue until Thanksgiving, planting earliest bloomers first. Choose some **daffodil** or small **tulips** for plastic pots. Plant and settle them into the ground, then use them to add color to spring containers. When in containers, they can be tucked into any annual or perennial combination. Plant winter-blooming **cyclamen** (*Cyclamen hederifolium* or *Cyclamen coum*) available at nurseries now. Their leaves and color brighten shady spots in winter.

Anemone tubers (*Anemone blanda*, or *Anemone coronaria*), resembling little buffalo chips, plump up and grow faster if soaked overnight in tepid water before planting. They produce brilliant spring flowers after their fall planting.

CARE

Zones 5-6: After the first light frost, dig and store summer bulbs.

Dahlia: Trim off dead foliage and gently fork the tubers up with a garden fork. Wash off soil and allow them to dry for three to four days in a sunny spot that won't freeze. Professional growers tie on an identification label immediately. Once dry, divide the tubers, minding the central stalk. Only tubers connected to the central stalk will bloom. Slice the tubers apart, keeping a bit of their stalk. Store tubers in sawdust or peat moss, barely damp.

Gladiolus: Dig and store in Zones 4 to 6. Hardy only to Zone 7, they can be dug and stored or left in the ground. If leaving them in the ground in Zones 7 to 9, trim off all dead foliage and mulch with three to four inches of compost. They produce dozens of small corms and grow better if dug at least every other year. They're also relatively inexpensive and easy to replace next spring for most satisfactory bloom.

Lilies: When true **lilies** turn thoroughly brown, divide them if crowded, replanting the largest bulbs (up to five years after planting). Dig slowly because it's easy to pierce a lily with the shovel.

Other tropicals: Most decline when temperatures drop below 45 to 50 degrees F. As night temperatures drop into the 40s, dig and store **tuberous begonias, cannas, callas,** and **caladium**. Follow the above directions for **dahlias**, except for the dividing. Simply shake soil off, let them dry for a few days, and place in storage boxes buried in dry peat. Store at about 65 degrees F.

Grape hyacinth (*Muscari armeniacum*) and **Dutch iris** send up green leaves in late September and early October, long before spring. Mulch with two to three inches of compost in the coldest Zone 5 to 6 areas.

Grape hyacinth

WATERING

When planting bulbs in containers, dampen the soil thoroughly before planting. This is crucial; soil may be dry below the bulbs, and roots need moisture to emerge.

FERTILIZING

Fertilize bulb plantings when installing, sprinkling granular bulb fertilizer over the surface.

GROOMING

Zones 7-9: Deadhead remaining flowers on summer-bloomers.

PROBLEMS

Mammals munching bulbs: Deer do not eat **snowdrops** or **daffodils** but enjoy **tulips** and **lilies**. If you have no deer fence, put vulnerable bulbs into containers to be safely moved in spring.

Protect **crocus** and **tulips** from squirrels with hardware cloth.

DID YOU KNOW?

Can you plant true **lilies** after the ground freezes?

Yes, but only if you prepare the soil in advance of freezing. Dig the hole to about twelve inches, removing prepared soil and stashing it in a non-freezing spot, and filling the hole with straw or other mulch materials.

(You can put the backfill soil back in the hole in a plastic bag.) Mark the location!

When **lilies** arrive, avoid leaving the bulb out in freezing air. Plant, then fill the hole, water soil to firm it, fill any air pockets, and mulch with four to six inches of leaves or straw.

NOVEMBER
BULBS, CORMS, RHIZOMES, & TUBERS

 PLANNING

All zones: If you "force" spring bulbs into bloom before its natural season, plan for the time they take to initiate roots. Most spring-blooming bulbs and corms need about ten to sixteen weeks of temperatures below 45 degrees F. A pot of **tulips** planted November 1st, sunk into the ground to the pot rim and mulched, produce roots ready for forcing by about January 10th. Around this time, bring the pots of rooted **tulips** into a cool basement. They need twelve hours of light a day placed eight inches above the pots. Keeping the lights on chains helps with raising them as foliage grows.

In the coldest zones, since you can't rely on moderate soil temperatures, look for "pre-cooled" bulbs, which need about three weeks at 40 degrees F. (in an unheated garage or an old refrigerator) to fill the pot with roots. Plant pre-cooled bulbs immediately and put them into 40 degree F. storage. If they sit about unplanted in normal household temperatures, they will lose their chilling. After the three weeks, bring the pot into warmth for further growth.

Choose one of the types that force well such as 'Single Early', pink 'Christmas Marvel', 'Bestseller', or 'Beauty Queen'. Another good forcer is the Fosteriana group, including what are known as the 'Emperor' tulips.

When **tulips** have set buds (three weeks or so), bring them into normal house temperatures and enjoy the show.

PLANTING

All zones: For easy, enjoyable flowers at the holidays, plant **paperwhite narcissus** (*Narcissus tazetta* hybrids). Nurseries will have them on hand now. Unlike every other **daffodil** type, these grow well without a "chill" period at cold temperatures. They originate in the south of France, are generally raised in Israel, and dislike cold weather.

They bloom in four to five weeks after planting at normal house temperatures. You may see them grown in gravel, but the bulbs do better in potting soil. A six-inch pot will hold about five bulbs for a good show. Tuck the bulbs in with about 1/3 of the bulb emerging at the top of the pot; you'll notice that most of them already have shoots. Keep them in a cool spot for ten days until rooted; water well. As shoots start to expand, put them in normal bright light.

Count back five to six weeks from the desired bloom date when planting. Bulbs planted November 15 will bloom for Christmas and New Year's. Keep extra bulbs on hand (stored in the dark but not in a refrigerator) and plant every two weeks until January or February.

Zones 7-9: Despite the weather, continue planting hardy bulbs and corms.

There are several options of mulching materials.

CARE

Zones 5-6: Put summer bulbs in storage if you haven't already.

True lilies grown in containers for summer color can't be left in their pots to freeze through winter. In warmer coastal zones, slide the lily out and plant it in the garden or bank the pot with ample mulch material. Those of you in inland and mountainous areas should sink the whole pot in the ground or move it to an unheated greenhouse.

Zones 7-9: Remove **tuberous begonias** from baskets, before the hardest frosts. Shake the soil loose. Lay them on dry newspapers until the foliage withers then store in dry peat moss, sand, or sawdust.

Divide stored **dahlia** roots, retaining a chunk of the stem with each tuber. Pieces of the plant without the stem will not produce growing eyes next season. Store in peat moss, and dampen with a light spraying of water. Store at room temperature (such as in a basement).

All zones: Mulch all newly planted bulbs with leaves, leaf compost, or regular compost. Shredded fallen leaves or pine straw to three to four inches deep will provide winter protection.

WATERING

All zones: If fall rains were scarce during October, water bulb plantings.

You brought the indoor **amaryllis** into storage in September. Repot it now. Shake off the soil and repot in moist, compost-amended mix. Bring it into warmth and begin watering now, even if you don't see growth. About the time **amaryllis** (*Hippeastrum* sp.) appear in nurseries for holidays, the stored bulb will begin its growth. Fertilize lightly then. Flowering usually occurs four to six weeks after watering.

FERTILIZING

Zones 7-9: Fertilize by top-dressing when planting bulbs.

GROOMING

Zones 5-6: Gardening is over for the season; if you didn't finish your clean up, it will wait for you until spring, under the ice and snow.

Zone 7-9: Complete fall clean up; if **dahlia** or **gladiolus** foliage had disease problems, don't compost it.

PROBLEMS

Sudden snowstorms or heavy rain and wind are common in November. Try to get planting done early in the month in zones 7-9.

LAWN FLOWERS

Bulbs in the lawn? Can you plant bulbs in the lawn to have an early-season "meadow" effect? This works well for *Crocus vernus*, the cultivated **Dutch crocus** with the four-inch flowers and bright colors. Use a circular bulb planter, excavate a hole, and drop crocus in, about three inches deep.

These complete their bloom early enough for mowing. Other bulbs like **daffodils**, even the smallest varieties, won't be ready for cutting until late May, which doesn't work on our lawns. If your lawn is Eco-turf, the combination of lawn grasses and perennial plants, the **crocus** might be particularly appealing.

DECEMBER
BULBS, CORMS, RHIZOMES, & TUBERS

 PLANNING

Gather planting records, tags, photos and notes—you may not have time to organize them this month, but getting them all into one spot will help with spring planning.

 PLANTING

All zones: Continue planting indoor bulbs for the holidays, choosing **paperwhite narcissus** and hybrid **amaryllis** that will bloom without exposure to cold.

 CARE

Indoor: **Amaryllis** (*Hippeastrum*) need warm temperatures; keep them out of drafts and where temperature stays at 65 degrees F. or above.

Paperwhite narcissus and other potted **daffodils** can take cooler temperature; they last longer when tucked on sheltered porches in cool temperatures in Zones 7 to 9. Bring them indoors if temperatures drop below 35 degrees F.

 WATERING

Indoor: Keep all indoor holiday bulbs evenly moist.

All zones: Outdoors, check moisture on bulbs in the ground and in containers. Rain and snow will have provided considerable soil moisture by now, but check any that are under eaves or spots where rain doesn't penetrate.

 FERTILIZING

Outdoors: Lime soil where **dahlias** will be planted; use dolomite lime, bearing in mind that it will require four to five months to be available to plant roots. Lime scattered over snow will also work into the ground as it thaws. Five pounds per one hundred square feet, used every three years, is generally adequate in western Washington and Oregon. In eastern areas, where soils may be alkaline, don't add lime without getting a soil test first. **Dahlias** do well at pH of 6.5 to 7.5. Add compost to dahlia planting areas because they are heavy feeders.

 GROOMING

Zones 5-6: If your garden clean up isn't done, relax and wait until spring.

Zones 7-9: Mild December days can provide good garden time relief for busy schedules; clear away all old remaining foliage and mulch over bulb plantings.

 PROBLEMS

All zones: If voles or squirrels have been bothering bulbs, lay hardware cloth over the plantings and cover it with mulch. Voles (which are the size of mice but resemble moles) live in the ground and will tuck themselves under mulch (perhaps keeping the slugs company). They especially favor **tulips**. If the in-ground tulips are continually bothered, try planting in containers next year. An enterprising cat will help out with vole management but often can't keep up with the population.

HOUSEPLANTS

Houseplants: the green ferny edges of a foliage basket or a Christmas poinsettia gleaming by candlelight—whenever we grow plants inside a home, we have what are commonly called "houseplants." Indoor gardening offers ease and portability—seldom will you contend with weeds or complex soil problems. You'll find as we go through the months that the indoor garden can change with seasons and celebrations. Color and texture are almost infinitely available with the different kinds of plants available for containers.

You'll find tips here for the year-round management of many different types of plants portably. Think of edibles like herbs on the kitchen window or citrus in the living room, the porch deck filled with miniature roses in pots, or tropical jungle plants that transform a room into a mysterious green world. Living with plants can reduce stress, and their benign influence is frequently noted as a source of comfort.

Garden designers and interior decorators work together: creating "outdoor rooms," where we

CHAPTER THREE

may cook in on a patio kitchen, where summer life goes on far into the dusk of evening. Just as the definition of living space has changed to include the outdoors, houseplants have become wanderers, contributing to the furnishings of the inside-outside home. Plants such as croton (*Codiaeum variegatum*), once considered strictly indoor dwellers, may find themselves tucked into a patio container during warm weather.

Whatever you grow in a container, the basics of managing the plant will be few: light, water, and soil. Yes, this sounds like the elements of outdoor in-ground gardening, but there are differences. Plants in gardens can extend roots to forage widely for nutrients, or can take in water from rainfall. Container pots cannot. When you put a plant in a container, your job resembles that of the zookeeper who cares for an enclosed animal. Everything the plant needs, you will supply. Plants in pots for our indoor garden will need management—a joy for those of us who gain energy from fussing about with plants.

LIGHT

Available light determines which plants to choose and how well they thrive indoors. Flowering or fruiting plants generally require more light than foliage plants. See November for more information on measuring light strength.

WATERING

The tricky necessity of watering leads to indoor complications, since it's not always easy to tote that bucket across a carpet. Planning for ease of watering will often dictate how many indoor plants are grown, and where they sit. How far away is the water source?

Some tools may help: Hose adapters exist to attach a hose to indoor faucets: if you have many plants this may be helpful. A well-equipped garden center can provide this tool. If you do have a hose set up, long watering wands are as useful indoors as they are outside, especially if your summer display gardening includes hanging baskets on an outside balcony or patio. A flexible plastic watering can with a fine-pointed end that waters small spaces will be fine if you have only a few plants.

How often to water? In gardening, many people say 'it depends" as an answer to questions. This surely applies to houseplant watering. See August for details.

POTTING SOIL

The medium that holds up your plants also helps to regulate water and fertilizer. Potting soil is certainly easier to amend than other elements of indoor gardening, but it's necessary to be aware of the components and how they work. See April for more information on potting soil.

ABOUT FERTILIZERS

Choosing fertilizer and using it carefully will help indoor gardens thrive. See February for more on fertilizer types.

CHOOSING A CONTAINER

Style: The container may be decorative glazed pottery or a plain plastic pot, but it must meet two requirements: does it hold enough soil for the plant's comfort? Does it drain water easily from the bottom?

Do not choose pots with "water reservoirs" or attached saucers; both those features will make managing the water at the root level more difficult. They may seem to offer immediate convenience, but are less well suited for a long-lived plant. And they are impossible for succulents like Jade plant or cactus type plants, or orchids—all of which need immediate and workable drainage.

Containers without drainage holes: But perhaps the container is a prized jardinaire from your family? You certainly don't want to drill the Limoges or the Wedgwood. Instead, choose a lightweight plastic pot that has drainholes and fits easily inside your selected container. The outer container then becomes a decorative jacket for the plant, but will not drain. When watering plants in such a situation, be sure to pour excess water out of the decorative container after

watering. You'll often see magazine articles with dinnerware or other household items used as exterior containers for plants. See September for more container information.

Once of the best parts of growing plants in containers is being able to observe them closely; the uncurling fern or the opening tulip will be particularly wonderful at close range.

Contemplate the home environment before selecting your plants—if you are fortunate enough to have a balcony or a sun porch, you'll have extra room and extra space to try pants. Whatever your particular home conditions are, you will gradually find the plants that adapt and settle down in your situation. Growing them will add to the pleasure and beauty of everyday life.

JANUARY
HOUSEPLANTS

PLANNING

In this season we appreciate indoor plants the most. Quiet greens and intermittent blooming delight us before spring arrives. This month will join December in having the lowest light levels of any during the year. Observe where growing conditions seem best on dark days.

PLANTING

Your favorite nursery may have a sale this month or next on houseplants. Read the tags carefully to see what light the plants need.

Houseplants from vegetables and fruit? This can be done any time of the year, with plants growing more vigorously during warmer weather. **Pineapple** tops, **sweet potatoes**, the reliable **avocado**, and even citrus seeds can step out as rooted and leafy interior plants. While not likely to produce edibles, they can produce intriguing plants.

For **avocado** and **sweet potatoes** suspend over water, holding them up with toothpicks or chopsticks so that $1/2$ is in water. (Avocado goes rounded end down.) Change water weekly. The avocado seed will split as it roots. When roots form, pot up and keep in a light window.

If your **orange** or **grapefruit** seed has opened and made a small root, gently pot it up in a 3-inch pot, covering the seed completely. Citrus grows slowly from seed but will grow handsomely as it adds leaves and branches.

Pineapple may or may not root. Pick one with healthy-looking top leaves. Cut it off about 1 inch from the leaves, cleaning the fruit away. Set it down on one side to allow the bottom area to dry a bit (2 to 5 days). Then set it on damp potting soil in an 8 inch pot, covering the plant up to the bottom of the leaves. You can also remove a few of the lower leaves to give the pineapple a longer stem to plant. Rooting may take up to 2 months.

CARE

Wrap any tropical plant you purchase this month when moving from warm nursery conditions to the cold, possibly freezing, winter car. Pre-warm the car interior. Many tropical plants, including **ferns**, can be damaged by temperatures lower than 50 degrees F., which makes winter transportation perilous.

If you're keeping flowering plants under lights, fertilize once a month.

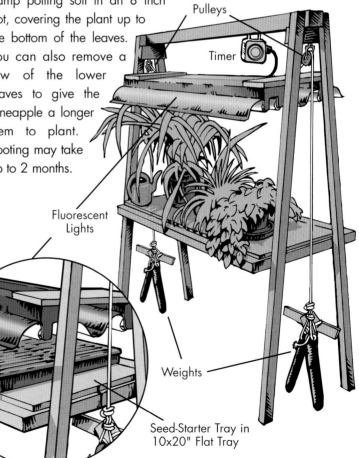

Pulleys

Timer

Fluorescent Lights

Weights

Seed-Starter Tray in 10x20" Flat Tray

Mid-winter often finds indoor plants lightly coated with dust. Rinsing or washing it off helps them look better and grow more efficiently. Give them a tepid, low pressure shower— if the plant is small enough to rinse in a sink, or light enough to lift into a bathtub. Do not soak, spray, or saturate **African violets** or any plants in the succulent or **cactus** families.

Plants don't need "leaf polish." Waxy or oily products reduce the plant's ability to get air through stomates, natural openings in the leaves. Save your polishing energy for cars, furniture or shoes.

Poinsettias: after their colorful leaf bracts drop, grow them as a tender house plant, keeping them in normal light, in a warm (65-75 degree) spot without drafts. Water when dry.

FERTILIZING

Winter life for indoor green plants? They slow down (perhaps like all of us). If the plant isn't growing, too much fertilizer may actually burn the roots. Fertilize in late fall, then only once a month with $1/2$ strength fertilizer through the winter.

Flowering plants, especially those under lights being forced into bud and bloom, will require fertilizer once a month—**African violets**, **flowering maple** (*Abuti-*

lon), **Cape Primrose** (*Streptocarpus*), and **geraniums** need this fertilizer boost if they're blooming heavily. **Amaryllis** (*Hippeastrum* sp.), just beginning to open their leaves or still blooming, need fertilizer every two weeks while in bloom with a full-strength fertilizer. (See Bulbs for more information on **amaryllis**.)

WATERING

Keep plants watered sparingly this month, allowing soil to dry to one inch. Take special winter care with succulent and **cactus** plants. **Jade plant** (*Crassula argentea*) needs water only once every six weeks in winter. It suffers from rot if over watered in winter. Let Jade plants dry out from mid-November through December, water once, and then wait until mid-February to resume normal watering.

Cactus: pretend it's in a desert. The cactus may look weary and withered, but it prefers dryness now.

With the common name **Kaffir lily**, *Clivia miniata* blooms during late winter with showy fragrant flowers. Do not water for 6-8 weeks in winter: stop around the first of December and resume when buds appear, usually in February.

PROBLEMS

Short days and gray skies combine to make January a dark month. Foliage plants already adapted to low light conditions will slow down, seldom producing new leaves.

Blooming plants show symptoms of insufficient light. They will turn a paler green, drop yellow leaves, or lean and stretch toward light. Flowering generally stops unless extra light is supplied. They 'll rally in spring.

Damage to plants may occur from touching cold windows. Close curtains to keep chilly air from reaching the plants. Air will be colder next to windows.

DID YOU KNOW?

Insect problems: plants may slow down in January, but insect infestations don't. If you see sticky, cottony wads where leaves meet stems, the likely problem is aptly named: mealybugs. These damage plants by sucking sap. Get an accurate diagnosis from a local nursery or WSU or OSU Master Gardener, then use recommended methods. Remove mealybugs with a cotton swab soaked in alcohol, but keep at it because they multiply faster than gardeners can wipe.

FEBRUARY
HOUSEPLANTS

PLANNING

Colorful flowers abound this month at florists and nurseries. You may find **primroses**, or **florist's cyclamen** in deep raspberry, pink, and white. Early spring bulbs, **crocus, daffodils**, and **tulips** will be available forced. Plan to add a few to perk up the indoor scene.

February often brings gift plants, a celebratory rainbow of potted floral offerings. Many can bring new color into the indoor garden. Some of these potentially become permanent house dwellers; others, such as **miniature roses**, will decline after several weeks indoors. That's fine; they can be considered long-lasting bouquets without the gardening struggle of keeping them alive in conditions they detest.

Review the houseplant collection: which ones do you like the best? Which need extra spring care and repotting? Late winter finds houseplants looking their worst; the well-adapted ones will be obvious now. Don't hesitate to discard unsatisfactory indoor plants. You'll have the pleasure of adding new plants. With limited indoor space, it's often necessary to discard some plants before embracing the new.

PLANTING

The edible indoor garden: Growing lemons indoors: this good trick is quite possible if you have a bright window exposure. The most commonly grown is called **Meyer lemon**, and it's often available for shipment in early spring. You can order the plants or you may be able to find them at a favorite nursery. Lemons offer fragrant flowers during winter months, shiny leaves, and often produce fruit once adapted to the location. Flowers and fruit appear on the plants simultaneously. Provide the brightest light possible. Lemon plants generally come in two or five-gallon containers: they will continue to grow into small tree forms. Repot in spring if they are rootbound, or immediately upon receiving the plant.

CARE

The tools of the trade: For indoor gardening, you'll find a small tarp, a good watering can with spout that aims well, small sharp clippers, a small bucket for dumping out water that's standing in saucers, and a trowel helpful. Grooming plants, a year-round activity, is easiest with a bucket or tarp to catch the removed bits.

WATERING

As February progresses, plants will require more water. Check the soil moisture and look for signs of new emerging leaves.

Jade plants and **cactus** may show some leaf shriveling. Water lightly this month for Jade plants. Use tepid water. Continue to be thrifty with water for the cactus and succulent family plants. They need increased moisture when the air temperatures are warmer, late March through summer.

Check all saucers under plants to be sure water has been absorbed by roots. You don't want accumulated water in the plant saucers. Logic might dictate the idea that water in the saucers is a good way to get extra moisture or humidity to plants. However, it often results in root rots from the constant sogginess. The only indoor plants adapted to sitting in water are those bred for growth in aquariums or in atrium water features.

FERTILIZING

Increase fertilizer toward the end of the month. If you've been mixing the product at $1/2$ strength and applying once a month, use it two times in February. Then move up to full strength in March.

In general, use a liquid fertilizer with moderate nitrogen but one containing trace elements. Fertilizers derived from living sources, such as kelp or fish, provide moderate nutrients. If you choose to use synthetic fertilizers, be sure to choose one with trace elements. Mix at the rate suggested, or at half strength for winter months. Never exceed the recommended concentration.

Why trace elements? All plants need very small amounts of a variety of materials, and it's easy to add them by choosing your fertilizer. Plants in garden soil can often receive what they need, but plants in containers benefit from fertilizer containing little bits of elements like magnesium, copper, and iron.

Gift plants—even those that aren't going to be a long-term part of the indoor garden—will look better if fertilized every 2 weeks while in the house. They

GIFT PLANTS RECEIVED IN SPRING

Hardy bulbs like **daffodils and tulips** bloom only once and then die down. They can be fertilized, watered until the foliage begins to turn brown, and then set into the outdoor garden for possible bloom next season. Daffodils return in following years more reliably than tulips. If you have no outdoor garden, discard the bloomed-out bulbs.

Florist cyclamen (*Cyclamen persicum*) will often have smaller buds tucked down against their leaves providing a long period of bloom. Keep them in a bright, light spot. Do not over water. Remove yellowing leaves.

Primroses look their best if they're kept in a light, cool spot, at temperatures below 60 degrees F. Baskets of them often grace mid-winter front doorsteps in zones 7-9. They'll survive front porch coolness where winter temperatures stay mild, but cannot be left out in freezing weather (they're adapted to greenhouse life.) After weather warms they can be set into gardens.

have been fertilized while at the nursery.

 GROOMING

African violets: if they've become dusty, use a soft brush such as a photographic lens cleaning

African violet

brush or a cosmetic brush to remove surface dust.

 PROBLEMS

Check garden **primroses** being used for indoor color; nurseries provide these in brilliant primary colors during mid-winter. Aphids may colonize their leaves. Use a magnifying glass—the tiny green aphids hide, being exactly the color of primrose leaves. Check other plants while you're aphid-aware. Rinse leaves with water to wash off aphids. For serious, repeated infestations, insecticidal soap will work. But any plants are seriously invaded, discard them to avoid starting an aphid riot in your other indoor plants.

MARCH

HOUSEPLANTS

PLANNING

Finish reviewing the indoor garden. Now, as you plan repotting and repositioning indoor plants, check growth of each, discarding any that have root problems or have been unsatisfactory. Consider how much space the indoor garden can claim. Plan to grow what fascinates you, be it orchids or cactus, and have all plants indoors thriving in excellent health. Healthy plants contribute energy to the indoor scene.

PLANTING

Spring's here. Indoor plants will grow again. Check any that need repotting. Repotting can continue from now through August, at your convenience. Roots recover from repotting best when the plant grows actively. Most larger plants will need new pots after about 3 years. Others can fill a pot with roots in only 1 year.

Signs of needing repotting: roots kinking out the bottom of the drainage hole. Slide the plant loose to see if roots have filled the container. If they have not, return it to the pot and top-dress lightly with fresh soil. Plants stuck tightly in the old pot sometimes emerge more easily if they've been without water for a few days. Tip the pot over and rap an upper edge on the floor to loosen the plant. Some truly stuck ones need to be pried out with a trowel.

Plants do best when potted "up" to about 2 inches larger than the old pot. If it's a very slow-growing plant, 1 inch larger will be fine. A kind of musical chairs shuffle may result if large plants require new pots, but others are able to step up into their vacated pots.

Prepare the new pot: terracotta pots should be thoroughly soaked before using. Wood or ceramic don't need this attention. Place a small piece of window screen, a bit of wall board tape, or a coffee filter over the hole. No rocks, gravel, pot chips, or layered material should go into the bottom. These amendments make drainage worse. Get rid of these if you've formerly used them, and fill the pot completely with soil mix. That seems illogical but it's been proven by years of scientific trials.

Place about 2 inches of soil on the bottom of the pot. Shake the old soil loose from the plant and spread roots a bit. Soak the root-ball in a bucket of water if it's hard. Trim off any roots circling the plant. Hold it with one hand and drop soil around it with the other. You'll need help for very large plants. Tuck soil in between roots, filling up air pockets. Water thoroughly, allowing water to run out of the drainhole.

Keep the plant in a low light spot for a week until the roots settle.

If you have no convenient indoor spot for repotting, wait until May when outdoor temperatures exceed 55 degrees F. Pick a mild, sunny day without wind. Wind can damage large-leaved tropical plants.

If it can be done easily, slide the plant out of its container to see if it's rootbound. If yes, then it's time to repot.

CARE

Houseplants must stay indoors this month; until mid-May or even June, outdoor temperatures in all zones remain too chilly for tropical houseplants.

When repotting, you may find plants that could be divided. **Clivia**, **tradescantia**, **tolmeia**, **philodendron**, and many others may have rooted sections that can be pulled loose and tucked into smaller pots.

WATERING

By the end of March you will see active growth on the healthy houseplants, so increase watering to the frequency you will use for the rest of the active growing season, through September.

FERTILIZING

When active growth begins, increase the fertilizer routine. You may wish to sprinkle timed-release fertilizer on the soil surface. This fertilizer type, sold as Osmocote™ and others, releases nutrients slowly over a period of months. Use it on flowering or fruiting plants where a higher level of nutrients is needed. It's most effective at temperatures of 70 degrees F. and

---

> ## DID YOU KNOW?
>
> Dealing with insect problems on indoor plants: even gardeners who are comfortable with insects outdoors draw the line at the indoor put up with an. In addition, living conditions indoors—lots of warmth—suit the insects perfectly, like an eternal summer. Aphids, scale, and mealybugs are most common. Scale resembles tiny turtles stuck firmly to the trunks, stems and leaves of plants; **indoor figs** like Ficus benjamina can be seriously invaded, as can **cactus**, **schefﬂeras**, **clivias**, and **palms**.
>
> Isolate or discard any plants with these insect symptoms to avoid infesting the entire indoor garden.

---

above, which obviously makes it a good houseplant fertilizer.

If the plant is in very low light conditions, or growing slowly, or newly potted up, avoid the timed-release fertilizer. Use $1/2$ strength liquid fertilizer twice a month until the plant begins sturdy growth.

For all other plants, increase the fertilizer to the levels you plant to use for the rest of the season.

GROOMING

Ferns of all types require frequent trimming of yellowing fronds throughout the year, but especially during winter when they aren't growing. A good range of ferns thrive indoors: **Maidenhair** (*Adiantum* spp.), **sword fern** (*Polystichum tsussinense*), and even **hare's-foot fern** (*Polypodium aureum*). They resemble hardier garden rela-

---

tives, but most grow best at temperatures above 50 degrees F.

Some indoor plants grow so happily that they will need regular pruning back. Plants pinched back now will make new growth much faster than those trimmed in colder, darker months.

PROBLEMS

Leaf stickiness on **figs** (*Ficus* spp.), **rubber plants**, results from insects, especially aphids or scale. Investigate for small green ovals in clumps. Aphids hatch frequently and can live happily indoors. Wash the plant's leaves gently with plain water. Then use a registered insecticide labeled for both that particular plant and for indoor use. Check with a nursery or OSU WSU Master Gardener for exact diagnosis and procedure.

APRIL
HOUSEPLANTS

PLANNING

Sort out pots, looking for those available for summer planting and for repotting. Pots, especially plastic ones, lose their integrity and attractiveness after several years. (They can be painted if intact; see May for details.) If any pot has contained a plant that died of disease problems, such as root rot, scrub it thoroughly and soak it in a mixture of 1 part household bleach to 10 parts water, for about 4 hours. Rinse thoroughly and air dry. This regime also works on outdoor garden pots.

PLANTING

Easter lilies can become part of the general garden. After bloom, trim the flowers off the lily, leaving a long stem. Water and fertilizer regularly. When garden temperatures warm, in May, remove the lily from its pot, untangle the roots, and plant in a part-shade, part sun area. Keep them watered until the leaves die back in late summer. These are usually *Lilium longiflorum*, forced into bloom. They may take 2 years to rebloom but can become permanent garden features. They're hardy in Zones 8 to 9, and in warmer parts of zone 7.

CARE

Potting mix: For all plants grown in containers, either for indoor or outdoor placement, the potting mix significantly affects root health, and thus the entire plant's health. Good potting mixes hold water, yet drain well to keep the plant from sitting in soggy, airless conditions. They're heavy enough to hold the plant steady.

Look for a mix containing organic components (in our region often "forest products"). The other vital component must be "gritty bits," particles of pumice or perlite that maintain air spaces and allow the soil to drain thoroughly. Give a prospective mix the squeeze test. Wet it, then squeeze. It should fall apart in your hand. If it clings in a wad and shows the pattern of your palm lines, it's lacking grit and will probably drain poorly. Add about 1/3 by volume of gritty material to improve this material.

Potting mix does NOT need: fertilizer, added microorganisms, or even "waterholding" beads. You can add your own fertilizer, depending on the types of plants and exposure they get. Microorganisms inhabit all composts and garden soils. If you wish to "up" the level of microorganisms in potting mix, add about 1/4 by volume of screened homemade compost or commercial compost.

Garden soil, scooped up and dumped into containers, doesn't work as a potting mix. It packs down and fails to hold enough air for the roots.

WATERING

Indoor garden plants will be growing strongly, and need regular watering. To test for dryness, poke your finger into the soil one inch in. If the soil feels dry at an inch, water. Dump all water out of saucers one hour after it's applied. "Waterholding" polymers, resembling gelatin when wet, aren't necessary for container gardening, and may indeed cause overwatering.

FERTILIZING

As with water, fertilizing is needed this month. Apply liquid fertilizer twice a month for most plants. **Cactus** and succulents need less. See March for more detail.

GROOMING

Remove all fading flowers and leaves to improve both appearance and health of plants. Do not allow leaves or flowers to fall

DID YOU KNOW?

Orchids add elegance to the indoor garden, and with hundreds of fascinating types available, gardeners have more selection than ever. New methods of cultivation including tissue culture produce more variety and more economical orchids. Orchids have become one of the most desired indoor plants, especially from an interior design viewpoint.

Some orchid growers encourage keeping the plant only through its first bloom, then discarding it. If your growing conditions do not suit keeping orchids for months or years, this may be a good solution. If you choose an orchid "in spike"—with buds forming—you'll have 6-8 weeks of beauty, or longer. *Oncidium*, *Dendrobium*, and *Phalaenopsis* orchids all make good household visitors.

Orchids—like all houseplants—vary in their temperature preferences, their water requirements, and their light needs. Hobby growers often invest in extra lighting, growing rooms to enlarge collections, and misting systems. If orchids catch your interest, talk to suppliers and invest in a good basic book: an excellent one is William Cullina's *Understanding Orchids* (2004).

Moth orchid

For more casual care, select an **orchid** suited to your own growing conditions.

Needing bright light: *Dendrobiums* and *Oncidium* hybrids. *Cattleyas* and *Cymbidiums*, need the brightest conditions. In protected zone 9 gardens, many *Cymbidum* hybrids survive outdoors nearly year-round.

If you have a part-shade windowsill where **ferns** and **African violets** thrive, you may want to try **moth orchids** (*Phalaenopsis* hybrids). **Orchids** require their own potting mixes and water regimes; though many are easy indoors, you'll do best by studying their individual care needs.

onto the surface of the soil and cause rot. Rotting plant parts can attract or worsen infestations of white flies.

PROBLEMS

No growth? If a plant sits still, doing nothing when others are moving into active growth, slide it gently out of the pot and check the root health. Healthy roots look firm and vigorous, not mushy or black. They may be white or tan or even yellow depending on the plant (and **fern** roots can be dark brown.)

Rotted roots generally mean the plant will probably die. Shake all the soil off and see if roots are healthy farther into the plant. Cut off dead roots and repot, perhaps into a smaller container (about 1 inch larger than the root ball) being certain that both potting soil and pot have excellent drainage. If the plant hasn't begun active growth within about 6 weeks, recovery is unlikely.

MAY

HOUSEPLANTS

PLANNING

Use your indoor plants for extra summer interest on the patio. Visit nurseries to find a few flowering plant inspirations to perk up the collection. Best suited for shade are **begonias**, **impatiens**, and **fuchsias**. Choose a shaded or semi-shaded spot, because plants adapted to indoor conditions will need protection from brightest sun. Even some **geraniums**—those in the Stellar series—will appreciate afternoon shade. Wait until warm nights before setting up the display.

Locate bricks, overturned pots, or wood stands for risers,

PLANTING

When repotting, make pots more manageable. Going smaller doesn't help. Larger containers give roots more room, hold moisture, and allow the presence of big plants like **fig trees** (*Ficus benjamina*). You can add a first layer of lightweight packing chips, filling about 1/3 of the bottom with the Styrofoam type. Be sure NOT to use the water-soluble so-called "biodegradable" type, which will dissolve to a messy glop when wet. Some gardeners crumple small flexible 4-inch plastic plant pots to make a raised layer instead of using the packing bits. After placing the packing chips or crumbled plastic, put a layer of window screen or landscape weed-barrier cloth (permable to water) cut to fit the pot above the chips. Water will go through screen and out the drainhole. Without this screening layer, your potting soil sifts down into the chips and gradually lowers the planting

and plan to enjoy the leaf shapes and textures, seeing them with a fresh eye when they're rearranged. Find some new pots to enhance those you're still planning to repot.

level so your plants slip weirdly down below the pot rim.

Plants will grow well in this combination. The foam bits or crumpled plastic won't act as a water-holder, thus doesn't harm plants by leading to soggy roots the way a bottom layer of gravel or chipped pottery will when topped with potting soil.

CARE

Indoor plants shoot into active growth in May when both light and warmth return. Check "shade-lovers" to be certain they aren't experiencing scorched leaves from more intense window light. Wipe leaves to remove dust, because anything impeding the plant's ability to receive light will reduce health.

Check beneath drainage holes to look for emerging roots; if the plant requires repotting, do it this month, or during summer through August.

WATERING

As spring advances, take special care with plants that sulk when they dry out: **Norfolk Island pines**, **ferns**, **grape ivy** (*Cissus* species), and **spider plant**. **Grape ivy** and **spider plant**s can return from a spell of wilting, but Norfolk Island pines and ferns

Jade plant

may subside, never to recover. **African violets** also need more water as they grow more vigorously, but never let their roots 'sit' in water. Allow the soil to dry on top before re-watering.

All indoor plants require regular watering now; use the 'knuckle' test, poking the soil to the depth of your first knuckle, about one inch, and watering if the soil feels dry.

Succulents like **Jade plants** (*Crassula* species) and cactus need moderate water, every three weeks or four weeks during active growth. If the plant shows signs of root stress stop watering and turn the plant out to check roots. Repot in a soil mix with about 1/3 pumice and watch the plant closely.

FERTILIZING

In May plants need higher levels of fertilization: for foliage plants like **philodendron** and **spathiphyllum**, fertilize twice a month with full strength liquid fertilizer. Use one with trace elements such as a fish or kelp fertilizer, and avoid very high levels of nitrogen. A 6-6-6 is fine for summering houseplants.

If the plant requires special fertilizer treatment, such as blooming plants that may pro-

---

DID YOU KNOW?

Paint plastic pots for summer cheer, either with latex house paint to match or contrast with a room, or with a plastic paint like Krylon™. The latex paint wears off quite quickly— it can look scuffed in a few months. The plastic paints hang on sturdily. Colors in the plastic paints lack variety but if you're looking for primary brights or 'let's hide' browns, they're available. If you're a fan of collecting inexpensive on-sale pots at yard sales, they don't have to remain drab.

---

duce leaves but few flowers, check the specific requirements with your nursery. The most usual reasons for limited flower production are lack of light and over use of nitrogen. Because indoor gardens contain so many different plant types, there's no "one fertilizer fits all" strategy, especially if you combine flowering and non-flowering plants, **cactus**, and **ferns**. Make a plan for each one.

GROOMING

Continue to remove withered yellowing leaves and spent flowers. Houseplants require regular tidying, because they're so much in view. Older leaves on **rubber plants**, **philodendron**, and **prayer plants** (*Maranta* species) may yellow at the bottom of stems. If new, emerging leaves on these plants turn yellow, that's a serious symptom of root problems,

potentially of root rot. New leaves are meant to be healthy and green. Don't allow fallen leaves to remain on soil surfaces.

PROBLEMS

Leaf diseases: fungus diseases often cause spotty leaves, but the exact cause can be elusive. Mildews, with gray powdery deposits on one or both sides of the leaves, result from poor air circulation or continually wet leaves. Isolate the plant. Remove all affected leaves. Then treat it with a fungicide registered for indoor use and safe for the type of plant. Checking with a nursery expert will help in selecting a product. If the plant does not improve, discard it. Miniature roses, often brought in for brief indoor color, are highly susceptible to powdery mildew.

JUNE
HOUSEPLANTS

PLANNING

In Washington and Oregon, gardeners face opposite summer conditions. In eastern Zones 4 to 6, where inland summers stay hot, the plants need shade. Plan shelter for tropical plants, such as **schefflera** and **rubber trees**, to keep them shaded and cool enough on dry, hot days. Gauge your local conditions before settling plants outside through the day. Leaves can frizzle without protection. Under a leafy tree, or tucked into an overhead arbor full of leaves, or in a shady lath house, the indoor plants will grow vigorously.

In Zones 7 to 9, particularly along the maritime areas of Washington and Oregon, nights can remain cold in June. In western areas, particularly the maritime, it's difficult to keep some of them—such as **angel's trumpet** (*brugmansia* sp) and **bird-of-paradise** (*Strelitzia* sp) warm enough for good bloom. In general, houseplants are generally tropical in origin, and can move outdoors when nighttime temperatures exceed 50 degrees F. regularly.

Flowering plants like **gardenias**, **princess flower** (*Tibouchina* spp.), and **flowering maple** will do well with morning sun in cool maritime areas but they also need shade protection from hottest afternoon temperatures.

PLANTING

Making more plants: early summer, when plants perk up and grow vigorously, you'll find that propagating new ones goes easily.

Plants grown from their own leaves: succulent plants like **Jade plant**, aloe, and sedums root readily from broken-off leaves. Cactus can be rooted from leaves also, but do not cover their leaves in plastic; allow them to root in open air once placed in the rooting mix.

For a potting mix with cuttings, use $1/2$ perlite or pumice and $1/2$ peat. Follow this process:

1. Break off a few leaves or plant sections (aloe will root from cut leaves)

2. Allow the leaf or section to dry for 24 hours.

3. Tuck the leaf about $1/4$ inch into moist—but not soggy—mix.

4. Label and date the planting. Popsicle sticks make good labels.

5. Slide the planting into a plastic bag, large enough not to touch the leaves (excluding **cactus**).

6. Place the planting in a light but not hot area.

7. Check for growth: after about a week, take the bag off. Keep planting moist but not wet.

8. Rooting may occur within three weeks; tug gently to check for roots.

Plant in a small pot when new growth shows.

CARE

In Zones 5 to 6: If garden conditions don't allow for summer protection from extreme heat and drying winds, sensitive indoor plants may survive better remaining in their winter positions indoors.

In all zones, be prepared to watch weather conditions for houseplant management. A

It may be difficult to keep bird-of-paradise warm enough for good bloom in cool maritime areas.

sudden spike of 90-degree temperatures in western areas along the coast can toast any exposed leaves left in sun. Thunderstorms and high winds can tear and damage leaves; hailstorms simply mash tender houseplants. Be alert to changing conditions.

WATERING

Whether indoors or out, all houseplants require more frequent watering in summer. Follow the routine of pouring water out of saucers after filling the entire pot.

FERTILIZING

Continue fertilizing plants as needed.

Cactus and **succulents**, which require relatively little fertilizing, can benefit from $1/2$ strength fertilizer once a month in summer.

Timed-release fertilizers: many indoor gardeners rely on coated fertilizers, such as Osmocote™, that provide nutrients over a period of months. As the plant is watered, the outer coating dissolves, and minerals are released gradually. Nurseries use them to reduce labor. In the indoor or patio garden, they are most helpful with large foliage plants that take a lot of summer fertilizer. They are not, however, a

---

DID YOU KNOW?

Can you reuse potting soil? Yes, container potting soils can be used year after year. But if the plants growing in it had insect or disease infestations, toss that batch out—into the garbage, not the compost.

Rejuvenating old potting soil isn't difficult. Dump it on a tarp, and shake out any old roots, removing them. Add about $1/4$ gritty material, like pumice or perlite. Mix it, then add about $1/4$ by volume of commercial bagged compost.

What you've done is to increase the air spaces, minimize compaction caused by constant watering, and add some microorganisms with the compost. Homemade compost is not recommended for houseplants because it's often not processed sufficiently to kill off disease organisms and weed seeds.

---

substitute for liquid fertilizers. Follow the package instructions when potting or repotting, adding it to the soil. Or sprinkle it on top of established plants. They last about 4 months (check the package) so should be used now rather than in fall when plants do not require as many nutrients.

GROOMING

Continue to deadhead flowers and remove dead leaves. Look over the plants for disease problems as you do this. Re-tie any vining plants left indoors for summer.

PROBLEMS

Take time during summer to scrub areas where houseplants are dis-

played; wash surfaces and the outside of pots with water and a bit of dish detergent.

Soak any empty pots in 1 part bleach to 10 parts water to prepare for future plantings.

Gawky plants, toppling in their pots, or vines scrambling too far, can be cut back this month, and will fill in by fall. Make bushier plants of **flowering maple** (*Abutilon* sp.), **asparagus ferns** (*Sprengeri* sp.), **begonias**, *Cissus*, **dieffenbachia**, **fatsia**, **fuchsia**, **geraniums** (*Pelargonium* sp), **philodendron**, and **tradescantia** by pinching them back. Summer warmth will help them fill in.

See July for ways to manage plants with trunks, such as **rubber plants**, that have become awkward and top-heavy.

JULY
HOUSEPLANTS

PLANNING

Review which plants you may want to coax into bloom for holiday color. If you've been carrying along **Christmas cactus**, **poinsettias**, **kalanchoe**, and others that take special care for winter bloom, check out the process required. **Christmas cactus** generally is easiest to manage; **poinsettias** may do best as a tropical summer houseplant to be discarded in fall. See September for details on fall needs for these potentially colorful plants.

Order **Christmas amaryllis** and **paperwhite narcissus** now from bulb catalogs.

PLANTING

Take cuttings the easy way, to grow in plain water. Plants that will obligingly root this way include the vigorous **grape ivy** (*Cissus* sp), any **philodendron**, **Swedish ivy** (*Plectanthus* sp.), and **zebrine**.

Make a cutting about 5 inches long, remove leaves that will be under water, and place the cutting container in light but not direct sun. Check and replace water weekly. Children can help with this and later in summer pot up and care for what could become their holiday gift plants.

CARE

Air-layering: elderly plants with trunks, such as **draecena**, **rubber plants**, or large overwhelming climbers like big-leaved **monsteras** (*Monstera deliciosa* and others) can be persuaded to become smaller by air-layering. The process is slow and somewhat unsightly, but if done when the plant is outdoors in summer, the new section should have rooted by fall.

Choose a spot below the healthy leafy section, where you want roots to form (figure 1).

Remove a bit of bark to induce rooting. Score it with a knife, all the way around the trunk, in two spots about an inch apart, and remove the bark between the scorings. Don't penetrate the trunk very far. You just want to remove the outer back.

Put rooting hormone on the newly exposed surface, and wrap moist moss around the area (figure 3). Two or three

Air Layering 1.

2.

3.

cups of moss is necessary to cover, not only the wound, but above and below it (figure 3).

4.

Bind the moss with twine. Then cover it completely with a plastic bag so that no moss is left uncovered. Moisture must stay inside,

Tie the bag on firmly with twine or electrical tape (Keep the tape off the trunk.)

5.

When roots are visible, cut off the stem below the roots (figure 4).

Pot up the new plant, watering carefully (figure 5). Place a stick to support it in the pot.

The old plant will often resprout from the roots if the trunk is cut off down to about 6 inches.

Tie up any tall **philodendron** or other vining plants like **hoya** (*Hoya carnosa*). When they grow strongly, they can fall away from their supports, resulting in stem breakage.

# WATERING

Sprinkling the leaves of houseplants summering outdoors may help remove dust from the leaves, but it's not a substitute for careful watering. Where air lacks humidity, the sprinkling or misting provides only quite temporary relief for the plant.

Houseplants in inland dry areas need special attention to watering from now through August; they can dessicate quickly on a hot afternoon, so doublecheck their shelter and move any that suffer from scorched leaves. Leaf scorch can happen even if plants are watered well.

# FERTILIZING

Continue summer fertilizing. If plants take off on a growth spurt that will make them larger than you want in the house, reduce fertilizer to once a month.

# GROOMING

Prune out any wind-damaged leaves. Prune back to a leaf growing point, just as you would for any outdoor plant.

# PROBLEMS

Give special attention to any tropical bulbs—**caladium**, **calla**, **canna**, or **elephant ear**—planted last month from nursery sales. New growth can be quick during hot weather but they are susceptible to slug attacks when growing outside. Hand pick slugs and put out either beer traps or iron phosphate slug bait (sold as Sluggo™ and other brands.)

AUGUST

HOUSEPLANTS

 PLANNING

August presents relatively few garden tasks. The combination of warmth and low rainfall causes all plants, including houseplants, to slow their growth. Check any plants that were not repotted in spring, to determine if their summer growth spurt results in outgrowing their current pots. Gently check the roots along pot sides and in the drainage holes.

Which plants deserve the house space throughout fall and winter? Disposing of unsatisfactory plants makes room for fresh choices, or larger spaces for plants that have expanded.

Nurseries may have sales on pots and potting soils during August and September.

 PLANTING

Making more plants: layering stems or small plantlets easily produces a new, vigorous plant. The technique works best with lax-stemmed plants such as **philodendron**, **Swedish ivy**, and **wandering Jew**.

1. Fill 3 to 4 inch pots with soil, well-moistened.

2. Pick out a long, healthy shoot. Pin it down firmly with a piece of wire or an old-fashioned hairpin, with a bit of soil over the shoot.

3. Keep it moistened but not soggy; in about three to four weeks when it roots, clip the plant loose from the parent plant. Water it carefully for a few months until it grows substantially.

 CARE

With vacations frequent in August, caring for plants in containers becomes a priority. The simplest and most obvious choice is finding a capable house and plant sitter; that prevents the need for special arrangements.

Plants will manage without care for two to three days but need attention if the vacation period is longer. Nurseries sell capillary mat systems that water from the bottom. They're most easily used in a splash-proof area like a basement workshop. You may also find drip systems that deliver water slowly from the top or bottom of the plants.

It's helpful to give these methods a trial period while you're still at home.

 WATERING

Watering depends on:

1. What are the plant's basic needs? Little or much? **Cactus** or **Boston fern**?

2. What's the season? Watering needs decrease during the late fall and winter, from November through mid-February. Plants need more frequent watering as they start active growth again in spring and during summer.

3. Before watering check the soil by poking about an inch down, with your finger or a probe like a chopstick. Some gardeners like using moisture meters which do 'read' the moisture level.

4. How is the plant physically set up for watering? In general, the best practice is watering just until moisture emerges at the bottom drain hole. A saucer or other form of water-catcher is necessary. Practice with the plant will help you understand how much to apply and how much will remain in the saucer.

5. Do not allow the bottom of the pot to stand in excess water. Roots can rot if constantly soggy. Good drainage and no standing water is vital for all plants in containers, both outdoors and indoors.

Pots with attached saucers or "self-watering" pots often result in wet conditions around roots. Stick to pots without these systems.

6. Allow water to sit overnight in order to reach room temperature when growing tropical plants, those that prefer their air temperatures over 65 degrees F.

For small seedlings such as **tomatoes**, tepid water is also essential.

7. Type of water to use? Some indoor gardeners collect rainwater for their plants. Others use distilled water, although this may be necessary only if the household water is alkaline or otherwise non-potable. Water straight from the tap is fine, also, with a few notes: if the water in your district has been fluoridated (has sodium fluoride added), this

Try overwintering potted tropicals indoors; you'll love the blooms next summer.

DID YOU KNOW?

One group of gift plants will not re-bloom or transfer well into the fall garden: **Miniature roses**, blooming **gerberas**, **eustoma**, **gardenias**, and **bird-of-paradise** do best treated as long-lived flower bouquets. Even **chrysanthemums** can be difficult to plant into the garden and winter over; they do not bloom again in the house.

Best chances for long life in the tender indoor garden come with **begonias**, **flowering maple** (*Abutilon* sp.), and **hibiscus**. They can be carried through winter as foliage plants and brought into flower next spring and summer.

fluoride is suspected of damaging plants in the *Dracena* family (**spider plant**, **dracena**, **lucky bamboo**) by causing brown leaf tip ends. Letting the water stand overnight will not reduce the sodium fluoride level. Using distilled water or rain water solves this problem.

FERTILIZING

Slower growth in August necessitates cutting back on fertilizer; reduce the amount to $1/2$ strength twice this month for plants like foliage plants.

Fertilize **cacti** or **succulents** lightly from now through winter.

GROOMING

Continue regular tidying of spent leaves and blooms. Yellowing leaves on lower parts of stems can be common toward sum-

mer's end. But yellowing leaves on the new tip growth often signal root or other disease problems.

PROBLEMS

Problems in watering: Water runs rapidly down the sides of the container?

1. The plant has dried out completely

2. It may have outgrown its pot, with roots filling the soil layer so that water can't infiltrate.

If either of these conditions apply, move the affected plant to a sink or bathtub where it can be set in water and allowed to soak the water up from the bottom. Once the plant has been thoroughly wet, it's easier to keep it watered. But if repotting is needed, the condition will repeat. Repot as soon as convenient.

September

HOUSEPLANTS

PLANNING

If you're moving, check with the Department of Agriculture to determine if live plants can be moved across the border. With a short move, it can be no more difficult than tucking plants in a closed vehicle, whether car or truck with overhead protection. The winds of even 35 mph can shred foliage plants and break fragile succulents.

Moving companies seldom take plants. The best option is to winnow the collection to three or four treasures that can be tucked into your own transportation. Watering well, then wrapping the plants in brown paper for protection, plus tucking them into boxes to prevent their toppling—these measures will generally take care of them for three or four days.

Plant lovers who've moved often will take small cuttings of heritage plants months before departure, to keep the plant descendant in the household but make the moving easier. Giving plants to friends allows visiting leafy favorites on trips back!

PLANTING

Choosing container types:

No one material is necessarily better than another: drainage is the single most vital need. If you've chosen a container without drainage holes, consider drilling about 3 holes in the bottom. This allows water to drain effectively.

Plastic containers come in many variations of texture and color: some copy clay pots accurately. Their advantage is lightness of weight, variety of sizes and shapes, and lower cost. Plastic pots do not "breathe," which means that plants in them stay moist somewhat longer.

Wood containers are also useful and can be painted. Wood gets heavy when wet and its rustic appearance may not suit a particular home interior. It's ideal for porch or balcony locations. Wood is slightly porous and lets some air and water through its sides, but also allows planting soil to hold moisture. Eventually it suffers slow disintegration.

Foam containers: what used to be purely utilitarian and less than gorgeous is going upscale with newer foam containers. Some mimic stone or concrete, others carry textured surfaces. Because they are molded, foam containers can copy just about anything the maker chooses. They excel in lightweightness, and hold water well. Be sure to take out the bottom hole-fillers; most foam containers are sold without the drain holes punched. Expense ranges from little to lots depend-ing on the size and type. The least expensive ones are easily broken or dented if bumped. The more costly ones nearly reach the durability of stone or pottery.

Pottery containers: beautiful stoneware and clay pots can add to décor. High fired stoneware is nearly indestructible unless dropped; clay and terracotta pots may be either quite soft and breakable or more durable. Soft clay pots "breathe" and may need watering more often than plastic. Many people love the classic look of plants in terracotta pots. They may show white deposits from salts in fertilizer, and should be scrubbed thoroughly when plants are repotted.

CARE

Bring houseplants in early this month, before night temperatures drop below 50 degrees F. For Zones 5 to 6, early rehousing of plants is vital, perhaps in the first week of September. Zone 7 to 9 should complete tucking in tender plants by the end of September.

Mid-September finds **poinsettias** and **Christmas cactus** ready for their manipulation to produce December or January color.

It's significantly easier to purchase new plants from nurseries than to get excellent results with recycled **poinsettias** from last

DO GREEN PLANTS IMPROVE INDOOR AIR QUALITY?

Peace lily

Humans, breathing out carbon dioxide, essentially make air more stale if they remain in a closed indoor space. Plants, giving off oxygen, do just the opposite. Architects and planners design plants as integral parts of new buildings, including circulating air through plant filled atriums in sealed buildings.

The basic idea explored by NASA scientists in the mid-1980s has been validated by later studies. Plants detoxify some indoor air pollutants. Don't count on a few plants cleaning the air entirely, but they'll help to freshen things up.

Mix different varieties, since it's not certain which combinations work best. Since most of our homes do have natural air circulation, it's likely that plants contribute to well-being psychologically but not necessarily by detoxifying the air. Basic low-light house plants suggested by researchers for air improvement include **spider plant**s, **dracenas**, the **Kentia palm** (*Howea forsterana*), and **peace lily** (*Spathiphyllum* sp.) Others are **weeping fig** (*Ficus benjamina*), **golden pothos** (*Scindapsus aureus*), and **Chinese evergreen** (*Aglaeonema modestum*).

year. They require complete darkness 14 hours per night and bright light for 10 hours, mid-September through mid-November. Both conditions are difficult to fulfill indoors. Nurseries manage by setting timers and using dark cloths that slide over plant areas.

See October for **Christmas cactus** management.

WATERING

Reduce watering as the plants slow their growth.

FERTILIZING

Fertilize once this month.

GROOMING

Prune back a few long shoots to shorten houseplants taller than their allotted spot. As with all pruning technique, removing an entire shoot keeps the plant from erupting in vigorous new growth as it might when shoots are tipped back. With vining plants, this isn't a problem, as they often grow better when slightly bushier. Plants pruned in September seldom add much growth from October to February.

PROBLEMS

Survey plants carefully before bringing them indoors. Slugs, aphids, and earwigs may wish to hitchhike inside. Thoroughly wash leaves and trim out any damaged by insects or diseases. Some gardeners set the plant in a bucket of water up to the soil line, then let it drain.

OCTOBER

HOUSEPLANTS

 **PLANNING**

Christmas cactus (*Schlumbergera* species) may need another nickname, since many bloom throughout winter. You may not think of jungles as containing cactus plants, but these naturalize in Brazilian tropical tree branches where leaves break down into nutritious soil. They bloom reliably with just a little fall care. These live for decades if well cared for and often become living family heirlooms.

1. To produce best buds, move plants every night to a dark spot starting in early October. Or cover with a black plastic bag if house lights are on.

2. Place them in medium light during the day. Continue this until the plant develops healthy buds. Note: buds may drop off after forming if the plant suffers stress from drying out (use rainwater or distilled water to moisten), or gets into a draft.

3. Keep the plant at the same orientation day and night: mark one side and keep that toward the light and do not alter that. This helps buds keep the same attachment, and prevents drop-off.

4. Do not fertilize during this period.

5. Dark treatment is not necessary once buds reach about 1/2 inch long.

6. Water generously during this period, keeping soil moist but not soggy during bloom. Allow top two inches to dry before rewatering.

7. Nip off segments that have bloomed once flowers fade, tidying the plant by cutting back to another segment. New flowers will form next year on sturdier branches. Floppiness accompanies unpruned *Schumbergera*.

 **PLANTING**

Plants propagated by cuttings or rooted plantlets in late summer: select small attractive pots and plant up any well-rooted new plants intended for holiday gifts. They'll look better when presented if they have 6 to 8 weeks in their new pots.

See Bulbs chapter, page 74, for information on starting **paperwhite narcissus** indoors for December bloom. Allow about 6 weeks from planting to buds and blooms.

 **CARE**

Zones 7 to 9: get all tender plants indoors by early October.

Tender blooming plants, some treated as annuals like **tuberous begonias**, can be wintered over, under light systems. **Geraniums** Stella series, **scented geraniums**, **florist's cyclamen**, and **African violets** bloom better with auxiliary light during winter when dark days throughout our region limit flower set.

Light "stands" are available commercially and might make a thoughtful present for a houseplant collector. Many are attractive enough for living room use. Or build it yourself. Simple con-

Cyclamen

struction of an A-frame with a shelf makes care easy.

Standard fluorescent bulbs work fine: 40-inch size with one cool-white and one warm-white in a shop-type fixture. Lights specifically designated for growing plants aren't necessary.

Foliage plants need less direct light but will thrive under a table-top lamp turned on at night—this obviously works with smaller plants like small **philodendron**.

WATERING

Plants need less water now; check surfaces and water only when dry 2 to 3 inches down, no more than once a month.

FERTILIZING

Reduce fertilizer to all non-flowering plants: use a $1/2$ strength mix once every six weeks in winter: mid-October, January 1, and February 15.

Do not fertilize succulent plants such as **Jade plant** or cactus-type plants until March.

Flowering plants require fertilizer once a month if growing under lights. The principles of fertilizer state: with more growth, more nutrients, with less growth, less nutrients. Winter dormancy helps plants grow and flower in spring, and true as that is outdoors, it's also true inside.

GROOMING

Fall conditions will result in greater leaf drop as growth slows in lower indoor light and darkening days. Keep all plants groomed and fallen bits cleaned off soil.

PROBLEMS

Check plants often in early fall for any insect or disease problems missed when plants were brought indoors.

Low humidity in heated homes will be a particular difficulty in colder Zones 5 to 6. Grouping plants together helps raise the humidity level with each plant benefiting from others. Misting plants, often recommended, gives a very short period of raised humidity and can contribute to foliage diseases.

Some gardeners place plants on trays full of small pebbles, with water up to the top of the pebbles but not touching the pot edge. (This prevents soggy roots). These set-ups may be difficult to maintain because they collect water when plants are irrigated.

Devices for raising house humidity for the entire family will also benefit houseplants, as will the old-fashioned "teakettle on the wood stove." Air dryness is a common winter problem for houseplants, along with light reduction. They'll recover in spring, even without special measures being taken.

DID YOU KNOW?

If you have ever stood under a tree when stressed, you know the presence of plants provides benefits that transcend the aesthetic. Being around plants helps heal and reduce physical stress, accounting for their presence in many hospital gardens and their value in therapeutic programs.

When entering a small conservatory or greenhouse space attached to a home, you recognize the freshness of the air and its contrast with air not containing plants. Even the few plants gracing your indoor garden can change the physical and psychological atmosphere.

NOVEMBER

HOUSEPLANTS

 PLANNING

Purchasing flowering plants now:

Look for **Christmas cactus** with large blooms: small buds often drop off when the plant is moved. Pick **poinsettias** late this month, with firm color on the bracts (the petal-like colored elements), closed yellow center blooms, and bright green leaves. Keep them out of drafts when moving them into chilly air. Warm the car and keep transportation time to a minimum.

Pots of forced bulbs, such as **daffodils, tulips,** and **paperwhite narcissus,** will thrive in cooler house temperatures such as an enclosed porch. They last longer at temperatures between 45 to 55 degrees F. than they do at normal house warmth. If given as a gift where they'll be in higher temperatures, bloom life is shortened. In Zones 7 to 9 they can be placed on front porches for decoration. Bring them in if temperatures drop below 35 degrees F.

 PLANTING

Terrariums—glass cases that hold small plants give rooms a touch of the Victorian Age when fern cases adorned every proper parlor. Discarded aquariums with glass lids cut to rest on top, or open round vases, or large canister jars will all work fine. The ideal terrarium balances water needs, requires no fertilizer, and thrive in warm spaces, moderate light. Avoid direct sun or total shade. Best plants for use are: small **ferns**, or foliage plants like **fittonia** or **peperomia**.

1. Clean the container thoroughly, inside and out.

2. Place about a 1-inch layer of charcoal on the bottom; unlike all other

types of potting, this is necessary for the closed environment.

3. Add about 3 inches of moistened clean potting soil (without fertilizer.)

4. Water plants before installing. Allow to drain.

5. Arrange plants, placing them close together.

6. Leave the top off for a few days, then cap it. Moisture on the sides is common in the morning but the area shouldn't be soggy.

A terrarium without a lid will provide humidity and shelter for plants, but takes more watering. Either method grows tender plants well.

 CARE

How can we measure light? The strange old historical term "foot candles" is still used to describe how much light radiates from a

Philodendron

source, even in these days of tensor lights and other electronic advances. Essentially it means how much light falls a foot away from a burning candle.

Light outdoors, whether the day is bright or dark, far exceeds the light inside a window.

A simple way to get a general idea of available light requires only a piece of white paper. Do this now to measure light in the "dark season" and do it again in March and June for seasonal changes. Note how different windows change as the sun moves monthly.

1. Place the white paper where you want the plant to grow.

2. Hold your hand about 12 inches above the paper during the brightest part of the day.

Now look at the shadow your open hand casts on the paper.

• A clear shadow, with crisp detail, signifies "high" light.

• A fuzzy shadow but distinguishable as a hand is "medium" light.

• A blurry shadow with no recognizable outline is "low" light.

• No shadow at all indicates that the area is too dark.

Obviously days without sun will differ from bright days. In fact, in Washington and Oregon, the "high" brightness areas of spring, summer and fall can be "medium" to "low" in winter. Individual patterns will vary during one day: areas with bright light at noon, facing east, may darken as the sun moves during the day. Becoming accustomed to how light moves and changes is a central skill of indoor (and outdoor!) gardeners.

Brighteners: light-colored walls, strategically placed mirrors, and moving plants into south exposures can help lift winter darkness. However they do not overcome winter sufficiently to grow flowering plants successfully. For that, you need a light system. (See October.)

WATERING

All houseplants need less water in winter when growth slows. Allow the top of the soil to dry

---

DID YOU KNOW?

Norfolk Island pine (*Araucaria heterophylla*) grows indoors, and can become a well-adapted permanent house plant that also serves as a Christmas tree year after year. Native to Norfolk Island in the South Pacific, they're in the same family as the odd **monkey puzzle tree** grown outdoors in Zones 7 to 9.

They require mild temperatures year round, and like household climates suitable to humans, with daytime temperatures of 68 and night temperatures a bit cooler, down to 50 degrees F. For best life, **Norfolk Island pines** need light; a bright window with as much light as possible suits them. Turn it $1/4$ turn per week to keep it symmetrical. If a light system is available, they benefit from 16 hours daily of artificial light.

Water it sparingly. The plant should be slightly damp but never soggy. Water with rainwater or distilled water. In winter allow the surface to dry before re-watering. Fertilize in early spring when new growth.

---

down to about 1 or 2 inches. However, plants with soft, bright green leaves such as **philodendron** or **Swedish ivy** will need close observation because they can suffer when too dry.

FERTILIZING

No fertilizing will be needed this month unless you are growing flowering plants under lights. Gift plants intended for a short stay in the house—three weeks or so—have been fed at the nursery and do not require anything extra. Bulbs like **paperwhite narcissus** being forced do not require fertilizing.

GROOMING

Thoroughly winter be meticulous about removing yellowed or fallen leaves. Keep the surface of the pot cleared of plant debris. Check for insect problems when grooming.

PROBLEMS

All plants will continue to adjust to lower light levels by ceasing active growth; the quiet of winter affects them too as they go into dormancy.

Just as the landscape garden has a rhythm, so does the indoor.

DECEMBER

HOUSEPLANTS

 PLANNING

Choosing indoor plants for winter holiday decoration, such as table-top **Christmas trees** or other living evergreens, requires thought.

Some catalog or nursery-available plants will thrive only briefly indoors:

Alberta spruce, for instance (*Picea glauca* var *albertiana*) can be ordered pre-decorated or plain. It's a perfectly shaped miniature **Christmas tree**. This tidy small tree, related to outdoor spruce, needs cool temperatures when indoors. It doesn't make a reliable houseplant because it's really a landscape tree requiring outdoor conditions.

When purchasing December decorative plants, check their tags for care requirements.

 PLANTING

No planting this month.

 CARE

When acquiring gift plants, or when wrapping plants for gifts, remove any foil or plastic wrappers. View a decorative cover as purely temporary. If your décor requires the colorful wrap, poke about 10 holes in it to allow water flow.

If you present a gift, make a care tag that identifies the plant and describes its needs. It's possible to get these laminated, which adds to their useful life. The best decoration for a gift plant will be this tag tied on with yarn, raffia or ribbon. Along with an attractive pot, no other wrapping is needed.

 WATERING

Holiday gift plants will need regular watering. **Florist's cyclamen** with butterfly-like white or red flowers, **Jerusalem cherry** (*Solanum pesudocapsicum*), **kalanchoe** (*Kalanchoe blossfeldiana*), and even **holly** can appear along with the **poinsettias** and **Christmas cactus**. Keep them evenly watered. Most of these will bloom 3 to 4 weeks before fading. But **kalanchoe**, with its brilliant red or yellow flowers, is most likely to thrive as a permanent member of your houseplant family.

Kalanchoe joins **jade plant** in the Crassula family, and must be watered more sparingly than the other holiday plants. Check to be sure it's dry at least 2 inches down before watering. Keep it in the brightest possible light at least four hours during the day. Move it anywhere you want to display it at night.

 FERTILIZING

Thankfully no fertilizing will be needed this month (since the month offers so many other enticements as well as chores).

 GROOMING

Poinsettias benefit from removal of spent leaves.

 PROBLEMS

Houseplants suffer from temperatures that are too hot at night; an evening drop of 10 to 15 degrees F. benefits many of them including orchids. **Orchids** will often rebloom better with cool temperatures.

LAWNS

AN OUTDOOR CARPET

Roll on it, picnic on it, chase the dog or the children on it—the outdoor carpet called *lawn* provides lots of summer pleasure. As a comfortable informal play surface, lawns are terrific. And year-round, a lawn sets off and frames the landscape, enhancing flower color and tree form. For many gardeners, only a grassy turf lawn offers the qualities needed for all these uses.

Growing a satisfactory lawn takes planning. But how hard, you may be wondering, can it be to grow grass? Doesn't it grow more or less all over the temperate world without much trouble? Yes, it does. But controlling the growth and producing a smooth, thick, picture-postcard lawn requires technique and time. Learning to manage a lawn isn't

difficult. The first requirement is considering and planning how the lawn fits your needs and determining its size. Do you need a new lawn? See August for information on total lawn renovation to determine if it's necessary to remove and replace the old lawn.

Do you enjoy caring for a lawn? Many people do. The odor of fresh-cut grass is considered by many to be enjoyable, a kind of summer aromatherapy, and the joy of walking barefoot on a healthy lawn can be energizing. The size and type of the lawn should suit the gardener's personal tendencies. In some situations, the turf quantity and placement can be part of residential requirements in developments. Even so, the lawn can be a source of pleasure for the homeowner.

PLANNING THE LAWN AREA

How will the lawn be used? Function counts for a lot. Will it get a lot of traffic, either for sports or for entertaining? Or does the lawn act as a small color spot, an oval or square of green in a larger design? Do you need a dog run? Or do you fancy a croquet court? For some uses, grass alone works. For other uses, such as entertaining, time spent planning and building a deck or patio may be more rewarding.

What are your standards for grass? Do you have a vision of just how it will look? Does the landscape require closely maintained grass, or can a freer "meadow-like" surface fit into the plan? For a play area, the turf may gradually be invaded by some volunteer grasses and weeds, kept mowed and fertilized, but not coddled. Perfection may not be required in a play area. If the lawn comprises part of a "show" area, a more detailed maintenance standard may prevail.

Are you determined to evict all weeds, or can you co-exist with some? People vary in their tolerance for lawn invaders such as weeds, moss, and moles.

What sun exposure does the area have? Lawn grass has noble relations that love sun.

The great staple foods of the world—rice, wheat, and corn—are all grasses. They require sun, deep fertile soils, and water to grow well. Lawn grasses also like these excellent conditions. Lawn specialists recommend a deep root run, 8 to 10 inches of soil under the lawn. Only rarely do lawns get that much root room. But you can provide it when installing a new lawn.

Lawns grow best in open, sunny conditions with deep, fertile soil. Turf grasses have specific growth needs, just as rhododendrons and roses do. Lawn should be planted where it gets at least six hours of light daily during periods of active growth.

Think of a prairie: Grasses are the dominant plants. They perform badly in cold, shady gardens. Poor soil, rocky or clay filled, will challenge their health. If the area you choose to plant in is a cold, shaded, rocky slope, the lawn project goes up in difficulty and may be inadvisable.

Neglected lawns: Perhaps you didn't plan the lawn, but it came with the property. Caring for a neglected or poorly installed lawn can be frustrating, but with some good choices, the difficulties may ease. See April for tips on lawn renovation.

The best instructions for lawn care emphasize good installation techniques, like building a house with a good foundation,

to make all subsequent lawn care easier. Although gardens and growing conditions differ, all lawns require attention to the basics: installation, watering, fertilizing, and mowing.

STARTING OVER

Simply tilling up a lawn does not work. The idea of turning the lawn under with a blade, then planting, might appeal, but it's not effective. The turfgrass keeps growing and creates a big weed problem unless it is removed or killed.

One method is to dig up the sod. Do this after a rain or after watering, since the tough sod succumbs better to removal when damp. You can dig it by hand (depending on the size of the task) or rent a sod-cutter.

Either way, pick up the sod, roots and all. Then if you have space to make an unobtrusive stack, pile the sod (roots up) and cover it with black plastic. Water the layers as you stack because if the sod's dry, it will not break down

Placing the roots upside down is important because if it's right side up, the grass will blithely continue to grow. In a year or two you will have some nice compost to add to your garden.

Killing the grass? The best way to do it, if you have time, is to cover the area with something. A thick layer of wet

INSTALLING THE NEW LAWN

Below is a quick recipe from Dr Tom Cook, Oregon State University turf specialist.

Timing on this will vary depending on the region. If you plant too early, seeds will rot in cold soil. If you seed late, such as too late in the fall, increase seeding rates.

Cook's Simplified List of Steps for Planting a New Lawn from Seed:

1. Choose the optimum time of year. May 1 to mid-June east of the mountains; April 1 to May 30 west of the mountains, August 15 through September 15 east of the mounts

2. Till and rough grade existing soil. Till in compost amendments (no more than 30 percent by volume) and lime if planting west of the mountains.

3. Spread imported soil (if using) and till together with existing soil.

4. Finish grading, raking and rolling to a firm surface.

5. Apply high nitrogen, pre-plant fertilizer, like a 21-7-14, at 2 pounds actual nitrogen per 1000 square feet. This is vital.

6. Apply seed with a drop spreader and lightly rake it in.

7. Apply 1/4 inch mulch with a wire basket mulch roller.

8. Water thoroughly and repeat with light applications as needed.

9. Keep seedbed moist for one to two weeks.

10. Mow as soon as the grass is tall enough to cut, about four weeks after planting.

11. Fertilize again with nitrogen based fertilizer four to six weeks after planting.

---

newspaper covered with compost, leaves, lawn clippings, or sawdust smothers it well. Allow this layer to remain until next spring, and you can plant right through the mulch and paper.

PLANTING

Installing a new lawn requires careful preparation. If the soil is compacted from construction damage or has a layer of hardpan close to the surface, grass roots can't penetrate and grow well. Similarly if the area chosen for the lawn has a very high water table, such as would happen adjacent to a lake, you may need professional assistance to manage drainage, grading of the surface, and bringing in new soil.

Good lawns need deep soils. Turf with an inch or two of sparse roots struggles to keep its blades growing. But turf can grow on various soil types. Sandy soil is harder to water, as it loses water easily. Clay soils give winter troubles with poor drainage that stays soggy. It's best to have 6 to 10 inches of well drained soil before the sod goes down or seeding is done. If a soil tests shows a need for lime or phosphorous, apply them before seeding. Without a soil test, you can get good results by incorporating 10 pounds of 10-20-20 per 100 square feet into the top 2 to 3 inches of the soil before seeding, or sodding will work. Or

use Dr Tom Cook's quick recipe (see above). It's vital to add fertilizer before spreading grass or installing sod.

Grass seed germinates best at temperatures between 50 and 80 degrees F. Obviously if the soil is colder than 50 degrees F., it will sit and do nothing (while birds peck away at the seeds). If your garden soil has warmed enough to grow lettuce seeds or spinach, grass seed will also germinate.

INSTALLATION

Turf Choices—Selecting the correct grass seed mix is essential.

WESTERN REGION

Kentucky bluegrass does not grow well in western areas.

Any of the following mixtures will work:

1. Turftype: Perennial ryegrasses alone or 50 percent fine-leaved fescues or colonial bentgrasses are good. Turftype perennial ryegrass needs full sun. Fine fescues and bentgrass blend in well with it and are better adapted to shade. The seeding rate is 5 to 7 pounds per 1000 square feet.

2. Fescues: Red or Chewings fescues, along with hard fescues, are the major types used throughout the Northwest. They require less water than turftype perennial ryegrasses and are good, drought tolerant, cool season grasses. Apply at 3 pounds per 1000 square feet when seeding fescues alone.

3. Colonial bentgrass at 1/2 pound plus 2.5 pounds of red or Chewings fescue per 1000 square feet.

EASTERN REGION

1. Kentucky bluegrass is good for sunny areas. It is long lived, and handles heat once established. It is good in a mix. Apply at 3 pounds per 1000 square feet of blended cultivars.

2. Apply Kentucky bluegrass at 2 pounds plus 1 pound red or Chewings fescue per 1000 square feet.

3. Apply turftype tall fescues at 6 to 8 pounds per 1000 square feet and buffalograss at 2 pounds per 1000 square feet for a drought tolerant lawn.

RENEWAL

Often the most important task is reviving an older lawn. See April for tips on lawn renovation. When preparing existing lawns for reseeding, it's good to till some compost into the soil. Do not exceed about 30 percent by volume; too much organic matter can result in a lumpy lawn as the components break down. The compost should be fully mature, not in the process of breaking down. If it is steaming or clearly immature, the area should lie fallow for about a month to complete the composting process. However, in the fall time is limited, and you wouldn't be able to wait this long, especially in coldest zones. So be sure to purchase fully mature compost.

PROBLEMS

Some people with lakefront property may find high water over bulkheads and across onto the lawn during winter storms, or low spots that fill with water and do not drain. Lawns won't survive over the long term in soggy ground. If it's impractical to install drainage or regrade to correct the drainage, remove the lawn from that area.

Moles probably cause the most lawn-grower frustration, next to moss! Sleek, muscular, and well-adapted to subterranean living, moles generate anger by rearranging lawns and flowerbeds. Their tunneling raises feeding runs and volcano-like humps. They aren't chewing on the turf or the roots; they are digging for soil-dwelling food. These mammals eat primarily earthworms and grubs; they don't generally munch roots, plant parts, or spring bulbs even though their digging may disturb growing areas.

Most home remedies for moles don't work, and many are environmentally unsound. Remember, these are mobile creatures, and they simply move out of the run when something noxious happens. Flooding, loud rock music, pouring drain cleaner or other toxic material down the runs—these do not work.

If you determine that it's not possible to live with the mole, trapping does work, using a scissors type trap. Get good instructions about how to set it into an active run. But do this only if you live in Oregon.

Washington state passed an anti-trapping law, I-713, in 2000, which states that scissors-type traps cannot be used. Despite legal review, Washington law (allowing mouse and rat traps), does not permit mole traps at this time.

Where you can't trap, dig a ditch 24 to 30 inches deep and bury "fences" of aluminum sheeting or 1/4-inch mesh galvanized hardware cloth. Bend the bottom 6 inches outward and allow 6 inches to extend above the ground surface. Be sure moles aren't present inside the created perimeter.

Keep flattening mounds and tunnels. Try to catch the moles digging. Some observers say that when the mole begins pushing up soil, the animal can be dug out with a spade if one is quick.

GRASS TEXTURE

Is the color and texture of your grass changing over time? Whatever you plant, whether sod or seed, will gradually be colonized by types of grasses that you did not start with, and the texture of the lawn will change. Lawns over five years old contain coarser, tufty grasses, as well as annual blue grasses that wave seedy stalks. This change in appearance can be accepted, being just as green, but it will not duplicate the original groomed look of the lawn.

WATERING

See individual month entries for watering tips.

FERTILIZING

You'll note that recommendations for fertilizers are generally given as a 3-1-2 ratio (3N-1P-2K). There are many fertilizer formulas for the Northwest that fit into these ratios (21-7-14, 6-2-4, and others). It is recommended that 4 pounds of actual nitrogen be applied over one year, in 4 different applications. If any fertilizer hits a hard surface (such as a driveway), be sure to sweep it up into the lawn or landscape, or it will become a non-point source of pollution when we irrigate or it rains.

What is the actual nitrogen? It's a simple bit of math to figure this. If you look at a bag of 21-7-14, not everything in the bag is nitrogen. (Thank goodness, since that would be explosive.) An easy way to figure out how much of a particular fertilizer to put on in order to get 1 pound of nitrogen is this: Divide the first number—the 21—into 100 using a calculator. The result is 4.76, which rounds off to applying 5 pounds of that fertilizer type to get the nitrogen rate. If the fertilizer were a 12-4-8, the result would be about 8.3 or rounded up to 8 1/2 pounds. Put that amount in the fertilizer spreader and spread it over 1000 square feet. If the lawn's bigger or smaller, adjust from the 1000 square foot rate.

MOWING

Mowing is crucial. Washington State University turf specialist Gwen Stahnke suggests cutting perennial ryegrass and perennial ryegrass-mixture lawns at 2 inches maximum height. Bentgrass lawns should be mowed no higher than 1 inch to prevent thatch buildup.

If you do nothing else for the lawn, regular mowing will help keep it looking good. If you add fertilizer 2 to 3 times a year, and water in summer, you should have an agreeable easy-care lawn.

JANUARY

LAWNS

PLANNING

Review the lawn's performance from last season but concentrate on the possible.

Dark shade, tree roots or other obstacles, poor drainage, or slopes too hard to mow make life tough for turf. When grass dies, weeds move into the comfy open spot left behind.

People with icy winter climates, in Zones 5 and 6 should not expect the lawn to look brisk and green at Christmas. Winter changes mean browner lawns. In the warmer areas west of the Cascades, gardeners often expect photogenic green lawns both winter and summer. (See June for managing lawns in the dry season.) Western area lawns that entered winter under stress will not be as thick and green as those with good fall care,

All zones: Review your lawn area during winter to check which areas hold water or freeze with puddles. If you have depressions in an older lawn, map these for renovation in April. Irregular surfaces will be harder to mow, and puddles can lead to poor grass growth

Does the lawn require renewal? Plan now for the time and tools to undertake this in March or April.

PLANTING

Zones 7-9: West of the Cascades, it's possible to lay sod this month and nearly every month. Construction project timelines sometimes require this. Sod is less available in December and January but can be found. Saturated soil also makes sod installation difficult.

CARE

All zones: Stay off frozen grass; walking on it will damage the turf. In warmer areas west of the Cascades, turf will thaw and resume very slow growth.

Keep leaves and fallen twigs raked up; west of the mountains, winds can bring these down, even as late as January.

Set up barriers if you have not already done so to prevent traffic on new lawns; walking on new seedlings or sod will slow down its establishment.

WATERING

Natural rainfall and snowfall provide moisture this month, no matter which zone you're in. If an unusual dry spell sets in west of the mountains in Zones 7 to 9, check the soil condition of new turf and water if needed.

FERTILIZING

All zones: Grass is not growing actively and does not need fertilizer. Sharpen mower blades and tune equipment.

MOWING

Zones 7-9: West of the Cascades, if January provides a week-long spell of mild weather, the lawn may need mowing. If it's getting long but rain continues, making the ground soggy, put off the mowing until mid-February. Because grass continues to grow, though slowly, through the winter, it may need 2 or 3 mowings between November and the end of February. East of the Cascades, and on inland landscapes, frozen and dormant grass won't require mowing.

Especially west of the Cascades, **moss** is so common that many people consider it inevitable. It's native to the region, with dozens of different types. The extended, cool, damp months of fall and early winter offer ideal growth conditions for moss. Moss can be annoying in lawns and is downright hazardous when it flourishes on walking surfaces like decks and sidewalks.

PROBLEMS

Moss grows in lawns where grasses have thinned or died out, leaving bare spots. Weed seeds will also take advantage of these gaps to move in. Too much shade, poor drainage, low fertility, and soil compaction all contribute to grass dying out. And any one of these, or often a combination, will open the gaps for moss to thrive.

Another way of stating this is that **moss** is a symptom of lawn problems, not a cause of them. Mosses, ancient and intriguing plants, can survive in distinctly different conditions than grasses.

To reduce moss problems:

1. Lawns need good light.

2. They also need fertile, well-drained soil to support roots that can penetrate 8 to 10 inches down, or even deeper, once established.

3, Poor drainage means that the area around the grass roots stays soggy and wet. Water stands on the lawn. Turf requires water but needs good drainage for root health. Any place in a lawn where water stands after rain or irrigation may result in moss.

4. Fertilize the lawn regularly. Correcting the overall lawn condition should be done with renovation when weather allows in March and April.

5. Many chemicals registered for moss management contain iron, in the form of ferrous sulfate, ferrous ammonium sulfate, or iron chelates, available in both granular and liquid forms. The moss will blacken after an iron application. Follow label directions carefully. Products containing iron will stain concrete and should be kept off sidewalks and patios.

Another type of moss control product contains potassium salts of fatty acids, a soap-type compound. These cause mosses to yellow and brown out, not turn black. Some yellowing and discoloration of the turf as well as the moss will occur. These soap-type products are more commonly used to remove mosses and algae from hard surfaces in the landscape than they are for applying to moss infestations in turf.

6. Whatever chemical is used on existing moss, the result will be areas of dead moss that must then be raked out. This process will leave bare spots. See March for renovation tips. You may find more satisfaction in waiting until March, then thatching, which pulls out a lot of the moss. Reseeding works well in spring.

DID YOU KNOW?

Grass seed can be scattered now, but the limited light of short days, plus cold temperatures and pounding rains, will prevent it from germinating evenly and getting good roots.

Established moss can be removed by hand raking, though this method doesn't control moss effectively. If the moss is raked out but nothing else is changed in the turf situation, the moss will return almost immediately when weather conditions allow.

Lime does not remove or kill moss in spite of the general perception that it does. What lime will do is correct the soil acidity that may cause the grass to grow poorly and to leave bare spots for moss to move in. Grass takes in nutrients better when the soil is not overly acidic.

FEBRUARY

LAWNS

 PLANNING

How big is the lawn? It's helpful to have the measurements and a knowledge of the square footage because fertilizer and other granular lawn treatments are stated in terms of pounds needed per 1000 square feet.

Review your lawn needs. If you plan to install a new lawn or renovate the existing one, gather supplies now for action in March and April. Seed choices, necessary soil amendments, and tool rental for thatching, aerating, and planting should all be on your list.

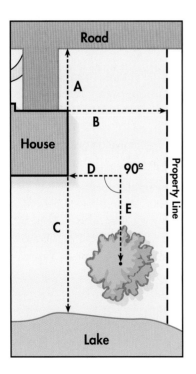

 PLANTING

Grass seed scattered now may come up in a mild spell but often rots out instead. Gather supplies as needed but wait until mid-March for all lawn renovation. In Zones 5-6, April is more appropriate.

 CARE

Lawn mower care: One more time, sharpen the blades and tune up the machine. Taking it in for work early in February helps beat the March/April rush of other gardeners whose mowers need work.

 WATERING

Watering generally isn't needed this month, unless February brings a spell of mild, warm weather west of the Cascades.

If you don't know your lawn area, measure it. Don't worry about being exact; an approximate square footage will be good enough to calculate seed and fertilizer needs.

 FERTILIZING

Do your lawn need a soil test? Soil tests measure the acidity level of the soil and also the availability of basic plant nutrients. When requesting the test, you'll be able to specify the use of the area: lawn, landscape, vegetable garden. Soil tests are advisable if you plan a large landscape installation and are unfamiliar with the characteristics of the property. This may be particularly important in eastern Oregon and other inland Northwest areas where soil pH can be high.

The other side of the soil test story is that it may not be necessary. Many people garden for decades without getting a formal soil test, relying on their experience and satisfaction with how plants grow. If you follow a regular lawn care fertilization plan, results can be entirely satisfactory even if no soil test is done. For information on where to find a soil testing laboratory, check the web site at **www.garden ing.wsu.edu**.

 MOWING

Zones 5-6: Cold weather and storms mean that this month is too early for mowing. (The very

thought of mowing a lawn now probably makes you laugh.)

Zones 7-9: Grass may begin to grow strongly in late February. Air temperatures affect this.

All zones: Mowing frequency and the final height of cut grass are both vitally important to the look and health of turf. Check the mower after the blade's sharpened to see if grass will be cut to the proper height.

Basics of mowing: Mow often enough that the turf doesn't get too long. Ideally, mowing should remove $1/3$ of the existing grass blades. If the lawn is 3 inches tall, you'd cut off only 1 inch. Shortening tall lawns? If the lawn has been allowed to grow to 6 inches or more, take it down in several steps. Do the first mowing down to 5 or 6 inches, remove the clippings, then allow the lawn to dry for a day or two. Then take off 2 inches. One final mow will get it to the desired height. Turf with growth that is too long will not look green when cut; it will take a few weeks of normal mowing to get it into greener condition.

Regular mowing keeps the lawn growing well. No matter what effort you've put into fertilizing or grass selection or weed control, without careful consistent mowing, the turf loses its beauty.

Mowing height and grass types: West of the Cascades, lawn seed frequently combines fine and tall **fescues** with **perennial ryegrass** and a little **Kentucky bluegrass**. Mow this to 2 to 3 inches.

East of the Cascades, where **Kentucky bluegrass** lawns grow (they prefer summer heat), mow them to 2 or $2^1/2$ inches. Avoid mowing too low, which will leave Kentucky bluegrass vulnerable to summer heat damage.

If the section you work with is rough-cut once a month or less often with a weed-eater, that's a field, not a lawn. The smoothness and texture of a proper lawn requires good mowing technique.

 PROBLEMS

Throughout the region, **red thread** is a common fungal problem. This fungal disease (*Laetisaria fuciformis*) disfigures the lawn appearance by causing the tips of the grass blades to turn a distinct reddish color as if the leaf blade were touched with red ink, later becoming brown-tipped.

Red thread often appears after a mild, wet winter, from fall through early spring west of the Cascades, or late summer through fall in east of the

Cascades. It affects a number of grass types that are commonly planted in western Washington, such as **perennial ryegrass** and **fine, red,** or **Chewings fescues**. **Hard fescue** seems to have some resistance to the disease.

There are no currently suggested chemicals for non-commercial use. The stronger the lawn is growing, the better the chance that it will outgrow the disease. Keep the lawn properly fertilized. Warmer, dryer weather also help the lawn recover.

Several tactics can also help manage the problem. If your lawn care practice includes "grasscycling," returning the clippings to the turf rather than bagging them, you should temporarily stop the grasscycling and bag the clippings for disposal in trash. (Do not compost them.) The fallen, diseased clippings should be removed from the lawn because the fungal organisms live on diseased grass and in soil. So if you were using the infected clippings as mulch, disease spread may occur.

Crane flies: See October, page 127, for information. Monitor lawns now and in March for damage.

MARCH

LAWNS

PLANNING

Specific timing for moving forward on lawn installation and renovation depends on both soil condition and air temperature. In the coldest zones, 5 to 6, April and May offer the best times for doing the work; mid-March through mid-April are the best times in Zones 7 to 9. If soils remain soggy, wait for a drying trend before proceeding.

PLANTING

Apply appropriate seed (see the chart in the introduction) at the rate of 5 to 7 pounds per 1000 square feet depending on the grass type. Roll it lightly to get good soil contact.

Natural rainfall can help keep the new seeds moist until they germinate. But be sure to water newly seeded areas if there's no rain; allowing the seedlings to dry out will kill the new shoots. They may need water 2 to 3 times daily for ten days. The thicker the lawn grows, the better it will resist weeds.

CARE

The following are done in late March in western zones and in April and May east of the Cascades.

Aerating: Does your lawn feel "spongy" when you walk on it? Or did it resist water penetration last summer? You can increase oxygen to grass roots and improve water retention by aerating. March and April offer good weather for this process. (If walking on it produces squish-squish, the turf is too wet for aeration. You want it damp but not saturated.) Two or three days after rain, or watering, is ideal for aerating. Aeration pulls "plugs" of old turf and roots, allowing water to penetrate the grass better. Gardeners sometimes stomp around the grass in spiked shoes, but the best way to aerate is to rent the machinery that yanks a plug, leaving a small open hole.

After aerating: allow the plugs to remain on the lawn where they will disintegrate.

Thatching: Another spring process, thatching thins out old dead material around the grass crowns, enhancing its growth. Thatch develops more readily in some types of grasses than in others. **Bentgrasses** get "thatchy." To determine if you need to thatch, dig out a chunk of turf, including the roots, and look at the brown section just above the roots where the grass begins to grow. If the thatch layer exceeds $1/2$ inch, lawn health will improve by thatching. Always remove thatch pulled out of the lawn.

Sowing: You must sow grass seed to fill in after aerating or thatching, overseeding with a mixture adapted to your area.

WATERING

Spring rains generally provide enough water for established lawns. Be aware of needs for newly seeded areas.

FERTILIZING

March isn't a good month for fertilizing anywhere in our region.

MOWING

Keep reciting the lawn-care mantra: "Good mowing makes good lawns." Regular mowing is easier than intermittent mowing, and the results show in a denser, healthier turf. Mow with blades

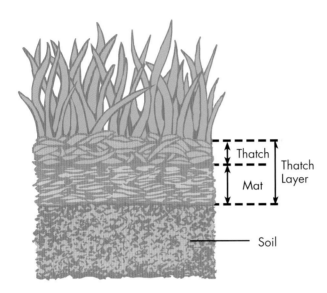

Thatch can build up, especially in bentgrass lawns. Dig out a section to check the thatch level.

sharpened every six weeks. Or follow the tip of having an extra blade on hand for the mower and switching every six weeks.

If you have begun this season's mowing, try "grasscycling," allowing the grass clippings to fall back onto the turf using a mulching mower or standard rotary mower. The clippings will break down and provide additional nutrients, including nitrogen, for the grass. This works effectively only if mowing is timely and less than $1/3$ of each grass blade is being removed. See July for more on "grasscycling."

PROBLEMS

Weed control: Weeds move in where lawn grasses have moved out. The best defense against weeds is a thick, well-maintained turf. Regular mowing can also help prevent weeds from going to seed.

If weeds are a problem, control is best in spring or fall. Depending upon the species, weeds can be pulled or spot treated with the appropriate herbicide in spring. The weed should be identified in order to select the best time for control. Take your weeds to a WSU/ OSU Master Gardener clinic or to a specialty nursery for identification.

Dandelions, one weed everyone can identify, can be dug by hand in small lawns but will need to be spot-sprayed on larger ones.

"Weed and feed?" Washington State University specialists do not recommend use of weed and feed lawn products except where weed infestation is severe. This type of pesticide/fertilizer combined product should only be applied once a year. Unfortunately, many gardeners are in the habit of using it more often.

If weed infestation is not severe, it is better to separate weed control from the fertilization. Use fertilizer alone and spot-treat weed problems.

Read all labels on pesticides before buying, applying, storing, or disposing of the material. Yes, weed and feed products are pesticides. The components in them can damage the roots of trees and shrubs near the lawn; if your plants show yellowing leaves or dead branches, it may be the dicamba in the weed and feed pesticide.

APRIL

LAWNS

PLANNING

Even though they look tired and beat up in winter, lawns in cold inland areas, Zones 5 to 6, will green up as warmer weather arrives. (Think of the grasses in pastures—that's why they call this season "green up time.") Lawns in warmer areas, which have stayed green—or nearly—through winter will begin a phase of stronger growth. Supporting the lawn now with regular mowing and fertilizing will get it into best condition for summer.

Plan to do any renovation needed now and in May. Spring gives the lawn grasses their best chance to grow from either seed or sod. Lawn seeding is not generally as successful between June 1 and August 15, largely because it's more difficult to keep the seed moist enough to sprout.

PLANTING

If lawn grasses have thinned out over winter, now's the time to fill in the gaps and prevent later weed invasions. Important: If you plan to allow the lawn to go totally dormant in the summer, without regular watering, *do not* overseed until fall.

Aerate or thatch first if your lawn needs this attention. Usually lawns three years old or older will begin to develop thatch and benefit from aerating and thatching. Don't be surprised at how scuffed, even scalped, the lawn appears afterwards. You've made the beginnings of a good seed bed for the renewed lawn.

For all parts of the Northwest, **perennial ryegrass** is suggested as a good choice if you are scattering seed over an existing lawn. It germinates and fills in quickly. When you're overseeding, apply turfgrass seed at about half the normal establishment rate. When using **perennial ryegrass**, overseed at 3 pounds seed per 1000 square feet after thatching or aerating the lawn.

Seed is best laid out with a rolling spreader, going evenly over the lawn in two directions. Mulch with a light layer of

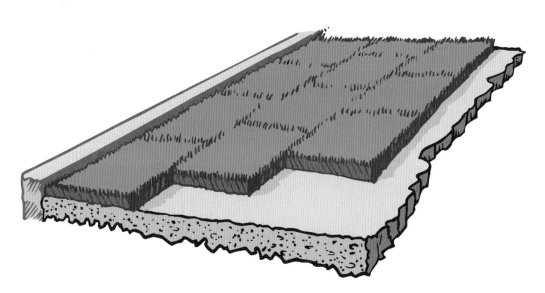

Be sure to tuck sod edges firmly together.

screened compost, about 1/4 inch. After seeding and mulching, roll the lawn to get seed in contact with soil. Water thoroughly. If the seed doesn't make firm contact with soil, it will not come up.

CARE

Sod installation: Correct any drainage problems before sodding. Prepare the soil for sod installation just as for a complete seeding. Till in 2 inches of well composted organic matter to a depth of 6 to 8 inches. Rake smooth.

WATERING

Watering isn't generally needed in April, but keep emerging seed grasses watered until they are at least 3 inches tall. If the seed dries after it begins growing, it will die.

New grasses have no reserve for surviving drought.

FERTILIZING

Do not fertilize immediately after seeding. If you aren't planning to overseed, fertilize in either April or May. The general requirement for lawns in our region is to apply 4 pounds of actual nitrogen per year. However, turf specialists suggest that when fertilizing this month or next, use only half the rate, applying only 1/2 pound of actual nitrogen per 1000 square feet. The objective is to avoid quick, lush growth that will require more mowing.

If soil temperatures are cool, use a chemically processed fertilizer for the first spring feeding. Any organic sources of nitrogen do not become available to the grass until soils warm and microorganisms can make the organics available for plants.

Zones 7-9: Fertilize in May, June, early September, and November or December.

MOWING

When mowing, look for symptoms. Does the lawn bounce in a spongy manner? Does it have lots of hollows and hills where the mower scrapes ground and scalps the turf? Is the grass patchy with bare spots? Do you see areas that you wish to improve?

PROBLEMS

Moles are more common where soils are neither very dry nor very wet (therefore easy to tunnel through) and where earthworms are plentiful. If you can coexist with the creatures, that's the easiest solution. But they can be troublesome as they start spring work. An irrigated lawn with a high organic content in the soil offers ideal living space for moles, especially if near a woods area. The better cared for lawns are definitely preferred by moles. See the General Introduction for control suggestions.

MAY

LAWNS

PLANNING

If the lawn is difficult to mow, is sloped and does not retain water, or is too shaded, consider replacing it with an adapted ground cover. See June for ideas on plant choices.

PLANTING

Seeding a new lawn: If the area is full of perennial weeds, spray with glyphosate (sold as Roundup™) and other names. This product must be applied to actively growing weeds on a warm, dry day. Weed kill may take two weeks or more.

Prepare a good seedbed, first correcting any drainage problems. Pick up big rocks, sticks, and other debris before rototilling to 8 inches. Wait until the soil is dry enough to crumble in the hand, but still damp.

Slope the lawn away from buildings. Fill in holes with extra soil; bringing in 6 inches of good soil may be needed but till it into the subsoil to help with drainage, unless the soil is compacted clay or hardpan. (See August for dealing with clay soils.) Level and smooth the area.

Apply a "starter" fertilizer before sowing seed; use 10 pounds of 10-20-20 per 1000

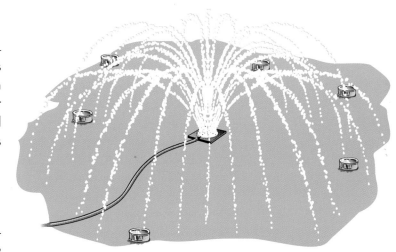

If you use a sprinkler system, you can easily check the flow by measuring how much water is collected during a certain time period.

square feet, raking it about 2 inches in so that seeds don't touch fertilizer granules.

Seed when soil temperature is 50 degrees F.; apply with a spreader in two directions, crossing over the first application at right angles. Use a lightweight roller to firm seed into soil. Mulch with 1/4 inch of compost; roll again lightly.

Keep it watered. Seedlings may emerge intermittently and aren't always immediately obvious. They start out as very fine threads of green.

CARE

Rope off any newly seeded or sodded areas to prevent foot traffic and leave the barrier in place

until the first mow is completed.

WATERING

Irrigate in the early morning. Late evening watering is also a possibility. Turn off water immediately if it begins to run off the lawn. If the soil is sloped or compacted, water will be easily wasted by run-off. In these conditions, irrigate for a brief period, just until run-off starts. Turn off the water, and turn it on again in about twenty minutes. Gradual slow watering will be most efficient, even though the process takes more time.

Irrigate to a 4- to 6-inch depth as needed. Deeper but less frequent watering will help lawn, and only 3 times per week maximum at the hottest part of the summer. (One inch of water per week.)

FERTILIZING

Zones 5-6: Fertilize this month, using a slow-release (not organic) fertilizer with a 3-1-2 ratio such as a 6-2-4 or a 12-4-8. Remember the specific dates for four separate fertilizer applications in the inland Northwest by these holidays: Easter, Memorial Day, Labor Day, and Halloween. Grass will be growing actively and require feeding.

MOWING

Alternate mowing direction each time you mow. If you mow in one direction only, the grass tends to lean. Mow at right angles to the previous mowing.

Mow often enough to remove only $1/3$ of the leaf blade; if the mower height is set at $2^1/2$ inches, mow when grass reaches $3^1/2$ inches. Dull mowers tear the grass blades, resulting in a dead, uneven area that can turn yellow. "Grasscycling," allowing clippings to fall back on the turf using either a standard mower or a mulching mower, saves

---

GRASS TYPES THAT WILL NOT GROW HERE

If you are new to the Washington and Oregon area, you may be accustomed to choosing many different types of grasses that aren't used here. **Zoysia, Bermuda grass, dichondra, centipede, carpetgrass, St Augustine,** and **mondograss** aren't successful lawn grasses anywhere in our region.

East of the Cascades, **buffalograss** is being tried; although it is dormant six to seven months of the year, it can be workable as a low maintenance, warm season grass.

---

nutrients and can help with lawn condition if done properly. It does not work if grass is too long or too wet.

PROBLEMS

Little heaps of soil on the surface of the lawn? This may be caused by **nightcrawlers**, which are sort of overgrown earthworms that are very beneficial to your garden soil. They shove little piles called castings, up to the soil surface. Some gardeners find this annoying.

Nightcrawlers draw their nutrition from the organic matter in the soil that passes through their bodies. The castings (what comes out the other end) are extremely fertile. In compact or poorly drained soils, the castings often appear on the surface of the soil. Ironically, the tunneling

of the worms will benefit these soils the most since it opens up soil and enhances drainage.

Getting rid of worms chemically isn't a good idea because it removes valuable garden dwellers and can also kill other beneficials like predatory ground beetles. You may see recommendations to kill the worms, but there are no legally registered chemicals to do so. Instead of removing, lightly rake the lawn area when you see castings. They will help with fertility. And if worms send up castings into bare soil under trees and shrubs, place an organic mulch over the soil. The castings will still be there, but you won't see them.

JUNE
LAWNS

PLANNING

Replacing the lawn where it isn't thriving? Check nurseries for ground covers called "Stepables™" (trademarked by the Under A Foot Plant Company). Shady spots? If the shaded area gets only occasional walking traffic, consider **Irish** or **Scotch moss** (*Sagina* spp.) or even the **common carpet bugle** (*Ajuga* spp.) You can find ratings for degree of disturbance by the traffic they endure, listed accord-

ing to their sturdiness. (www. stepables.com)

Sunny areas where the lawn needs replacing will give you more choice in plants: **creeping sedum, creeping thyme,** and **blue star creeper** (*Pratia pedunculata*) offer texture and color but require light. A cultivar of blue star creeper called 'County Park' endures some foot traffic. Since all ground covers need time to establish, it's easier to replace lawn a few square feet at a time.

Native ground covers include **kinnikinnick** and low **mahonia**, although neither of these will stand foot traffic. They would be best on a sunny slope along with native sword fern.

Blue star creeper

PLANTING

Removing a lawn: Perhaps this should be called "un-planting." Preparing a former lawn area for planting flowers, trees, or shrubs requires time, often up to two months or longer. Given the time required, summer is a good time to alter a lawn. See the General Introduction to find information on lawn removal.

A fast way to kill turf during warm weather, when it is in active growth, is with an herbicide. Round-up™ (glyphosate) in its various formulations and trade names is the most common choice. Round-up must be applied on actively growing grass, not on the dormant brown type. It works only on plants that are in full growth. This product kills both grasses and broadleaved plants. Because it breaks down rapidly in the soil, you can replant relatively quickly after the grass has died. Follow the label directions carefully. The lawn grasses can take up to four weeks to die out. Some people till after this and remove the dead clumps and dead roots, then prepare for planting.

CARE

Does it feel bouncy or spongy when walked on?

Start by analyzing the spongy feeling. Thatch, which builds up at root and crown, is an intermingled layer of dead material and living crowns. Thick layers of thatch, when they dry out in summer, repel water and can keep rain or irrigation from reaching turf roots.

Next, check the lawn for soil compaction. Has your family been making new traffic patterns on the lawn? Grass roots get shallow when walked on. Aeration helps get oxygen and water into the root zone. Aeration isn't advised in June —wait until next fall when rains resume. You can't aerate a dormant lawn with summer-dry soil.

WATERING

Irrigation: Depending on what type of grass you have, if you decide to let the lawn go totally dormant, do not begin watering the grass in midsummer and revive the grass, then turn the water off again. This will damage the grass. **Bentgrass** lawns can go totally dormant and recover in the fall. This is the best lawn type to survive a dry summer west of the Cascades.

Perennial ryegrass and **fine fescue** lawns will need to have some moisture in the soil to keep the grass from severely thinning out by fall. If you do not provide an inch of water a week, at least give the lawn a deep watering

twice a month. Renewing a dead lawn in fall may not be worth what's saved in resources by eliminating summer water but water restrictions may require reductions.

Limit traffic on dry grass: Footprints and scuffs add to stress on crowns and roots of grass.

FERTILIZING

Zones 5-6: Inland gardens—if you did not fertilize on Memorial Day weekend, in early June, use a slow-release or organic source of nitrogen to limit growth to provide a source of food when irrigation or rain is available. However, if you do not plan to water your lawn this summer, do not apply fertilizer now.

Fertilize moderately to prevent lush overgrowth of grass. The more grass food, the greater the water requirements. If you "grass-cycle," returning the clippings to the lawn, the grass clippings will break down into water and nutrients. Studies show that regular grasscycling can provide up to 25 percent of the total nitrogen needs during a year. This means that if you were planning to fertilizer 4 times, you could skip one—and the June application is a good one to skip.

Pull or spot-treat weeds as you see them. Fertilizing and growing a thick lawn will help keep weeds from gaining ground.

MOWING

All zones: Mow regularly. Do not allowing blades to grow overly long. Remove only $1/3$ of the growing blade.

PROBLEMS

What if you had a new lawn put in last year and the first dry days find it declining? Many people have the unfortunate situation of finding themselves with a lawn that looks fine at first but declines rapidly after a few months or years. This is often traceable to poor soil preparation. Even the best quality sod can't cope with bad soil. Sod is sometimes unrolled over two inches of soil with hardpan beneath. If your lawn is persistently soggy, dies out in spots, or is hard to keep watered in summer, dig out a one foot square section and check the soil quality under the roots. Plan to renovate the lawn in fall.

JULY
LAWNS

PLANNING

Think of the principle in landscaping called "Right Plant, Right Place." Some of the difficulties presented by lawns relate to misplaced grass—the hopeful optimism that a lawn will grow anyplace we want. Lawns have specific growth needs, just as **roses** do.

Is the lawn getting enough sunlight? As summer days lengthen, maximum sun finally reaches light-starved gardens. Turf should be placed in the open, where it gets at least six hours of light daily.

If the lawn is in a sunny spot, isn't on a steep slope, drains well, and has good soil for 6 to 8 inches under its roots, that's a great start to a satisfactory lawn.

PLANTING

Summer weather conditions prevent seeding lawns this month. It's possible to install sod, being sure that the soil is well prepared and thoroughly watered before laying the sod. Keep the sod watered until fall rains return. Sod has been regularly watered and fertilized at the sod farm. Without water it will decline quickly no matter the original quality of the sod.

CARE

Aerating and thatching should be completed in spring for best results when the lawn grows in summer. Do not attempt to aerate a dormant lawn on dry soils during the summer. Consider these as fall renovation techniques once rains return.

WATERING

Water wisely. Do not over-irrigate. Check the water levels at the root depths by probing with a trowel to determine how well water is penetrating.

Be sure to keep newly-seeded and newly-sodded areas watered throughout the summer until the grass is well established. Check the corners and seams of sod particularly, because these sections can pull apart if too dry.

If you haven't checked your soil type, do so now. Sandy soils need more frequent watering for shorter periods because they do not hold water well. Clay soils absorb water slowly and will take longer periods of watering.

To get a quick idea of your soil type, dig out about a cup of soil from the lawn area. Put it in a quart jar, and fill the jar with water, adding 1/2 teaspoon of soap. Cap the jar and shake it

It's fun but also useful to test your lawn's soil type.

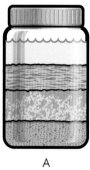

A
Loamy

B
Clay

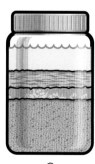

C
Sandy

Clay

Silt

Sandy

thoroughly. Let it sit for about a week. Coarse sands and gravels will fall to the bottom; silt and clay particles settle on top. A heavy clay soil may require longer to settle out. The result is a general sense of the balance of sand/gravel to clay in your soil. Organic bits like fallen leaves will float on top.

FERTILIZING

Do not fertilize established lawns in July or August.

MOWING

Turn off irrigation or stop irrigating one day before mowing to avoid sogginess, which might catch up the wheels in the soil.

Mow on a regular schedule—every five to seven days during rapid growth. Remove only about $1/3$ of the grass blade and no more than 1 inch at a time.

Mow when the grass is dry and keep mower blades sharp.

PROBLEMS

If your lawn is struggling with a summer weed load, try not to allow the weeds to go to seed now. Keep the lawn mowed to prevent weed seeds. Tall, flexible weeds can lie down and slide

DID YOU KNOW

Grasscycling allows clippings to drop back on the lawn rather than being caught in the catcher bag. Some gardeners have done this for years. It can be done with any type of lawn mowing equipment or with a specially equipped mulching mower. Mow often enough to keep the clippings short. If the lawn is too long, leave the catcher on for the first mow; then mow again letting the clippings fall. Mow dry grass; wet grass clippings won't scatter into the lawn. Only the most efficient new model **mulching mowers** can handle grasscycling in wet grass. Accept some scattered clippings on the lawn surface if you use conventional mowing equipment.

The hand push mower, a neighbor-friendly and energy-efficient machine, produces evenly-scattered clippings on the lawn surface. If the lawn is too long, grasscycling with a push mower won't work at all. A push mower is a reasonable option only for very small lawns that get regular care.

Older conventional **power mowers** get best results on short, dry grass and when only about 1 inch of the grass blade is removed per cutting. They will leave clumps and rows of grass clippings on the lawn if the grass is too long. These clumps eventually break down into the lawn, but some raking may be necessary.

Retrofitted mowers. Various kits can be used to retrofit older mower blades. They give mixed results; like the standard equipment, they work best on shorter, dry grass.

under the mower, so check the weeds a few days after you have mowed.

Hand dig the weeds if your lawn is small enough to make this feasible.

Spot-spray persistent perennial weeds. However, do not use any garden pesticides when temperatures are above 85 degrees F. The selective chemicals that target broadleaf weeds but not grasses work best on weeds that are actively growing. If the weeds, and the lawn, have

turned brown and crispy, dig by hand or water well a few days before treating the weeds. Read pesticide labels carefully before spot-spraying.

Do not use weed and feed type mixtures during summer when lawns aren't growing well. Limit your use of these to once a year if you choose to use them.

AUGUST

LAWNS

PLANNING

By the end of August, summer's difficulties show up as rampant weeds and inconsiderate grass decline. Perhaps lawns tire of being sliced off, working to grow back, and being mowed again, again, and again. Late summer weather conditions haven't helped. After caring for the lawn all summer, your expectations of the size you wish to maintain may have changed. Take time this month to plan changes in the lawn that will bring it closer to your landscape's needs.

Fall rains help dormant grass revive, but they can often be late in arriving, making watering important when you choose to overseed or renovate.

PLANTING

Zones 5-6: August has poor conditions for any planting, especially in the inland high desert. If, however, you are able to water, seeding a lawn between August 15 and September 15 gives the best opportunity in coldest areas to get it established before winter.

CARE

What conditions mean the lawn needs replacing? Taking out the lawn and replanting is a sufficiently big task that it's important to do it only when improving the lawn isn't possible by overseeding. Several years of neglect can result in a lawn outnumbered by weeds. Or construction damage during house remodeling or landscaping can kill part of a lawn. Difficulties caused by diseases or insect damage are far less common. If you plan to kill out the grass and start over, wait until grasses resume growth. Then herbicides like Roundup™ will work.

First, to re-do an established old lawn, be sure that the grass is as free as possible of big, perennial weeds such as dandelions. Dig them out or spot-treat them with an herbicide such as glyphosate (sold under a number of trade names including Roundup™). If you do use glyphosate, be aware that it's also toxic to grass—wipe it individually on weeds and don't get it on the desirable lawn areas. Glyphosate kills weeds thoroughly, but it still takes about three weeks to fully remove them.

WATERING

Water lawn moderately during dry months. Watering in late afternoon or early evening may benefit the roots rather than having the heat of midday burn off the moisture. If you have not been watering weekly, be sure the lawn gets at least one deep watering this month.

FERTILIZING

Don't fertilize during the height of summer. Do apply slow-release fertilizers in late autumn, using a 3-1-2 formulation for Pacific Northwest lawns. A September fertilization could be skipped in favor of a November/December application, which is the most important timing west of the Cascades.

MOWING

Watch the growth of the lawn and mow when turf has added 1/3 of its height. Get lawn mower blades sharpened this month.

PROBLEMS

Whatever you plant, whether sod or seed, will gradually be colonized by types of grasses that you didn't start with, and the texture of the lawn will change. Lawns over five years old contain coarser, tufty grasses. This change in appearance doesn't mean it's not green, or attractive, or useful, but it won't duplicate the groomed perfection of golf courses.

If your lawn is beginning to look better now, do not let the turf go into drought stress during the dry end of the summer. Keep it moderately watered to support the roots and crowns of the plants for strong future growth and recovery.

GRASS MIXTURES USING BROADLEAF COMPONENTS

Do you want a meadow-like, casual lawn? Years of research at OSU have given gardeners in our region the chance to grow an innovative mixture of grasses and broadleaf plants that uses less water in the summer. The result gives grass a mixed texture that has some blooming components before mowing but resembles an all-grass lawn when mowed. The texture variation makes this an individual-choice lawn. It's appealing to some, odd-looking to others.

Sold as "EcoTurf" and "Fleur de Lawn" as well as others), these mixtures contain both grasses and broadleaf perennials such as **yarrow, strawberry clover,** and **English daisies.** Why isn't this the same as just allowing weeds to colonize the lawn? The seed mixtures for these lawns are balanced for good growth—primarily west of the Cascades. They start with a **perennial ryegrass** basis, up to 80 percent ryegrass, to keep the lawn looking grass-like.

These mixtures grow best when used as a new lawn or a complete replacement lawn. Some of the seeds are perennial broadleaves and they do not germinate as well when used for overseeding. Seed the new lawn at 2 pounds per 1000 square feet after soil preparation, exactly like that for any other newly seeded lawn. The perennial plants fill in rather slowly and require two years for full coverage.

To protect nearby bedding plants from drift, cut out the bottom of a plastic gallon jug if you spot treat broadleaf weeds in your lawn.

SEPTEMBER

LAWNS

 PLANNING

Review the lawn now, considering what it contributes to the landscape. Do you wish to remove some of it to make next year's landscape beds? Follow the tips in the June entry for details on lawn removal.

Slopes remain one of the most difficult areas for lawns; water applied doesn't get into the soil evenly. Now, when planting and transplanting conditions improve, consider terracing sloped sections and replacing the lawn. Low-water-use plants, such as smaller **juniper** cultivars, can be both attractive and serviceable in difficult sections. (Check nurseries for evergreens that are drought-tolerant). Making this change takes both time and work initially but will be better looking over time.

 PLANTING

Using either seed or sod, following these dates for planting:

Zones 5-6: Plant new lawns between August 15 and September 15. Weather may turn to sudden freezes after September 15, making new grass growth difficult.

Zones 7-9: Plant between September 1 and October 15. After October 15, cooler darker weather inhibits grass seed establishment.

If you aerate and thatch now, overseed with a locally appropriate lawn mixture. (See the introduction for lists of seed mixes.) **Perennial ryegrass** is a good choice for areas that will get traffic, such as play areas. Be sure to water newly seeded areas carefully if fall rains stay away.

Aerating is a helpful renewal process, allowing better water penetration on older lawns. But be sure to water a few times before aerating or choose a time when a few good rains have left the soil moist; otherwise, the cores won't hold together to be pulled out.

 CARE

During September, you can do all the lawn care chores that were possible during April and May. September is an ideal month to renovate or install new lawns.

If you fertilize, be sure to water in September before rains return. Grass roots can't absorb nutrients without water to carry the fertilizer into the ground. If water isn't penetrating to the root depth, aerate or thatch during September.

 WATERING

All lawns will need water during September, especially if fall rains return late. Continue to apply water deeply.

 FERTILIZING

Regular, balanced fertilizer applications will help the lawn resist weed and moss invasions by growing thickly. Use a fertilizer with a 3-1-2 formulation or one close to this: 3 percent available nitrogen, 1 percent available phosphorus, and 2 percent available potassium.

Zones 5-6: Apply on Labor Day and again on Halloween to get the lawn into best winter condition.

Zones 7-9: Lawn fertilizer in a 3-1-2 ratio in early September and again in late November or early December will supply nutrients for healthy winter growth. In the warmest zones only, if you choose to give up one of these

COVER CROPS

Do you have a lawn prepared for planting but need to wait until spring to do it? Or is there bare ground around a home under construction? A "cover crop" can be sown in September to enrich the ground and keep the weeds down.

Another term for cover crop is "green manure." These are crops sown specifically to be dug back into the soil when they reach maturity, before they go to seed. Bare ground calls to weeds; whenever possible, keep bare ground covered with mulch or cover crops. Another good use for cover crops is in a place where the summer vegetable garden has finished producing and the gardener does not wish to put it in a fall or winter garden.

Fall and winter are good times to grow cover crops. Crops in the legume family, such as **crimson clover**, are excellent for adding nitrogen to poor, acidic soils. **Crimson clover, vetch,** and **field peas** can all be planted from late August to mid-October. (Or mid-August to mid-September east of the mountains.) After mid-October these crops fail to sprout sufficiently well to act as a good cover through winter.

Allow the cover crop to grow up, and then till it under in February or March when the soil is workable. Do not allow the cover crop to go to seed. Let the area rest for a month after tilling to allow the green manure to compost..

---

two fertilizations, skip September but don't skip late November.

All zones: Use a fertilizer with a fall/winter formulation. Don't be tempted to apply more than the recommended level of fertilizer—it won't help. A light fertilizing in early September will often be sufficient, around Labor Day, using 1 pound actual nitrogen per 100 square feet.

In all zones, if you've been "grasscycling," it's possible to skip a fertilization because the nitrogen in the fallen clippings raises the fertility level of the lawn, adding at least 25 percent of the year's requirement. So if grasscycling is part of your lawn

care routine, you're already providing part of what the lawn needs and may skip the early September application.

 PROBLEMS

Infestations of crane flies are scattered and sporadic throughout the region. Crane flies get a lot of attention this time of year, in part because the adults emerge in late August and early September, resembling large non-biting mosquitoes. If you see adult **crane flies**, do not think that the outcome will automatically be spring lawn damage from lar-

vae chewing your lawn. Other animals eat them. Both adults and larvae are necessary food for many creatures such as birds, fish, and other insects like yellowjackets. September is not the time to treat the lawn for crane flies, and even before treatment, you'll want to check for damage. See October for more details.

OCTOBER

LAWNS

PLANNING

People with icy winter climates don't expect the lawn to look alive at Christmas, but in the Northwest we want photogenic lawns both winter and summer west of the Cascades.

PLANTING

Grass seeds do best if they have at least six to eight weeks of growth time after they germinate. Follow up aeration or thatching by spreading seeds over the bare spots, using those adapted to your area. In zones 5 to 6, in the eastern inland areas, October will be too late for seeding.

Plant until October 15 in western warmer areas. Good grass types include **perennial ryegrass** and **fine fescues**, usually sold mixed. Later fall plantings may be colonize by winter weeds that like cool temperatures, especially if they have not filled in evenly. The later you plant, the more grass seed you will need to put out to ensure coverage.

CARE

Preparing the lawn for winter in all zones:

Mow as long as the grass keeps growing. This can be nearly year-round west of the mountains in Zones 7 to 9.

Rake tree leaves off the lawn regularly, to keep the lawn from being smothered.

Water the lawn deeply east of the mountains before hard freezes. This will help reduce winter injury from dessicaiton.

Stay off the lawn during winter. West of the mountains the soil may be saturated, which can compact if stepped on. Aerate in spring if winter compaction occurs.

Fine fescue is a good choice for western warmer areas.

 WATERING

Fall rains will help with water needs; be sure to keep any newly seeded emerging lawns watered if rains are scarce.

 FERTILIZING

Zones 7-9: Keep in mind that pH measures the acidity of the soil on a scale of 0 to 14, with 7.0 being neutral. West of the Cascades, soils are often around 5.0 naturally, but is close to ideal for most vegetables and flowers. Many plant nutrients become unavailable in acidic soil. Sometimes a soil will be very fertile, but plants show nutrient deficiency symptoms because the pH is too low for nutrient uptake. Below 6.0, phosphorous is less available, and at 5.5 (or lower) nitrogen, potassium, sulfur, calcium, and magnesium uptake is also diminished.

Many lawn grasses can grow at fairly low pH, such as the 5.0 to 5.5 level common along the western areas. However, it's advisable to get a soil test for a new lawn, particularly a large one, to determine pH and get recommendations for potential lime additions. Apply lime to the new lawn area before tilling, then till it in. The lime and fall fertilizer stimulate grass growth to help the turf fill in and compete successfully with moss.

Lime takes a while to become available and should be worked it at the rate suggested by the soil test at least a month before fertilizing and seeding. Do not apply lime and fertilizer at the same time.

Zones 4-6: Conditions east of the mountains can be opposite to those on the west side. Soil can be more alkaline and certainly will never need lime.

 MOWING

Mow regularly. With a sharp blade and a grass catcher, mowing over a light layer of leaves on the lawn will work fine. The leaves and grass, chopped together and scooped off the lawn, will make fine compost if dumped in a compost holder and allowed to mellow.

 PROBLEMS

In late summer, lawns can look pitiful without any help from crane flies. Often, it's a result of compaction, lack of nutrients, thatch buildup, or even lack of water. Crane fly damage seldom shows up before spring: winter cold temperatures and bird predation tend to reduce the populations. So treating for them in fall makes no sense.

To check for crane fly larvae, look for bare or dying spots in the lawn with holes. In late winter or early spring, the larvae may even be out of the ground on the top of the soil or sod. Birds may be feeding in flocks. If you see these signs in late winter, dig up a square foot of lawn and count the larvae. If the square footage has 40 or fewer crane flies, the lawn is probably able to outgrow the damage if the lawn is healthy and growing fast. Do not use chemical treatment until you have checked out the damage level.

NOVEMBER

LAWNS

PLANNING

Anyone who has lived in Ohio, North Dakota, or eastern Oregon knows that the normal winter color for grass is doormat brown. But here in Western Washington, our mild winters allow the lawns to struggle forward in some shade of green. Gardeners expect no less, hoping that the lawn will set off winter shrubs and conifers with magazine-photo, emerald color. Not surprisingly, lawns that look best through winter have had good care during the other three seasons.

PLANTING

Zones 5-6: It's too late for planting lawns of any type now.

Zone 7-9: West of the Cascades, install sod through November 15 in the cooler spots. Along the coasts, in protected maritime areas, sod can go in nearly any time throughout winter as long as ground isn't saturated and can be well prepared.

CARE

What if your lawn is full of **mushrooms**? Mushrooms, which are the fruiting bodies of fungus living underground, are not harmful in gardens. During dry weather the underground web of fungal life isn't obvious, but in fall the spore-producing bodies appear. They are non-chlorophyll producing entities that live on decaying or dead organic matter. Many of these fungi, in current studies, are being found to serve beneficial roles in the health of tree roots, assisting the roots in taking in mineral nutrients and other necessary growth components. They help out in the growth of trees.

Knocking them over and raking them up is about the most benign prescription for getting rid of them. There are no chemicals registered for mushroom control, nor should there be, as they are not harmful. Another approach is to observe and appreciate these mushrooms as parts of the web of life.

WATERING

Since November is generally a wet month, irrigation won't be needed this month. Secure and settle the irrigation system for its winter rest.

FERTILIZING

This is the correct time to apply winter fertilizer west of the mountains.

Zone 7-9: The general rule for fertilizing is that turf needs about 4 pounds of actual nitrogen applications per year, in 4 installments. Dr. Gwen Stahnke, turf agronomist at Washington State University's Puyallup Research and Extension Center, suggests doing this for winter between Nov. 15 and Dec. 7 then waiting until April 15 for spring fertilization, repeating June 15, and again Sep- tember 1. If you are grasscycling, you could eliminate at least one fertilization, perhaps the June 15 date.

The main need of the turf during this season is nitrogen. Choose the fertilizer type carefully. You want one with a nutrient ratio of about 3-1-2. Also choose a slow-release fertilizer such as "sulfur coated urea."

In cold soils, the inorganic fertilizer types provide nutrients faster, but one choice might be to use a mix of inorganic and organic fertilizers, about half and half. Both types are slow release, which reduces nitrogen leaching to water and gives better color over a period of months. You don't want to choose something like a 33 percent ammonium nitrate, a quickly soluble "instagreen" that's potentially dangerous to water quality.

Choose a slow-release form of fertilizer in late November because it provides nutrients gradually through winter. Some fall fertilizers also contain sulfur, and there is research demonstrating that sulfur can help slow down lawn diseases like red thread during damp, cold winter weather.

MOWING

Zone 7-9: For the rest of winter, keep leaves and twigs raked, mow as needed (don't wait until spring), and enjoy the win-

---

DID YOU KNOW?

Gypsum is calcium sulfate. It is sometimes recommended to add calcium to an alkaline soil since it doesn't increase the pH like limestone. It has been promoted as a soil conditioner that can magically improve soil structure. In fact, it can produce rather miraculous results, but only in soils with an excess sodium problem. Such soils are rare in Washington and Oregon and never occur on the moist side of the Cascades.

---

tergreen lawn. Sharpen those mower blades! And stay off a frozen lawn—footsteps can harm the good results your care has produced.

PROBLEMS

Washington State University Extension Specialists suggest that fall is not the time to treat

for any crane fly infestation, in spite of what industry advertising might indicate. The best line of defense is to allow natural controls to work on the population over winter.

There are several types of fertilizer spreaders, including the old-fashioned one of broadcasting by hand. But a mechanical-type spreader provides more even coverage.

December

LAWNS

PLANNING

Lawn experts remind us that grass behaves differently during winter in separate regions of the state, depending on winter temperature. West of the Cascades, it keeps growing and never really develops cold tolerance. When there's a sudden Arctic freeze on the west side, grass blades may be nipped, turning brown at the tips. A prolonged freeze on the west side can result in damage, especially if the lawn gets foot traffic while frozen. This can cause dead areas.

In Zones 5-6, east of the Cascades, grasses go dormant and stop growing in winter. Short, cold days slow down grass growth, and the plants store nutrients for spring growth. Even if they look totally brown and dead, the turf will stay alive and be ready to grow again with warm spring temperatures.

Moisture loss, when the grass plants dry out from wind or exposure, can result in dead turf. Windy sections of the inland regions and the Columbia Gorge can expose the grass to conditions that kill it. Tops of hills or mounds, or other areas particularly exposed to wind, can be most affected. Bitter cold will not kill turf during winter when it's dormant.

A sudden spring freeze can nip new, emerging grass—it's susceptible to freeze damage when growth begins again.

PLANTING

Sod can be installed in warmest zones, 7-9, but only when temperatures are above freezing and ground isn't water saturated. Keep seams and corners well watered if winter rains cease for a week or more.

Do no seeding or lawn renovating this month.

CARE

Keep wielding the rake and get all fallen leaves off the lawn.

FERTILIZING

Here in the Northwest we want photogenic lawns both winter and summer. One way to help is fall fertilization: Application of lawn fertilizer in a 3-1-2 ratio in September and again late November or early December will supply nutrients for healthy winter growth.

If you choose to give up one of these two fertilizations, skip September but don't skip November. (Choose a slow-release form of fertilizer in late November because it provides nutrients gradually through winter.) Some fall fertilizers also contain sulfur, and there's evidence that sulfur can help slow down lawn diseases like red thread during damp weather.

MOWING

Keep lawns mowed if they are actively growing. Mowing once or twice in December, January, and February may be necessary in warmest areas.

PROBLEMS

Winter conditions may reveal symptoms resembling lawn diseases. Red thread (see page 111), and fusarium patch can be common on both sides of the Cascades. Fusarium patch, caused by fungal agents, creates round watersoaked spots up to 6 inches across, often with masses of white or pinkish mold. Symptoms may show up more during cold weather when grass grows slowly; sometimes called "snow mold" because it appears under snow east of the mountains. Good air circulation, moderate and not excessive nitrogen fertilizer, and dry weather conditions can help prevent this. Get an accurate diagnosis.

NATIVE PLANTS

Native plants are those that naturally occur in a given region and are a longstanding part of the local ecosystem.

Each plant in our gardens has its origins in a native species from somewhere. As people and plants have moved together around the world, it may not always be easy to tell which plants are truly native. Earliest settlers brought along European plants they relied on as medicinal herbs. One of these, foxglove (*Digitalis purpurea*), has so easily blended with natives west of the Cascades that many people mistake it for a native wildflower.

Throughout history, plant explorers have wandered the globe in search of new plants for use back home. During the early 1800s, this area proved to be a rich resource for plant explorers. Scottish botanist David Douglas was perhaps the most productive of these explorers, identifying and naming a great number of our local species, many of which remain popular garden plants in Europe to this day.

Several garden cultivars and varieties have been cultivated from our natives. The red flowering currant (*Ribes sanguineum* 'King Edward VII') has larger, deep-pink flowers and a compact habit. *Acer macrophyllum* 'Seattle Sentinel' has a very narrow, upright form. Vine maples (*Acer circinatum* 'Monroe' and 'Elegant') have finely cut leaves reminiscent of Japanese maples.

VEGETATION ASSOCIATIONS AND CLIMACTIC ZONES

Oregon and Washington host a diverse range of climactic conditions with distinct vegetation types (see General Introduction). Getting acquainted

with the plant associations (plant combinations which grow together in the wild) and the growing season of your location will improve your gardening success with native and garden selections alike.

WHY GROW NATIVE PLANTS?

There are many good reasons to build native plants into your landscape, either in exclusively native landscapes or as garden companions. Whether in the arid high desert or along the misty coastal ranges, our native species help define the natural character of the region. Adding natives to your garden honors the natural history of your locale and is one strategy for environmentally friendly gardening. From the butterflies that lay their eggs on willows to the eagles that nest in the tallest Douglas firs, native plants are important to a wide array of local creatures that depend on them for their survival. Sited correctly, native plants can be grown with much lower requirements for irrigation and cultural care than many other garden plants. Existing natives also foster microclimate conditions supporting the growth of additional native plants.

Using local flora to landscape a vacation cabin is much more sensible than adding cultivated garden plants. Native selections can be placed in the aestheti-

cally pleasing arrangements of a planned garden while still looking like they belong to the territory. They can be left to grow with less worry for their continued maintenance or risk of their potential escape into the surrounding wild lands.

NATIVES AS GARDEN COMPANIONS

Many of our native species blend beautifully with different types of garden styles. Conifers provide a dramatic evergreen backdrop to colorful ornamental specimens. Vine maple (*Acer circinatum*) and rock maple (*Acer glabrum*) are lovely small trees suitable for intimate garden settings. Evergreen huckleberry (*Vaccinium ovatum*) is beautiful as a naturalized screen, a trimmed hedge, or a companion with rhododendrons. Bleeding heart (*Dicentra formosa*), coastal strawberry (*Fragaria chiloensis*), and *Sedum* species are reliable ground covers. Choose adaptable native species to add variety, color, contrast, and durability to your landscape scheme.

NATIVE PLANT PRESERVATION

Your home garden may abut or contain existing native plants. These remnants of native vegetation merit special consideration and care. When some garden plants infiltrate wild lands, they can displace native species

and disrupt wild habitats. Those that are particularly invasive and destructive have been identified by State noxious weed boards (see pages 288 and 289). Be vigilant about keeping out known invasive species and avoid using cultivated plants that spread vigorously, especially in garden areas that border wild lands.

Existing and restored native landscapes in developed areas require continued stewardship. Expect to periodically weed out non-native trees, shrubs, vines, and herbaceous plants that may seed or creep in. Fill vacant spots with new native plants. Protect bare soil with organic mulch while young native plants become established.

Regional conservation districts through State Department of Natural Resources and through County offices often offer inexpensive native saplings. Some areas have programs for obtaining salvage plants from properties being cleared for development. Never dig plants from their wild homes outside of such programs. Collecting seeds is one way to start some types of native plants. Others are better acquired as whole plants from other sources.

RIGHT PLANT RIGHT PLACE

As with all garden plants, natives need to be located in microcli-

mate conditions to which they are adapted: sun or shade, damp or dry soil, fertile woodland or mineral desert soil. Just because a plant is native to the region doesn't mean it can be planted anywhere. Native plants are no more capable than exotics of surviving in unsuitable locations. Space remains a primary consideration—our tallest growing, broad spreading conifers are ill suited to the confines of small urban lots but will beautifully grace large gardens.

Check your landscape and garden conditions to identify natives existing there. Use a good handbook or the resources offered by local native plant societies to help you identify unknown plants. Talk with nurseries and walk natural areas to get acquainted with the characteristics of local vegetation. It is vital to understand the cultural needs of the plant and how it will look as it grows and matures. Native plants can be small herbaceous perennials, trillium (*Trillium ovatum*), mid-sized shrubs like red huckleberry (*Vaccinium parvifolium*), medium- sized trees like vine maple (*Acer circinatum*), or very large trees like Pine (*Pinus ponderosa*) or Douglas fir (*Pseudotsuga menziesii*). Make note of species commonly found growing together.

Shop close to home to find selections best suited to your area. Many natives in Washington and Oregon grow in other locations—they're not exclusive to us. Red stem dogwood (*Cornus sericea*) grows in Maine, Alaska, Southern California, and elsewhere. Plants propagated and shipped from other areas will not be as well adapted to our climate as those locally grown, even though they are the same species.

MAINTENANCE PRACTICES

The basic techniques for planting, pruning, and irrigation covered in the other chapters carry over to the care of native species. Native trees and shrubs can be pruned for structure, form, and appearance. Minimal fertilization is even more critical when it comes to native species, particularly if you are gardening around existing native trees. Natives in the garden will do well to have nutrients supplied through organic sources in the form of coarse mulches and leaf mold.

Planting: native species doesn't necessarily spell a "care free" garden. The soil and light conditions in many urban and suburban garden sites are highly altered from those in natural habitats. Just like cultivated plants, natives will suffer when placed in soil or light conditions to which they are poorly adapted. Sites where the native soil has been heavily compacted or disturbed by construction will require extra attention to soil preparation before native species can be expected to grow well. Woodland species placed in too much sun or in dry areas may suffer scorched leaves and stunted growth.

Native plants often respond to garden cultivation with more compact, lush growth, and greater bloom. They will grow well with far less water and no fertilizers in comparison to many cultivated plants. Manage the mulch layers and watering to resemble that present in wild habitats. In some locations, native species may require some supplemental water over summer—they may lose more moisture and have less soil area for roots to penetrate than their wild counterparts.

Native species are not completely without insects and diseases. Slugs will chew trillium; Oregon grape (*Mahonia aquafolium*) can get powdery mildew. This doesn't make them poor garden choices; consider it one part of the plant's role in the ecosystem. Some problems, however, can become severe enough to compromise plant health and growth, such as anthracnose leaf fungus on Western dogwood (*Cornus nuttallii*) and fatal root rot diseases which can afflict native conifers and maples.

JANUARY
NATIVE PLANTS

 PLANNING

Conifers are nearly synonymous with Northwest trees, and their contributions to the landscape are especially evident in winter. The long periods of moist weather, moderate temperatures, and overcast skies west of the Cascades provide ideal growing conditions for the **Douglas fir** (*Pseudostuga menziesii*), **Western red-cedar** (*Thuja plicata*), and **Western hemlock** (*Tsuga heterophylla*) that define the character of the coastal northwest. East of the Cascades, **ponderosa pine** (*Pinus ponderosa*), **lodgepole pine** (*Pinus contorta* var. *latifolia*), **Western larch** (*Larix occidentalis*), and **Western juniper** (*Juniperus occidentalis*) dominate the scene. Native conifers provide year-round interest to woodlands and gardens alike.

The numbers of native conifers are rapidly diminishing in populated areas. Some are displaced by construction, while others slowly succumb to the stress of construction damage. Planting new ones where space and site conditions allow is vital to maintaining our regional heritage of native evergreens.

Extra care and attention is needed to successfully preserve existing native trees where new construction and gardens are to be installed nearby. Mature trees are not very resilient to dramatic changes to their immediate surrounds, though it often takes several years for the damage to kill or sicken the trees. Take the time early in the planning process to consider the potential impacts on valuable trees. Call an ISA certified arborist for help with an evaluation and preservation plan for existing native trees (see Trees chapter, April).

 PLANTING

Zones 5 -6: It is typically too cold for Planting:.

Zones 7-9: Evergreen and deciduous woody species can be planted and transplanted during warmer periods with low temperatures in the 40s and soil that is not sopping wet.

 CARE

Zones 5-6: Winter desiccation can occur. Needles on evergreens can dry out when soils are frozen and sun and wind exposure occurs. When establishing young plants, make sure evergreens go into winter well watered. Damaged needles may be shed and replaced the next growing season.

 PRUNING

Zones 5-6: It is generally too cold for pruning work.

Zones 7-9: Dormant season pruning for deciduous and evergreen trees and shrubs can be done during periods of mild weather.

 WATERING

In high desert regions, newly planted trees and shrubs will benefit from occasional supplemental water their first year or two when soil conditions remain dry.

 FERTILIZING

No fertilizing is needed now.

 PROBLEMS

Winter storms can take a toll on trees: snow, ice and wind can break limbs. Trees in waterlogged soils may begin to lean or even fall over. Check on your trees after any severe storm or wind events. Pruning to thin out dense canopy in conifers can help reduce wind sail (see Trees, January).

FEBRUARY

NATIVE PLANTS

PLANNING

No matter which part of the region you reside in, the local native species can be incorporated into cultivated gardens as companion plants. It can be as simple as adding **ferns** and ground covers or replacing lost ornamentals with native species offering similar ornamental and functional qualities.

Sometimes native plants will find their way into your garden on their own. Before you yank them all out along with the weeds, stop to see if they might fit within the existing landscape. This happens most easily with ground cover species that seed in, though a new shrub or tree might also happen to sprout in a good position. If several plants have cropped up in one spot, choose the best one and weed out the rest.

PLANTING

Zones 5-6: Not while winter conditions remain below freezing.

Zones 7-9: All types of nursery stock can be planted when soil and weather conditions are not too soggy. Many types of native plants are available as restoration stock from specialist nurseries, as well as through State DNR and local conservation district programs. If you are restoring native plants to a large area, mulch the entire area first. Rake the mulch away to bare soil for each planting hole. Mulching can be done weeks ahead of planting and should be about 2 to 4 inches deep.

CARE

Zones 7-9: Add mulch beneath large trees where the soil has become bare. Remember to keep mulch a few inches away from the base of the trunk. With their varied particle size and bits of leaf, wood, and bark tissue that emulates the natural mulch (duff layer) found in forests, wood chips from tree and shrub trimmings are an ideal mulch material.

Clear away weeds and thick vegetation from the base of tree trunks so the root flare area is clear and visible on all sides.

All zones: Winter storms may still occur throughout the region. Inspect trees for damage after storm events (see Trees).

PRUNING

Zones 5-6: Evergreens and deciduous plants can be pruned in late winter.

Zones 7-9: Continue dormant season pruning as needed for trees and shrubs. See Trees and Shrubs chapters pruning notes.

WATERING

Zones 5-6: In high desert country, newly planted trees and shrubs will benefit from an occasional winter watering during periods when the ground is not frozen.

Zones 7-9: Soil moisture is typically ample at this time of year.

FERTILIZING

None this month.

PROBLEMS

Zones 7-9: True **firs** (*Abies* species) grown in gardens can develop severe infestations of the native wooly fir adelgid. It is evident on older trees with white "flocking" on the main trunk and on young trees when branch ends become swollen and knotty. Dormant oil applications can be helpful (see Trees).

MARCH

NATIVE PLANTS

PLANNING

Early blooming natives herald the arrival of spring. Look for spots in your garden that may host them. For naturalized plantings west of the Cascades, **Indian plum** (*Oemleria cerasiformis*) marks the start of spring with its early white blooms and freshly emerging leaves. About the same time, bright yellow bracts of **skunk cabbage** (*Lysichiton americanus*) poke up along damp areas. Two beautiful garden additions are the red flowering **currant** (*Ribes san-*

guineum) and the fragrant western **azalea** (*Rhododendron occidentale*). Western **serviceberry** (*Amelanchier alnifolia*) performs beautifully in nearly all zones of the region, bearing delicate white blossoms.

PLANTING

Plant native trees, shrubs, and ferns as temperatures warm and soils remain moist. Many nurseries ship bare-root trees for planting in March and April (see General Introduction for planting details).

Several native shrubs can be grown from live stakes—stem cuttings that are placed directly in the soil in early spring: **red stem dogwood** (*Cornus sericea*), **black twinberry** (*Lonicera involucrata*), **Pacific ninebark** (*Physocarpus capitatus*), and **willow** (*Salix* species). It's a great technique for restoring vegetation to large naturalized areas.

CARE

Replenish mulch as needed, especially for newer plantings that are less than three years old.

PRUNING

Multi-stem native shrubs can be maintained with selective thinning of the longest, thickest stems: **wood rose, mock orange, Indian plum, shrubby cinquefoil, Oregon grape, ocean spray,** and others (see Shrubs chapter).

Old, shabby fronds on sword fern may be cut back to the ground before new growth begins, but be careful to protect coiled new fronds.

HELPFUL HINT

Learning about and using native plants is a fine adventure, one that opens new worlds and helps us experience the beauty of our region in more depth.

NATIVE PLANT INFORMATION

Native Plant Society of Oregon
PO. Box 902
Eugene, OR 97440
503-248-9242
www.npsoregon.org

Washington Native Plant Society
7400 Sand Point Way NE
Seattle, WA 98115
206-527-3210
www.wnps.org

Gardening with Native Plants of the Pacific Northwest by Arthur R. Kruckeberg. University of Washington Press, 1982. (Covers eastern and western regions).

Native Plants in the Coastal Garden, revised and updated by April Pettinger. Whitecap Books, 2002.

WATERING

Zones 5-6: In high desert regions, give new plants a deep soaking every few weeks if precipitation has been low.

Zones 7-9: Seasonal rains typically provide enough soil moisture.

FERTILIZING

None this month.

PROBLEMS

Zones 7-9: Search through the native plant borders for invasive seedlings of evergreen woody weeds such as laurel, holly, and ivy. They are easy to pull when only a few inches tall.

NATIVE CONIFERS FOR THE SMALL URBAN GARDEN

There are smaller growing conifer species and cultivars suited to all parts of the region. Ornamental and functional, some merit use as single specimens or can be used in mixed plantings.

- **Mountain hemlock**, *Tsuga mertensiana*—slow growing to 30 ft.; 'Cascade' and 'Glauca' with blue foliage (Zones 5-9)
- **Shore pine**, *Pinus contorta* var. *contorta*—40 ft. (Zones 7-9)
- **Brewer's spruce**, *Picea breweriana*—slow growing to 50 ft. (Zones 7-8).
- Dwarf forms of **Western red cedar** (*Thuja plicata*): 'Aurea', 'Zebrina' and columnar 'Hogan' (Zones 5-9)
- Dwarf forms of **Lawson cypress** (*Chamaecyparis lawsoniana*) including 'Alumni' and 'Wisselii' (Zones 4-9)
- **Alaska yellow cedar** (*Chamaecyparis nootkatensis*)—45 ft. Cultivars 'Compacta', 'Pendula', 'Stricta' (Zones 4-9)
- **Incense cedar** (*Calocedrus decurrens*)—tall and narrow habit (Zones 5-9)
- **Rocky mountain juniper** (*Juniperus scopulorum*)—30 ft. Cultivars 'Argentea', and 'Columnaris' (Zones 5-9)

Alaska yellow cedar

APRIL

NATIVE PLANTS

PLANNING

This is the month to honor, preserve, and celebrate the bounties of our natural earth. Earth Day is observed on April 22 with many community volunteer efforts going into environmental stewardship projects. These projects also offer first-hand opportunities to learn more about the heritage of native vegetation unique to your corner of the region.

Good results in urban areas comes not only through matching the correct species to the site conditions but also through grouping plants in combinations as they occur in the wild. This holds true for both naturalized and landscape plantings. A common association west of the Cascades includes **Douglas fir** (*Pseudotsuga menziesii*), **madrone** (*Arbutus menziesii*), **salal** (*Gaultheria shallon*), **sword fern** (*Polystichum munitum*), and **Oregon oxalis** (*Oxalis oregana*). Where **shore pine** (*Pinus contorta* var. *contorta*) occurs in coastal areas, it may be joined by **kinnikinnick** (*Arctostaphylos uva-ursi*), *Sedum spathulifolium*, **coastal strawberry** (*Fragaria chiloensis*), and **Nootka rose** (*Rosa nutkana*). Wetland areas host **willow** (*Salix* spp.), **hardhack spirea** (*Spiraea douglasii*), **red stem dogwood** (*Cornus sericea*), and **skunk cabbage** (*Lysichiton americanum*). **Western junipers, sagebrush** (*Artemisia tridentata*), and **pines** co-habit in high desert areas.

See page 136 for regional native plant information sources.

PLANTING

Zones 5-6: Plant bare-root, container, and balled-and-burlap nursery stock. Conservation districts offer bare-root seedlings for restoration plantings.

Zones 7-9: Finish planting before the end of the month to lessen transplant stress during the coming summer.

CARE

Mulching is one of the best care practices you can provide for native plantings. Look to the natural habitats near you and mimic the natural conditions and types of organic input to the ecosystem.

PRUNING

Multi-stem shrubs may be pruned to maintain form and size. Thin out the oldest and longest stems from **wood rose, mock orange, Indian plum, western azalea, shrubby cinquefoil, ocean spray,** **Oregon grape, ninebark,** and others. (See Shrubs chapter.)

WATERING

As temperatures warm and precipitation decreases, begin monitoring new plants for water needs. Use a trowel to check soil moisture levels.

FERTILIZING

On most soils, native plants will not require supplemental fertilization. While some may tolerate being fertilized alongside their cultivated neighbors, keep fertilization minimal around native species for best results. Native species that inhabit naturally infertile sites are not tolerant of nutrient rich soils.

PROBLEMS

Zones 7-9: Native **dogwoods** (*Cornus nuttallii*) in key locations that have suffered from **anthracnose** may benefit from extra care. Very young trees may be protected with fungicide sprays as buds open and leaves expand, but spraying full sized trees is not always feasible. Contact your OSU or WSU Cooperative Extension for information on managing anthracnose.

MAY

NATIVE PLANTS

PLANNING

Rock gardens are a great choice for arid sites, particularly with our native alpine species. Well drained soils with spring moisture and crushed rock mulch to emulate mountain scree conditions are important cultivation elements. Many rock garden plants can be found at nurseries that specialize in native and rock garden plants. Never collect live plants from the wild.

Lovely blooms are found on *Lewisii* species, **shooting star** (*Dodecatheon conjugens*), **penstemon**, and **Douglasii** (*Douglasii laevigata*). Foliage interest is provided in shadier rockery crevices with **rock brake fern** (*Aspidotis densa*), **spleenwort**, (*Asplenium trichomanes*), and **parsley fern** (*Cryptogramma crispa*). For extended bloom, add **pussy-toes** (*Antennaria* spp.). Grassy looking **sandworts** (*Arenaria* species) are among the easiest rock garden plants to establish.

PLANTING

Planting should be completed before summer temperatures arrive.

CARE

Naturalized native plantings and remnant stands of native vegetation need continued observation and weeding to keep non-native plants out.

PRUNING

Prune spring flowering trees and shrubs after blooms fade (see Trees and Shrubs chapters).

WATERING

Newly planted native plants will need regular watering during their first two to three years of establishment. Check new transplants for watering needs at least once a week.

FERTILIZING

The best nutrients sources will be natural. Utilize local sources of organic materials to replenish organic matter in the garden each season.

PROBLEMS

Be careful about choosing commercial wildflower or meadow seed mixes. Commercial mixes packaged for a very broad region may include seed foreign to your area, such as a Western US mix that includes California and Arizona plants. Some species may behave as noxious weeds when grown out of their range. Many "wildflower" mixes contain non-native species. **Oxeye daisy** (*Chrysanthemum leucanthemum*), **Queen Anne's Lace** (*Daucus carota*), and **knapweed** (*Centaurea* spp.) are commonly included in wildflower and meadow mixes and are all prohibited species.

Seed packets or locally collected mixes blended for a specific range such as Puget Sound Prairie or eastern Oregon shrub-steppe are safer options.

JUNE
NATIVE PLANTS

 PLANNING

Many native plants and their cultivars can be used in ornamental containers with as good effect as commonly used ornamentals. Go all native, or combine them with similarly adapted horticultural selections. Place **kinnikinnick** (*Arctostaphylos uva-ursi*) to drape over edges of pots or raised planters. Evergreen **huckleberry** (*Vaccinium ovatum*), **mountain hemlock** (*Tsuga mertensiana*), and **sumac** (*Rhus glabra* 'Laciniata') make lovely container specimens alone or in combination with native **ferns** and perennials such as *Heuchera micrantha*, **pussy-toes** (*Antennaria* spp.), or **fleabanes** (*Erigeron* spp.). Fleshy-leaved **sedums** in pots or an old floral basket make beautiful drought tolerant accents. For a fun project with children, have them plant some *Sedum oregonense* in an old shoe to set out along a garden path.

Kinnikinnick

PLANTING

This is not an ideal time for planting, especially where water is scarce. If you must plant now, do it during periods of cool damp weather. Thoroughly soak rootballs beforehand, and check them daily the first weeks after planting. Don't forget to mulch.

Save seeds of **Indian plum**, *Oemleria cerasiformis* and **Western serviceberry** (*Amelanchier alnifolia*) to dry for fall sowing.

NATIVE OR INTRODUCED?

For the newcomer to Pacific Northwest native plants, some of the introduced species that have colonized disturbed areas and existing forests can appear to be part of the native flora. Not all the plants you see "growing wild" belong there. With its delicate leaves and fine pink blooms, herb **Robert** (*Geranium robertianum*, Europe) readily mimics local wildflowers. Harvesting **Himalayan blackberry** (*Rubus discolor*, Europe) is a treasured summer tradition for many, though this is one of the more aggressive noxious weeds species to colonize open ground. State Extension and native plant society web pages include useful photos and resources for plant identification of invasive intruders.

CARE

Create broad, soil rimmed basins around new plants to aid water penetration.

PRUNING

See Tree and Shrub chapters for summer pruning techniques. Trim back dried bloom stalks as needed on herbaceous plants and save seeds from desirable plants.

WATERING

About once per week, check plants which have been added over the past three years.

Use great caution when adding new irrigation near large native trees. Keep irrigation systems and cultivated plants that require summer moisture beyond the drip line of native trees. Locate sprinklers so that water spray stops short of hitting the trunk. Mature trees, including **madrona** and **Douglas fir**, are not adaptable to new summer irrigation, and continual moisture in the root flare area can contribute to root rots and early death. Spot-water or use irriga-tion tubing with emitters placed by new plants to help establish ferns and ground covers beneath existing native trees.

FERTILIZING

None this month.

DID YOU KNOW?

Native species are essential to providing butterfly and hummingbird habitats. Add some of these for their nectar, as well as food sources for caterpillars.

WOODY PLANTS:
- **Wild lilac**, *Ceanothus* spp.
- **Elderberry**, *Sambucus cerulea, S. racemosa*
- **Huckleberry**, *Vaccinium ovatum* and *V. parvifolium*
- **Hardhack**, *Spiraea douglasii*
- **Kinnikinnick**, *Arctostaphylos uva-ursi*
- **Mock orange**, *Philadelphus lewisii*
- **Ninebark**, *Physocarpus capitatus*
- **Oregon grape**, *Mahonia* spp.
- **Red flowering currant**, *Ribes sanguineum*
- **Salal**, *Gaultheria shallon*
- **Serviceberry**, *Amelanchier alnifolia*
- **Sumac**, *Rhus* glabra
- **Twinberry**, *Lonicera involucrata*
- **Western azalea**, *Rhododendron occidentalis*
- **Wild rose**, *Rosa* spp.
- **Willow**, *Salix sp.*

HERBACEOUS:
- **Bleeding heart**, *Dicentra formosa*
- **Campanula**, *Campanula rotundifolia*
- **Penstemon**, *Penstemon* spp.
- **Western columbine**, *Aquilegia formosa*

PROBLEMS

Pine shoot moth damage may appear on 2-needle pines, including **shore** and **lodgepole pine** (*Pinus contorta*). Clip out and destroy damaged shoots, particularly on young trees.

JULY

NATIVE PLANTS

PLANNING

Choosing what to plant in barren areas beneath large native trees can be a perplexing challenge. Trying to alter soil and moisture conditions usually produces poor results in the long run. Improvements can be gained with a little patience and using the right plants. Start by observing which native shrubs, ground covers, and wildflowers are normally found around these trees in the wild. Remove dead or undesired plants now, being careful not to disturb tree roots. Cover bare soil with mulch. Assemble a shopping list for fall planting season.

Don't attempt to install plants too close to tree trunks. Work nearer the drip line where root competition is less intense. Native ferns are some of the best adapted plants for under trees. Include plant species that will naturally spread to fill in open spaces, such as **Oregon grape** (*Mahonia* species), **salal** (*Gaultheria shallon*), **Oregon wood sorrel** (*Oxalis oregano*), and **inside-out flower** (*Vancouveria* spp.) While these plants may expand very slowly during their first years, they provide durable cover over the long run. Herbaceous plants such as **woodland strawberry** (*Fragaria vesca*) and **piggyback plant**

(*Tolmiea menziesii*) spread more rapidly and can be included to achieve quicker cover.

PLANTING

The peak dry heat periods of summer bring some of the worst conditions for planting. Focus instead on collecting seed of native plants for fall sowing.

Collect seed of *Ribes sanguineum* when berries are blue black.

Try softwood cuttings of *Ribes sanguineum* and *Potentilla fruticosa* (see New Woody Plants from Softwood Cuttings on page 290).

CARE

Many native species cope with extended dry periods by going into summer dormancy. However, they may remain green under cultivated conditions with continued moisture, provided they are not over watered.

PRUNING

Summer pruning may be provided as needed for trees and shrubs. Dried flower stems from **fringe cup** (*Tellima grandiflora*) may be cut back for a tidier appearance.

WATERING

Native trees and shrubs placed in urban settings may not be as drought tolerant as they are in their natural environments. Supplemental water may be needed to compensate for exposure to reflective heat or restricted rooting areas. Provide infrequent, deep watering if plants show leaf scorch or wilting.

Just the opposite problem can affect existing native trees which suffer from added irrigation when highly cultivated gardens or lawns are added beneath them. Maintain their health by using companion plants adapted to the existing conditions.

PROBLEMS

Zones 5-6: Off-color foliage and stunted or dead branches may indicate root disease problems, such as phytophthora on **Port Orford cedar** and verticillium wilt on **big leaf** and **vine maple**. Contact your OSU and WSU Cooperative Extension agent for more information.

The bright red and green leaf galls which may appear on **kinnikinnick** are not usually serious to plant health. They may be clipped off and disposed of.

AUGUST

NATIVE PLANTS

PLANNING

It is perhaps on the most sweltering days of summer that the cooling shade of trees is most appreciated—or missed. Consider some of the better shade tree candidates among native species. On larger properties where space is ample, don't overlook the potential for **big leaf maple** (*Acer macrophyllum*) and **Oregon ash** (*Fraxinus latifolia*) to develop into classic shade tree dimensions. The 'Seattle Sentinel' **big leaf maple** is a smaller, columnar form more suitable for urban sites. **California black oak** (*Quercus kelloggii*) and **Garry oak** (*Quercus garryana*) are elegant, drought tolerant trees highly worthy of ornamental use in western Oregon and parts of Washington.

Where space is more limited, **vine maple** (*Acer circinatum*) can be trained to a single trunk for a moderate-sized shade tree. It is best placed away from reflected heat. Its hardier cousin, **Douglas' maple** (*Acer glabrum*), is a good choice east of the Cascades.

Hardy throughout the region, **serviceberry** (*Amelanchier alnifolia*) and its cultivars can be used as a small garden specimen tree to shade a patio or entry walk. It is covered in delicate white spring blooms with small, clean summer leaves which burst into hues of red and yellow in fall. The smooth gray bark is lovely in winter. Its small summer fruits, reminiscent in look and taste to **blueberries**, are tasty for gardeners and birds alike.

Some native trees don't work well along streets and sidewalks. Check with your local municipality before planting since many require permits for planting along streets.

PLANTING

This is a good time to collect seeds from many different types of native plants for fall sowing.

CARE

Do not allow heavy vines to grow high up into trees where they can add weight and shading on tree branches. Keep watch for and remove invasive species such as **English ivy, old man's beard,** and **kudzu** that sneaked into native woodland stands (see Vines chapter).

PRUNING

Carry out light pruning as needed to remove the occasional dead or errant woody branch in cultivated gardens. Dead branches can remain in wildlife plantings, as they are an essential habitat component.

WATERING

Watering should not be a concern for native plants, which are so well adapted to our pattern of dry summer seasons. However, don't ignore them completely. Those recently planted, or growing in containers and other areas with limited soil volume may require some supplemental water. In extremely warm, dry years, even natives growing in the wild can suffer drought damage.

FERTILIZING

None this month.

PROBLEMS

Fall webworm nests may appear on **willow, poplar,** and **alders**. Part of the native ecology, these caterpillars have been feeding all summer and generally do not damage native trees.

September

NATIVE PLANTS

PLANNING

Ground covers offer one of the easiest, most effective ways to include natives in your garden, and early fall is a good time for establishing them. Though some can be slower than others to get a grip, they are durable and tenacious once established and are well worth the wait. Evergreen *Vancouveria hexandra* and the low growing **Oregon grapes** (*Mahonia nervosa and M. repens*) are among these slower growers. **Wild strawberries** (*Fragaria* spp.), **piggyback** (*Tellima grandiflora*), and some of the **sedums** can be counted on to provide quicker cover.

PLANTING

Fall planting is ideal for many native plants. Remember to water and mulch if soils and weather conditions remain dry.

This is also an optimal time to add companion ground covers and **ferns** beneath large trees (see Ground Covers, October).

Harvest and plant seeds from native shrubs. Clean seeds from most berries before fall sowing.

Zones 5-6: Planting seeds now is beneficial for those species requiring a cold period prior to germination. Planting now also means taking advantage of seasonal moisture to support germination and early root growth.

CARE

Retain natural leaf litter beneath natives whenever possible. In more cultivated garden settings or where heavy leaf cover may smother smaller plants, shred the coarse native plant debris and return it to the site. This not only helps the soil but also enhances habitat for beneficial native insects.

PRUNING

To preserve existing native meadow plant communities, mow down and remove dry stalks by fall each year.

WATERING

Water recently planted container and balled-and-burlap nursery plants. Check the original rootball soil, as nursery soils dry out more quickly than native soil.

FERTILIZING

Apply organic mulch or compost to maintain soil nutrients. This timing coincides with the natural nutrient cycle as shed leaves drop to the ground at the end of the season.

PROBLEMS

Zones 7-9: The appearance of brown *inner* leaves on **Western red cedar** (*Thuja plicata*) at this time of year can be alarming. In fact, it is a normal shedding process. However, brown foliage extending onto branch tips and new growth can signal health problems.

COMBINATIONS FOR FALL COLOR

These cultivars of native trees and shrubs offer the adaptability of local plants with additional ornamental features for cultivated garden spaces. Contrast the vibrant, lacy foliage of *Rhus glabra* 'Laciniata' with evergreen *Chamaecyparis lawsoniana* 'Pembury Blue' or low *Juniperus communis* 'Nana'. **Vine maples** (*Acer circinatum* 'Monroe' and 'Elegant') are at their prime in autumn. **Western service berry** (*Amelanchier alnifolia* 'Altaglow') blends shades of yellow, oranges, red, and purple as its leaves turn before falling.

SELECTED NATIVE GROUND COVERS
FOR CULTIVATED GARDENS

Name	Zone	Conditions
Kinnikinnick, *Arctostaphylos uva-ursi*	5-9	sun
Strawberry, *Fragaria* spp.	5-9	sun to light shade
Sedum, *Sedum* spp.	5-9	sun
Creeping Oregon grape, *Mahonia repens*	6-9	sun to light shade
Pacific bleeding heart, *Dicentra formosa*	7-9	damp shade
Piggyback, *Tolmiea menziesii*	7-9	damp shade
Foam flower, *Tellima grandiflora*	7-9	light shade
Inside out flower, *Vancouveria* spp.	7-9	open shade
Wild ginger, *Asarum caudatum*	6-9	moist shade
Wild lily of the valley, *Maianthemum dilatatum*	7-9	damp shade
Woodsorrel, *Oxalis oregana and O. suksdorfii*	7-9	light shade
Low Oregon grape, *Mahonia nervosa*	7-9	light shade
Prostrate juniper, *Juniperus communis* var. *montana*	5-9	sun

Maidenhair fern

FERNS

WOODLAND FERNS, ZONES 7-9
Maidenhair fern, *Adiantum pedatum,*
deciduous
Deer fern, *Blechnum spicant*
Oak fern, *Gymnocarpium dryopteris*
Licorice fern, *Polypodium glycyrrhiza*
Sword fern, *Polystichum munitum*
Anderson's sword fern, *Polystichum
andersonii*
Chain fern, *Woodwardia fimbriata*

ROCK CREVICES, ZONES 5-9
Spleenwort, *Asplenium trichomanes*
Lace fern, *Cheilanthes gracillima*
Parsley fern, *Cryptogramma crispa*
Bladder fern, *Cystopteris fragilis*
Polypody fern, *Polypodium hesperium*

ARID FERNS, ZONES 6-9
Rock brake, *Aspidotis densa*
Cliff brakes, *Pellaea* spp.
Woodsia, *Woodsia oregana,
W. scopulina*

OCTOBER

NATIVE PLANTS

 PLANNING

Native plants are the backbone of landscaping for wildlife. Whether incorporating selected native species in a conventional landscape or developing a full scale habitat planting, these plants will support a wider array of native organisms and wildlife than you may imagine. Native plants in gardens can provide wildlife with vital links between nearby green belts or wild areas. As the native species in your garden increase, so will the appearance of birds, butterflies, beneficial insects, and other creatures. The benefits are many, from aesthetics to water-wise plantings to natural pest suppression.

To learn more about enhancing the habitat qualities of your garden, contact your OSU and WSU Cooperative Extension office. A great guide with practical information for east and west of the Cascades is *Landscaping for Wildlife in the Pacific Northwest* by Russell Link, University of Washington Press, 1999.

 PLANTING

Dormant season planting is ideal for native plant restoration. A good layer of mulch improves plant establishment. Be sure to keep it from covering the lower trunks and stems of woody plants.

 CARE

Where leaf fall is heavy, gather them for shredding and composting into leaf mold to use as mulch throughout the year.

Install protective collars around the base of young trees where winter rodent damage is a problem.

 PRUNING

Keeping some dead branches and snags (dead tops) in trees are helpful in bird habitat—both to perch on and to host insects that provide food.

 WATERING

Watering should not be needed as fall rains return, but keep an eye on new plants.

 FERTILIZING

Autumn mulches slowly add nutrients to the soil as they decompose.

 PROBLEMS

Zones 7-9: Fallen leaves of **big leaf maple** can overwhelm smaller plants below them. Clear them off the tops of plants before they are smothered by heavy, water laden leaves.

All zones: Native species can insert themselves into garden areas where they become weeds instead of welcome companions. Fast growing **poplar, alder,** and **birch seedlings** may overwhelm gardens or pop up against building foundations. Suckering stems of tall **Oregon grape** (*Mahonia aquafolium*) and **hard hack** (*Spiraea douglasii*) may extend their reach into other plants. Some judicious weeding may be required to maintain the right balance of plants. Deep rooters are most easily dislodged from moist autumn soils and may even be transplanted now if useful elsewhere.

NOVEMBER

NATIVE PLANTS

PLANNING

Many local species are a "natural" choice for winter interest. **Silk-tassel bush** (*Garrya elliptica*) from southwestern Oregon is a hallmark winter garden plant with its dramatic, long tasseled flowers and broad evergreen leaves. Cultivars and hybrids with this species include 'Evie' and 'Pat Ballard'. The dormant branches of 'Pacific Fire' **vine maple** are brilliant against a backdrop of native conifers. Bright red stems of *Cornus sericea* **dogwood** stand out against snow and evergreen foliage throughout the entire region. **Limber pine**, *Pinus flexilis*, and its cultivars 'Firmament' and 'Vanderwolf's Pyramid' are beautiful pine forms for dryer inland communities.

Perhaps one of the most striking and picturesque trees in winter is the **Pacific madrona**, *Arbutus menziesii*. Its glossy evergreen leaves and large sculptural limbs with variably smooth, peeling, and rough bark in hues of cinnamon to dark mahogany stand out against an otherwise bleak landscape. It is found on high dry bluffs near salt water, often in association with **Douglas fir, snowberry, salal,** and **sword fern**. With older trees dying out from fungal cankers and other causes and young trees being difficult to transplant, it is most worthwhile to preserve existing trees. Intolerant of cultivation around their roots and perennially shedding plant debris, they are best grown in naturalized beds with companion ferns and shrubs.

PLANTING

Zones 5-6: Planting: stops as deep cold, wind, and snow arrive.

Zones 7-9: Fall planting can continue as weather and soil conditions permit.

CARE

Keep up on the removal of undesired plants, such as **blackberry, ivy, scotch broom,** and other woody weed plants. They are more easily uprooted from damp soils at this time of year.

PRUNING

Large conifers with extremely dense canopies may be lightly thinned to reduce wind resistance. Have large dead limbs removed from tall trees before winter winds arrive (see Trees, "Preparing for Winter Weather").

WATERING

November marks the start of heavy rainfall season throughout the region.

Zones 4-6: In arid locations, provide recently planted conifers and evergreens a deep soaking before winter temperatures set in.

FERTILIZING

None.

PROBLEMS

Some native plant species are commonly foraged by deer, which can be welcome or a nuisance depending on the location and function of the plantings. Some of the favored plants include new growth on **Douglas fir, western red cedar, serviceberry, mock orange, snow berry, wild rose, deer bush** (Ceanothus spp.), and **salal.** East of the Cascades, **sagebrush** may also be browsed. Some feeding is to be expected and is one role for habitat plantings. However, if damage becomes intense, protective fencing may be needed, especially while younger plants are still being established.

DECEMBER

NATIVE PLANTS

PLANNING

Native ferns are versatile companion plants for many types of landscape settings. They come in a range of sizes, shapes, and textures. Ferns are ideal for planting under trees, where they are more amenable than most plants to being swamped in autumn's fallen leaves and are also tolerant of the dry shade of evergreen trees. Arid regions have drought tolerant **rock ferns**, with some more at home in damp rock crevices. Many of these arid ferns are adaptable to cultivation in dry, sunny rock gardens.

Combine native ferns with other wildflowers and perennial plants. A solid drift of ferns makes a cooling, defining statement in the woodland or shade garden area. And what is more inviting than a shady walkway lined in ferns? **Evergreen ferns** provide a lively winter accent and contrast amid winter interest plantings. Venture out to get acquainted with the winter appearance of native ferns in your area and see how they may be included in your garden areas. See page 145 for a list of native ferns.

PLANTING

Zones 5-6: It is typically too cold for planting this month.

Zones 7-8: Planting deciduous and evergreen woody plants as well as evergreen ferns can continue as weather and soil conditions permit.

CARE

Native plants in landscape uses will often require similar care as their cultivated counterparts for winter season protection in cultivated gardens.

PRUNING

Save some of your dormant season pruning tasks to provide interesting branches for holiday decorations with native plants. Always use thinning cuts when collecting greens so the pruning looks natural and inconspicuous.

Outstanding cut greens are found among our native trees and shrubs. **Western red cedar** (*Thuja plicata*) is a standard for wreaths and garlands, and **salal** (*Gaultheria shallon*) and evergreen **huckleberry** (*Vaccinium ovatum*) are lovely in seasonal floral arrangements. Stems from **pines, Port Orford cedar** (*Chamaecyparis lawsoniana*), **incense cedar** (*Calocedrus decurrens*), and **Oregon grape** (*Mahonia* spp.) have lovely foliage for greens. For contrast, collect deciduous stems from **red stem dogwood** (*Cornus sericea*), **vine maple, red huckleberry,** or berry laden **snow berry** (*Symphoricarpos albus*).

WATERING

Not this month.

FERTILIZING

None this month.

PROBLEMS

Woody weeds like **Himalayan blackberry** and **English ivy** are readily visible and can be removed as weather permits.

PERENNIALS &
ORNAMENTAL GRASSES

Perennials tucked under trees and shrubs give the garden its "understory." Gardeners often comment about the "sterile" gardens composed of bark, a few shrubs, and one tree often seen around new houses. The missing element is the foliage and added color given by perennials that soften a harsh landscape. The most monotonous garden could leap into year-round interest with the addition of herbaceous perennials and well-selected ground covers.

Choosing them often includes looking at their total virtues, not just their flowers. Many have long-lasting foliage that gives strength and vigor to garden designs. Others act brilliantly as ground covers and give nearly year-round presence in the garden.

To care for herbaceous perennials, you must be sensitive and responsive to the rhythm of their growth that coincides with the seasons. Observation will tell you that the plants are actually showing you what to do: dead stems in spring with new growth beneath—trimming is the action needed! Taller growth in May that begins to fall sideways—then staking is required. The individual tasks aren't difficult, but because we bring so many different types of perennials into the garden, the

DID YOU KNOW?

Microclimates Can Extend the Zones

Planting tender plants (those not adapted to your particular zone) has become part of nearly every herbaceous perennial garden. The joy of stretching zones makes the garden even more adventurous. Take advantage of possible garden microclimates, try tucking more tender plants into the landscape. A position against a sheltered, south-facing wall could make herbal **rosemary** likely to survive in Zone 5, especially the most hardy of the cultivars. A stone edged, raised bed could also help with plant survival, as long as protection from the worst drying winds also results. Garden buildings can be sited to provide shelter. Take some time this winter to determine where the garden naturally stays a bit warmer, where snow and frozen ground melt early, and where winds seem less penetrating. Mark those spots for next year's experimental plantings.

A Gift That Keeps on Giving!

Written resources on herbaceous perennials can make staying inside during winter more enjoyable.

A few "must haves" for our region include the *Sunset Western Garden Book* (Menlo Park, 1995) and Graham Stuart Thomas *Perennial Garden Plants* (Sagapress, 1994). For maintenance specifics, Tracy Sabato-Aust's *The Well Tended Perennial Garden* (Timber Press, 1998) offers thorough information on individual plant care. The timing she suggests is most helpful for the colder zones, 4 to 6 because the book was written in Ohio. But it's also useful in Zones 7 to 9 and is an excellent resource for understanding the growth habits of herbaceous perennials. Lauren Springer's *The Undaunted Garden* (Fulcrum Press, 1988) cheers any gardener confronted with extremes of heat, cold, or drought in our region.

Perennials as Cut Flowers

For all zones: Aster, fall (*Aster novae-angliae*)

Spring: Anemone (from fall planted rhizomes: *Anemone coronaria*); **bleeding heart** (*Dicentra spectabilis*); **bellflower** (*Campanula lactiflora* and others); **daffodil** (*Narcissus* spp.); **Christmas rose** (*Helleborus orientalis*); **tulip** (*Tulipa* hybrids)

Summer: orange coneflower (*Rudbeckia fulgida*); **purple coneflower** (*Echinacea purpurea*); **foxglove** (*Digitalis* spp.); **iris** (all types: Siberian, German, and bulbous) **lily** (*Lilium* spp.); **peony** (*Paeonia* spp. and hybrids); **yarrow** (*Achillea* spp. and hybrids).

Late summer/fall: *Aster* hybrids and species; *Chrysanthemum* hybrids; *Dahlia* hybrids; **shasta daisy**, *Leucanthemum* x *superbum*.

To enhance good perennials for cut flowers, choose garden shrubs such as **heavenly bamboo** (*Nandina* spp.) and **flowering quince** (*Chaenomeles* hybrids) that can also add greens and texture to flower arrangements.

Purple coneflower

rhythm may be different for different plants. And as we divide and add plants, some may be at different stages of growth. Those not established will need extra water. Others, well settled, will thrive even through dry summers.

Growing perennials from seed allows experimenting with new cultivars. Some that start well from seed include bellflower, *Campanula* sp., blanket flower, *Gaillardia* hybrids, poppies, *Papaver* sp., and yarrow, *Achillea* sp. Set up one place where you can watch and care for the emerging seedlings rather than scattering them into the established garden where they can become lost among bigger plants. Most take several weeks to germinate, but check the packages because some may grow more slowly.

Sowing the seeds takes more investment of time than buying plants but can give satisfactory plant volume. Be ready to protect the emerged seedlings in a cold frame or other unheated winter protection site after they've reached transplanting size.

Perennials that bloom in the first year from seed: Depending on garden conditions, you may get first-year bloom from smaller

Delphinium

Delphinium elata, some of the garden pinks (*Dianthus*), and biennial hollyhock (*Alcea* hybrids.) Other perennials sown from March through May will form big enough plants to set in a permanent spot in fall and will bloom next season. Growing from seed is the best method for acquiring very rare plants if you have the conditions to care for them. Choose plants adapted to your zone, and group them according to water and light needs. With perennials, choosing for foliage color and texture, flower color, and adaptation to your garden means you have multiple choices. One good way to start is to select a small area and plant it, get started, and move forward by stages. The variety and joy of using herbaceous perennial plants give gardeners daily pleasures.

JANUARY
PERENNIALS & ORNAMENTAL GRASSES

PLANNING

Photograph the garden regularly and note where light strengthens and wanes. A series of photographs on the first of January, first of April, first of July, and first of October, from various angles, helps you know where sun- or shade-loving plants go. Or you may choose to photograph on the solstice and equinox. Learning the movement of light across the garden will be as important as studying the soil.

Herbaceous perennial plants may bloom less when shaded by taller plants, and the "sunny" spots may gradually move into becoming part sun or even shade. Gardens require revising as time changes them. Change the scene by adding and subtracting plants. One joy of perennials is their easy mobility; their root structures aren't complicated like established trees and shrubs.

Herbaceous perennials are improving constantly. New cultivars become available for sale. Read catalogs, attend winter study classes on perennials, or check the newest information by computer to stay up-to-date. Exotic plants found world-wide or cultivars developed by breeders continue to enhance our choices.

PLANTING

Weather makes planting this month impossible throughout Washington and Oregon. Avoid walking or digging on frozen ground or on ground that's sodden from winter rains.

CARE

Zones 5-6: Plants may "frost heave," emerge out of the ground because of alternate freezing and thawing. This exposes roots to damaging freezing temperatures. If you have not covered the most vulnerable plants with mulch or evergreen boughs, do that now, treading the ground as little as possible. Hope for snow, which is an excellent insulator.

Take time this month to research what mulch is available in your area because mulches differ regionally. For upcoming spring mulching, choose mulch with a fine texture such as composted yard waste or shredded leaves or even pine needles. "Fertile" mulch with animal manure additve, such as aged dairy manure mixed with com-

post, also adds nutrients to the plants. These finer-textured mulches are pleasant to spread and look finished when tucked around plants. They also break down as the season progresses and add to soil tilth. Unfortunately, seeds dropping or blowing onto their surface will germinate rapidly. This may be welcomed if you want extra plants from your perennials, but it's bothersome when the newcomer is a weed. However, the

There are many mulch options including straw, shredded leaves, pine straw, and grass clippings. Evergreen boughs can also be used.

texture of fertile mulch makes the weeds easy to pull when young.

Although the size of the mulch remains a matter of personal taste, chunky mulches like big of bark or shredded tree prunings may not encourage thriving growth for flowering and foliage plants like herbaceous perennials. They will be fine tucked around shrub, tree, and ground cover areas.

WATERING

No watering this month. Check under eaves and anywhere plants may be tucked away from normal rainfall to be sure they are receiving moisture. Indoors, water any tender perennials being wintered over.

FERTILIZING

No fertilizing this month.

PRUNING

Zones 5-6: Frozen ground prevents pruning. Wait until spring to trim back the older leaves left over the crowns. Brown leaves help to insulate plants when snow is scarce.

Zones 7-9: Trimming back dead leaves from perennial plants on a mild January day is fine, but if weather fails to cooperate, the task can wait until February.

Epimedium spp.: **Bishop's hat** should be trimmed this late month or in earliest February before new growth emerges. Old leaves resemble torn vinyl; carefully cut them back but watch for new, small, soft foliage. Trim carefully. In March, plants will look renewed with a whole new set of leaves setting off their small spring flowers.

PROBLEMS

Zones 7-9: Slugs! Slugs invade crowns of *Delphinium*, *Iris*, *Pulmonaria*, and *Brunnera* now when leaf stalks have grown only an inch or even less. If winter weather stays freezing, this is less likely to happen, but it's necessary to check closely and pluck out the offenders.

Some gardeners in Zones 7 to 9 rake away mulches during late winter to remove cozy spots where slugs hide. Many plants need the mulch for protection now. But if you're growing *Delphinium*, mulch isn't needed because most are hardy to Zone 3 (with winter temperatures of 30 degrees F.) Temperatures in Zones 7 to 9 actually stay mild enough in winter to aid early growth on *Delphinium*, months before their flowering in June.

EASY CLIPPING

Grooming or pruning herbaceous perennials goes more easily when you understand their different growth habits:

1. Fully herbaceous perennials die to the ground and come back from a "crown" just above the roots. Their stems become brittle, stop growing, and don't show a "green" inner core when broken. Remove all old stems without chopping new emerging stems beneath the dead bits.

2. In warmer areas, some herbaceous perennials become nearly "evergreen," with foliage staying lively through winter. In late spring, pull out dead leaves on **coast iris**, (*Iris douglasiana*) and allow new foliage to fill in. Trim evergreen **daylilies** (*Hemerocallis* spp.) all the way to the ground.

FEBRUARY

PERENNIALS & ORNAMENTAL GRASSES

 PLANNING

Contemplate your existing garden. Does it have bare spots requiring ground cover, or vines, or perennial flowers? Do you want a cutting garden where you can gather flowers for the house?

Plan for interior paths within planting areas for passage into and out of the garden. Otherwise, working among herbaceous perennials might be difficult, especially when fully grown. Making working space can be simple: a few flat stones, some mulch spread to make a path, or small bricks laid over the soil. Spring planting will be simplified by easier access.

 PLANTING

All zones: No planting this month

 CARE

All zones: Keep mulch and evergreen boughs over perennials this month

Zones 7-9: Perennial plant growth will often start before the end of February, especially on the earlier flowering types. Increasingly move away mulch as plants increasingly grow. If a hard freeze is predicted, lay an old bedsheet, spun-bonded garden cloth (sold as Reemay and other names), or burlap bags over the tender emerging plants for a night or two. Remove this during the day as temperatures moderate.

Mulch will be invaluable for weed management and moisture retention. Some gardeners—particularly those growing warm-temperature plants including vegetables—do their spring renewal mulching after the soil warms. In Zones 7 to 9 along coastal areas, summer temperatures stay cooler than they do inland, even though the inland areas have colder winters. If your garden is situated in a coastal area, allow sun to warm the soil until May or even June before applying another two to three inches of mulch.

Try to stay off of frozen or soggy soil, especially if it's clay; it will be harder to work later on. To check the composition of soil, put a handful in a quart jar. Fill up the jar with water, adding a teaspoon of dish soap. Shake vigorously As the water and soil mix settles, you will see layers of different texture: pebbly sands, fine sand, and brownish silt or silt loam. The finest grayish or bluish particles are clay. Floating on top may be organic material such as bits of leaf mold or composted bits. (Settling may require a few days.) Of course, if the soil clings to boots in globs and warms slowly in spring, you'll already have identified a clay component. (See the General Introduction for more material on soils and soil management.)

 WATERING

All zones: Check perennials under eaves to be sure they're damp. Also check on any perennials sowed from seed last fall. If rain is scarce in February, probe the soil around emerging perennializing bulbs to make sure roots are damp.

Feather reed grass

Blue fescue

Similarly, tug low clumping **blue fescue** (*Festuca glauca*); it pulls out like fur tufts. If they've stayed in good color all winter, lift the edges to find last year's dead growth where they touch the ground and pull that out. If they are brown, trim to the ground.

Hardy ferns: The native evergreen **sword fern** (*Polystichum munitum*) and other hardy ferns need clipping in earliest spring. Trim off all the foliage from previous years. Without this attention, the plant acquires a misshapen ground-level collar of dead foliage. Before trimming, spread the old fronds gently to see curled crosiers near the crown. These will unfurl into new leaves. Protect those when cutting.

FERTILIZING

Zones 5-6: No fertilizing until March.

Zones 7-9: If weather allows in late February, sprinkle granulated fertilizer on the perennials.

GROOMING

Ornamental grasses:

All zones: Trim back or groom all ornamental grasses.

Tallest types: On warm-season grasses such as six-foot **feather reed grass** (*Calamagrostis* x *acutiflora*), and **eulalia** (*Miscanthus sinensis*) cut down to one foot. Huge clumps are better managed if lassoed by rope into pillar shapes before cutting.

Smaller types: Prune to four to six inches, removing the dead grass blades and allowing for March's new foliage.

Grooming only: The cool-weather grasses, which grow well in spring and set seeds before heat arrives, will fill in quickly early in the season. In Zones 7 to 9, some need only minor grooming if they've kept their foliage color. Many cool-weather grasses, such as **blue oat grass** (*Helictotrichon sempervirens*) maintain some leaf color through winter and require tugging out dead foliage rather than cutting to make room for the new. These plants cycle foliage through several seasons rather than having it go dormant all at once.

PROBLEMS

All zones: By the end of February, spring weeds germinate. Winter weeds go to seed now through March. Yank troublemakers like chickweed and shotweed before they spread trouble all over the garden.

MARCH

PERENNIALS & ORNAMENTAL GRASSES

PLANNING

Review what is in the garden now looking for what has survived winter. What do you want and need? Make lists to take to nurseries and garden sales. Impulsive discoveries can be wonderful, but finding your "must-have" is best.

PLANTING

When the perennials you've ordered from catalogs arrive they are ready to grow and need immediate care. Open the boxes and check over the order. Discrepancies or plant damage need prompt reporting to the company. Look on the shipping documents for any special handling instructions.

Ideally, you'll plant them as soon as possible in their chosen garden place. They can stay in packages opened at the top to admit air only for a day or two.

If you can't plant, remove the plants from their packing bags. Shake off the packing material. Settle them in appropriately sized pots with potting soil and water well. In case of plant arrival during inclement weather, pot them up and keep them in a sheltered outdoor place. If below freezing weather persists, move

them to an unheated garage or basement. They won't need light for a few days. But for a long period of storage—a week or more—provide light from overhead fluorescent tubes.

All zones: Plant groups according to their individual water needs. Sufficient irrigation will be the main task of the summer once they're actively growing. Check with nurseries when selecting plants to determine their needs.

Zones 7 to 9: March is the opportune month to make layout or plant changes. Move the plants to more suitable spots as roots stir into growth and have small foliage. They'll recover faster from changes made now than they would from later transplanting. In fact, many perennials dislike summer transplanting when in full growth.

CARE

All zones: In early spring, divide crowded perennials to increase them. Although plants can be divided in fall in warmer zones, spring suits all zones, and most plants. (See September for dividing **peonies**).

Zones 4-6: Remove winter protective coverings. Gradually move away the mulch in the coldest areas, keeping some extra

sheets or burlap close by to cover plants in case of a sudden freeze.

WATERING

Set up soaker hoses to make watering chores easier. It's simpler to work with watering systems after plants have been installed or divided. Most herbaceous perennials, especially those with robust blooms and foliage, require more water during their growing season than our region provides. A simple system with a faucet timer will work, but be certain that all plants in the bed are receiving sufficient water to root depth.

Check sprinkler or bubbler head placement so that plants don't get skipped; ensure performance now before you'll need to rely on it in the dry season.

FERTILIZING

Zones 4-6: Fertilize using the instructions for warmer zones, but do it after all winter protection has been removed in late March to mid-April.

Zones 7-9: Fertilize bulbs when they are between two and four inches tall.

Late February or early March, fertilize all emerging perennials with a moderate nitrogen formula like a 9-6-6 or 5-10-10. Fertilize once a season when the ground is damp. Water after the application (or fertilize happily during a light rain!). Using a fertile mulch in spring (containing composted animal manure) will also keep perennials growing well.

PRUNING

All zones: Clear away last year's foliage from plants, stepping carefully to avoid emerging shoots. Keep any diseased foliage out of compost.

Some perennials with woody branches are "sub-shrubs," meaning their woody structure persists, and among these are herbs like **lavender** and **rosemary**. These can be evergreen (keeping foliage through winter) in Zones 7 to 9, although many are too tender for Zones 5 to 6. They grow new leaves from the existing wood. Trim them gently, shearing lightly to shape and take off last year's spent flowers. (See July for care of **lavender**.)

PROBLEMS

All zones: Slug control! **Delphinium** stalks may be in danger.

BE CAREFUL ABOUT GARDEN BULLIES

Observe whether plants become unfriendly, space-grabbing hogs in the garden. Delicate plants can be overtaken by more rugged, vigorous types. They may be good looking, but are they badly behaved? A few notorious ones include **plume poppy** (*Macleaya cordata*), **Welsh poppy** (*Meconopsis cambrica*), and **yellow archangel** (*Lamium galeobdolon*).

Remove mulch from delphinium and use iron phosphate slug bait or beer traps. When delphinium gets two feet tall, they toughen up and slug damage diminishes, though it doesn't disappear.

Carefully prune any remaining perennials with diseased leaves that you didn't in the fall. Don't compost diseased foliage.

Perennial weeds are among the worst invaders of perennial gardens. Dandelion, bindweed, or quackgrass interfere seriously with garden success. If possible, dig out the roots. Spot treat returning pests with a registered herbicide, painting it on with a small brush. For large infestations, it's necessary to remove the desired perennials and treat the weeds with a registered herbicide or cover the site with cardboard and deep mulch for a year.

For weed problems, check with trained Master Gardeners from OSU or WSU Extension Offices. Don't select a chemical control without knowing the weed's type, habit, and name.

Lavender

APRIL
PERENNIALS & ORNAMENTAL GRASSES

 PLANNING

Will summer winds blow through your perennials? If so, find perennials that are "low to the ground." Many wonderful cultivars grow to lower profiles. **Asiatic lilies**, at two to three feet, manage wind better than the six- to seven-foot hybrid **Oriental lilies**. **Larkspur** (annual flowers) substitute nicely for taller **delphinium**. Or select compact perennial delphinium 'Summer Blues'. Many of these also suit smaller garden spaces.

Wind stress can reduce soil moisture, especially during summer. Where winds and high temperatures prevail during summer choose herbaceous perennials adapted to dry conditions.

 PLANTING

All zones: Plant herbaceous perennials before fully grown in moist soils. when soils. Work carefully around older plants expanding their leaves now. In Zones 4 to 6, it's not too late to divide overcrowded perennials.

If catalog orders arrive bare root, without soil over the roots, soak them briefly (one or two hours) in tepid water or follow any instructions sent with the plants. Plant in their chosen gar-den spot or containers and wait for appropriate planting time. (See March for handling plants shipments.)

Zones 7-9: As soil warms plant summer-blooming bulbs, which go directly into soil and don't need indoor starting. **Crocosmia, agapanthus,** and **dahlias** can go in the garden or containers now.

 CARE

All zones: Set supports or stakes now while plants are small or when planting bulbs. Staking or support is needed for tall plants, like the larger **lilies**, or for those with weak stems and/or top-heavy ample flowers, like herbaceous **peonies**.

Use bamboo poles, slender wood poles, metal poles, or plastic stakes for plants with single stems. The stake should be about three-quarters the height of the plant's final size. Tie the plant stem as it grows, using flexible plastic or string ties. When staking large **lilies**, don't pierce the lily bulb.

Bushy or floppy plants require short stakes surrounding it— three or four short stakes with crisscrossed string will support well. Commercial wire hoops and supports also work.

 WATERING

All zones: Set soaker hoses or check the irrigation system for all garden areas. Watering becomes necessary from mid-May through September, or even into October, throughout our region. The systems install more easily when plants are still small.

 FERTILIZING

All zones: If you have not done so in March, fertilize plants in active growth once this spring using a low-nitrogen formula like a 5-10-10. If your garden is near a water source or aquifer, apply fertilizer moderately, especially not during a rainstorm when granules can wash off. Herbaceous perennials generally thrive on moderate to low levels of fertilizer, particularly if you've applied fertile mulch (see February).

"Waterwise" plants such as herbs, **artemisia**, and **yarrow** become floppy and unattractive if overfertilized. If the herb garden grows well and plants look strong, no fertilizer is needed.

Caution: Do not fertilize newly divided plants until they show new leaves, the sign that the roots can take in nutrients.

Be sure to fertilize around clumps of emerging **Siberian iris** and **German iris** (*Iris germanica*) using 5-10-10 or similar fertilizer.

Fertilize all spring-blooming bulb clumps during or just after bloom to help with formation of flower embryos for next year. Use a 9-6-6 (or similar) bulb fertilizer, following instructions on the package. Water granular fertilizers into the soil using a gentle spray.

 GROOMING

Prune to clean up damaged plants. Don't put diseased plants in the compost.

 PROBLEMS

Aphids hatch as the plants begin growth. Once active leaf formation starts, they're vigorous and hungry. As leaves mature, plants endure a certain amount of aphid activity, but aphids can damage young leaves. Wash them off with a gentle stream of water, encourage beneficial insects, and use mild insecticidal soap for the worst infestations.

Avoid toxic insecticides that harm ladybugs, lacewings, and other beneficial predators.

FLOWERS CAN ATTRACT BENEFICIAL INSECTS

To help increase the "good guys," add a variety of flowering plants. **Angelica, fennel, dill,** and **yarrow,** as well as **catnip, rue, thyme,** and **alyssum,** can all provide nectar for numbers of helpful insects.

If you've planted handsome perennial ground covers, they offer great hiding places for slugs. Trim foliage a bit above ground and avoid laying fresh mulch until plants finish their spring growth and soil dries a little. Handpicking, beer in traps or saucers, and mild baits containing iron phosphate will all help. Lift the dangling foliage on brick or rock walls to find more slug hiding spots.

Place a wet board or wet newspaper on the ground and checking under it in early evening or morning for slug invaders. Check underneath pots and on decks and patios. Vigilance helps because no single system will manage slugs.

All zones: **Peonies** succumb to fungal botrytis, especially west of the mountains. Stems will show blackening.

Clean up all dead stems if that hasn't been done. Watch emerging foliage for signs of black patches.

Fennel

MAY

PERENNIALS & ORNAMENTAL GRASSES

PLANNING

Photograph or sketch the garden to recall its spring glories for future planning. Look at spring bulbs. Could next year's planting use some "perennial disguise" at their feet? These have been referred to as "shoes and socks," disguising the ankles of the bulbs with perennials. You can install a gentle edge in front of the bulb plantings. These "edgers" help subdue the effect of bulbs turning brown and returning to dormancy. **Lady's mantle** (*Alchemilla mollis*), **perennial candytuft** (*Iberis sempervirens*), and **prostrate rosemary** (*Rosmarinus officinalis* Prostratus Group) clothe garden margins nicely.

PLANTING

Zones 4-6: May days are ideal for planting new perennials from pots and divisions. Settle in those purchased and water thoroughly after each planting. Perennials plant best at three to five inches high. But they can adapt at other heights.

Zones 7-9: As the garden fills with foliage, buy and add plants for late summer and fall color: **yarrow, black-eyed Susan** (*Rudbeckia* spp.), **Japanese anemone** (*Anemone japonica*), and **white boltonia** (*Boltonia asteroides*).

CARE

All zones: After you've tidied, divided, planted, fertilized, and watered, apply "finishing" mulch. Once soil warms a bit and plants are in growth, mulch is the last touch. Keep mulch two to three inches deep and don't apply it over the growing crowns. Also, don't apply mulch over a dry soil. (This can be early April in Zones 7 to 9, depending on spring weather.)

Zones 4-6: Stake (or support with twigs or metal) emerging **delphinium, peonies**, *Helenium*, *Asters*, and other potential floppers.

WATERING

Perennials planted—or divided—during spring will need careful watering throughout the summer. Many, such as the waterwise *Artemisia* and most herbs, require less irrigation in following years once their root systems are established.

FERTILIZING

All zones: Fertilize when plants show new growth. Do this in May only if you have not done it earlier in the year. One spring application is enough for perennials if soil is also enriched with fertile mulch.

Zones 7-9: Native soils west of the Cascades in both Washington and Oregon tend to have an acidic pH. Soil amendments such as compost can change the acidity, but it's not always necessary to add lime when growing perennials. For example, **peonies, German iris, delphinium, dianthus,** and perennial **baby's breath** prefer soils at the 6.5 or higher pH range. If they are growing fine, no action will be needed. Some Westside growers mulch sensitive plants with limestone chips to provide a very slow drip of lime. Consider testing your soil.

Inland gardens, east of the Cascades, generally have neutral pH (7.0) rather than acidic. No lime of any kind is needed to grow lime-loving plants effectively.

PRUNING

Zones 4-6: Clean up old perennial foliage as summer-blooming plants grow. Do this early in the month. You'll see new growth starting up in the centers of plants.

All zones: As spring bulbs finish blooming, allow leaves to die back without interference. **Snowdrops, crocuses, hyacinths,** and **tulips** need thoroughly brown leaves, indicating that the bulb has ripened. All **daffodils** (*Narcissus* spp.) may be cut back six to seven weeks after bloom finishes.

All zones: Trim back foliage of spring-blooming perennials. Perennial **candytuft** (*Iberis* spp.), **rock cress** (*Arabis* and *Aubrieta* spp.), and **ground cover phlox** will form renewed fresh foliage after dead flowers are removed, providing a cleaner summer appearance. All of these take shearing with hedge trimmers.

Pinching: Remove the top three inches of growth from fall blooming **asters** and **chrysanthemums** to make the plants bushier. The British say: "Pinch your Mum on Mother's Day and the Fourth of July." Two pinches will help the fall plants.

Summer bloomers like **beebalm** (*Monarda* spp.) and **tall phlox** (*Phlox* spp.) benefit from one pinch.

LATE RISERS

Some perennials like **hosta** and **lilies** emerge from the ground later than others. Be sure to mark their locations so that you don't accidentally plant another treasure on top of them.

 PROBLEMS

Now and in June, look for spittlebugs, tiny green nymphs of insects hidden inside wads of white froth. Simply wash them off plants. They aren't generally harmful (except on **strawberries**), but their numbers can build up, reducing the attractiveness of the garden. Check **columbine, daisies,** and **iris,** which spittlebugs seem to favor.

Slugs reach their peak in late April and May just as all foliage is crisp and delectable (see April). The plants most bothered by slugs include **hosta, iris** (all

types), **true lilies** (*Lilium* spp.), and **day lilies** (*Hemerocallis* spp.).

Ants wander onto **peonies** as they develop. People sometimes say "the ants make the peonies bloom," but the ants have just arrived for the sticky, sweet residue on the buds. When picking peonies for bouquets, swish the flowers in a bucket of water—outside—to remove ants. They do not harm the peonies, but they alarm dinner guests.

Keep weeding. Avoid using pre-emergent herbicides; they can stop annual and perennial seed germination. Some types containing the chemical dichlobenil damage emerging bulb shoots and new perennial roots.

Pinch back mums to develop bushier plants with more flowers.

JUNE
PERENNIALS & ORNAMENTAL GRASSES

 PLANNING

Photograph the color and layout of the June garden. Spring and early summer flowers like **campanula, columbine, iris, Oriental poppies,** and **lupine** bloom in one splendid burst. Many will stay in blossom for three weeks or so, making June a garden celebration. Keeping a calendar of "first and last" bloom on individual perennials will be useful.

 PLANTING

All zones: Planting is more difficult this month because of all the plant growth. If you're new to growing herbaceous perennial flowers, observe how large the plants can become even in their first year. Take note of crowded plants and move them in earliest fall. The ultimate size of these plants depends on soil type, light availability, and the amount of water provided.

Heat-loving, non-hardy plants started indoors early this spring can move outdoors now.

If you do find perennials in nurseries this month, plant them where you see a gap, treading carefully to protect existing plants. **Peonies** may be sold by nurseries in bloom this month. Leave the plant in its nursery pot and dig a hole to accommodate the pot and the plant in the garden. In fall, when the plant loses its leaves and goes dormant, take it out of the pot and plant it. Do not disturb the roots in summer.

 CARE

If the heaviest flowering of the perennial plants have not been staked, do this now, as early as possible in the month. The larger the plant is when staked, the greater the chance of crushing or damaging leaves and stems.

Bananas (*Musa* spp.), tender **tropical ferns,** and **caladium** prosper best when night temperatures stay above 60 degrees F.

Inland summer temperatures, warmer than those on the coast, suit these tender plants perfectly if they can be sheltered from drying winds.

 WATERING

Gauge the effect of water stress. Some herbaceous perennials, such as tough **shasta daisies,** recover well after leaf wilt. Others, especially the water-lovers like *Astilbe* and *Ligularia,* may collapse to the ground in an approximation of fainting. Continual water stress can kill some plants.

All zones: Watering will be the main task for the summer garden. Apply enough water to wet plant roots thoroughly. Allow the top of the mulch to dry one to two inches down. Watering once a week should work for most gardens, unless heat accompanies lack of rain. Determine whether plants need water by probing the root zone and checking for moisture.

 FERTILIZING

If fertilized earlier in spring, most perennial plants won't need any fertilizer now, except **dahlias** and **delphinium** which benefit from a low-nitrogen fertilizer boost six weeks after the first application.

GROOMING

All zones: Begin deadheading, the practice of removing flower heads from stems when they finish blooming. Many perennials bloom longer and stay more attractive if they don't go to seed. Removing the first spent flower will result in new side shoots and more bloom on **campanulas, coreopsis, day lilies, lupine, lavender, sages** and many others.

Trim back any spring bloomers that are finished. Some plants, such as **columbine**, produce seeds freely and will plant themselves in corners and cracks. Columbine seedlings aren't always the same color as their parent plants.

Once established, herb gardens produce far more than any one gardener will need. Tidy up **thyme** by selecting the longest shoots to give as small gifts. **Rosemary** varies in its productivity depend on the zone. In Zones 5 to 6 it needs winter protection, taken indoors for the freezing season. A few cultivars of including 'Madeline Hill', may survive to -10 degrees F. But in Zones 7 to 9 they have no weather problems. The larger cultivars can grow to eight-foot bushes and need clipping to keep them neat.

Pick up and stake, or prune off, vigorous branches that grow over neighboring plants now.

PROBLEMS

Are your **peonies** failing to bloom but producing healthy leaves? They may be too young; herbaceous peonies take at least two to three years to bloom after planting. If the "eye," or growing point, is deeper than one to two inches below the soil, the plant will look fine but will not bud. If yours is planted too deep, allow it to grow normally this summer.

GETTING A SECOND WIND

Some perennials, when cut back just after bloom, produce new stems with secondary flowers later in the summer. **Penstemon**, hybrid **foxglove** cultivars, and **delphinium** will offer fresh flowers on new stems. Often the repeat flower isn't as tall or broad as the original but is still attractive.

Dig it and reset it in September or October.

Slugs continue their ravaging, but it is less noticeable as plants get tougher through summer.

The columbine sawfly larvae obviously goes for the **columbine**, which can look terrific one moment and skeletal the next. Cut out all affected foliage, preferably when you see the critters. (They are a quarter-inch long and the exact green of fresh columbine foliage.) New foliage will come up and fill in the spot.

Tall **German iris** can get leaf spot with brown blotches on the older leaves. Cut these out of the plant. Apply a fungicide like sulfur (but don't use a chemical until you have precise identification of the problem).

Foxglove

JULY
PERENNIALS & ORNAMENTAL GRASSES

PLANNING

Browse tempting sales at nurseries. You may bring home some plant bargains. Since this isn't a good month to add small plants to the perennial garden, grow them in containers. Buy your plants intentionally, for dry, moist, or damp conditions.

Some plants can manage with little irrigation once established and may do fine with water twice a month in summer. Excellent species and cultivars available to enhance the low water-use garden include **yarrow** (*Achillea* spp.), various **artemisias** (*Artemisia* 'Powis Castle' holds up well), **coreopsis** (*Coreopsis verticillata* 'Moonbeam'), **cottage** and **cheddar pinks** (*Dianthus plumarius* and *D. gratianopolitanus*), **purple coneflower** (*Echinacea purpurea*), and **sun rose** (*Helianthemum* spp.). During their first two summers, they need deep watering every ten days until root establishment.

Moist or Damp Conditions: Perhaps you have a pond or a spot that stays damp year round. If you can provide sufficient water to keep the area thoroughly moist throughout summer, choose **astilbes** in red, pink, or white (*Astilbe* spp.), **filipendula** sometimes called Queen of the Prairie (*Filipendula rubra* 'Venusta'),

Coreopsis is a great water-wise plant; this one is 'Moonbeam'.

ligularia (*Ligularia dentata* 'Desdemona'), and **globe flower** (*Trollius europaeus*).

PLANTING

To install perennials brought home now, choose big containers, at least twelve inches across, to allow enough root room. Big black nursery pots work well, though lacking elegance. They provide good temporary storage and room to grow. But be sure to keep anything in a black plastic pot wrapped with burlap or can-

vas. If hot sun strikes the plastic, roots can cook. Provide ample drainage for the new plants.

Set four-inch plants about four inches apart; keep them watered well. They have received fertilizer at the nursery, but will need fertilizer when new growth commences.

CARE

Plants such as **delphinium** may require tying or re-staking.

WATERING

Continue watering and soaking perennials to the root depth once a week, or often enough to keep them from moisture stress. Random sprinkling or waving the hose about above plants doesn't have the same beneficial effect.

Reminder: Even plants notoriously "waterwise" are susceptible to suffer, stress out, and even die when they are newly planted or exposed to severe conditions in the hottest months of summer.

FERTILIZING

Do not fertilize **chrysanthemums** after July. **Delphinium, dahlias,** and **roses** can use one last application early this month. Use the same fertilizer you've previously applied.

Be more generous with the tropicals. Fertilize tropical tender plants and all perennials in containers—except those just installed—once a month through summer.

PRUNING

Fall blooming plants, such as **chrysanthemums** and **asters** grow sturdier flowers and bushes if pinched back. Remove about three inches of their growing tips.

Lilies: When bloom finishes, cut back to the first leaf below the flower. All lilies must keep green foliage intact until brown and crisp and fully dormant in fall.

Lavender: For sachet and potpourri, the scented oils preserve best if flowers are gathered just as the buds show color before they open.

A few summer bloomers such as **hardy geraniums** and **catnip** (*Nepeta* 'Six Hills Giant') will set flowers again if sheared now. Cut off all blooms and leave four to six inches of foliage. Water them after cutting back to assist in new flower formation.

PROBLEMS

Hollyhocks, glorious bloomers, can increasingly suffer from rust throughout summer. A few cultivars seem less rust-prone, but even with rust-resistant types it's a problem, especially in damper areas. Although the "black" or dark-flowered types have been popular, it's the old-fashioned pastels that do better. Look for yellow *Alcea rugosa* or **fig-leaved hollyhock** in pink, yellow, or white (*Alcea ficifolia*).

Check your nursery and catalogs for herbaceous perennials resistant to powdery mildew that appears in midsummer and continues into fall. "Resistance" means they'll show less damage or get symptoms less heavily.

For all plants, resistant or not, planting in sunlight with good air circulation reduces powdery mildew. Prune out just a few affected leaves or wash the plant with water.

Resistant plants:

Phlox: white *Phlox carolina* 'Miss Lingard'; *P. paniculata* 'David'—both white and fragrant, 'Orange Perfection', and 'Starfire')

Beebalm: *Monarda didyma* 'Purple Mildew Resistant' and 'Rose Queen'

Roses: *Rosa rugosa* and its cultivars

EARLY DORMANCY OF SPRING AND SUMMER BLOOMERS

Early blooming perennials disappear this month, or even sooner. You'll discover foliage dying back on **jack in the pulpit** (*Arum italicum*), **true poppies** (*Papaver orientale*), and on native and cultivated **bleeding heart** (*Dicentra* spp.). The plants simply turn yellow and lie down on the ground. This is normal.

Other plants may bloom more sparsely when stressed by hot, dry weather. July, August, and September put strain on plants.

AUGUST
PERENNIALS & ORNAMENTAL GRASSES

 PLANNING

Visit gardens now to get ideas for late summer garden plantings. August finds gardens stressed by hot weather and often lacking in flowers—so if you discover a cleverly designed and attractive one, take photos. Container plantings and late summer bloomers like **asters** will help liven up the scene. Ornamental grasses—especially the warm weather grasses like *Miscanthus* and *Calamagrostis* shine this month, with plumes of bloom that haven't yet turned brown.

Autumn work, planned now, will carry the herbaceous perennial garden plants over winter and into their next blooming season. Make notes of which plants you wish to move in early September when the weather cools.

Review last spring's photographs of hardy bulbs. Look at the garden now to consider which ones you'll add this fall and where they will look best.

Drying perennial flowers for bouquets: **quaking grass** (*Briza media*), **globe thistle** (*Echinops* spp.), **statice** (*Limonium* spp.), **pincushion flower** (*Scabiosa* spp.), **strawflower** (*Helichrysum bracteatum*), and **yarrow** (*Achillea* spp.) are among the types of flowers that preserve well if picked just as flowers show color. Pick well formed flowers, strip off all foliage, and bundle them for hanging upside down in a dark, dry place. If you find that making dried bouquets pleases you, plan to add perennial plants that expand your range of dried flowers next year.

Hang flowers upside down to dry.

 PLANTING

Heat and dry weather combine to make August nearly impossible for planting in all zones.

 CARE

All zones: **German iris** (with rhizomes) will have finished their flowering, unless you have a culti- var that reblooms quite late such as white iris 'Immortality' (to Zone 3) or blue-purple 'Recurring Dream'. Rebloomers (also called "remontant") can send up new stalks through August, September, and October, so this type should not be divided now. When clumps get crowded and bloom less freely, usually after four years, divide the rebloomers in August with other **German iris** types. Divide spring-blooming perennials now and in September.

Water them carefully and thoroughly when resetting; cover roots with mulch to protect them from drying winds and heat.

Zones 5-6: In the coldest areas, **iris** need to be established with new roots before freezing weather and should be moved by mid-August. (See Bulbs on page 66.) Water thoroughly after dividing, and watch for new growth, keeping plants moist. If you are planting in a scorching, full sun area, mulch lightly over the spot before planting.

Zones 7-9: Pacific Coast **iris** (*Iris douglasiana* and their cultivars) will stay nearly evergreen through winter but can be divided now if you're careful, with clumps carefully split apart and reset in shade or semi-shade, in good soil.

Weeding continues. No matter how dry the soil or hot the day, weeds find a way to multiply.

GROOMING

Lavender that finished blooming needs light shearing to remove flower stems. Though not as fragrant as earlier, they still carry fresh scent. Do not cut deeply into the branch wood but remove only the flower stems and enough leaf to reshape the plants.

Continue to deadhead spent flowers of **coneflower, Shasta daisy, cosmos,** and **hardy geraniums**. If you haven't sheared off flowers of **catmint** (*Nepeta mussini*), cut them back now.

Cutting to ground now? The tattered foliage of some plants, like **daylilies** (*Hemerocallis* spp. and cultivars), **Siberian iris** (*Iris sibirica*), and **lady's mantle** (*Alchemilla mollis*), can be cut back now if that suits your own garden sense of tidiness, or it can be allowed to remain until early spring. Some gardeners remove the most unattractive bits and allow the rest to go on (a compromise between doing nothing and cutting the plant off entirely). If the perennial is only marginally hardy in your area (say, a Zone 6 plant in Zone 5),

leave the foliage on to provide some winter root protection.

Seedpods? You'll start to see full seed development. **Siberian iris** produces intriguing stalks of seedpods that dry well and can add to winter garden interest or dried flower arrangements.

WATERING

Some fall blooming plants won't bud up well unless watered. These include **asters, chrysanthemum,** and **dahlias**. Allowing dahlias to dry out causes them to stop setting buds.

Pay attention to watering any plants that were newly installed this year or have been divided or transplanted. Many herbaceous perennials develop sturdy root systems over time, but their first year requires extra water to allow roots to expand.

General garden watering continues; check the soil to make sure roots receive water.

In the herb garden, woody, gray-leaved herbs such as **lavender** and **rosemary** may need watering only once every three weeks; soft-leaved herbs like

mint, oregano, and **catnip** need once a week watering.

FERTILIZING

Delphinium can use one more booster fertilizer this month. Use a liquid formula, with a moderate level of nitrogen (5 to 6 percent). Granular fertilizers require water to wash them into the roots, so do not apply them on dry soil and water after applying.

Do not fertilize other plants; strange as it seems, in this hot month, plants begin now to alter their growth and rhythm toward "hardening off" for winter. Growth slows, and many perennials start into dormancy.

PROBLEMS

Powdery mildew affects many herbaceous perennials, as well as shrubby plants, again this month, intensifying with hot days and cooler night temperatures, especially west of the Cascades. Check July for more information; a registered fungicide can help on vulnerable perennials or vegetables. If the plant is annual and about finish its life cycle, treatment isn't necessary. Simply remove it from the garden. Treatment is also unnecessary for **deciduous azaleas** that will soon drop the affected leaves.

DID YOU KNOW?

Birds appreciate seedheads on perennial flowers. Goldfinches and chickadees will gather for **dahlia,** annual **sunflower,** and **daisy** seeds. As will the squirrels! You may wish to allow some plants to set seeds for bird attraction.

September

PERENNIALS & ORNAMENTAL GRASSES

 PLANNING

Photograph the garden again this month to note the full expanse of completely grown plants. Draw a map of locations for planting spring bulbs—a simple pencil sketch will assist in planning. If you've planted bulbs previously, get out the photos and drawings to recall where last year's bulb plantings are.

Map plants that require moving or dividing; in Zones 7 to 9 this can be done throughout the fall; in Zones 4 to 6, finish at least one month before hard freezes to allow roots to settle and grow well before they're halted by winter.

 PLANTING

All zones: Nurseries will carry an excellent variety of hardy perennials this month; select and plant by early October in the coldest zones, and by mid-November in Zones 7 to 9.

Zones 5-6: Complete your planting of spring-blooming, hardy bulbs, tucking them into gaps between perennials or perennial ground covers. Or transplant rooted ground cover perennials over them. When planting in September—whether bulbs or perennials—dig the required hole then fill it with water. Allow the water to drain out. This assures that emerging bulb or perennial roots will meet damp soil. Often at this time of year, soil has become deeply dry and doesn't dampen well when watered from above alone. Mark the edge of planted areas with small twigs or popsicle sticks to prevent accidental disturbance later.

Zones 7-9: Seeds of very hardy perennials can be sown in a nursery bed outdoors early this month (as well as in spring).

 CARE

Zones 5-6: Preparation for cold weather: Gather frost covers (sheets, clothes, or burlap bags) to cover perennials if a sudden early frost threatens. Keeping them protected during the first frosts will allow enjoyment in warm days that often follow initial spells of cold.

 GROOMING

Perennials can provide seeds or winter protection for birds. **Dahlias**, all the composite flowers like **daisies** and **cosmos**, and clumps of flowering grasses produce edible seeds. If the grass can become invasive from seeding, such as **Mexican feather grass** (*Stipa tenuissima*), do not allow seeds to remain in winter.

Gardeners differ on whether they do or don't cut back perennial foliage in the fall. For gardeners in milder areas desiring a tidy look, spent foliage may be removed between now and November. In coldest zones, dead leaves help provide winter protection to roots, although the same assistance can be provided by mulching. In all zones, remove any foliage that has shown damage from disease.

 WATERING

Watering will be needed this month, even though plants begin to slow their growth for fall and winter. Fall rains often return by month's end but may not.

 FERTILIZING

No fertilizing is needed now.

 PROBLEMS

Plan to clean out any foliage from plants with disease difficulties such as powdery mildew, rust, or botrytis. As leaves fall, clean up and destroy them. Do not compost any diseased plant parts.

Cut **peony** stems to the ground. Don't compost the foliage. The exception is **tree peony**

DIVIDING TO SUCCEED IN MULTIPLYING

Many garden perennials establish well and don't need dividing often. Keep an eye out for crowded clumps, diminishment of bloom (in the case of **lilies** or **iris**), or plants that have simply outgrown their space. The garden will often thrive for three or four years before much division is needed. Spring division suits all zones of our region best, but some plants must be divided in fall. The most demanding are **peonies**.

Herbaceous garden peonies—the kind with leaves that die to the ground in winter—divide and install best in September and October. Look for tubers now, or follow up on orders placed last spring during blooming time. All types of peonies dislike disturbance, so the closer they are to winter dormancy when moved, the better. September is the ideal month for **peony** division or installation in Zones 5 to 6.

Divide **herbaceous peonies** only when the plants are older than four years, and remember that garden peonies can grow for several decades (fifteen to twenty years) without requiring division. Once they begin to grow and bloom, they are best left alone. They do not relish being planted or transplanted.

But circumstances sometimes require division, especially if you are moving a garden or redesigning. Choose a cool fall day when the ground is moist but not soggy wet. Cut back all foliage to the ground when peony foliage has started to die down for winter. Carefully fork up the roots. You'll have a tangle of heavy, crossed tuberous roots slightly thinner in diameter than a garden hose. Spray to remove dirt from the roots. Cut into sections with three to five "eyes" or more. The spots where old foliage emerged, that's an eye. In spring, they will be the pinkish growth points that will be new shoots. Sections with more eyes bloom faster. Do not allow peony divisions to sit in hot sun before planting.

Amend the soil with compost then plant the roots with the eyes one to two inches below the soil surface, no deeper. Set divisions about one foot apart and share extras with fortunate friends.

Division may retard bloom; don't be concerned if their bloom stays sparse for two years after division. Mulch around the plants but only lightly over the crown; remove mulch over the growing area early in spring.

Newly installed **peonies** will also bloom slowly or reluctantly, often until their third or fourth year. Do not fertilize newly planted or divided peonies until growth begins next spring.

Tree peonies, which form permanent woody branches, can be planted in fall. They do not divide well once established. You'll get better results allowing the plant to remain in place, expanding slowly by the year and becoming more beautiful as it grows.

(*Paeonia suffruticosa*), technically a shrubby plant, which grows permanent branches. Do not prune or trim the plant, but do rake up and discard fallen leaves as they drop off.

Spray the peony roots so you can see what needs to be cut when you divide them.

OCTOBER

PERENNIALS & ORNAMENTAL GRASSES

 PLANNING

October gets so busy in all zones while gardeners dash to beat the weather.

Review and mark satisfactory or unsatisfactory perennials. If the plant has had two or three years of trial and remains unsuited to the garden or of a type or color you definitely dislike, remove it while doing fall garden clean up. Sharing and trading with friends is as much fun in fall as in spring.

 PLANTING

Zones 5-6: Planting of both hardy spring-blooming bulbs and herbaceous perennials should be finished about four weeks before hard freezes. If temperatures produce a glancing freeze with mild days, continue to plant in early October.

Zones 7-9: October offers fine conditions for adding new perennials to the garden. In the coldest zones, any new plants should go in at least one month before hard freezes.

Any hardy perennials used as container subjects this year need to be removed in October. If their roots have filled the container, plant the perennials in ground for winter protection. When perenni-

als in pots get too crowded, they cannot receive enough water or nutrients efficiently and may decline. They also become susceptible to winter freezes.

Replant containers with winter-hardy plants like small **evergreens, kale,** and **pansies**. Use large containers to allow extra soil around the roots for winter freeze protection. (About three inches between the edge of the pot and the rootball of the plants will help.)

 CARE

All zones: Rake fallen tree leaves off garden beds. Add them to compost, or shred them and use them directly as mulch. Deciduous leaves packed into plastic bags and dampened, then left for six months to a year, will yield the useful soil amendment called leaf mold. It's not moldy, but rather deliciously dark brown and crumbly. If the leaf supply is too big to deal with easily, consider making at least one new stack of them, inside a wire cage. Wet them thoroughly before stacking and allow them to break down over winter.

Zones 5-6: Prepare a "nursery bed" or spot to receive perennials acquired either small, late in the season, or grown from seed. (This practice can extend even into Zone 7a.) If you don't have

a place in the permanent garden for them until spring, remove them from their display pots or plastic pots and cover them with soil, allowing the crowns to rest just at the soil surface. When the ground freezes, mulch over the entire bed with a light fluffy material like pine needles; four inches will be adequate to protect plants with disturbed roots. This effort is needed because plants in small pots freeze all too readily and the contents are often killed. In the garden, mulch after the ground freezes.

Dig and store **agapanthus, begonias, calla lilies, cannas,**

Store dahlias in peat or a similar material for the winter.

dahlias, and **gladiolus** after the first frost.

GROOMING

On ornamental grasses, allow fall seedheads and tawny foliage to remain for winter display. They stay attractive through the early snows, though they can become flattened in midwinter. Even when tumbled, they respond to weather by moving in wind.

WATERING

Zones 4-6: Fall rains generally return this month, adding welcome moisture to our gardens. If the weather continues dry, water the perennial garden deeply. This is especially necessary so that roots go into winter well hydrated.

FERTILIZING

No fertilizing will be needed this month.

PROBLEMS

Slug eggs: Look for small patches of eggs, about 1/16 inch in diameter, from 40-100 in a stack. They resemble small seed pearls, with a yellowish gray sur-

COLD CAN BRING GOLD, ORANGE, AND MORE

Chrysanthemums: Their scent alone recalls autumn. Their cooperative nature in florist cultivation has these former fall-only plants available year round. Nurseries offer them in colorful bud through the fall months. It's difficult to imagine a Halloween porch display without orange and yellow chrysanthemums. In some gardens, especially in the coldest areas, they are treated as fall annuals and not expected to winter over.

But many cultivars do emerge again in spring, grow through summer, and bud up in fall. They are "short day" plants requiring darker days, with less than twelve hours of light, to set buds. Reliably hardy ones (often cultivars of *Dendranthema* x *grandiflorum*) include the Prophets series from Yoder Brothers. Many of these have girlish names such as the orange 'Vicki', peach 'Zesty Jean', and dark yellow 'Carrie'. Ask your nursery about current selections because their availability and their names will change yearly. A few older hardy cultivars include pink 'Clara Curtis' and rose 'Mei-kyo' (also sold as its look-alike plant 'Anastasia').

In all zones, plant perennial **chrysanthemums** with protection from drying winds. Do not fertilize after July. Give roots good drainage, keeping plants moist in fall (which rain will usually do) but avoiding boggy soil. Do not take stems off the plants after flowering; deadhead them in spring. Mulch over the crowns with a fluffy mulch, like pine needles, when mulching the entire garden.

face. They will be tucked unto mulch, under the edges of rotting wood, or even down in the soil. Scoop them out with a trowel, drop them on a piece of newspaper, and crush them.

Slug eggs may be visible throughout the year, but the heaviest mating periods are in August and September, resulting in clumps of eggs in fall. Getting the eggs now will prevent them from hatching in spring to attack new foliage. Perennials most damaged by slugs include **dahlia, delphinium, hosta, lilies, narcissus, tulips, primroses,** and **pansies**. Observe your own garden records this year to determine which plants have been attacked. Some gardeners, especially on the wetter west side of the Cascades, choose not to grow hostas because of slug depredation.

November

PERENNIALS & ORNAMENTAL GRASSES

 PLANNING

November and December bring welcome quiet to the garden, a good time to ponder its past year. Consider the length of time perennials stay in bloom (two to three weeks may be the average) when selecting new plants or redesigning the garden. Variety in the range of performance of herbaceous perennials helps because some give much longer bloom, including those primarily grown for foliage effects, such as **epimedium** and **hosta**. For lengthy flowering, your garden will get weeks of attractive bloom from **hellebore, echinacea, coreopsis,** most **euphorbia,** hardy **geraniums, phygelius,** and fall blooming **Japanese anemone** 'Honorine Jobert'.

If keeping the garden's water needs met this year has been an uncomfortable chore, consider revising the existing irrigation system. There are no systems that work without the gardener's help, but you may wish to simplify or to add more piping. Rain barrels will fill this month, but the average collection size—about 45 gallons per barrel—doesn't handle summer garden needs. It's good to have the barrels set up, because they fill rapidly from even a scant rain and act as good reminders to conserve water.

 PLANTING

Zones 4-6: Cold weather usually prevents planting this month.

Zones 7-9: Early November is good for getting in all spring-blooming bulbs along with the ground covers over them. Planting them now is not simply a matter of workable soil conditions. Hardy bulbs and corms require a specific "chill period" with weeks of root growth underground, ranging from ten to seventeen weeks depending on the plant. If put in too late, they do not bloom or develop normally.

Some warmer gardens can leave **gladiolus** and **dahlias** in growth all winter.

 CARE

Zones 5-6: Lightweight winter mulch, such as **pine** needles, should go down now where perennials are exposed without protection from walls or fences or buildings. If you've planted, transplanted, or divided, be sure to carefully watch those that are recently planted. Be sure to use mulch across the area. Mulch is essential for those with new, tender roots that are damaged if they freeze and thaw in cycles throughout the winter. They are better off staying solidly frozen.

Aim to finish this covering by mid-November.

Zones 7-9: Weeding needs completing—though it's never fully over. Weed out seedlings of perennial plants if they aren't wanted.

If you do want to nurture a seedling, it can stay in place next to the parent plant until spring and be moved into a permanent place then. Some seedlings, such as those of **hepatica** (*Hepatica americana* and other species) may take two to three years to reach transplantable size.

When time permits, it's also possible to lift and pot herbaceous perennial seedlings and tuck them into a nursery bed with other plants started from seed. If you do not have a cold frame to shelter those plants through winter, it's easy to make a small hoop house with plastic pipe, then covering it with clear plastic. Nurseries and garden centers sell hoops and clips for making these protective covers.

 GROOMING

All zones: Cut off dead stalks of **euphorbia**. Fresh blooms will form for spring.

Zones 7-9: Continue trimming back plants that have completed their flowering. Remove and get rid of any foliage that has become diseased—keep it out of the compost bin.

Do not cut back **hardy fuchsia, kniphofia, hardy cyclamen** (allow all the leaves to remain), **epimedium** (wait until early spring), or ornamental grasses (unless too tall and knocked down by a November wind and rainstorm). Large leaves on **bear's breeches** (*Acanthus mollis*) may stay attractive through winter unless slugs have shredded them.

 WATERING

November rains will soak the garden this month; check all plants tucked under big tree roots or against house foundations where water may not penetrate. Even small conifers can prevent water from reaching adjacent ground covers and flowering perennials.

Check on water needs of any plants in winter cold frames or plastic protectors: They should stay moist from the recirculation of water within the frame, but they still require observation all winter.

 FERTILIZING

No plants require fertilizer this month.

Bear's breeches

 PROBLEMS

Keep any diseased foliage out of the compost. Many disease problems, such as peony botrytis, persist through winter on the affected foliage. Get rid of these.

Zones 5-6: Check plants for frost heaving, when the roots become exposed to air. Push them gently back down and renew the mulch.

If soil becomes saturated with rain, do not walk on it. Compaction of wet soil can lead to loss of air spaces required to supply oxygen to plant roots.

December
PERENNIALS & ORNAMENTAL GRASSES

PLANNING

Catalogs will be enticing this month. Ponder the spots that could benefit from a bit more color, or a larger leaf for show, a broadleaf evergreen ground cover. When ordering for spring delivery, make a note about the eventual placement of the plant. Or add it to your existing sketch of the garden. Ordering plants in winter can be delightful, but it's helpful to have a specific destination for new plants.

Remind yourself when planning new perennials of the fact that they grow slowly. Plants that seemed small during this year will expand during the next. And after two to three years, they'll have reached their full size. For plants that will eventually make low, mounding pools of foliage, order and plant three or more of a type. Then plant them in a triangle and let them fill in.

PLANTING

All zones: Perennials lie nearly dormant this month.

Zones 5-6: It's too cold this month to plant. Withhold planting until mid-March.

Zones 7-9: Ground cover perennials in containers can be planted on milder days

CARE

If mulch still awaits spreading, do it now. Soil will be frozen in Zones 5 to 6 and growing cold in 7 to 9. Don't bury the center crowns of the plants.

Use evergreen boughs from holiday decorations to add a layer of protection over the most tender perennials. Their coverage can prevent damage in coldest exposed areas.

Zones 7-9: Watch for emerging spring bulbs and do not leave the evergreens piled over them. The garden may show slight inch-high leaves of **crocus, snowdrop, muscari,** and early **daffodils**. They will survive cold temperatures and possible snow without damage, ceasing their growth when weather threatens. *Arum italicum* will show full-sized green leaves throughout winter, drooping only when temperatures reach the low 20s.

PRUNING

Zones 5-6: Wait until spring for further garden tidying.

Zones 7-9: A few mild days may entice gardeners into raking, picking up windfall limbs, or trimming a few spent plants. Allow all foliage and stems to remain on hardy **fuchsias** and **chrysanthemums**.

WATERING

Water, either liquid or frozen, comes to gardens this month. Be sure that drain holes flow freely on any winter container plants so that the roots will not get soggy.

FERTILIZING

No plants require fertilizer this month. In cold weather, they are not growing actively.

PROBLEMS

Zones 7-9: Watch the garden for drainage difficulties; far more perennials die from drowning in soggy soil than are lost to cold. Check under gutters in particular to see if water stands over any plants. If water stays in puddles in one part of the garden, it's worth the trouble of digging out the affected plants and moving them to a well drained area of the garden.

ROSES

Roses fascinate gardeners with their vivid colors, fragrance, garden presence, and the nostalgia and memories. Simply reading a list of rose names excites us! Roses may be first choices for beginning gardeners or cherished specialties for the most advanced horticulturalists. Portland, Oregon, known as "City of Roses," headlines these plants, but they're renowned for their beauty throughout the region.

All gardeners can grow roses in Washington and Oregon. Roses carry a reputation for being "difficult," but they aren't when you choose what suits your own garden. Know your climate zone, your garden exposure, and space available for the rose. Consider what level of time, effort, and care you will provide. Intentionally choose rose types adapted to your individual garden style and your climate. You'll be happy you did.

Plan first and then succumb to roses at your nursery or from a catalog. This chapter clarifies some best choices and timely action to care for them from selection, to planting, to final winter tuck-in.

Effect of the climate zone: Check the map on page 20 to determine your USDA hardiness zone. Fortunately for gardeners throughout Washington and Oregon, roses hybridized for all our climate

zones exist. In the coldest areas of our region, Oregon's eastern high desert and northeast Washington, temperatures can drop to -20 F. or lower. Rose selection in the extreme temperatures of Zones 5a or 4b is vital. Roses grown in Zones 6 and below require winter protection. (See October for details.)

Freezing winter temperatures aren't the only seasonal factor. In milder winters with temperatures characteristic of Zones 7 to 9, roses grow vigorously, resisting winter dormancy. They produce leaves and buds deep into December, which makes them susceptible to damage from sudden frigid spells. (See November.) In addition to winter's diversity in our region, varying summer weather can affect bloom in different ways. For example, where summers are cool, as in western Washington and Oregon, low temperatures retard bloom. Familiar beauties, such as 'Chrysler Imperial,' that typically grow well in the steamy Midwest languish west of the Cascades.

Sadly, rose diseases such as blackspot thrive vigorously in humidity and mild temperatures. Selecting for disease resistance is another way to ensure contentment with your rose garden.

Rose growers in all our regional zones enjoy experimenting with new species and cultivars and demonstrating their particular adaptation to our region. Visit the appendix to locate show gardens in your own area. As your garden experience with roses develops, you'll identify your own favorites.

IS A ROSE A ROSE?

Sizes, growth habits, and garden impacts vary from rose to rose. Rose breeders and producers concentrate on giving us new choices; there's a rose for nearly any landscape situation from the smallest windowbox to sprawling acreage. Colors range widely from any color found in a tropical sunset to whites and purples. It's helpful to choose a rose type first for its growth habit to suit your situation then for its color within that category.

How large will it grow? One good way to "sort" roses is by eventual mature size, from miniatures as the smallest (twelve inches to three feet), to rambling climbers like 'Bobbie James' that may scramble forty feet over a roof.

MAKING THEM FEEL AT HOME

Roses share their plant family—the *Rosaceae*—with many of our most delicious fruits, like apples and pears. Think of them as fruiting plants. But rather than fruit, you're encouraging blooms! Sun, well-drained and prepared soil, water, and nutrients bring roses to their best growth, just as they do edible fruit. Indeed, roses grow happily anywhere you can produce a good tomato—though you certainly don't want to evict the vegetables.

Choose a location with ample light (at least six hours of full sun per day) and open breezes for air circulation. (Air flow will help reduce, though not eliminate, rose diseases.)

A very few roses tolerate shade (four to five hours of part sun per day). You'll get fewer flowers but will enjoy their presence on woodland edges. (See March for a list of shade-tolerant roses.)

TYPES OF ROSES, SIZES, AND GARDEN USE

The quick reference guide below shows rose types in order of the least space required to the most. However, the general tendency of size and shape can often be altered or managed by pruning techniques; it's best to select one suited to your situation rather than coping with tangled thorny overgrowth.

MINIATURES

Small roses inspire words like "darling!"—they have the familiar shapes and forms of larger roses with buttonhole-sized blooms on small, upright plants.

Bloom time: continuous throughout season

Size: one foot to over three feet

Colors: all found in larger roses

Use: cut flowers, or containers, patio plantings, houseplants (with ample light)

GROUND COVER ROSES

Often wider than tall, ground cover and "landscape" roses are new to gardens, with all-season flowering and easy management, as well as disease-resistance. They're garden dream plants for ample color.

Size: eighteen inches to five feet tall, three to five feet wide

Colors: all Flower Carpet™; Dream™ Roses; Pavement™; Meidiland™ series

Use: hedges, slope covering, color masses in garden beds, herb or perennial bed edgings, walk edges

FLORIBUNDA ROSES

Floribundas bloom throughout summer, flowers forming clusters at the ends of stems, with a firm upright growth form. Double or single, they offer garden variety.

Size: 'Patio' types can be two to three feet; others range from three to seven feet but can be kept shorter by pruning

Colors: all ('Betty Boop', red and white, or 'Sunsprite', brilliant yellow)

Use: cut flowers, patios, containers (for smaller types), garden beds

HYBRID TEAS

Familiar to all rose lovers, hybrid teas form one classically-formed blossom per stem; they also bloom continually. Usually narrower than tall, with upright form.

Size: five to seven feet

Colors: all (fragrant ones include 'Just Joey', apricot colored, and 'Double Delight', red/white)

Use: cut flowers, (these are the florist's rose), in perennial borders, display beds, or sunny shrub areas, mixed foundation plantings

SHRUB ROSES

Often large, shrub roses contain many of the most delightful rose types; they are often cold-tolerant and excellent for filling big spaces. Continuous bloomers include the 'English' roses such as the David Austin and Harkness series, the species *Rosa rugosa*, and modern shrub roses like the hybrid 'Golden Wings'. Generally continuous bloomers.

Size: arching form, vigorous, both wide and tall, spreading broadly three feet to eight feet wide by four feet to ten feet tall

Use: fragrance, cut flowers, hedges, larger landscape beds, some can be trained as climbers

OLD GARDEN ROSES

Used in gardens before 1867, old garden roses bloom once generally without repeat. Fragrant, fascinating but also thorny and often large.

Size: five feet to eight feet wide by eight feet tall

Color: predominantly pink, red, purple

Use: fragrance (gather for potpourri), screening landscapes, tie up against buildings, heritage gardens

CLIMBING AND RAMBLING ROSES

Either once-blooming or continuous, climbers and ramblers send up long flexible canes that can be tied or trained.

Size: both wide and tall, from four to twelve feet wide by eight to thirty feet tall

Colors: all

Use: fragrance, sculptural effect, covering fences and buildings, trellises and arbors

JANUARY
ROSES

PLANNING

All zones: Gather catalogs and books—explore them to get good ideas about both rose types and cultivars and those best suited to your particular garden situation and zone. Talk to neighbors and experienced gardeners about their rose successes.

Climbers: need plenty of room and firm structural supports. Plan to build and reinforce the structure for climbers. You'll need a strong trellis, fence, or arbor.

Hedging roses: often used as shorter hedges to separate garden areas, the newer landscape roses such as bright pink 'Carefree Beauty'™ are ideal for mass planting, growing to five feet. Hedging roses need eighteen to twenty-four inches of space between them depending on the eventual plant height. For a tall hedge, David Austin 'Mary Rose' grows over six feet and stays healthy even when plants touch each other. Plant a row either straight or slightly staggered to produce a wider hedge.

Ground covers: measure the spot to be covered, allowing four square feet for each rose. They'll spread beautifully over flat areas or moderate slopes (if pegged down and kept watered).

Garden accents: **floribunda**, **hybrid tea** roses, or **shrub** roses can be striking when combined with flower borders or placed in sunny areas with other shrubs. Allow at least a 3-foot circle for floribundas, hybrid teas, and shrub David Austin roses.

Backgrounds and barriers: *Rosa rugosa* and its various cultivars such as 'Hansa', can make an attractive and nearly impenetrable barrier. Allow four to five feet between plants and stand back as they fill in with thorny, fragrant, and blooming thickets.

PLANTING

All zones: Review the technique for planting roses.

Zones 7-9: Late in the month in the mildest areas, plant bare-root roses during moderate weather. Planting continues through February until leaves begin growing. Soak bare roots six to eight hours (up to twelve hours maximum) in lukewarm water before planting. Dig a hole with a conical center to spread roots over. Install with the graft union above ground. Mulch deeply after planting, insulating the graft union against sudden February freezes. Dormant roses may be moved from one spot to another when the temperature is above freezing and the ground isn't squishy wet.

Zones 5-6: No outdoor planting or transplanting is possible during this month (no surprise!).

CARE

All zones: Leave winter protection on the established roses. Tie up any canes that whip in the wind.

WATERING

All zones: On a day that is above freezing, monitor and water any roses planted close to eaves or tucked against walls where water may not penetrate. Roses that dry out at the roots are more susceptible to cold damage.

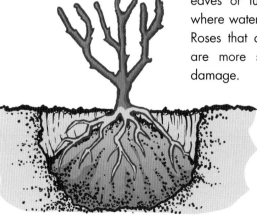

Dig a hole with a conical center to spread roots over.

DID YOU KNOW?

Roses are available in one of three ways: Bare root, bare root in packages or boxes, and in containers surrounded with soil.

Bare-root roses are available only when plants are dormant in late winter and early spring. They are shipped in moist peat-packing material like sawdust or peat moss. Bare-root plants alarm gardeners with nude roots, but they're easy to plant and grow quickly as weather warms. Be ready to plant them soon after they arrive.

Packaged roses, also bare root, rest in colorful boxes—often showing the rose in bloom—with moist packing material protecting the roots. Purchase packaged roses before they begin to show leaves and slide them gently out of the box, shaking soil off and planting as if bare root. In colder areas if purchasing packaged roses before planting time, place the entire package in a cool but not freezing place and regularly check packing for moisture, watering as needed to keep roots hydrated.

DO NOT plant the box, even when some box instructions may advise this practice. In the summer-dry climates of all Washington and Oregon zones, boxes can wick water away from roots and prevent proper rose growth.

Container roses provide more flexibility for planting times. They're planted by nurseries in pots and can be available throughout the growing season. Plant them as you would any ontainer shrub; planting earlier in the season allows them to establish well for the current year. Container roses planted later in the year will bloom better their second year when roots settle in.

Grafted or "own root" roses? Traditionally, roses combine two parts: the named variety on top grafted onto the "rootstock," the graft showing as a distinct knob just above the roots. Rootstock can vary, but *Rosa multiflora* is reliable for winter survival; many roses also use 'Dr Huey' as their rootstock. Grafted roses can thrive and produce handsome plants. The disadvantage of grafting is that roots may send up canes of their own. If possible, choose roses grafted with a rootstock appropriate for your own climate.

"Own root" roses are just that, shrubs grown from cuttings so that the blooming top and the roots are the same plant genetically. They have no knobby graft union. In the coldest zones, growers observe that if the upper branches of an own-root rose die in winter, the roots may live to send up new canes that reproduce the desired rose. They will be strong and productive in the garden. Hedged own-root roses may thicken up faster than grafted roses as new canes spring up from the roots and add growth identical to the variety.

 FERTILIZING

All zones: Fertilizer is not needed this month because plants aren't actively growing.

 PRUNING

All zones: No pruning yet. But you can get pruners cleaned and sharpened at nurseries.

When the temperature is above freezing, trim and prune back any branches that winter has ripped or broken.

 PROBLEMS

Zones 7-9: Rake up and discard any leaves or fallen petals left around roots; do not compost these. Removing old rose parts now will reduce disease potential later.

FEBRUARY

ROSES

 PLANNING

If you haven't done it in recent years, test the soil to determine pH levels. Roses grow well in a wide pH range of about 5.6 to 7.2, slightly acid to neutral. If your soil grows **tomatoes, carrots,** or **peonies** well, it should manage roses without amendment.

 PLANTING

Zones 5-6: Bare-root roses require installation as soon as possible. Freezing or stormy conditions may prevent immediate planting. If so, leave them in their packaging in a cold, protected location such as an unheated garage for up to seventy-two hours. Do not allow them to freeze. If there is a longer delay you can "heel in" the plants. Proper heeling-in takes about the same time as planting, but it is a good investment for the health of your plants if the weather is severe.

1. Soak the roots in water for six to eight hours.

2. Prepare a trench, slanting the soil so that roses will rest at an angle.

3. Lay the unwrapped roses against the ground, slanted with the roots down and canes up; cover both roots and canes with about eight inches of soil. Four inches of mulch can help if the weather turns very cold.

4. Water thoroughly.

Zones 7-9: Plant and transplant whenever the ground is workable and air temperatures are above freezing. Finish moving and transplanting roses by the end of the month, before they start full growth. Plant container roses growing in nursery pots. (You can continue this into late spring or into summer.) Water thoroughly after planting or transplanting even during rain. Water settles roots and eliminates air pockets in the soil.

 CARE

Zones 5-6: Tie up climbers or any roses torn loose by wind. Keep protective winter coverings snug around the plants.

Zones 7-9: Unless February is unusually cold, gradually remove winter protection after mid-February, taking four or five days to reveal the plant completely.

 WATERING

Irrigation is not needed until roses move into active growth.

Indoors: Miniature roses need frequent watering. Remove foil wrappers or decorative frills that could keep soil from draining well. Dump extra water out of saucers. Indoor roses will bloom briefly for three to four weeks.

FERTILIZING

Newly planted roses, those you order and plant bare root or from boxes, cannot process granular fertilizer until their roots establish. Bring them into your standard fertilizing regime during their second spring. Some growers do feed them with liquid foliar fertilizer in midsummer if they have begun to bloom.

Zones 5-6: East of the mountains, plants aren't growing, so fertilizer is not needed.

Zones 7-9: After pruning, apply the first of the season's fertilizer. Whatever you choose, water it in well if rain is lacking.

PRUNING

Trim off canes with small leaves to manage the overall structure of the plant. Roses respond to pruning by producing new, stronger leaves and buds. Check for pruning demonstrations in public rose gardens. Observing and learning from experts will give you the confidence and skills to prune properly.

Zones 5-6: In these zones and in higher elevations, winter continues its grip—you won't prune in late March or early April.

HOW OFTEN TO FERTILIZE

Fertilizer enhances rose growth, and it's often suggested to fertilize monthly during the growing season. However the dangers of over-fertilization make it necessary to moderate timing and amount.

Once-Blooming Roses: Fertilize all **once-bloomers** twice a year, once when new growth starts and again just after bloom in late June. **Species roses**, "**old roses**," and once-blooming **shrub roses** can thrive with this simple regime.

Continuous Bloomers: Hybrid teas, floribundas, grandifloras, and "English" roses that bloom all summer can use fertilizer three times at six week intervals: when new growth starts, mid-May, and the first of July. However, you can fertilize only twice a year, using the once-blooming schedule, for good results. Rose growers who grow for shows and exhibitions use the more frequent feeding schedule. Choose fertilizer that supplies moderate amounts of nitrogen and also includes micronutrients (called "trace elements").

Container roses, those in nursery pots, may have established root systems if they've been in the container for months. Or they may be "new" and young like bare-root roses. The later in the season you purchase containerized roses, the more mature their root systems will be. Summer-planted container roses can tolerate and require liquid fertilizer if they have good leaf coverage and are blooming.

Zones 7-9: You will often prune in late February, traditionally around President's Day. Cold weather can push this into March. Earlier pruning risks freezing damage.

PROBLEMS

Zones 7-9: If the roses had disease problems last year, use a registered fungicide after pruning except on *Rosa rugosa*, which does not tolerate chemicals. Blackspot, if present, infects canes as well as leaves. Rose growers recommend using fungicides now and regularly throughout the growing season on susceptible plants. Low toxicity fungicides for roses include neem oil, potassium bicarbonate (Remedy™), and sulfur. Follow label instructions.

MARCH
ROSES

 PLANNING

Rose gardens need sun, sun, and more sun. Roses grow best when they receive at least six hours of sun daily. (Don't we all?) But, east of the Cascades where summers stay hot with drying winds, they also need protection from excessive sun exposure and heat. Allow roses plenty of room. Their roots need oxygen and don't grow well if they're walked on, dug over, or crowded.

Lavender, rosemary, sage, and other herbs look handsome with roses but need far less water. Roses in containers could enliven herb beds while being watered separately. Or, design separate planting areas so the herbs thrive nearby, adding color and scent. You could mix drought tolerant *Rosa rugosa* and its various cultivars with herbs.

 PLANTING

Plant bare-root and boxed roses this month, the first two weeks in Zones 7 to 9 and later in the colder areas as the ground thaws. Roses need excellent drainage. Add organic matter or compost to the entire planting area (not just individual holes) or use compost as a mulch if the planting bed has already been amended. Do not use fresh manure.

Companion Planting: Give the rose its space, but let the companion plants fill in, occupying the front or the sides of the area. Combine roses with perennial **ground covers,** blooming **shrubs,** or summer bulbs like **lilies** and **dahlias.** Pretty accompaniments are **lady's mantle** (*Alchemilla mollis*), annual **violas** grouped in masses, or low **catmint** (*Nepeta mussini* 'Six Hills Giant') with blue flowers. Be sure to combine roses with plants requiring the same growing conditions.

Zones 5-6: In the coldest inland areas, plant the graft union about 3 to four inches *below* the soil level. Roots may develop above the graft in colder areas, adding vigor to the plant. Mulch thoroughly after planting using two to three inches of compost, keeping it away from the rose trunk. (See Tree and Shrub chapters for more information on mulching technique.)

Zones 7-9: Set the graft union above the soil level where you can see it.

 CARE

Zones 5-6: Remove winter protection later in the month, gradually exposing roses as weather moderates. Do this before pruning.

 WATERING

Drip irrigation, soaker hoses, or low bubblers help keep rose foliage dry and encourage strong roots. Getting water systems set up now before plants expand prevents damage in the long run. Rainfall usually keeps plants well watered in March, but be prepared for dry spells ahead.

 FERTILIZING

Choose a slow-release, balanced N-P-K fertilizer (nitrogen-phosphorous-potassium) with "micronutrients" and apply after pruning while the soil is still cold. Avoid very high nitrogen applications which produce excess leaves instead of blooms. Water before and after feeding. Many growers use non-organic fertilizers for the first spring application and then switch to organics for the second, when the warm soil and its microorganisms can break down the fertilizer's contents. Organic fertilizers, such as alfalfa pellets, guarantee the presence of essential trace elements. They're always present in soil, but roses, being heavy feeders, respond well to additional trace elements.

 PRUNING

Zones 7-9: Complete pruning.

Zones 5-6: Begin pruning when temperatures rise above freezing. Many experienced growers say "prune when the forsythia blooms," often around the end of March or April 1 in colder zones.

Basic rose pruning technique:

• Identify the type of rose you have. If you don't know, prune it lightly this year, removing only about 1/3 of each cane. When the rose blooms, take a spray to a nursery for identification of the type.

• Remove dead and diseased wood on all rose types (such wood will look brown and may break readily). Cut back to green cambium (it's almost the color of a Granny Smith apple, with clean white pith inside).

• Proceed according to the rose type. (Note: After the first spring pruning, paint the cut ends of the largest canes with white glue to deter cane borers. Do not compost debris.)

Hybrid teas: These need "heavy pruning," with all canes cut down to one foot to one and one-half feet above the ground. Remove all small, weak canes (pencil size or smaller) down to the ground, leaving four to six strong canes.

DID YOU KNOW?

Disease-resistant roses: can reduce maintenance needs and increase satisfaction. But they don't guarantee total immunity. Some of the best for all zones are *Rosa rugosa*, **shrub rose** 'The Fairy,' **old garden rose** 'Louise Odier', and **climbers** 'America' and 'Altissimo' (Zones 6 to 9).

Shade-bloomers: Roses tucked into part shade bloom less bountifully. However, some will display color. **Ramblers** such as 'Bobbie James' compensate by climbing trees for light. *Rosa rugosa* 'Delicata,' and *R. polyantha* 'The Fairy' are good choices. Try **shrub roses** like white 'Sally Holmes' and yellow 'Golden Wings'.

Shrub roses: These keep more wood than **hybrid teas**. Saw out any dead canes to the bud union or trunk. Balance and tidy up the shape and remove only one-third of each cane, cutting each cane to an outward facing bud.

Climbers: Allow canes to grow for two years, tying the strongest ones to the trellis, arbor, or fence to form a framework. Remove weak, small, or non-blooming canes. After the second year, canes develop blooming side-shoots emerging from the tied up structure. Don't remove the structural canes, but shorten side-shoots and remove any dead canes. If you cut a climber down to the ground, you'll lose at least a year of bloom.

Ground cover roses: Once they're established, shear off at least six inches of growth now before buds begin to form.

Aphids on rosebuds

 PROBLEMS

For rose diseases, apply fungicides just after pruning. Cover the canes of any roses that suffered from blackspot last year. Roses that resisted disease last year do not need fungicides. Do not use fungicides on any of the *Rosa rugosa* or its hybrids; these disease-resistant roses suffer leaf damage from chemicals. Aphids may be washed off with water.

APRIL

ROSES

PLANNING

Nurseries will have container roses this month. Select one or two miniature roses for a patio or deck container. Use a large pot to combine the rose and a selection of annuals. **Miniature rose** 'Gourmet Popcorn', a white fluffy bloomer, looks great in a deck pot with **cosmos** 'Sonata' and deep pink **New Guinea impatiens**. All these love sun. Compose a scheme that suits your favorite colors. Some miniature roses will thrive in hanging planters, producing spreading branches that hang attractively over the edge. Try miniature 'Sweet Chariot' with rosy-pink flowers combined with annual trailing **lobelia**.

PLANTING

Zones 5-6: Finish planting bareroot roses early in April. Watch weather reports, and plant when night temperatures rise above mid-20s. Remember to install grafted roses with the bulbous graft union three to four inches underground.

Zones 7-9: Perennial and annual flowers grow quickly this month; if adding nursery container roses to established flower beds, do it as early in the month

as possible, and tread carefully around emerging plants.

CARE

Yank weeds out of rose beds. Do not use a pre-emergent weed killer labeled for use only around established woody plants. Chemicals (like dichlobenil—sold as Casoron™ and others) damage young roots.

Mulch reduces weed problems by preventing seeds from sprouting. After setting and checking soaker hoses and giving a good watering, add two to three inches of fluffy mulch over the rose roots.

WATERING

Watch rainfall this month. Poke gently with a trowel around established roses and new plantings to be sure moisture reaches roots deeply. Roses—with the exception of established rugosas and **old shrub roses**—bloom better with regular watering,

How much water you apply depends on temperature, soil type, and mature root establishment. A sudden heat spell, especially when accompanied by wind, stresses water reserves. Newly set plants succumb to dry soils faster than old, sturdy roses. Roses in pots or hanging baskets also lose water quickly. A mini-

Miniature rose 'Gourmet Popcorn'

mum of one inch of water weekly—four inches a month—is often cited. Check the root dampness to determine if this is enough. Plants do best with slow, deep soaking rather than shallow frequent sprinkles.

Rainfall this month varies throughout the region: Seattle averages less than three inches in April; Spokane may receive only 1.25 inches; Bend, Oregon, less than one inch. Gray skies and misty mornings may delude gardeners into thinking that moisture is reaching the soil and the rose roots, but such days often yield no rain whatever. Also, the month's entire rain budget can fall in one day's deluge, leaving the rest of the month dry.

FERTILIZING

Fertilize all roses immediately after pruning, using a slow-release type (either chemical or organic, depending on your choice). Apply fertilizer to damp ground, work it in, and water it thoroughly.

Reminder: Do not fertilize bushes planted in the current spring season. When the bush blooms, roots have established and you can fertilize with a liquid foliar type once, about the first of July.

PRUNING

Zones 5-6: Complete spring pruning on all roses, perhaps as late as the third week in April.

PROBLEMS

The three main diseases can be easily identified: rust (looks exactly like the name, with orange bumps on leaves), powdery mildew (leaves, buds, and flowers appear dusted with gray talcum powder), and rose blackspot (leaves seem splashed with

INSECTS ON ROSES

In Washington and Oregon, insect pests generally bother roses far less than diseases. If you've moved into our area from another part of the United States, you may be surprised—and certainly pleased—to discover that the dreaded, destructive Japanese beetle (*Popillia japonica*) doesn't appear in Oregon or Washington. Gardeners here avoid saying "Japanese beetle" when standing in front of roses for fear of jinxing this present good fortune.

Aphids, a common sucking pest, can gather on the new leaves and shoots. They annoy the roses (and us) more in spring than any other time. Washing them away with a gentle stream of water gets them off the leaves. Too much water pressure can snap brittle new foliage off. Aphids multiply quickly—and will be back! Many garden friends like birds, ladybug beetles, and lacebugs devour aphids happily. Use low-toxicity insecticides or none at all to keep your beneficial insect helpers alive.

dark ink blotches). But the most harm is done because leaves affected by disease can't create the nutrients that feed and support buds.

Fungicides, pesticides that affect fungus organisms, help reduce the severity of the problem but don't eliminate it. To be effective, apply fungicides before disease symptoms appear. Think of them as a raincoat and the disease organism as falling water drops. Using the least toxic type helps protect beneficial insects; one example is neem oil, which is produced from a Southeast Asian tree (sold as Rose Defense™ and other names). Another low-impact fungicide is potassium bicarbonate (sold as Remedy™ and under

other names). Do not apply any pesticide without exact identification of the problem.

Use a registered fungicide. Follow all directions exactly and wear gloves and goggles for protection. (Check with your local WSU Extension or Oregon Extension office, or with a trained WSU or OSU Master Gardener.) Pesticide names and brands differ from year to year as companies alter their packaging. Be sure to get clear information and identification of the problem before selecting a rose fungicide.

MAY

ROSES

 PLANNING

Note when roses first bloom, how bountifully they produce, and their special attributes like fragrance. List newly planted roses; if you're inclined, add a color picture. Most of us have notebooks with pencil comments and muddy fingerprints—a color photo now and then provides real glamour! All of us learn what plants do from the intimacy of growing them, which is far different from scanning their photos in catalogs. You may find that you'll want to alter your rose collection, adding or subtracting according to performance. Be cautious and forgiving in your judgment of newly-planted roses; they often reach full glory in their second or even third year.

 PLANTING

Roses growing strongly in nursery containers may be planted from now through late summer. Water thoroughly before planting. Trim roots that "girdle" or "circle" around the rootball. Tease roots loose and spread them in the planting hole to ensure long survival of the rose bush.

Indoor roses: Gift **miniature roses**, often in three- or four-inch pots, don't thrive in household conditions. They require light and good air circulation. After all frost is past, set these roses into patio pots or out into the garden, perhaps on the edge of perennial flowers. For about a week, set them outside in shade during the day and bring them in at night. Then plant outdoors. It's a garden gamble but worth a try. Prune lightly and fertilize after two or three weeks outdoors.

 CARE

Look at canes being produced by **climbers**, and tie up those you wish to keep as the "framework" of the plants.

 WATERING

Continue checking roots' water needs. This month can be rainy, with several inches in the Portland and Seattle areas; or it can be dry with less than an inch of rain during the entire month, especially east of the Cascades.

 FERTILIZING

Whether you choose processed chemical or organic fertilizers, roses will grow. Apply fertilizer after pruning or early in the spring when leaves and new shoots have started growing. Apply regularly every four or six weeks. In all zones, roses will put out new shoots this month. Water thoroughly before and after fertilizing.

When you cut roses, trim back to a place on the stem with a five-leaf grouping.

PRUNING

Once major pruning is completed, shaping and caring for the established roses continues.

Look at the bush to find any "blind shoots," skinny ones with no flower buds forming. Remove these. Flower buds take on the classic "rosebud" shape when very small, so they're easy to distinguish.

For newly planted roses, don't prune now. Allow the canes to form whether or not they have bloom. You want the growth to develop so roots and plant can become stronger.

As you cut roses, trim back to a place on the stem with a five-leaf grouping. New buds will form and bloom in about six weeks if the rose is a repeat or all-summer bloomer. (**Old roses** produce flowers only once a year, generally in June.) This trimming method is traditional, although some experts now say you'll get new buds also by cutting back to three leaves, which gives more choice when looking at a rose cane. Cut to a leaf node facing out toward you. New branching will head outward instead into the center of the shrub.

PROBLEMS

Check rose leaves for blackspot and rust. Powdery mildew often shows toward the end of summer. Remove all affected leaves and trim back any canes showing inky blackspot lesions. Repeat fungicide application, using an EPA registered product. Follow directions exactly. The rose grows better without diseased canes, even if you remove those already leafing out.

Insect problems? Avoid using fertilizer/insect killer combination products. You may see combination fertilizer and insecticides, which offer both rose feeding and insect killing. These will not help with any rose leaf disease problems like blackspot. Toxicity is the worst side effect of the insecticide disulfoton (also called DySyston™, an organophosphate) commonly included in these combo products. It kills all insects, even the good guys like lady beetles who munch aphids. Read the label. Broad-spectrum insecticides like this one are also poisonous to birds and mammals: that's pets and children! You'll grow better roses by fertilizing with plant nutrients alone and treating problems separately.

ROSES WITHOUT PESTICIDES

When treating roses for disease problems, it's not necessary to use chemicals if that approach doesn't suit your garden philosophy.

1. Choose roses adapted to your area and noted as disease-resistant. *Rosa rugosa* and its hybrids, for instance, stay nearly disease-free. It's the most easy-care rose type. Check the list of cold-tolerant roses in the introduction and talk to your local rose growers and nursery staff.

2. Plant in sun. Provide necessary fertilizer and water.

3. Separate rose plantings by placing other shrubs or perennial flowers between them so that if one rose is diseased it won't infect its neighbors. (Spores can be wind borne, and infection can travel.)

4. Plant roses far enough apart for air movement between them and prune to allow good air circulation. Remove old leaves and any diseased canes.

5. Keep the rose area clean and clear of fallen leaves, raking and disposing of them (not in the compost).

6. Monitor the rose carefully, pruning off any diseased leaves.

7. Tolerate some leaf imperfection and enjoy the flowers!

8. If a rose persistently shows bad disease symptoms, consider removing it.

JUNE
ROSES

PLANNING

Revel in roses this month. Once-bloomers like **old garden roses**, **climbers**, and **species roses** throw out festivals of flowers They're joined by those that will bloom throughout the summer—**hybrid teas**, **floribundas**, **English roses**, and **miniatures**. Summer light shines over the rose garden, and long evenings invite us to linger until dark.

Rose shows abound in this most flowery of months. Seeing roses on display, and talking to experts will boost your rose knowledge. Keep your notebook handy to record those you like best.

Visiting local public rose gardens also engages our senses this month. You'll see the form and growth habit of different rose types and how they are pruned and trained by specialists. Public rose gardens show best bloom from mid-June to the end of July, though you can visit throughout the season.

PLANTING

All zones: Roses available in nursery pots can go into the garden now. Plant them early or late in the day to protect them from fierce sun. Set up shade protection for the first week after planting. Lath house shading, greenhouse cloth, snow fencing, or muslin or burlap cloth stapled to stakes helps the roses adjust. If leaves droop even when the plant is watered, replace the shading.

CARE

Continue weeding as needed. Mulch will keep most weeds under control, but seeds can blow into the top layer of the mulch and sprout happily in a rose bed's excellent growing conditions. Fasten climbing canes to their supports. **Climbers** tied horizontally to a fence or across the top of an arbor form more ample blooms. Horizontal positioning can improve flowering. Old-fashioned trellises, for example, benefit rose growth with gentle arching shapes.

WATERING

All zones: Careful watering tops the list of rose chores this month. Use any method that gets a deep soaking to at least one foot; some gardeners set "bubblers" to fill the root zone. Form a shallow, circular "moat" around the rose by piling up soil and mulch three inches high and eighteen inches in diameter. This holds the water while it soaks into the roots. If using the less effective sprinkler, water early. Leaves need the whole day to dry to avoid disease.

FERTILIZING

All zones: This is a vital month for fertilizing; apply fertilizer according to your rose type schedule, every four weeks or six weeks. Water before and after applying fertilizer.

Do not use granular fertilizer on this year's newly planted roses. If they are growing well and setting buds, coat the leaves with a spray of mild foliar fertilizer, such as fish fertilizer.

PRUNING

All zones: Pruning this month should be called "grooming." Your fingertips for pinching, your clippers for cutting flowers and branches—both these gentle techniques will shape and tidy the rose. Prune out "blind shoots," weak canes with no buds.

Procedure with once-bloomers: For large bushes like **ramblers** and **old garden roses** like 'Cécile Brünner' and the **Alba roses**, do *not* trim off withered bloom. As the flower petals fall, once-blooming roses set brilliant red seed, in the form of hips—more

DID YOU KNOW?

Throughout Washington and Oregon, visitors can ramble through local public gardens that inspire and teach. In addition to this list, check your rose catalogs. Many growers have display gardens to demonstrate their own plants.

OREGON

Eugene
George E. Owen Memorial Rose Garden
524-682-4800

Portland (The "City of Roses")
International Rose Test Garden
Washington Park, 503-823-PLAY
Ladd's Rose Garden, SE 16 and Harrison,
503-823-PLAY
Peninsula Park and Rose Garden
6400 Albina, 503-823-PLAY

Salem
Willamette University, Sesquicentennial Rose Garden, 503-370-6143

WASHINGTON

Chehalis
City of Chehalis Municipal Rose Garden

Bellingham
Fairhaven Park and Rose Garden
www.barstop.com/parks

Kenniwick
Lawrence Scott Park Rose Garden

Olympia
Priest Point Park

Seattle
Woodland Park Rose Garden

Spokane
Manito Park/Rose Hill.

Tacoma
Point Defiance Rose Garden. 253-591-5328

---

genteelly called 'heps' by the British. They'll ripen and add to the garden's color in autumn.

Repeat-bloomers: **Hybrid teas**, **floribundas**, **landscape roses**, and **English roses** (David Austin and others) will set new buds on canes after the first flowering. Deadhead spent flowers, cutting back to an outward-facing leaf bud to encourage fresh growth. New flowers require about five to six weeks to form.

Disbudding: To encourage one large flower at the end of a **floribunda** or **grandiflora** branch, pinch off two out of three flowers in a cluster to encourage one showier bloom.

 ## PROBLEMS

Deer seek out roses and many other plants in the rose family, such as apples. If you want to attract deer in the garden, plant roses. If you do not want deer, construct a formidable eight-foot fence. Deer-repellent chemicals do exist. Your nursery knows which one can be used on roses in bloom; do not spray at mid-day when hot sun is on the leaves. Mix up just the right amount. Deer repellent can burn young leaves if it's left mixed in the sprayer and applied days later.

Aphids continue to flourish this month. They can cause rose leaves to curl and pucker. Birds and beneficial insects are your allies against aphids. For intractable infestations, spray insecticidal soap directly on the aphids. Aphids multiply astonishingly fast, so be sure to look under the leaves and check again four to five days after spraying. Again, do not spray on young leaves in hot sun.

To fight against diseases, use fungicides at the interval suggested on the label on new growth and buds of susceptible plants. Pick off leaves affected by blackspot; do not put them in compost. Roses resistant to disease do not need treating.

JULY
ROSES

 PLANNING

Keep visiting public gardens—the best way to learn rose realities in your area is to consult successful local gardeners. The rose demonstration gardens throughout the United States are fun to visit when traveling, but you'll learn most by observing what thrives in your area.

 PLANTING

You may take advantage of summer nursery sales. Select by color but also inquire about the local adaptability and disease-resistance. To reduce stress plant in the cool of the morning or at dusk.

If you wish to propagate a favorite rose, such as creating new shrubs from a family heirloom, take cuttings in both June and July in all zones and in early September for the milder Zones 7 to 9. The best candidates for cutting are **shrub roses**, **old roses**, and **climbers**. Some newer hybrid roses, protected by patents, cannot be propagated. Look at the tag.

Follow these steps:

1. Prepare a pot full of clean sand or with perlite and sand mixed 50-50. Wet it.

2. Select a strong shoot of this year's growth with four leaflets. If the thorns break off with a "snap," the shoot is ripe for propagating.

3. Keep the two top leaflets with about three inches of stem below them.

4. Dip the cut end in a rooting hormone.

5. Poke the soil and set the cutting with the lower leaf is just above the soil surface. Firm the soil around it, eliminating air pockets. Some growers start several in a circular row around the edge of a container.

6. Water and cover with a plastic bag. Keep it in a shady spot, and check for moisture routinely. Rooting takes about eight weeks. Success isn't guaranteed, but it's great fun when a cutting "strikes root."

 CARE

Continue weeding (it never ends).

Has foot traffic started to make a path and compact soil in the rose garden? Roses need oxygen at the roots, so gently loosen compacted soil and put up a friendly barrier of twigs, small stakes, or decorative edging.

 WATERING

Watering is the most crucial task this month. Water slowly and deeply once a week so that the moisture goes down eight to twelve inches; allow the soil to dry slightly between watering. When using soaker hoses, bubblers, or drip irrigation systems, it's difficult to measure the "inch a week" typically recommended. Instead, gently dig and check how deep the water penetrates.

FERTILIZING

All zones: Early July is the last time to fertilize outdoor roses. You don't need to fertilize once-bloomers if they have finished their cycle. But **hybrid teas, floribundas**, and **grandifloras** producing flowers need one more application before going dormant.

For container plants, fertilize twice a month since regular watering will wash nutrients through the soil. If using a liquid form, such as a fish fertilizer, spray some on the leaves.

If newly planted roses bloom, spray a low-nitrogen liquid fertilizer on the leaves and around the roots. If newly planted roses have not bloomed, leave them alone. Fertilize them next spring at pruning time when the roots are fully established.

PRUNING

Continue grooming the repeat-blooming roses, deadheading thoroughly. Leave any rose hips that form on once-bloomers.

PROBLEMS

All zones: Cooler, more humid regions suffer more from black-spot than the hotter, drier areas. Remove leaves severely affected by blackspot and use a registered fungicide on unaffected leaves. For minor infections, simply clip off the leaves.

If you see ball-shaped, mossy growths, suspect gall wasp damage. The wasp, a beneficial insect, makes a small sphere that looks like **sphagnum moss** tucked on a branch. Trim off the hosting stem and lay the cut piece elsewhere in the garden where the larvae can grow and emerge. The wasps don't do much damage to roses.

If leaves show "calligraphy" patterns of yellow, the rose may have a viral infection. The plant and virus can coexist but the plants grow weaker each year. Removing the rose is the only way to manage the disease.

EATING ROSES

Roses add romance and sweetness to parties, from wedding showers to anniversaries. People generally don't nibble on bouquets. But you and your guests can eat petals as a garnish or in rose hip jelly. To ensure safe eating, stop using pesticides and fungicides at least eight weeks before the intended meal. Or, grow a disease-resistant type without chemicals. You may wish to use *Rosa rugosa* species or hybrids *of Rosa rugosa*, which are damaged by pesticides and should never have them sprayed on. Their petals are deep pink ('Roseraie de l'Hay') or reddish-purple ('Hansa') or even white ('Blanc Double de Coubert') and deliciously fragrant, often chosen for potpourri. *Rosa rugosa* prove hardy at least to -20 and work in all Washington and Oregon zones. Plan include special roses at a party next year and start growing now.

Caution: The most toxic pesticides, the combination fertilizer and insecticide types sold with the active ingredient disulfoton (also called DySyston), *should not be used at any point* in the season if you plan to eat the roses. Florist roses, generally treated with pesticides, should not be eaten.

Make friends with a rain gauge, soaker hose, and mulch—you won't regret it.

ROSES

PLANNING

August is a quiet garden month, with plants completing their bloom. Take time as cool evening comes to settle and enjoy the garden's late summer ripening. Roses produce slightly less bloom this month, but many will be forming strong buds for the show that September's cooler weather brings.

Start reviewing rose performance, photographing for your records. If some developed intractable disease problems or didn't please for some other reason, remove them. Giving up on a plant every now and then just leaves space for another with better characteristics.

PLANTING

This is absolutely the last month to do it. Roots need to get settled before winter, especially in Zones 5 and 6. If installing roses from containers, unpack them carefully because pots will be full of roots. Presoak roots and plant on a cloudy day, early in the morning or in the evening.

CARE

Mulch around newly planted roses this month. The later in the summer that a rose is planted, the more susceptible it will be to freezing and winter kill.

Rake up fallen leaves, especially if defoliation is the result of diseases such as blackspot. Trash or burn them if that's allowed. Do not put them in the compost.

PRUNING

Deadhead the plants until the end of August. After that, allow the blooms to form natural seedpods, the heps.

Remove suckers that have developed during the summer. What are suckers? They're random shoots emerging from the roots of grafted plants. They do not occur on own-root plants.

Zones 5-6: When the graft union is underground, suckers may still emerge from the root stock, though it happens less often. It may be necessary to pull, tug, and dig to get them out.

Zones 7-9: Look around the roots. Are there suckers springing up from the rootstock?

FRAGRANT ROSES

Some good choices in all zones for distinctive fragrance:

***Rosa rugosa* x hybrids:**
- 'Roseraie de l'Hay' (deep red-purple)
- 'Thérèse Bugnet' (lavender-pink)

Shrub roses:
- 'Distant Drums' (lavender/bronze)
- 'Golden Wings' (yellow, single flower)
- 'Stanwell Perpetual' (soft pink)
- 'Henry Hudson' (white—Explorer rose)
- 'Jens Munk' (pink—Explorer rose)

Floribunda:
- 'City of London' (soft pink)

Shrub rose:
- 'Gertrude Jekyll' (lavender/pink—David Austin rose)
- 'Abraham Darby' (apricot—David Austin rose)
- Floribunda 'Sunsprite' (yellow)
- 'Iceberg' (white)

Hybrid tea:
- 'Just Joey' (apricot)
- 'Double Delight' (red/yellow blend)
- 'Dainty Bess' (pink)
- 'Fragrant Cloud' (red/salmon)

Visit nurseries to survey roses arriving throughout this month.

Remove all canes growing below the bud union.

Suckers are strong growers and will become too vigorous and compete with the chosen rose type. They are unlike the blooming canes, with different leaf type and even different bark. If suckers grow in canes and remain long enough to develop bloom, the rose color and shape will differ. Gardeners sometimes say, "My white rose turned red!"

WATERING

This is a vital task this month. August may have no measurable rainfall throughout the region. Even with occasional storms, the cooler air and moistened leaves may be too slight to help the rose that needs water at the roots.

Be sure to get water eight to twelve inches down and concentrate in particular on roses that have been newly planted. Large, established **shrub** roses and **climbing** roses will be going dormant at the end of the month and need less water.

FERTILIZING

No fertilizing is needed this month. The roses you pick now and in September developed from July's application. There's one exception: Container roses on patios and decks need liquid fertilizer mid-month for best health.

PROBLEMS

You may see the fuzzy, gray, powdery spores of powdery mildew appearing, not only on roses but on many other garden plants. Cooler evenings and dry days increase the fungal activity as can excess fertilizer. Review your records to assess how much fertilizer (especially nitrogen) you've applied to the rose. Overfertilizing causes soft, weak foliage that's more susceptible to aphids and powdery mildew.

Fungicides such as potassium bicarbonate (sold as Remedy™) can reduce powdery mildew, even after it shows on the plants. Other diseases like rose rust and rose blackspot need to be treated before the symptoms show to be effective at all.

> ## DID YOU KNOW?
>
> **Miniature roses** combine smaller flowers with charming short plant stature. They settle happily in containers and come in as many styles and types as larger roses. Some can grow as tall as four feet, but most hover between eighteen inches and three feet. Blooms are petite compared to the smaller bush size. You might find the perfect shape of the **hybrid tea** rose but only one inch in length, or a fragrant **floribunda** style with a three-inch spray of bloom.
>
> Rose growers and breeders on the West Coast, especially Ralph Moore in California, produced some of the first miniature roses forty years ago. Moore's rose 'Beauty Secret', a classic warm rosy red, received several American Rose Society awards of excellence. New miniatures appear yearly. They're among the easiest to buy and care for in bloom, and you'll find them throughout the summer in nurseries. Several beautiful ones include 'Rainbow's End', a warm shimmery red and yellow blend; and 'Little Artist', red with white centers. Miniature roses aren't grafted; they grow on their own roots. In all zones, when planting them, set them at the same level at which they previously grew.

SEPTEMBER

ROSES

PLANNING

Review the last burst of bloom this month, noting your favorites. Perhaps you'll find a local rose show this month. September is a beautiful month for bloom.

For ideas about roses, try going online to the American Rose Society at www.ars.org. (Be sure to stick to those best adapted to your area and climate zones.)

Have the perennials planted with the roses done well? Are they scrambling all over the rose roots? Roses don't grow well when their root systems are smothered with competitive plants. For Zones 5 to 6, move perennial plants this month, mulching well. For zones 7 to 9, move anytime into mid-November. Or even later if the ground stays unfrozen.

PLANTING

All zones: Do not plant or move roses this month.

Zones 5-6: If you have a container rose in a nursery pot that hasn't been installed, sink it into the ground, pot and all. Then cover it with four to six inches of fluffy, mulch-like pine needles, keeping the mulch away from the plant's trunk.

Zones 7-9: Rose cuttings may be started this month, following directions in the July entry.

CARE

Continue to check your rose cuttings for even moisture. Any rose cutting started eight weeks ago will develop roots by now if it's going to be successful (not all will be). Tug gently on the stem to determine if they've rooted. Remove the plastic covering if they have and set them in a partly-sunny, partly-shaded place. In Zones 5 to 6, prepare a sheltered spot for rose cuttings to winter over: A cold frame is ideal, or a spot in a cool greenhouse that doesn't freeze. If neither is available, sink the pot with the cutting in the ground in a site protected from wind. Mulch over it deeply with pine needles or other loose mulch when it starts dropping leaves late this month (or in early October). Let the mulch protect them through the winter but remove it incrementally in spring. Allow them to stay in their pot until growing strongly.

Clean up fallen leaves and prune out diseased twigs to get a head start on fall clean up. You'll be glad you did next month.

A cold frame is an ideal spot to overwinter rose cuttings.

WATERING

All zones: September rain can vary from ample to nonexistent and everywhere in between. If rain is scarce, water as you have done through the summer to preserve the last blooms and hydrate the roots for winter.

FERTILIZING

Do not fertilize roses in the garden. If you have miniature roses in pots you're bringing indoors for winter, give them one more fertilization this month, using half of the amount you've applied previously.

PRUNING

Celebrate the beauty of roses by cutting one final splendid bouquet. In Zones 7 to 9 flowering continues into October but slows as days shorten. Allow most blossoms to remain on repeat-blooming roses for rose heps, the seedpods of the rose. Forming heps helps the plant enter dormancy and stops the vigorous production of new leaves and flower buds.

DID YOU KNOW?

Is your soil diagnosed with "rose replant disease"?

You may have heard that when a rose is pulled out of a garden spot, another rose should not be planted in that place. Rose experts differ on the truth of this rule and whether or not it is a true "disease."

In fact, some roses do decline and die when replanted where another rose was, especially if the rose grew there for more than ten years. Some experts believe that the former rose exuded a chemical that inhibits growth of the new rose. Other causes, however, may be more typical and include nutrient deficiency/excess and poor drainage that encourages fungal spores that cause root rot.

If you transplant a healthy rose, the remaining soil may readily accept a new rose. Many growers advise adding compost with the new planting; some replace all soil where new roses are to be planted, no matter what the condition of the removed rose.

If a newly planted rose does poorly and nothing explains its difficulties, you can amend the soil with compost or replace the soil. Consider putting another type of plant in that spot. But if you don't want to give up yet, review the different factors essential for rose performance, such as well drained, nutrient-rich, moist soil.

PROBLEMS

Powdery mildew remains troublesome this month. Your choice to treat it depends on the severity of the infection, the garden prominence of the rose, and how soon the first frosts will arrive. You can choose to take no action, knowing that the affected leaves will drop off with cold weather (then rake them for disposal). Or you can spray with a registered fungicide to reduce the infection on emerging leaves right now.

OCTOBER

ROSES

 PLANNING

October is a busy garden month in all zones. Planting of spring-blooming **bulbs**, general clean-up, and the last of summer's chores arrive just as the daylight dwindles steadily, reducing garden time. For rose gardens, identify places to install next spring's bare-root roses and evaluate performance of existing plants.

 PLANTING

Zones 7-9: Transplanting—moving a rose from one spot to another—is best done when the plants have dropped their leaves and gone into dormancy, which may start happening at the end of this month. New rose bushes may be planted if available.

 CARE

All zones: Rake up and discard all fallen leaves and petals under roses to reduce disease organisms. Don't put them in compost.

Standard roses, or "rose trees," require winter protection. These elegant grafted trees, with their single straight trunks and formal rounded tops, need spe-cial winter care. They have two graft unions, one at the crown just above the root and the other just under the branching and blooming section. They're vulnerable to freezing in all zones. Start by removing all leaves after the first cold weather. If they've grown in containers sink the containers in the ground or move them into cold storage where they won't freeze. Wrap the exposed trunks with foam pipe insulation, snuggling it against the entire trunk with twine. You may want to use a double layer.

Zones 5-6: Hill up the plants. What is "hilling up"? This technique protects graft unions from freezing. Pile soil or a mixture of soil and aged compost over the graft in a cone shape. Bring in a separate supply rather than scooping it up from around the plants, which can expose and disturb roots. After the ground freezes, cover the whole rose crown with a foot of pine needles or other fluffy mulch. Some wrap the top branches with burlap, making the outline of a lollipop.

Zones 7-9: Allow leaves to fall or remove them after the first freeze, and mulch over the plants in November. Toward month's end, remove all remaining foliage from roses. Strange as this seems, it gets diseased leaves off the plant and also forces the plant into needed winter dormancy. It's easy to do with smaller bushes but will be impractical for large scrambling climbers or huge shrubs. For those, raking under the bushes and spring pruning will assist removal of old, overwintering leaves.

Mulch doesn't prevent freezing, just fluctuating freezing and thawing. Pine needles were recommended by local experts in Spokane, Washington because they drain easily and are easily obtained. Compost, fallen deciduous leaves, or aged sawdust may be substituted.

If you need an example of how hilling up for the most sensitive roses is done, visit a local rose garden. (See June for listings.) Or talk to a nursery specialist.

 WATERING

As roses go into dormancy and fall rains return, the need for watering usually ceases.

Zones 5-6: If storms don't provide deep moisture, water roses thoroughly before applying winter mulch. Roses will need well hydrated roots to help with winter freeze resistance.

FERTILIZING

All fertilizing is over for the season, even on container plants on patios in the warmest zones.

PRUNING

Zones 5-6: Remove ragged growth and shorten very long branches on shrubs and **old roses** and **floribundas** to help with winter protection. Also, look at bushes (especially at the ends of branches) to identify "bunchy" growth where snow could pile up and possibly break the branch.

Zones 7-9: Major pruning waits until spring. Trim back long canes that may tear in winter winds.

PROBLEMS

Mossy balls on roses? You may see these oddities after leaf drop reveals the structure of branches

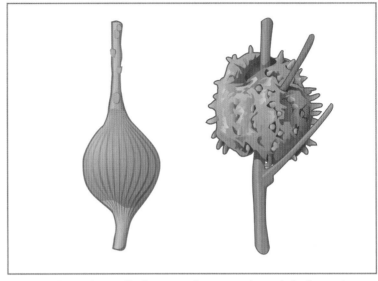

Insect galls are basically the same shape, a spherical "ball" inside which insect larvae reside.

and trunk. If you find strange, fuzzy, mossy-looking balls on a stem or stems, they're the work of an insect, the mossy rose gall wasp (*Diplolepis rosae*). Mossy rose galls are spherical and quite soft to touch. About the size of a fifty cent piece when mature, the gall holds young wasp larvae inside. Adults emerge in spring. Prune these out of the plant and place elsewhere in the garden. They can't

sting or harm you because they are tucked inside undeveloped. Gall wasps seldom harm roses other than reducing bloom or leaf on branches. They're almost more of a curiosity than a rose-threatening problem.

Gardeners often forget that wasps and other members of their family are generally beneficial in the garden, eating aphids and other undesirables.

VIRAL DISEASES

Roses can be affected by viruses, which cause odd markings on leaves and may result in stunted bushes. The most noticeable symptoms include distinct mottling or yellow lines in irregular patterns on the leaves (not following the vein structure); these can show up at any time during the growing season. Nothing helps.

The plant, once infected with the virus, cannot recover. Have a nursery specialist or WSU or OSU Extension Master Gardener volunteer diagnose the viral problems. If it's viral, the whole plant must be removed from the garden. Use the fall garden time to pull these out and dispose of them.

NOVEMBER

ROSES

 PLANNING

Get lists of roses from local societies, gather catalogs, and transcribe your notes of summer garden visits. Preparing a list of roses now will help you order from catalogs or locate plants from nurseries when they begin arriving in late winter and early spring.

 PLANTING

Zones 5-6: Weather prevents planting or transplanting this month.

Zones 7-9: November is often perfect for moving and transplanting existing roses once they go dormant. Before proceeding, check drainage. If the spot drains slowly, the soil may be too compacted or dense for the rose to thrive. Choose a day above freezing when the soil is workable, not sodden from November's frequent rainstorms.

If moving a large rose, prune off about one-third of the height and bind the branches together with twine towards the center of the plant. Dig the hole as deep as the rootball and twice as wide. Settle the rose in place, firm the soil around it, being sure it's not deeper in the ground than

it was at the original location. Untie the rose and use pruners to trim back any broken twigs or cracked branches.

Water the rose to finish. Cover the bud union with mulch, using soil or compost, and mulch about three to four inches deep over the roots after planting.

COLD HARDY ROSES

These roses can overwinter in Zones 4 to 9, and occasionally in zones 2b to 3 as in the Parkland series)

- **Albas:**
  - Carefree Series™:
    - Carefree Delight (pink)
    - Carefree Beauty
- **Canadian Explorer Series Roses:**
  - Henry Kelsey (dark pink)
  - Henry Hudson (white)
  - William Baffin (Pink)
  - John Davis (pink)
  - John Franklin (red)
- ***Rosa rugosa* and hybrids:**
  - Blanc Double de Courbet
  - Hansa
  - Hunter (red)
- **Griffith Buck Roses:**
  - Applejack (single pink)
  - Winter Sunset (apricot)
- **Kordesii:**
  - John Cabot (pink)
  - William Baffin (pink)
- **Meidiland series:**
  - Magic Meidiland (pink)
  - Red Meidiland (red, white eye)
- **Parkland series:**
  - Morden Ruby
  - Morden Snowbeauty
- **Shrubs:**
  - Stanwell Perpetual (light pink)

All of these roses are classified as shrubs, and many are repeat bloomers.

They're also disease-resistant and generally easy to grow, making them good choices for warmer zones also. Many other roses survive beautifully in Zone 5. Many Zone 6 roses, including hybrid teas, do well in Spokane's Zone 5b if given winter cover. You'll have lots of choices.

 CARE

All zones: Rake away any fallen leaves and debris around the roses.

Zones 5-6: Some of the most cold-hardy roses, such as the Parkland and Morden series, generally manage winter with a layer of three to four inches of mulch over the roots.

Zones 7-9: Remove leaves late in the month to force dormancy on **hybrid teas** and other winter-tender roses. Leave rose hips; if picking a few for brilliant house decoration, leave the rest on the bush for birds.

Pull mulch up over the graft union and cover the roots with two to three inches of fresh mulch generally completes what is needed west of the Cascades.

 WATERING

Zones 5-6: Thorough watering is needed before covering roses for winter. Be sure to water well if there is no rain so roses go into winter freeze with a good supply of moisture at their roots.

 FERTILIZING

All zones: Because roses are going dormant this month, fertilizing is not advised.

 PRUNING

All zones: Avoiding fall pruning also contributes to winter survival because the plant is not shocked into producing tender, vulnerable new foliage during mild weather. Major pruning waits until early spring as rose growth starts.

Zones 7-9: Tidy up this month, nipping back any large branches that will whip in the wind. Tying branches for stability also helps.

 PROBLEMS

Dead wood on dormant roses in winter is sometimes hard to distinguish from wood that has simply lost leaves. While this isn't a good month for pruning, you'll find that checking over plants after high winds will enable you to trim out broken branches. Clip the branch down below the breakage.

Truly dead wood will look ashy gray or dead brown, often with flaking bark. Dead wood is harder to cut; it resists the shears. Live wood will have fresh white pith inside. Do as little trimming as possible this month, but definitely care for storm damage.

CHOOSING DISEASE-RESISTANT ROSES

Rose specialists evaluate the best choices in their own areas. Lists will differ according to the evaluation of different growers and local growing conditions.

Roses often noted as disease resistant by many different evaluators include: **hybrid teas** 'Dainty Bess' (pink), 'Just Joey' (apricot) and 'Honor' (white.) **Ground cover roses**, as a class, were bred for disease-resistance, including 'Pavement' roses.

Landscape roses like pink 'Carefree Beauty'™ and 'Carefree Wonder'™ handle cold weather to Zone 4 and thrive without disease problems. *Rosa rugosa* 'Hansa' (red-purple) lives up to its reputation for toughness. 'Henry Hudson,' (white) part of the Explorer series, grows easily, as do others in that series hybridized in Canada. **Species roses** in general and the category called **old garden roses** (in gardens before 1867) often resist disease. One of the oldest of all known historic roses, *Rosa gallica* 'Versicolor' (also known as 'Rosa Mundi') wafts great fragrance from pink and white blooms—without disease problems.

December

ROSES

PLANNING

Review your satisfaction with this year's roses. Catalogs tantalize with new cultivars—perhaps you want to try some **ground cover roses** or some of the newer **landscape roses**. Check with the supplier or nursery about the disease resistance of the new rose for your particular region.

Observe drainage conditions during winter storms; if you're planning new rose installations, mark low-lying or wet spots holding winter water so that you'll avoid planting roses there. To test drainage, dig a hole twelve inches deep and twelve inches wide. Fill it with water. Look for at least one inch of water drop per hour. Sandy soils will lose water much faster than this. If the hole still contains water after twenty-four hours, the soil drainage is inadequate for roses.

PLANTING

Zones 5-6: Inland regions generally experience hard freezes by early December, or before. Planting or transplanting is not possible now.

Zones 7-9: West of the Cascades, transplanting may continue if the ground is workable—unfrozen and not too wet.

CARE

All zones: Finish winter protection for roses.

Zones 7-9: Fill a few large plastic bags with fallen deciduous leaves as emergency insulation around cherished plants in case of temperatures descending below 20 degrees F.

PRUNING

Roses did not go dormant? Grooming the plants will encourage dormancy.

Zones 7-9: Mild December temperatures may have your roses covered in leaf and poking out the occasional blossom. You may like picking roses on Christmas Day and find the emergent buds charming. However, the roses need dormancy.

Remove foliage from **hybrid tea**, **floribunda**, **grandifloras**, and **English roses** that continue to grow. Allow buds to stay on to develop heps and seeds.

WATERING

Watering is not necessary for outdoor plants, but check any roses under overhangs where rain may not reach, and water these.

FERTILIZING

No fertilizer is required this month. If you didn't keep records of application this year, resolve to start a record book next season.

PROBLEMS

Rake and dispose of any fallen leaves or twigs that may carry rose diseases. Don't compost them.

SHRUBS

Shrubs are the most serviceable plants of the garden. They have permanent woody stems like trees, and a variety of floral color and leaf texture like perennials. Some shrubs can last for generations, as the old lilacs and rhododendrons surviving from old farmsteads remind us. With the countless new forms and cultivars becoming available each year, there is a shrub to fit just about any garden purpose or condition. Shrubs will reward you with years of beauty and practical function in return for modest levels of care through the year.

Winter blooming camellias and witch hazels (*Hamamelis*) in western Oregon and Washington, and forsythia, rhododendrons azaleas and lilacs mark spring throughout the region. Summer blooms arrive on mock orange (*Philadelphus* spp.) and hydrangea. Shrubs provide sweet fragrances and interesting foliage. Brilliant fall color can be found among cranberry bush viburnum (*Viburnum opulus*), winged euonymus (*Euonymus alata*) and chokeberry (*Aronia* spp.). Strawberry tree (*Arbutus unedo*) adds small white blossoms to the fall mix west of the Cascades. Many shrubs with

distinctive berries, colorful stems, or evergreen foliage add to winter interest.

Landscape functions: With their permanent woody structure, shrubs fulfill many important landscape functions. Shrubs bridge many of the landscape features provided by trees and perennials. Smaller shrubs serve as ground cover. Upright forms work as a hedge or narrow screen for privacy and to define garden spaces. The traditional "foundation plantings" soften the edges where house walls meet the earth. Compose a colorful border with a grouping of evergreen and deciduous plants of various leaf colors, textures, blooms, and fruit. Shrubs provide low cover, food, and nesting sites for bird habitat. Taller species function as a petite specimen tree for the small garden. Several species tolerate the rigorous pruning techniques required for tightly sheared hedges, the flat plane of an espalier, or the specialized shapes of topiary. Small shrubs grown in large containers provide focal interest.

Shrubs offer excellent landscape solutions for problem spots. Cover a difficult to access slope with a dense, mounding shrub that spreads by underground stems, such as box leaf honeysuckle (*Lonicera nitida*) or cutleafed stephanan-

dra (*Stephanandra incisa* 'Crispa'). Twig dogwoods and winter berry holly (*Ilex verticillata*) are well adapted for open sites with very wet soil. Create a narrow screen with tightly columnar evergreens. Low growing drought tolerant shrubs such as *Potentilla* or rock rose (*Cistus* spp.) are a pleasing replacement for a poorly performing patch of lawn on a sunny slope.

SHRUBS COME IN MANY SHAPES AND SIZES

Most garden shrubs are multi-stemmed; they are made up of several trunks or canes emerging from the soil, with new stems appearing each year. Some grow in clumps, such as mock-orange (*Philadelphus* spp.), deciduous azaleas, or hydrangeas. Others spread widely by underground stems (stolons), such as Oregon grape (*Mahonia* spp.). Several species and cultivars have neatly mounded shapes. Place them with enough room to reach their natural spread, and they rarely need pruning. Rock roses (*Cistus* spp.), evergreen azaleas, spirea, and some dwarf conifers have this mounding form. Tree-like shrubs develop strong central trunks: *Camellia*, *Pieris japonica*, rhododendrons, and others. Low, spread-

ing prostrate shrubs such as creeping juniper (*Juniperus horizontalis*) and Point Reyes ceanothus occupy the ground-cover plane.

WHEN IS A SHRUB A TREE?

It can be confusing as to when a plant is above a "large shrub" and crosses over into a "small tree." A practical definition centers on the height, structure and permanence of the trunks. Trees are generally distinguished by growing more than twelve feet in height with large main trunks. New growth extends from buds along the branches. Red maples (*Acer rubrum*) are a classic example of the tree form. Shrubs are typically shorter than twelve feet and most can be rejuvenated with early spring pruning that remove stems at ground level—a technique which could kill or permanently disfigure trees.

Several taller growing shrubs hover at the boundary between tree and shrub: some species of rhododendron, *Camellia*, *Osmanthus*, and *Viburnum*. But, unlike trees, these may be effectively regenerated by pruning the trunks down close to ground level. Lilacs grow mostly as multi-stem shrubs, but merge into tree form when tall gnarled older trunks are preserved. In very mature gardens of 40

years or more, old shrubs that have reached "small tree" dimensions are common.

There are a few rugged tree species so tolerant of rigorous pruning they are commonly sold for use as shrubs and hedges. Cherry laurel (*Prunus laurocerasus*), Portuguese laurel (*Prunus lusitanica*), and *Photinia* commonly reach twenty to thirty feet or more in height with broad spreading crowns when left un-sheared. Many people may not recognize them as the same plant in their natural state. Their large growth habit can make them difficult to maintain as hedges on many sites, making them a nuisance in the landscape.

CHOOSING THE RIGHT PLANT

Select shrubs adapted to your specific garden conditions, and position them with enough room to expand. Ignore the common notion that shrubs can be "easily maintained with pruning." The all too common sight of hedges that have devoured entire sidewalks or shrubs that are pruned into odd shapes reminds us that, in the long run, pruning cannot make up for the wrong size shrub. Plants grown in their preferred light and soil conditions will thrive with fewer pest problems and maintenance needs.

Pay close attention to specific cultivar names and their tagged descriptions when shopping for shrubs. A species, such as *Camellia sasanqua*, may have many different cultivars with different bloom colors. If you want a red one, check the tag. Likewise, mature size can be very different among cultivars: 'nana' and 'prostrata' are two common cultivar names for smaller versions of a species. Consider the sizes listed on nursery tags as a general guide, not a steadfast rule. Climate, garden microclimate, and care regime also affect eventual growth. Visit public gardens or nursery display gardens to see living full grown examples in your area. Nurseries have good supplies of plants "in season"—shop during fall for leaf color and berry set, and in spring for flower color.

PLANTING PRACTICES

Review the general steps under planting trees and shrubs in the General Introduction. Shrubs are mostly sold in containers, some as balled and burlap, and only occasionally bare root. For zones 4 to 6, plant them in early fall and mid-spring. In the absence of extreme cold or wet conditions, you can continue to plant throughout winter in zones 7 to 9. If you are planting a large area, aim to complete

planting by the end of March for better plant establishment with lower watering needs the first summer. Container shrubs planted later in the season will require greater after care—watering, mulching, and weeding—throughout summer.

If you need to move a shrub to a new spot, most are easily transplanted while dormant in fall or early spring. When the soil is damp and holds together well, smaller shrubs are easily dug up and moved. Be sure to capture as wide a section of roots as you can, at least half again as wide the above ground width. Protect bare roots from drying out during the process. When moving deciduous multi-stem shrubs, it can be helpful to prune out some of the bigger canes and to tie spreading stems together for easier handling. Some multi-stem shrubs such as lilacs or spirea may be easily transplanted by slicing out just a portion of the stems and roots, much like taking a division from an herbaceous perennial. This leaves the original plant in place while creating a new transplant.

Planting too close to the foundation walls or sidewalks is the most common planting error with shrubs. Don't be deceived by the small stature of young container plants, they will

expand rapidly! Shrubs can be economical for landscaping because they grow so quickly. Once planted, smaller plants sold in one-gallon containers easily catch up in size with those from larger, more costly containers. Allow them enough room to grow without being overcrowded. Add low ground-covers, perennials, or annuals to temporarily cover open ground until the shrubs fill in.

PRUNING

Match mature size to the space, and your shrubs may rarely need pruning. Follow their natural growth patterns to determine the best pruning practices for optimal growth and performance. Resist the urge to trim all shrubs into geometric forms—it can mean more work, and flower display and leaf attractiveness usually suffers. Unless your garden design requires highly man-aged plants for hedges or sculptural effects, keeping plants informally shaped with save time and effort.

Older stems on species such as *Forsythia* and red or yellow stem dogwoods (*Cornus sericea* cvs.) become dull in color or bloom poorly as they age, and should be removed to make way for vigorous young stems. However, older stems are kept on tree-like shrubs such as rhododendrons or camellias. Hedge shears are best used for hedges, not on specimen or foundation shrubs. Loppers and hand shears with curved by-pass blades will provide the cleanest cut for woody stems.

For general shrub pruning, start with thinning cuts—remov-ing branches all the way back to the ground, or to a larger stem. Final cuts should be made near but not quite flush to the bark on the remaining stem. Don't leave stubs; they are unsightly and can invite the start of decay. Inspect for dead, bro-ken, or over-crowded stems and remove them first. Next, remove

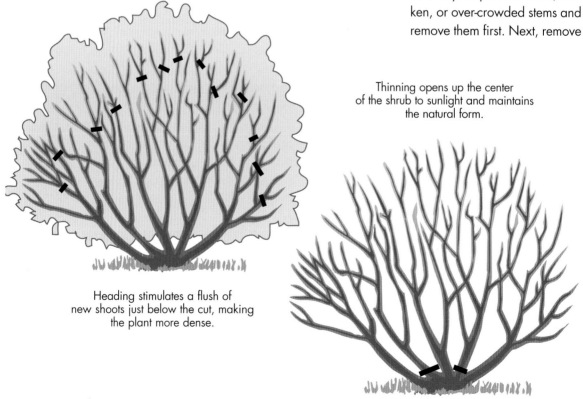

Thinning opens up the center of the shrub to sunlight and maintains the natural form.

Heading stimulates a flush of new shoots just below the cut, making the plant more dense.

any stems that are growing out of proportion or against the predominant direction of the rest of the branches. You can also reduce size using thinning cuts to remove the tallest and longest stems back to the base or inside the crown. This pruning technique maintains the natural shape of the shrub, allows good light and air circulation to the inside, and reduces the amount of future pruning needed.

Heading cuts remove the ends of branches back to a strong bud. Vigorous new shoots will grow from the buds directly beneath the cut end. Cut to buds that point in the desired direction for the best results. Use heading cuts to shorten and stiffen long and whip-like stems, and to increase the number of side shoots on those stems.

Most shrubs can be lightly thinned during the dormant season to keep them vigorous and blooming well, removing no more than $1/4$ of live branch area. To rejuvenate overgrown multi-stemmed shrubs, prune them hard in late winter, removing about one-third or so of the oldest stems down to the ground each year over three years. Vigorous shrubs may be pruned completely to the

ground in late winter, though a year's bloom is usually lost. Summer follow up pruning will be required to thin out the thick crop of new sprouts that result from this style of rejuvenation.

Summer pruning has a dwarfing affect, and is helpful for slowing growth rate when size control is important (See August). Additional shrub pruning techniques are presented throughout the monthly tasks listed in this chapter.

WATERING, MULCHING, AND FERTILIZING

Shrubs require less water and fertilizer than perennials and annuals—a great plus for developing water-wise gardens. Excessive tender growth and plant stress can occur if they are treated with the too much water or fertilizer. If you have a landscape planting that combines trees, shrubs, flowering perennial flowers, and bulbs, manage for the woody plants first. Water and fertilize according to their needs. Then provide individual applications to non-woody plants as needed.

The greatest demand for water is in early summer when growth is most active. Coarse textured mulch applied early in

the season will conserve soil moisture by suppressing weeds, reducing evaporation, and aiding good penetration when water is applied. Mulched soil holds dampness longer into the summer. Allow the soil underneath the mulch to become partially dry before watering. A mulched soil may look dry at the top, but be moist beneath. Or the surface can be damp and the soil below dry. Check the soil before and after watering: Use a trowel to get a handful of soil several inches below the surface and squeeze it to check soil moisture content. (See the General Introduction for more information on watering practices.)

Most common pest and disease problems can be minimized with proper plant selection and good cultural care. Accept some imperfections and choose the least-toxic controls when pest damage is great enough to threaten plant health. Birds, spiders and predator insects naturally supress aphids and other insect pests. Avoid the use of broad spectrum insecticides which kill beneficial insects as well as plant damagers. (See pages 285-287 for information on Integrated Pest Management.)

JANUARY

SHRUBS

PLANNING

As colder weather drives us indoors, and outdoor activities for the garden diminish, garden shrubs still have much to offer to our winter existence. Pause to take in the views and lighting of your garden at this time of year. What do you see from your favorite windows? Is the view interesting or not? Is there a spot to add a winter focal point? Take pictures and save them for making garden changes later in the season. Begin an album that tracks the progression of seasonal change as you look out from inside.

Look at the shapes and textures garden plants take on in the winter, and what scenes are most pleasing to look at. A balance of evergreen and deciduous plants will bring color and dimension to an otherwise subdued winter landscape. Evergreen shrubs provide a dramatic backdrop when combined with deciduous shrubs and trees, highlighting branch structure, colorful bark, and bright berries. Dramatic patterns and details emerge when plants are dusted in snow or outlined with frost.

Warmer sections of our region can have winter gardens can alive with fragrance and bloom, **Zones 7-9**: *Mahonia* hybrids with bright yellow floral spikes attract hummingbirds, **witch hazel** (*Hamamelis* spp. and cvs.) casts a gentle sweet scent, and the intense perfume of **sweet box** (*Sarcococca confusa*), brings a tropical hint to the dreariest of winter days.

Nurseries in milder parts of the region often keep a selection of plants with winter interest in stock at this time of year. Or visit local gardens to view interesting winter season plants.

PLANTING

Zones 4-6: It is typically too cold for planting.

Zones 7-9: Evergreen and deciduous shrubs can be planted and transplanted during warmer periods when low temperatures are in the 40s, and soil is not sopping wet. Roots suffer freeze damage at higher temperatures than stems. Store shrubs in containers where they will not be exposed to freezing temperatures. Mound mulch or compost around the pots to insulate them, or store them in a bright, unheated garage.

CARE

Zones 4-6: Check on winter protection installed for evergreens and tender shrubs (those margin-ally hardy to your growing zone). Upright evergreens such as yews and junipers may need binding with rope to keep their upright stems together. Evergreens vulnerable to desiccation from winter winds and sun can be wrapped with burlap.

Snowfall can occur in all regions this month. Gently shake snow loose with a soft broom to lighten loads on bent over stems. If conditions are icy, touching the branches may risk breaking frozen stiff stems. Allow plants covered with ice to thaw naturally unless broken branches need to be removed for safety.

PRUNING

Evergreen and deciduous shrubs can be pruned when conditions are enough above freezing to be comfortable working outdoors. Look for dead branches on evergreens. Thin out some of the larger, oldest canes on multi-stemmed shrubs such as **mock orange**, **forsythia**, and **spirea**. Prune out any broken branches from snow or ice damage.

Zones 7-9: Bring branches of **flowering quince** (*Chaenomeles* spp.), **forsythia**, **daphne**, and **witch hazel** inside to force into early bloom. Soaking the entire branch in tepid water for a few hours accelerates bloom.

SHRUBS FOR BIRD HABITAT AND WINTER INTEREST

These shrubs add winter interest while providing birds with shelter and food. Some birds feed on winter berries. Others, such as the small bushtits and brown creepers, scour the stems for aphids, scale insects, and other insects that live and over winter in the bark. Avoid using pesticides on your shrubs as most birds in our region feed on insects. For best habitat qualities, keep shrubs pruned to an open form. You'll be able to see into the plant. Don't shear them, as flower and fruit production will be reduced, and the growth can become too dense for birds to get through. Position some of these shrubs where you can observe their color and creatures from your favorite windows. Consider adding a feeder to attract a wider variety of birds.

Zones 4-6:
• **Cranberry viburnum** (*Viburnum opulus, V. trilobum*)—red winter berries
• **Firethorn** (*Pyracantha coccinea*)—orange-red winter berries

• **Japanese barberry** (*Berberis thunbergii*)—branch texture, winter berries
• **Red** or **yellow twig dogwood** (*Cornus sericea* and cvs.)—colored stems
• **Sagebrush** (*Artemisia tridentata*)—evergreen
• **Snowberry** (*Symphoricarpos albus*)—white winter berries

Zones 7-9, in addition to the above:
• **Cotoneaster** (*Cotoneaster lacteus*)—evergreen, berries
• **Darwin barberry** (*Berberis darwinii*)
• **Dwarf strawberry tree**, *Arbutus unedo* 'Compacta')—evergreen,
• **Evergreen huckleberry** (*Vaccinium ovatum*)—glossy foliage
• **Winter blooming mahonia** (*Mahonia* x 'Arthur Menzies'), 'Charity'—nectar for Annas hummingbirds.

WATERING

Zones 4-6: If the weather has been milder than usual and snowfall sparse, garden evergreens may need supplemental water, particularly if they went into winter with dry soil. (See November Watering.) Check the soil and water these plants when temperatures are well above freezing.

Zones 7-9 If rainfall has been short, planting beds that fall under building eaves or the canopy of dense conifers may become too dry. Provide water for any plants that are in very dry spots.

FERTILIZING

No fertilization this month.

PROBLEMS

Check the base of shrubs to be sure no leaves and mulch have blown or fallen against the trunk, which can provide a warm haven for rodents to chew on the bark. Use fencing as a barrier to surround young plants vulnerable to damage from deer browsing.

Be prepared for cold snaps—young shrubs that were planted this past season can be more vulnerable to freeze damage. Use light blankets, bushel baskets, or evergreen boughs for quick cover. In mildest areas, remove covering when temperatures moderate above 35 degrees F.

FEBRUARY

SHRUBS

PLANNING

Gardening catalogs reminds us to plan for a new gardening season. Look back at your pictures and notes. Many of last year's landscape problem-spots can be solved with good shrub plantings. Tired of mowing grass on a steep bank? Replace the turf with a bed of dense growing shrubs. Make mowing and edging easier by round out odd-shaped corners into a smooth line. Need a low screen that won't need constant trimming? Plant upright shrub cultivars that reach 4 feet, such as the **English yew** (*Taxus baccata* 'Standishii'), **American arborvitae** (*Thuja occidentalis* 'Rheingold'), *Rhaphiolepis* 'Gulf Green', or **heavenly bamboo** (*Nandina domestica* 'Gulf Stream').

Extremely damp turf areas that are hard to mow might be changed over to a shrub bed with deciduous species that thrive in damp soil, such as **winterberry holly** (*Ilex verticillata* cvs.), **stem dogwoods** (*Cornus sericea* cvs.) and **shrub willows** (*Salix purpurea*). For smaller spaces, look for the dwarf versions.

PLANTING

Zones 4-6: Conditions are typically too cold for planting shrubs.

Zones 7-9: This is a good time to plant fruit trees and deciduous shrubs, including bare root nursery stock. Plant when temperatures are above freezing and the soil is not sopping wet. Working on wet soils will damage soil structure, resulting in compaction and poor drainage. See the General Introduction for information on soil management

CARE

Zones 4-6: Check on plants to see that winter protection remains intact.

Zones 7-9: As weather warms, remove any winter protection used on tender plants and rake away mulches that have been used for freeze protection. Clean out any winter weeds that have cropped up among shrubs and groundcovers. Weeds can thrive at more challenging temperatures than we imagine.

WATERING

Garden conditions typically remain moist this month. Continue to check on container plants, and those in the dry shadows of eaves or evergreen canopy. Monitor recently transplanted shrubs.

FERTILIZING

Nitrogen readily leaches out of soil during heavy winter precipitation, and it is not a good time for fertilization.

PRUNING

Zones 4-6: Begin pruning deciduous multi-stem shrubs when conditions are mild enough to work comfortably outdoors. To enhance form and floral display for spring, thin out a few of the largest old canes on multi-stem shrubs such as **mock orange**, **forsythia**, **quince**, **lilac**, and **spirea**. Remove these and any broken stems as close to the ground as possible. Do not shear or head back any of the remaining stems, or you'll be removing flower buds. Bring **quince** and **forsythia** branches inside to force into bloom. Remove any branches that have been broken during winter weather.

Zones 7-9: Prune shrub conifers and broad leaf evergreens in late winter. Repair winter damage. Begin pruning on summer blooming shrubs that flower on new growth, including **glossy abelia** (*Abelia* x *grandiflora*), **bush cinquefoil** (*Potentilla* spp.), *Hypericum*, and **summer sweet** (*Clethra alnifolia*). Thin out old unproductive stems to the ground,

NATURALLY NARROW PLANTS FOR EASY CARE HEDGES

Rapidly growing shrubs that tolerate heavy shearing are often chosen for new hedges. But they also require frequent trimming once they've grown. With patience for slower growth, choose cultivars with naturally narrow forms to build a hedge with lower pruning requirements. Avoid planting hedges and screens too close to sidewalks or fences. Space the plants according to their mature spread: the center of shrubs which grow to 4 or 5 feet in diameter should be placed about 2 feet from sidewalk edges, and on 2 to 3 foot centers within the row. Here is a brief list of narrow shrub cultivars which can be trained informally, treated as a hand pruned screen, or sheared into formal hedges:

Zones 4-6:
• **American arborvitae** 'Rheingold' (*Thuja occidentalis* 'Rheingold') 5 feet height x 3 feet width
• **Barberry** 'Helmond Pillar' (*Berberis thunbergii* f. *atropurpurea* 'Helmond Pillar') 6 feet height x 2 feet width

• **Boxwood** 'Graham Blandy' (*Buxus sempervirens* 'Graham Blandy') 8 feet height x 1½ feet width
• **English yew** 'Standishii' (*Taxus baccata* 'Standishii') 4 feet height x 1½ feet width
• **Irish yew** (*Taxus baccata* 'Fastigiata') 20 feet height x 4 feet width
• **Japanese holly** 'Jersey Pinnacle' (*Ilex crenata* 'Jersey Pinnacle') 6 feet height x 4 feet width
• **Japanese holly** 'Mariesii' (*Ilex crenata* 'Mariesii') 3 feet height x 1½ feet width

Zones 7-9, in addition to the above:
• **Dwarf yeddo rhaphiolepis** (*Rhaphiolepis umbellata* Gulf Green™) 3 to 4 feet height x 2 feet width
• **Heavenly bamboo** 'Gulf Stream' (*Nandina domestica* 'Gulf Stream') 4 feet height x 2 feet width
• **Japanese euonymus** 'Green Spire' (*Euonymus japonicas* 'Green Spire') 15 feet height x 6 feet width

removing no more than about one quarter of the shoots. Remove dead and damaged stems.

Hedges that need to be reduced in size can be cut back hard to bare stems late in the dormant season. Reduce width one side at a time to maintain some foliage cover. **Yews, laurel, photinia, privet** and others that produce new shoots on bare stems can be greatly reduced. Beware, conifers such as **pines, junipers, arborvitae** and others don't produce new shoots on the bare stems, and often die when pruned too heavily.

Prune **hydrangeas** every spring just as buds green up and swell. Thin out some of the older, very crowded, and very spindly canes, removing them at ground level. Remove dried flower heads, cutting the stems just above strong buds; use heading cuts on remaining stems if more dense growth is desired.

PROBLEMS

Webworm nests with patches of brown foliage may be seen on junipers and prostrate **cotoneaster**

(*Cotoneaster horizontalis*). Trim out and dispose of these nests before caterpillars emerge. Horticultural oil can be sprayed on evergreen and dormant deciduous shrubs where webworm, scale, aphids, and mites were severe the previous year. Apply on dry days when temperatures are above 40 degrees F. Applied once during the dormant season, the oil suffocates eggs and small insects on the plant. Follow label directions carefully. Contact WSU or OSU Extension for positive identification and control recommendations.

MARCH

SHRUBS

PLANNING

This is a busy time of year for tending shrubs. Take a moment to review the shrubs in your garden and their pruning requirements. Are they blooming well each year? How often do they need to be pruned? Have they become difficult to manage? Plan now for garden changes and to schedule pruning that will address these problems.

If you have to rigorously prune a shrub more often than every three to five years to contain its size, it is probably too large for the site. Don't struggle trying to contain it. Remove it or transplant it to a roomier location. Replace it with a smaller growing shrub. If growth has been especially long and lush, cut back on water and fertilizer to help moderate growth.

Another option is to wait until summer to prune these shrubs, using thinning cuts to remove the longest branches. Less new growth will be stimulated from this mid-season pruning. (See August.)

PLANTING

This is a good month for planting. Temperatures are warming and soils are moist. Shrubs planted and mulched now will establish quickly with lower summer irrigation requirements. Bare root plants can be installed in all zones. (See General Introduction for Planting details.)

CARE

Zones 4-6: As the weather warms up, remove coverings and mulch used for winter freeze protection.

Zones 7-9: Bring container plants out of winter storage. Lightly top-dress with fresh potting soil or screened compost. Water thoroughly. Apply a slow-release fertilizer according to label directions. Repot plants where roots are coming through the bottom or have become so dense containers are difficult to water.

In the landscape, apply or refresh the organic mulch to 2 to 4 inches deep around new plants, and for plants that suffered drought stress last season. Early season mulching helps retain moisture, suppresses weeds, and replenishes nutrients and organic matter. See the Introduction chapter for more information on mulches.

WATERING

Zones 4-6: Check for dry soil under evergreens and provide a deep soaking to support new spring growth. Keep container plants watered.

Zones 7-9: Look over your watering equipment from last season to see what repairs, replacements, or additions may be necessary. Get rain barrels ready for the season and be sure screen-covered lids are in place to keep debris and mosquitoes out.

FERTILIZING

Zones 7-9: Acidifying fertilizers such as cottonseed meal and products containing ammonium sulfate are helpful for **camellias, azaleas, heaths, heathers, rhododendrons**, and other shrubs adapted to acid soils. Some rhododendron growers suggest fertilizing before buds begin to swell and once more after flowering. Fertilize in moderation, and only as needed.

Provide slow release fertilizer for ornamentals in containers.

PRUNING

Zones 4-6: Pruning of deciduous shrubs can begin. Thin out about

DID YOU KNOW?

Hand pruners with curved by-pass blades provide the cleanest cut for woody plants. Use them on branches up to $1/2$-inch diameter. **Loppers** with a similar, but larger by-pass blades and long handles will cut stems up to 2 inches in diameter. **Pruning saws** are designed to cut on the pull stroke, and those with three-sided razor teeth and tapered blade thickness make rapid cuts with less binding. Nine-inch saw blades are effective for stems up to 4-inch diameter. For larger stems, go to a saw with a longer blade that has self-cleaning, raker teeth to clear away sawdust as you cut.

Clean and dry your tools after each use. Use steel wool and coat lightly with oil, especially when used in wet weather or gummed with sap and pitch. **Be sure the bolts are tightened and joints oiled.** They'll make poor cuts if there is any wobble between the blades. Use a fine file or wet sharpening stone to keep cutting edges sharp. Replace worn saw blades or take them to a professional for sharpening.

A coat of bright red or yellow paint will protect wood handles and make tools easier to spot on the ground when you are working.

one quarter of the old canes on multi-stem shrubs such as **lilac**, **mock orange**, **weigela**, and **viburnum**. Remove any broken or dead stems.

Zones 7-9: Prune **rhododendrons, azaleas, camellias, silk tassel** (*Garrya* spp.) and **sweet box** (*Sarcococca*) as their blooms fade, and before new growth emerges. Use thinning cuts. Remove any dead or damaged stems, and those resting along the ground.

All zones: To invigorate tired shrubs, prune them just before new growth begins in early spring. Extremely overgrown, vigorous shrubs such as **forsythia** or **firethorn** (*Pyracantha* spp.), may be completely pruned to the ground. Good results are also

achieved by removing about $1/3$ of the oldest and most crowded stems each year over three years.

For **buddleja**, remove a few of the very oldest stems to the ground, or cut to a framework of stems about 3 feet tall. **Buddleja** is proving to be invasive in many areas of our region. Put a reminder in June to trim summer blooms as they fade, before they go to seed. Better yet, remove it now and replace it with another flowering shrub. **Butterfly bush** (*Buddleja davidii*) is now on invasive weed lists in both Washington and Oregon. While butterflies take its nectar, they will not lay their eggs on it. *Buddleja* seedlings often displace native willows that are

an essential food source for native butterfly caterpillars. While researches develop seedless cultivars, gardeners are being encouraged to replace *Buddleja davidii* and weed out new seedlings wherever they are seen.

PROBLEMS

Zones 4-6: Horticultural oil can be sprayed on those evergreen or deciduous shrubs where insects such as webworm, scale, aphids, and mites were severe the previous year (see February Problems zones 7-9).

APRIL

SHRUBS

PLANNING

Early-flowering shrubs mark the beginning of warmer days, blooming alongside spring bulbs. Dress up early spring color with the addition of some early bloomers such as *Forsythia x intermedia* 'Lynwood Variety', *Rhododendron* 'Cornell Pink', or *Fothergilla gardenii*. Place them in full sun with evergreens behind for brilliant contrast. Visit local gardens and nurseries to hunt out the most attractive early blooming shrubs in your area. Shrubs purchased this month can be planted right away for immediate results.

Sweet scented **lilacs** grace May gardens. Choose among white, pink, and purple hues. 'Sensation' has white-edge purple blossoms, and 'Belle de Nancy' has pale, double purple blooms. Spokane became the City of Lilacs in the 1930s when local garden clubs launched an intensive **lilac** planting campaign. Plan a visit during the third week of May to take in the annual Lilac Festival.

PLANTING

Take your planting plan to nurseries with you. Choose plants with healthy leaves, plump green buds, and no broken or dead stems. Stay away from very small plants in large pots, and very large shrubs in very small pots. Avoid potted plants with roots growing out of the bottom, or with thick woody roots visibly circling the top of the container.

Zones 4-6: Plant all types of nursery stock this month—bare root, B&B, and containers. Transplant dormant deciduous shrubs before the leaf and flower buds begin to swell and open.

Zones 7-9: Woody plants installed before the end of April will suffer less drought stress than those planted later in the spring. Create a shallow basin with 2- to 3-inch rim of soil to aid watering. Mulch bare soil around new plants and keep mulch from covering the stems.

CARE

Zones 4-6: Bring container shrubs out of winter storage: shrubby fuchsias, marginally hardy **rhododendrons** or **azaleas**, **rosemary**, and others. Clean up dead leaves and stems. Lightly top-dress with fresh potting soil or screened compost and slow release fertilizer. Repot those which have outgrown last year's containers. In the landscape, apply or refresh the organic mulch as needed for new plants and those which were drought stressed last season. See General Introduction chapter for more information on mulches.

Weed growth accelerates this month. Focus early season weeding on those that go rapidly from bloom to seed, such as dandelions and mustards, to suppress their continued spread. Practice weed birth control—don't let them propagate. Immediately cover exposed ground with mulch or more ground covers.

WATERING

All zones: Nursery soil mixes often dry out sooner than the surrounding soil, causing drought stress. Set up soaker hoses or irrigation products with low volume emitters to supply water to newly planted materials. Directing water to those plants that need it most. Well established plants require less water. Test automatic irrigation systems and make needed adjustments or repairs.

FERTILIZING

An annual application of a slow-release fertilizer for young plants can be done this month or later (see General Introduction).

Nitrogen is the most essential element utilized for spring growth. Established plants don't require annual fertilization. If your plants show yellowing leaves, get the problem diagnosed before applying fertilizers.

PRUNING

Zones 4-6: Shape and thin early blooming deciduous shrubs—**rhododendrons** and **azaleas**, **forsythia**, **honeysuckle**, **spirea**—after blooms fade. Prune summer blooming shrubs such as **hydrangea** before new growth begins (see February and March pruning for Zones 7 to 9).

Zones 7-9: When buds on hardy **fuchsia** (*Fuchsia magellanica* and others) begin to show color, remove dead stems and thin out overcrowded canes. Avoid heading cuts to keep growth open and arching.

All zones: Prune **bluebeard** (*Caryopteris x clandonensis*) back to a framework of 6 to 8 inches tall stems before new growth emerges.

PROBLEMS

Zones 7-9: Aphids show up on succulent spring shoots (don't fertilize until you've got them under control). Allow natural predators to arrive and do their work.

TIPS FOR SHEARED HEDGES

Shape new hedges the year after planting to develop dense branching. Keep the top narrower than the bottom so lower branches don't become shaded out. Round the top if you live where snowfall is routine to reduce load damage. String a level line to guide even pruning at the desired height. Remove no more than 1/2 to 1/3 of the shoot length at each trimming, less from needle-leafed evergreens.

Faster growing shrubs such as **laurels** and **photinia** need more trimmings per year than slower growing **osmanthus**, **arborvitae** or **yew**. Scissor style hedge shears provide a cleaner cut than power trimmers and are a good bet for smaller hedges. Powered trimmers are faster, and useful for larger hedges with fine leaves. For the neatest job with either type, they must be kept sharp.

Choose plants with smaller leaves for formal sheared hedges:
- **Japanese holly** (*Ilex crenata*)
- **Box honeysuckle** (*Lonicera nitida*)
- **Osmanthus** (*Osmanthus delavayi*)
- **Privet** (*Ligustrum*)
- **Barberries** (*Berberis*)
- **Boxwood** (*Buxus*)
- **Yews** (*Taxus*)

Control persistent aphid problems with insecticidal soap, a hard spray of water, or hand removal. Aphids diminish in hot weather, and low populations won't do much damage to most shrubs. Avoid broad spectrum insecticides to protect beneficial insects.

Aphid

West of the Cascades, in a rainy spring, bacterial blight can increase on **lilacs**. Young shoots and flower clusters turn brown and die back. Grow lilacs in full sun, and thin dense growth to improve air circulation. Cut out blighted stems as soon as they appear. Disinfect your tools with rubbing alcohol and coat with light oil. Disease resistant selections include 'Maud Notcutt', 'William Robinson', 'Rutilant' and 'Guinevere'.

Colder zones can rejoice because **lilacs** grow better there. Cold winters and dry summers benefit them.

MAY

SHRUBS

PLANNING

Spring flowering shrubs come into their glory with a variety of color and scents. Take pictures for documenting and explore the wealth of different flowering shrubs beyond **rhododendrons** and **azaleas**. Peruse nurseries for interesting new selections, and rediscover reliable old-fashioned shrubs such as **spirea**, **deutzia**, and **weigela**. While you admire the flowers, pay attention to leaf qualities which come into full view as the blooms fade. Cultivars with variegated, purple, or lime colored leaves provide beautiful summer color and contrast: *Weigela florida* 'Variegata', *Berberis thunbergii* 'Crimson Pygmy', *Fothergilla gardenii* 'Blue Mist', **Black Beauty elderberry** (*Sambucus nigra* 'Gerda'), and yellow to lime hues found in *Spiraea japonica* 'Fire Light', 'Magic Carpet' and others. Deep green leaves with bold textures offer dramatic backdrops to summer perennials.

PLANTING

Woody plants installed this month will need extra care to reduce transplant stress.

Softwood cuttings of many shrubs can be taken just before succulent new shoots begin to harden.

CARE

If newly planted shrubs in full sun keep wilting and are difficult to keep watered, relieve the moisture stress with a temporary shade cover. Shaded leaves lose less water. Shade cloth lasts longer than sprayed on anti-desiccants which wear away as leaves expand. Use a light mesh fabric or shade cloth available in garden centers. Construct a simple teepee with long poles for smaller plants. The shade can be removed later in the summer when no longer needed.

WATERING

Routine water applications should start as the weather warms up and soaking rains diminish. Cover bare soil with coarse mulch. Remove weeds to reduce moisture competition. Check the soil with a trowel and water when it's slightly damp.

Two common errors with automatic irrigation systems are either leaving them at the same setting all summer, or not watering deeply enough. Monitor the soil for wetting depth, and adjust the settings for deeper, less frequent applications. Upgrade your system with sensors that adjust irrigation according to soil moisture. Keep track of rainfall in your garden notebook.

FERTILIZING

Established shrubs should not need annual fertilization. A single slow-release application can be given to new shrubs planted in the last years and to selected shrubs as indicated by growth problems the previous year. Use moderate rates: about 2 tablespoons of a 19 percent nitrogen product per 4-foot diameter circle provides 1 to 2 pounds actual nitrogen per 1000 square feet. (see Introduction page 14 on fertilization applications).

Hydrangea bloom color is affected by soil pH. Blues are maintained under acid conditions, with aluminum sulfate or other acidifying fertilizers. Add lime and floral hues shift to pink.

PRUNING

Zones 7-9: Prune evergreen **rhododendrons**, **azaleas**, and other broadleaf evergreen shrubs just as they finish blooming. Spent blooms can be removed from **lilacs** and **rhododendrons** for neater appearance. Use hand pruners on **lilacs**; **rhododendrons** can be deadheaded by hand.

Be careful not to snap off new buds. Some growers feel next year's bloom is improved when plant energy isn't spent on developing seeds. Other experts have indicated the practice is most useful for appearance. You might choose to dead head those plants that are easily reached and in prime viewing spots in the garden.

All zones: Natural form is best preserved when winter damaged stems are pruned all the way back to the ground or a bigger main stem, rather than near the break. Note where new growth is absent and prune out entire weak or dead stems.

In very cold winters, less hardy shrubs may die back completely to the ground. Don't be too hasty to dig them up, as new growth may still emerge from the roots. Cut away the dead stems, and mark the spot with a stake. Watch it the rest of the summer for signs of new sprouts. Some plants may take until the next year before sprouting new shoots.

PROBLEMS

Twisted, puckered leaves indicate heavy aphid feeding. When populations increase past beneficial insects control, and damage becomes prolonged, apply insecticidal soap, repeated every 7 to 10 days as new eggs hatch.

Voracious leaf-feeding caterpillars can appear almost overnight, camouflaged by their green color as they chew away. Leaf rollers hide by curling the edges of leaves around them. Squish them on sight for immediate control.

Check new growth of all **rhododendrons** for disease symptoms. Begin fungicide applications for powder mildew on plants diagnosed last year. (See June).

Notched leaf edges on **rhododendrons**, **evergreen azaleas**, *Pieris,* and **strawberry tree** (*Arbutus unedo*) indicate adult root weevils. This is a common malady in this region. To reduce damage, keep lower limbs pruned up off the ground (adults come up from the ground to feed at night). Using a flashlight after dusk, drop hand picked weevils into soapy water. Or shake them off onto a large sheet laid on the ground first. You can drench the soil with beneficial nematodes that feed on the larvae. Apply when soils are moist and temperatures are above 55 degrees F. Use this combination of techniques to suppress weevil damage without reliance on broad-spectrum insecticides like acephate (Orthene, Ortran) that are very harmful beneficial beetles and other insects. See page 223 for a list of **rhododendrons** less prone to root weevil damage.

Contact OSU or WSU Cooperative Extension for positive pest identification and control options if problems persist.

It's not all rhododendrons or azaleas—try planting pieris, also known as Japanese andromeda for something different.

JUNE
SHRUBS

 PLANNING

Shrubs create colorful, drought tolerant containers, especially in combination with perennials. Buy shrubs in 6-inch or 1-gallon pots, with a plan to place them out in the garden in fall. Use larger containers (5 to 10 gallons or more) for greater soil volume and water holding capacity. Single specimens of dwarf conifers can be kept in large containers for a few years. Choose among dwarf shrubs for striking foliage color and texture: *Hypericum* x *moserianum* 'Tricolor', *Weigela* 'Florida Variegata', *Spiraea japonica* 'Limemound', **smoke bush** (*Cotinus coggygria* 'Royal Purple'), or the many selections of colorful **barberries**. Cool green maple-like leaves of the petite *Viburnum opulus* 'Nanum' are elegant solo or in combination plantings. Blossom laden stems of hardy **fuchsia** gracefully drape over container edges. Blooms to last the summer can also be found among cultivars of *Potentilla fruticosa*, **pink elf hydrangea** (*Hydrangea macrophylla* 'Pia') and *Caryopteris* x *clandonensis* 'Worchester Gold' with deep lavender flowers over golden foliage. Woody herbs such as **Spanish lavender, rosemary**, and variegated **sages** provide colorful drought tolerant container specimens.

 PLANTING

All zones: Do not transplant during active growth. Plants installed now will need more mulching, weeding, and watering. If you still have shrubs to plant, do it during the coolest conditions possible. Water nursery stock thoroughly the day before planting. Use these same techniques for potting up a decorative container of shrubs.

Take softwood cuttings from shrubs at this time of the season. Look for strong shoots which are firm but not yet woody.

 CARE

Keep shrub beds weeded, especially around new shrubs. Minimize soil disturbance to avoid stirring weed seeds up to the surface. Dry soil makes weeds hard to pull. "Shave" them at the soil surface and cover the ground with mulch. Any weeds that grow back from roots will be easier to extract from mulched soil.

If you have not already done so, replenish mulch to a total depth of no more than 3 to 4 inches for coarse materials, thinner for finer textured mulches.

 WATERING

Pay extra attention to new plants. If the garden's verdant growth swallows them, mark them with a bright ribbon tied to a stake. Containers will need to be checked if not watered daily. On extremely hot days, smaller containers may need water twice in a day.

If you have an automatic system, make sure water is being delivered properly and penetrates 6 to 8 inches deep, which promotes deeper root growth. It is very hard to re-wet the soil if it dries out completely. A light rain dampens the surface making the perfect time for your irrigation to push moisture even deeper into the soil.

FERTILIZING

Annual fertilization is not required for established shrubs. What if you see yellow leaves? Yellowing leaves can signal different plant problems including root rot, poor soil drainage, and some leaf diseases. Get an accurate diagnosis before adding fertilizer. If the plant suffers from root rot, fertilizer will not help and may make the problem worse.

FROM OVERGROWN SHRUB TO SMALL TREE

Several shrub species train beautifully as small trees, including the larger **rhododendrons**, **camellias**, **red vein enkianthus**, and taller **viburnum**. This technique allows more light in while requiring less follow-up pruning than trying to keep them trimmed low. Smaller plants can be added beneath to enhance the effect.

First, identify the lowest branches to be kept. As a general rule, the canopy should take up about $2/3$ to $3/4$ of the total height.

Remove the lowest branches at the main trunk. Leave no stubs, placing cuts at the slight bulge of the branch collar and not quite all the way flush.

If the canopy is very dense, thin out a few long branches to allow filtered light through the crown and enhance the appearance without making it look like a lollipop.

This pruning can be done in winter or summer for both deciduous and evergreen shrubs.

 ## PRUNING

 ## PROBLEMS

Some shrubs start to sprout "wild hairs," branches that shoot out of control. Prune these and other vigorous shrubs that need more restraint than encouragement. Prune both deciduous and evergreen shrubs now.

Shape hedges with the base wider than the top. Informal hedges can be shaped by thinning out the longest shoots with hand pruners.

Zones 4-6: Deadhead large spent blooms on **rhododendrons** and **lilacs** (See May).

All zones: Remove spent blooms of *Buddleja* before they go to seed to reduce undesirable spread of seedlings. Plan to remove shrubs that can't be deadheaded.

Spittle bugs may appear along the stems of many plants. These clever insects coat themselves with a layer of tiny slimy bubbles to deter predators. They are rarely numerous enough to worry about.

Rhododendron powdery mildew (*Microsphaera* spp.) often shows up with paler green patches on top of the leaf, with brownish or purplish splotches on the underside. It lacks the white dusting seen with the powdery mildew that afflicts deciduous shrubs. It is difficult to control, and can be fatal after several years of infestation. To avoid it, grow **rhododendrons** on well drained soil with organic mulch, good air circulation, summer irrigation and minimal fertilization. If you noticed symptoms last year, new growth may be protected with a fungicide

Shrub after training to small tree form.

before symptoms appear. Some **rhododendrons** appear to be less susceptible, including *R. yakushimanum*, many of its small 'Yak' hybrids and tree-like *Rhododendron augustinii*. If you suspect this disease is on your **rhododendrons**, take a sample to an OSU of WSU diagnostic clinic, and ask for information on resistant varieties.

JULY
SHRUBS

 PLANNING

Before you rely only on annuals and perennials for summer color, remember that these herbaceous bloomers demand both water and time. There is a hidden treasure of bloom, color and texture on woody stems waiting to be gathered into our summer gardens. Well-placed shrubs with summer colors and textures stick around for repeat performances in other seasons. With lesser requirements for irrigation than herbaceous plants, they make for more water-wise seasonal color.

Plan to include a few of these favorites: **Oakleaf hydrangea** (*Hydrangea quercifolia*) bears large creamy white blooms against large, leathery leaves—with the added joy of orange autumn tints. Several forms of **St. John's Wort** (*Hypericum*) such as 'Hidcote' and others produce sunshine-yellow blossoms by mid-summer. **Virginia sweetspire** (*Itea virginica* 'Henry's Garnet'), has fragrant white blooms and dynamic fall color for damp woodland gardens. Drought tolerant **tree anemone** (*Carpentaria californica*) bears large white flowers with bright yellow centers gaily set against evergreen foliage.

 PLANTING

Avoid installing shrubs during periods of clear, hot weather in all but the shadiest garden spots. If you must plant now, keep plants cool and moist in the days before planting. Plant them late in the day so they have the cool overnight hours to adjust. See the June "Care" notes for setting up shade tents. Or put off planting until fall planting season. To protect containers from heating up in direct sunlight, surround the sides with mulch to shade and cool them. Repot to a larger container if you see roots coming out the bottom. Take softwood cuttings of **barberry**, **flowering quince**, **hydrangea**, **heavenly bamboo**, **rhododendron**, **azalea**, and many other deciduous and evergreen shrubs.

Check for rooting where low branches of garden shrubs have made contact with the soil. This is called "layering," and the rooted section can be clipped free and dug out as a new plant. This can be done intentionally by pinning one of the lower branches to soil and waiting patiently for it to root.

 CARE

Keep companion ground covers strong by removing weeds before they've advanced in size or gone to seed. If the area to be weeded is very large, take it by one small manageable plot at a time, immediately mulching the area you've weeded.

 WATERING

This starts the warmest, driest part of the growing season throughout the region. Use your

Oakleaf hydrangea

finger to probe and ensure container soil is moist. If water is racing through the container without soaking into the soil, add a few drops of dish soap to the watering to improve water penetration. You may need to keep pouring water through the container until the soil has soaked it up. A saucer to hold excess water is helpful for smaller containers.

FERTILIZING

No general fertilization is needed for this part of the growing season.

PRUNING

Remove dead, damaged, or diseased stems with thinning cuts all the way to the ground, or where they attach to a larger branch. Thin out wild stems that grow out of bounds or against the main direction of growth.

Pruning for reduced size: Midsummer is also an optimal time to prune shrubs you wish to keep smaller in size, as fewer new shoots will be stimulated now than in early spring. Remove no more than about 1/4 of the total leaf area when pruning at this time of year.

Prune or shear hedges and topiary as needed to maintain their shape and size. Hedges with large shiny leaves have a nicer appearance when shaped with loppers and hand pruners to selectively remove longer shoots. It avoids shredding the leaves and often means longer intervals before shaping is needed again. It also prevents the accumulation of thick branch stubs that become too thick for cutting with hedge trimmers—a common problem with English laurel hedges.

PROBLEMS

Leaf scorch symptoms may appear on drought-stressed plants as leaf tips and margins turn brown. It can be a signal that a shade-loving plant is getting too much sun. Excess fertilization can cause leaf scorch symptoms even where soil is moist. Remember to dig under the soil to check conditions before watering these plants, as they may need additional care beyond watering. Plants most likely to scorch include **rhododendrons, skimmia,** and **hydrangeas.** Scorch damage will remain on the plant until affected leaves are shed and replaced. Make a note to provide mulch and additional watering next season for plants with repeated droughts stress.

Root rots and wilts: Shrub conifers such as **arborvitae** (*Thuja* spp.) suffering from phytophthora root diseases will suddenly turn brown. Curled leaves and single wilted branches may appear on **rhododendrons** and other shrubs infected with verticillium wilt. This fungus clogs up the vascular system of many different types of woody plants, including **hardy fuchsia, heather, lilac, privet, sumac,** and **viburnum**. These soil-borne diseases travel on bits of soil clinging to tools and shoes. Root rot diseases are more severe on waterlogged, poorly drained soils that lack organic content. Once the symptoms appear the plants are not treatable. Contact OSU and WSU Cooperative Extension for diagnosis and management for nearby plants. Watch for signs of spider mites—dusty, off-color foliage with visible webbing—on **arborvitae** growing in hot sunny exposures. Washing down infested foliage with water spray helps suppress spider mites. Wasps activity can be more noticeable now, and a nuisance to gardeners who get too close to their nests (See August).

AUGUST

SHRUBS

 **PLANNING**

Green hues tire to dull khaki during these pre-autumn days. The best and worst of shrub performance will show this month. Some plants experience a drought-induced dormancy in late summer. Repeated years of such drought stress can hamper plant health. Examine the soil where these plants are growing. Provide a slow, deep watering to re-hydrate roots. Cracked, dry soil conditions can be corrected with coarse organic mulches and better irrigation applications next season. (see March).

Go with the flow. Don't coax struggling plants into better shape; replace them with the right species for your garden. August is a good month to visit nurseries and see drought-tolerant selections for different garden settings.

 **PLANTING**

Wait for cooler weather to install new plants. If you've picked up new nursery stock, keep the pots watered and store them in a cool, shady place until planting time.

If you feel like braving the weather and want to do some gardening, this is a good time to

prepare the planting sites. Remove dead or failing plants. Apply 4 to 6 inches of mulch in open areas to be planted. Wet the area down thoroughly. By fall planting time, the soil will be easier to dig, weeds will be suppressed, and mulch will be in place for planting. Rake the mulch away to expose the soil before digging planting holes. Do not dig wood chips or bark into the soil! Keep coarse mulch on the surface.

Take more softwood cuttings this month, and check the those you've started. Remove any that have mildewed or are shriveled. Remember to open plastic coverings periodically to vent moisture and bring fresh air to the cuttings.

 **CARE**

Continue weeding and mulching around shrubs as needed.

 **PRUNING**

Summer pruning can continue during the first part of the month (see July). Immediately remove any branches with solid green foliage on variegated or colored leaved shrubs to keep the whole plant from reverting to the plain foliage.

Watch for the occasional errant stem that drapes into walkways, or is growing out of bounds. If dead branches are numerous, insect or disease problems may be a culprit. Get the problem identified to deal with the source of the dieback.

 **WATERING**

Watering should be less frequent toward the end of the growing season as plants head into dormancy, but don't let plants get too dry. Shrubs whose inner leaves turn yellow and drop are likely showing a drought stress response, as oldest leaves are shed when water supply becomes short. If drought gets severe, early fall color and total leaf drop can occur. A word of caution: These very same symptoms can show up when too much water drowns roots. Dig below the surface. If you find waterlogged soil that smells bad, soil drainage or irrigation applications probably need to be corrected.

 **FERTILIZING**

Top dress with compost or organic mulch.

PROBLEMS

Don't head for the wasp spray right away! These summer fliers can be a menace and hazard, but they are also one of the most beneficial insect predators. Wasps differ from pollen collecting bees that lazily buzz through the garden. Wasps are strong, fast flyers and primarily meat eaters (aphid, whiteflies, and caterpillars besides the fare at your barbecue). They are more interested in their prey than people. One wasp can deliver repeated painful stings, unlike bees which sting only once.

Before diving in to work on thick growth, take a few minutes to study the landscape first. Wasps are most active at the warmest, brightest periods of the day. If there is a nest, you will see a strong pattern of wasp flight to and from its location. The northern paper wasp makes a large round, papery hanging nest, the bald faced hornet makes a similar smaller hanging nest, and the German yellowjacket nests in the ground. If you see a nest, and can postpone the task until mid-winter, leave the colony to complete its summer life-cycle.

Commercial products sold for clearing out nests advise to work after dark but there may still be some "scouts" crawling over the nest. Proceed with great care, and consider calling professional help. Some professionals vacuum wasps from their nests for their beneficial use in medical allergy treatments.

Camellias looking black and oily? The appearance of dark black sooty mold on plant leaves is a signal of an infestation of scale (camellia, holly, and maple scale) or aphids. The black mold grows on the sticky honeydew excreted by aphids, and by itself is not harmful. When winter comes, horticultural oil can be applied to smother aphid eggs and scale insects over wintering on the plants. To improve appearance, heavy sooty mold on evergreen foliage can be washed down with mild soapy water, though it's sometimes quite a scrub to get it off **camellia** or **photinia** leaves. Pruning out some of the affected branches can help improve air circulation on dense shrubs.

Virginia sweetspire has multiseason interest. In addition to white blooms now, it has fantastic fall foliage color.

September

SHRUBS

PLANNING

Planting and transplanting time returns. Now you can think about rearranging shrubs for better growth and function. Move plants with too much shade into a sunnier spot. Notice the microclimate affects in your garden, and adjust plants to more favorable spots as needed. As the landscape changes over time, some plants may no longer perform as well as they once did, while others thrive. This often occurs where sun-loving plants become shaded out as young shade trees that were planted with them grow larger, shifting the surrounding garden area from full sun to partial shade. Likewise, the loss of a large tree or the removal of a tall wooden fence can suddenly expose plants growing comfortably in that shade to more sun than they can handle. If they haven't recovered after the second growing season, they should be moved or removed. This is also a time you can work on adjusting the spacing of plants that are too crowded, or too far apart. Continue to take photos to document landscape changes.

PLANTING

As the days get cooler and daylight shorter, it is great time to plant woody shrubs. Make sure any plants you have been holding over summer remain well watered until planting. Many nurseries have sales this time of year to reduce stock for winter. This is also a good time to transplant evergreens, provided they are not in the middle of a new flush of growth. Wait until leaves have fallen from deciduous plants before transplanting them. Be sure the ground is well watered before digging.

Softwood cutting can still be taken of several plants: **strawberry tree**, **aucuba**, **camellia**, **holly**, and **yews**.

CARE

Zones 4-6: Get containerized shrubs ready to bring under winter protection before the first frost.

WATERING

Non-irrigated areas are usually their driest at this part of the growing season before fall rains return. Established evergreen and deciduous shrubs will benefit from a good soaking if the ground has gone dry, so they can go into winter with roots well hydrated. Coarse mulch put over bare soil before watering can help infiltration. If soil has become so crusted and hydrophobic that it repels water before it can soak in, pre-wet the surface soil with a mild soap solution to break the surface tension.

Newly planted shrubs should be checked at least once a week for watering. The small rootballs may dry out quickly even though surrounding soil may be moist.

FERTILIZING

If shrubs have not been fertilized yet this year, this is another time in the growing season that a *very light* application of fertilizer may be given to woody plants. Use 1 pound of actual nitrogen per 1000 square feet, preferably a slow release formulation (about 2 tablespoons of 15 percent nitrogen product for a 3-foot diameter circle). The soil must be moist for roots to take it up. The nitrogen absorbed now will be stored to fuel expanding buds and shoots in the spring. **Caution:** Be very careful not to over apply fertilizer at this time of year. It can cause unwanted results in plant growth, and with heavy rains coming, the extra nitrogen is easily washed through the soil and leached into ground water and streams.

PRUNING

Pruning efforts should be minimal this time of year, just enough to take care of the occasional errant branch that blocks a walkway or window. Wait until later in the season to begin dormant pruning.

Camellia is too pretty too let it succumb to a scale infestation.

It is not necessary to prune all shrubs at planting time, but do remove any branches that are weak, dead or broken.

PROBLEMS

By the summer's end, the effects of powdery mildew may be evident on many garden shrubs. The good news is that powdery mildew seldom kills a plant. Some basic plant care techniques can help. Make sure that plants have good air circulation. Avoid shearing shrubs that have been prone to powdery mildew in the past, and do some remedial thinning in the dormant season. Likewise, light thinning of crowding limbs from adjacent trees and shrubs can improve air circulation for affected plants. Rake away fallen leaves under plants that have been affected to reduce spore sources for next year.

Begin control efforts early in the season before powdery mildew has had time to build up on the leaves. Overhead sprinkling by mid morning to wash off spores has been found helpful for some plants (except roses). Ultra-fine horticultural oil and neem oil provide good suppression for moderate infections. Fungicides containing sulfur or potassium bicarbonate are also useful when started early in the growing season. Sulfur and horticultural oils should never be used at the same time. If powdery mildew remains a looming battle each year, consider transplanting or replacing the affected plants with less prone selections. **Deciduous azaleas**, some native *Mahonia*, **privet** and **lilacs** are particularly susceptible to powdery mildew.

Treat **rhododendrons** and other shrubs that have been severely chewed by root weevils with a soil drench of parasitic nematodes. Soil must be damp before hand. Consider replacement plants that have shown resistance to root weevil damage, including *Rhododendron* 'P.J.M.' (pink) 'Dora Amateis', (white) and any of the *R. yakushimanum* hybrids (pinks and whites).

West of the Cascades, prune out twigs killed or infected by juniper twig blight. The tips of branches turn brown first, with dieback continuing down the stem. Sanitation—cutting out and disposing of infected stems—can help suppress it. It is less problematic on older plants.

OCTOBER

SHRUBS

PLANNING

While massive shade trees dominate our images of great fall color, don't overlook the many shrubs whose blazing colors complement and complete this seasonal tapestry. Visit nurseries now to see shrubs in peak color, and bring some home to plant for instant gratification. Reliable fall color is found on several deciduous shrubs: *Aronia* 'Autumn Magic' with red to purple hues, **beautyberry** (*Callicarpa* 'Profusion') in almost iridescent violets, and the most intense of reds on compact **burning bush** (*Euonymous alatus* 'Fire Ball'). *Fothergilla* delivers a warm golden color, beautiful next to the deep wine colored foliage of **oakleaf hydrangea** (*Hydrangea quercifolia*). *Viburnum* species turn to lovely shades of yellow, orange, and red, with all three colors appearing together in the cultivar *Viburnum dentatum* 'Autumn Jazz'.

PLANTING

Fall is a great time for planting shrubs throughout the region, although in zones 4 to 6, less hardy species will fare better

Burning bush displays an intense red fall foliage.

if planted in spring. See the Introduction chapter for shrub planting details. You may still need to water in newly planted shrubs if rainfall has been light. Don't forget to provide a generous mulch ring around each new shrub. Be sure to keep mulch from touching the stems.

CARE

If falling leaves from deciduous trees pile up on top of shrubs they can quickly smother the life out of them, especially on evergreen shrubs. Rake them away, but don't be too tidy about removing all leaves. Allow smaller leaves— such as those from Japanese maple, katsura, or birch—to join the mulch on the ground beneath adding to nature's seasonal pattern of cycling of organic matter back to the soil. Clear away any leaves that have accumulated directly against the stems near the ground. Be especially careful not to allow deep layers to accumulate over rhododendron root balls.

Save larger leaves in garbage bags, or shred them, to make leaf mold mulch for shrub beds. Piles need to be kept moist. Close the tops of leaf-filled bags, and poke some small holes for air exchange. Let them sit, or turn them over occasionally to speed up the composting process. Fall saved leaves are usually ready to use for spring mulching. If leaves are lacking in your garden, apply other organic mulches to renew those that have dwindled over summer. Autumn mulching also helps suppress growth of winter and early spring weeds.

Zones 7-9: Prepare shrubs in containers for winter as first frost

dates approach. Be prepared to move more tender species under cover if deep freezes are forecast. Have some old blankets or bubblewrap ready to provide quick insulation for pots that won't be moved under cover. With cooler weather less watering is needed, though rainfall rarely wets containers very well.

WATERING

General irrigation needs diminish as days become cooler and shorter, and fall rains return. Start putting your irrigation equipment away for the winter. Winterize automatic systems where freeze damage can be a problem.

Zones 4-6: Winterize irrigation systems and protect exposed hose spigots. Clean out rain barrels for winter storage.

Make sure evergreens that have been dry over summer are well watered as they go into the dormant season. Plants that go into winter cold temperatures suffering from drought stress can get more severe freeze damage than those with roots hydrated.

FERTILIZING

Discontinue fertilization as heavy rains return to the region. Organic mulches can still be

---

SHRUBS FOR SMALL GARDENS

If your yard is the proverbial postage stamp, you'll want to look for dwarf varieties of shrubs that will stay in scale without constant pruning or crowding headaches. Here is a sampling of some choices to get you started:

Rhododendron impeditum—1 1/2 feet x 1 1/2 feet
Rhododendron 'Ruby Heart'—2 feet height x 3 feet width
Rhododendron 'Yaku Princess'—3 feet x 4 feet
Berberis thunbergii 'Crimson Pygmy'—2 feet x 3 feet
Bluebeard (*Caryopteris x clandonensis*)—3 feet x 3 feet
Fothergilla gardenii—4 feet x 3 feet
Dwarf hinoki cypress (*Chamaecyparis obtusa* 'Nana')—
 3 feet x 3 feet, slowly
Green island holly (*Ilex crenata* 'Green Island')—
 3 feet height x 6 feet width
Dwarf cranberry bush (*Viburnum opulus* 'Nanum')—
 2 feet x 2 feet
Dwarf heavenly bamboo (*Nandina domestica* 'Wood's Dwarf'), 'Harbor Dwarf'—2 1/2 feet x 2 1/2 feet

---

applied now, and will slowly add nutrients to the soil as they decompose.

PRUNING

Not much pruning should be needed at this time of year. General shrub pruning needs will begin later into the dormant season.

PROBLEMS

Spider webs can be seen glistening with early morning dew at this time of year. Their beautiful patterns stretched across shrub beds indicate the presence of effective natural pest control on duty. Spiders actively hunt and feed on insects throughout the growing season. Some work from webs, while many roam through plants in search of prey. Spiders thrive with the protection of dense plant growth (such as shrubs and ground cover plants), leaf litter covering the soil and some moisture. Maintain some plant debris on the ground throughout the year to provide adequate habitat, and resist the urge to stomp them when they catch you by surprise: They do very important work in suppressing problem insects.

NOVEMBER

SHRUBS

PLANNING

As the garden is readied for winter, it is a good time to reflect on the progress of your garden over the last year. Look over pictures taken at different seasons. Enjoy the images of your garden at its best moments. Review the plants and planting areas that have provided the best function and enjoyment with minimal care demands. Make plans to repeat those successes in other areas of the garden.

Look at which shrubs contribute to the winter scene now that leaves are down. Both deciduous and evergreen shrubs provide continuity and structure through the seasons.

West of the Cascades, broadleaf evergreens thrive and are plentiful in gardens. Many bear colorful blooms at some point in the year: **rhododendrons**, **camellias**, **glossy abelia**, **silk-tassel** (*Garrya* spp.), and *Pieris*. The flowers of some are discreet (*Sarcococca* and **boxwoods**), while others show off colorful berries, such as hollies, **heavenly bamboo** and **skimmia**. All provide rich textures in green that compliment the garden the year round.

East of the Cascades, the winter landscape is highlighted by needle-leaf evergreens such as pines, **juniper**, and **arborvitae** as well as deciduous shrubs with colorful stems or berries. The deciduous **winterberry holly** (*Ilex verticillata* 'Winter Red'), **beautyberry** (*Callicarpa dichotoma* 'Early Amethyst') and *Aronia melanocarpa* 'Morton' (Iroquois Beauty™) all offer strongly colored winter berries and thrive in zones 4-6. All prefer damp soils and sun.

PLANTING

Transplanting can be done in all zones, weather permitting.

Zones 4-6: Fall planting should wrap up early in the month before freezing weather sets in.

Zones 7-9: Continue planting shrubs as long as weather permits; not too wet or freezing.

CARE

Install winter protection for tender plants as needed in all zones. Move tender container plants under cover for winter storage and water them thoroughly. In areas with heavy snow fall, wrap vulnerable evergreens with burlap or twine protect against snow load damage.

In areas where deer browsing increases in fall and winter, set up protective cover or fencing as needed.

WATERING

This is typically the wettest month of the year throughout the region.

Irrigation systems should be drained and winterized by now where freezing is concern.

FERTILIZING

Hold off on broadcasting fertilizers, as heavy rains can result in rapid leaching of nitrogen before plant roots can absorb them. Organic mulches may still be applied. Choose drier days to avoid tromping over soggy ground.

PRUNING

No major pruning is needed at this early part of the dormant season. Attend to dead or damaged limbs as needed. Clip stems with attractive fruits or seed pods to enjoy indoors: **beautyberry**, **winterberry**, and **spirea**. Use your imagination; look beyond the usual for interesting textures in bud, bark, and fruits. Always use thinning cuts back to the ground or a larger stem, and leave no stubs.

HELPFUL HINTS

Shrub-Size Conifers

Bare winter stems of deciduous shrubs call for the company of rich evergreen foliage found among the many forms of dwarf conifers. These are smaller, slower growing versions of tall needle leaf trees. Check labels and cultivar descriptions carefully—some "dwarf" conifers grow to be smaller trees of the parent species. Others dwarf conifers remain diminutive they remain in scale with rock garden plants. Dwarf conifers are available in a wide variety of sizes, shapes, and colors. They require plenty of sun and well drained soil. Here is a brief sampling:

- **Dwarf hinoki cypress** (*Chamaecyparis obtusa* 'Nana Gracilis')—5 to 10 feet height
- **Dwarf cypress** (*Chamaecyparis obtusa* 'Kosteri')—3 to 4 feet height
- **Grey Owl juniper** (*Juniperus virginiana* 'Grey Owl')—4 to 5 feet height, spreading
- **Dwarf Norway spruce** (*Picea abies* 'Procumbens' and others)—3 to 4 feet height
- **Mugo pine** (*Pinus mugo* 'Oregon Jade' and others)—3 to 6 feet height
- **Dwarf yew** (*Taxus cuspidata* var. *nana*)—2 to 3 feet height
- **Dwarf arbor vitae** (*Thuja orientalis* 'Aurea Nana')—2 feet height

Deer-Deterring Shrubs

Browsing damage from deer can occur between late fall and early spring. As winter food sources diminish and deer get very hungry, repellent methods often lose effectiveness (with the exception of tall fences). It can take a lot of work to keep up on protection measures, and it still may not be possible to protect all your favorite plants from deer damage. There are, however, several shrubs that deer avoid eating which you can incorporate into your garden. Make note of which parts of your existing landscape remain unscathed, and use this list to build a garden less inviting to deer appetites. Locate vulnerable plants far from observed deer trails. Feeding patterns will vary with seasonal conditions, alternate food sources, and taste preferences of the local population. Expect to protect young, newly planted shrubs until they reach larger, less tender dimensions.

- **Barberries** (*Berberis* spp.)
- **Boxwood** (*Buxus* spp.)
- **Forsythia** (*Forsythia* spp. and cvs.)
- **Leucothoe** (*Leucothoe* spp.)
- **Lilac** (*Syringa*)
- **Mexican orange** (*Choisya ternata*)
- **Mountain laurel** (*Kalmia latifolia*)
- **Pieris** (*Pieris japonica*)
- **Potentilla** (*Potentilla fruticosa*)
- **Red vein enkianthus** (*Enkianthus campanulatus*)
- **Rhododendrons**
- **Sagebrush** (*Artemisia tridentata*)
- **Silk-tassel bush** (*Garrya* spp.)
- **Smoke bush** (*Cotinus coggygria*)

Native plant species commonly foraged by deer include:

- New growth on **Douglas fir, western red cedar, mock orange, snow berry, wild rose, deer bush** (*Ceanothus* spp.), **salal,** and **sagebrush**.

PROBLEMS

Zones 4-6: Protect tender evergreens from drying winter winds.

Set up burlap wind breaks, or wrap individual shrubs with burlap and twine. To reduce freeze damage to evergreen and deciduous shrubs, give the roots a last deep soaking if recent rainfall has not been sufficient to do so.

December

SHRUBS

 PLANNING

The addition of shrubs with winter interest can brighten gloomy days and add beautiful details against a backdrop of snow: **junipers** with waxy green cones, arching stems of **cotoneaster** lined with neat red berries, tight spiraled stems strung with golden catkins on **Harry Lauder's Walking Stick** (*Corylus avellana* 'Contorta').

Visit garden centers for gardening gifts in the form of shrubs with winter interest, or fine garden tools, in anticipation of the coming growing season. Gardening books with ample color photographs inspire ideas for enhancing your shrub plantings and solving landscape challenges.

 PLANTING

Zones 4-6: No more planting or transplanting now.

Zones 7-9: Continue planting as weather permits. Transplanting can be done for evergreen and deciduous shrubs.

 CARE

Zones 4-6: Apply a layer of mulch after the ground freezes to prevent frost heaving. Snow cover that remains at 2 or more inches will also provide good insulation.

All zones: Heavy snow fall can bend and break branches. Use a small broom to lightly shake them free of snow. Leave them alone during icy conditions, which can cause stems to snap. Inverted baskets and light blankets can provide a quick cover to protect tender shrubs when a cold front descends.

 WATERING

Check containers in winter storage or under porch or deck shelters and water if they are dry.

 FERTILIZING

Not this month.

 PRUNING

When temperatures are above freezing, you can gather holiday greens by providing some of your shrubs a light thinning. Evergreens such as **holly**, *Sarcococca* and **conifers** are good choices. Use your imagination as you save trimmed stems for winter arrangements, looking for interesting colors and textures found in deciduous stems with remnant berries or seed pods. Long, whippy stems might be coiled as a base for a wreath. When you cut for decorating, follow standard pruning practices of thinning cuts and leaving no stubs.

 PROBLEMS

Rodents may chew bark and cause damage, especially where there is thick snow cover. To help deter them, don't allow mulch to be piled up against the trunks of shrubs. Install a ring of 8-inch tall wire mesh around the base of shrubs vulnerable to winter rodent chewing.

Harry Lauder's Walking Stick

TREES

BENEFITS OF TREES

Trees have been described as the backbone of the garden. They bring dimension and definition to garden spaces. A well-placed specimen becomes a focal point. Trees provide sheltering shade for companion plants and garden visitors. As we enter natural spaces, adults and children alike are drawn to the embrace of trees, for limbs to climb on, or shade to rest beneath. The quality of our gardens, of our very lives, would be diminished without trees.

Among all the garden plants we use, trees offer the greatest aesthetic, ecological, and economic benefits. In urban communities trees contribute to storm-water management, air quality, and energy conservation. In rural areas, trees are used as valuable windbreaks and shelterbelts in wide open spaces. Healthy trees enhance the property values. They provide bird habitat. Urban tree lined streets have been linked to lower crime statistics and better shopping activity in business districts. Sadly, the number of trees in urban areas has been steadily declining over the past few decades. The benefits of preserving exiting trees and planting new trees reach far beyond the single yard to the larger community.

These gentle woody giants are more vulnerable to damage from gardening and construction activities than many people may realize, further complicated by the fact that the resulting damage symptoms may not be evident until a few years later. With some basic understanding of how trees grow, many problems can easily be avoided.

HOW TREES GROW

Trees develop a permanent woody structure of trunks, limbs, and branches, with smaller shedding parts in leaves, flowers and fruit, cones and seed. Each season, new layers of wood are laid down over last year's—the growth rings counted on a cut stump that tells its age. The height and spread of the crown extends from growth at the branch tips. Trees reach their mature size slowly. Some species can live more than 100 years.

Their woody structure serves as physical support and to store the energy from photosynthesis that is used for growth and development. The vascular system (xylem and phloem), which moves water and nutrients through the tree, lies just beneath the protective outer bark. Also beneath the bark is the bright green cambium layer, where new layers of wood form each year. If we damage the bark, we can also damage these vital growth structures.

It can be surprising realize how much of a very large tree's root system is in the top foot or so of soil. Tree roots grow where the soil offers enough oxygen, moisture and nutrients. Some roots become very large and woody with age, and serve to anchor and support the tree. How deep they go depends on the soil (they do not mirror the size and shape of the crown). The finer textured feeder roots that grow nearer the surface do the essential work of absorbing water and nutrients and are where beneficial mycorrhizal fungi attach. Tree roots typically extend far beyond the drip line of the canopy.

GARDENING NEAR TREES

Gardening near trees can present challenges, but by keeping in mind where and how tree roots grow, these challenges need not be so difficult. Keep digging and planting activities to a minimum directly beneath trees, especially right next to tree trunks. Choose species well adapted to the existing conditions and start with small plants. Stay away from those which require annual digging and cultivation. Concentrate irrigation on establishing the new plants without over watering the entire area beneath existing trees. Don't allow irrigation spray to repeatedly wet tree bark. Finally, don't add or remove soil under trees, as grade changes can harm roots. Consult with a certified arborist before hand if grade changes are planned around large established trees.

TYPES OF TREES

Trees are generally distinguished from shrubs as growing more than 12 feet in height and having large, permanent main trunks. They may be as small as 15-foot Japanese maple (*Acer palmatum*) specimen in a small garden, or as large as an 70-foot red oak (*Quercus rubra*) shading a sprawling backyard. Evergreens come with needles, such as pines and firs, or with broad, leathery leaves as found on evergreen magnolia or holly. Deciduous trees shed their leaves each autumn, changing colors as they lay their branches bare for winter.

Trees come in many shapes and sizes. **Pyramidal** trees have a strong central leader with branches growing more narrow toward the top, as found on conifers and deciduous trees such as sweet gum (*Liquidambar stryaciflua*). Many shade trees have several large main limbs, or scaffold branches, making up a **rounded** or **spreading** shape. The branches of **vase-shaped** trees are broadest at the top of the crown. **Upright** or **fastigiate** cultivars remain narrow with upswept branches. The branches of **weeping** trees drape toward the ground. **Globe** forms retain a tight round shape. The mature crown shape is not always evident in the young tree. It pays to find out the mature crown spread and shape as well as height when choosing trees that will fit well into your garden space.

CHOOSING TREES FOR PLANTING

The advice of putting the right plant in the right place is even more essential when it comes to trees. They are not as readily transplanted as are shrubs if they prove to be in the wrong spot or grow too large for their location. Match tree size (height and spread), as well as light, soil and moisture requirements to those in your garden. Medium to large growing trees should be placed 10 feet or more away from buildings—remember the trunk and crown will need room to expand without colliding with foundations and roofs. Do the math now to save yourself and your tree problems in the future.

Buy only strong, healthy nursery stock. Small young trees establish faster than very large stock. Trees are sold in containers and balled and burlapped. Look for sturdy trunks, free of wounds or tears in the bark. Side branches should be well spaced along the trunk, not crowded together at one spot, and there should be a single central trunk on upright trees. Check the top of the root ball where the trunk meets the soil—you don't want specimens with circling woody roots that will girdle the trunk. Pass on very tall skinny trees growing out of very small pots, as they are not likely to develop into strong trees after planting.

Buying bare root trees is an economical, easy way to plant many types of deciduous trees. Nurseries ship dormant bare root trees to coincide with the appropriate planting dates for your location. If you are looking to install larger specimen trees, you may want to enlist the help of a nursery or garden center that offers warranted planting services.

WHEN AND HOW TO PLANT

In zones 5-6, trees may be planted in fall while soil is still warm enough for some root growth to occur. Use mulch to help keep the soil warmer longer. Trees planted in late winter and early spring will also have some time for some root growth before new shoots expand. Planting can continue through winter in zones 7-9 when conditions are not too cold or soggy. Trees planted by early spring will have less transplant stress than those planted later.

Before digging the hole, prepare and measure the root ball. Water it well beforehand. Slide containers off and gently shake or rinse off some of potting mix. On balled and burlapped trees, untie the cords and burlap at the top of the root ball. Gently rake your fingers over the soil near the trunk to remove any

None

CHAPTER NINE

excess soil that may have piled up against it during digging process at the nursery (it will be looser than the root ball soil). Next, measure the depth of the root ball, and dig the hole about an inch shorter to allow for settling. Dig the hole at least 2 or 3 times wider than the root ball, *without disturbing the bottom of the hole.* Roughen the sides of the hole. For bare root trees, place a small mound of soil in the bottom to center the roots over. Lift the tree from the root ball or by grabbing the trunk just above the roots.

Cut the burlap away from the root ball after it is placed in the hole. On both container and b&b plants, gently tease outer roots away from the old root ball shape. This will help direct them to grow out into the surrounding soil. Protect exposed roots from drying out during the planting process, using dampened burlap or newspaper and keeping them out of the sun. Refill the hole with the original, loosened soil and taper it to thinly cover the root ball. *Do not mix any compost, amendments or fertilizers with the backfill.* This can result in problems with settling and impedes root growth into the surrounding soil. Organic amendments or leftover container mix may be spread on the soil surface after planting. Fertilizer is not essen-

tial at planting. Water slowly and thoroughly to settle the soil (but don't tamp it down). Shape a 2 to 3 inch soil rim to create a broad basin to hold water over the root ball. Finish with 2 to 4 inches of coarse organic mulch. Be sure to keep soil and mulch off the base of the trunk.

Use stakes only if the tree is not able to remain upright on its own, most common with bare root trees. Drive stakes into undisturbed soil outside the root ball. Attach ties low on the trunk so the top can flex in the wind. Flexible rubber straps are a good tying material, not wire or

nylon cord that can quickly dig into the bark. Remove stakes during the first year, as soon as they are no longer needed.

It is *not* necessary to prune newly planted trees to balance the roots. Those branches and leaves are needed to support new root growth. Prune only as needed for dead or damaged branches.

PRUNING

Proper pruning when trees are young will help them develop strong structure with less future pruning requirements. Trees should be pruned

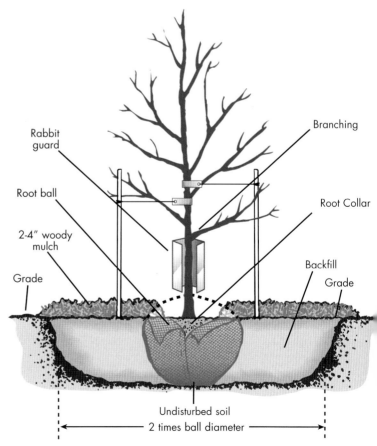

232

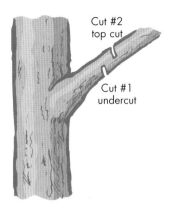

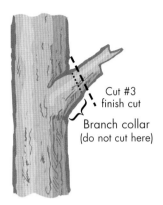

Cut #2
top cut

Cut #1
undercut

Cut #3
finish cut

Branch collar
(do not cut here)

Location of saw cuts to remove a branch.

with respect to their natural architecture, using thinning cuts to remove branches at main trunks or larger side limbs. Branches should never be cut flush, nor with stubs left behind. Cut just outside the branch collar, the natural bulge where the branch meets the trunk. Pruning for size, removing lower limbs, or cleaning out dead and broken branches is all best done with thinning cuts. Use by-pass style pruners and loppers, and good pruning saws (see Shrubs, page 211).

Check your trees each season for dead, damaged or diseased limbs. Prune with moderation, removing no more than about ¼ to ⅓ of the total branch area. Unlike shrubs, trees do not lend themselves to rejuvena-tion pruning, and may be permanently harmed if over pruned. The only exceptions are those rugged tree species so tolerant of rigorous pruning they are commonly sold for use in hedges, but even this training must start with young plants. Laurels (*Prunus laurocerasus, P. lusitanica*), holly (*Ilex* spp.) hedge maple (*Acer campestre*), hemlock (*Tsuga* spp.), and hornbeam (*Carpinus* spp.) are some tree species that tolerate pruning as hedges.

Pruning for very large trees and any work off the ground is best done by a professional arborist trained and equipped to work safely in trees.

MATURE TREE HEALTH CARE

Taking good care of your trees is an investment in their long-term health, safety and beauty. Routine care helps reduce potential problems. When large trees develop health or structural problems, they can become hazardous. Some problems, like large dead limbs are easily managed through pruning. Other problems may require timely removal. Take a close look at your trees throughout the year, paying attention to any changes from its usual appearance. Hire an ISA certified arborist to help with your large tree care needs. See April for more information on tree care and hiring an arborist.

JANUARY
TREES

PLANNING

Conifers are nearly synonymous with Northwest trees. The long periods of moist weather, moderate temperatures, and overcast skies west of the Cascades provide ideal growing conditions for native **Douglas fir** (*Pseudostuga menziesii*), **Western red-cedar** (*Thuja plicata*), and **Western hemlock** (*Tsuga heterophylla*) that define the character of our forests and cultivated landscapes alike. East of the Cascades, **ponderosa pine** (*Pinus ponderosa*), **lodgepole pine** (*Pinus contorta* var. *latifolia*), **Western larch** (*Larix occidentalis*), and **Western juniper** (*Juniperus occidentalis*) are the predominant species.

The wide variety of cultivated conifers offers a wealth of choices to match a variety of garden spaces and conditions. These evergreens add texture and color to a monochrome winter and provide year-round interest. Existing and newly planted native conifers can be easily incorporated into the landscape. Use them so they complement rather than dominate the plantings. Existing large conifers can be utilized as a dramatic backdrop, their dark hues illuminating the colors of branches, leaves, and flowers on adjacent trees and shrubs. Intersperse them among deciduous trees for accent and seasonal interest. Many shades of greens, blues, and gold can be found among garden conifer cultivars.

Look to the native species that thrive in your area as indicators of which types of cultivated conifers will also do well in your garden. The range of colors and textures provide immense opportunities for combinations with other garden elements.

PLANTING

Zones 4-6: It is typically too cold for planting.

Zones 7-9: Evergreen and deciduous trees can be planted and transplanted during warmer periods with low temperatures in the 40s and when soil is not sopping wet.

CARE

Zones 4-6: Winter desiccation means needles on evergreen trees can dry out when soils are frozen and sun and wind exposure occurs. Needles may be protected with a spray-on anti-desiccant when temperatures are above freezing. Smaller trees might be wrapped with burlap, as is done for shrubs. Make sure evergreens go into winter well watered. Damaged needles may be shed and replaced the next growing season.

PRUNING

Zones 4-6: It is generally too cold for pruning work.

Zones 7-9: Dormant season pruning for deciduous and evergreen trees can be done during periods of mild weather.

WATERING

No irrigation should be needed during the wet winter season, except in high desert regions where evergreens and new trees will benefit from supplemental water if soil conditions remain dry.

Douglas fir

THE PITFALLS OF TOPPING TREES

Some people believe that trees should be topped to keep them from getting too big, or to make them safer. Tops and large limbs are lopped off in the effort to control shape and size. Tree topping often occurs in the first years after a property is acquired, though few people are pleased with the resulting appearance. Some have the idea that the profusion of stimulated shoot growth is good for a tree. But pruning trees back hard like a rose bush or hedge will permanently damage structure, strength, appearance, and long-term health.

The truth is, topping is harmful to tree health and safety:

• Topped trees have a shortened lifespan and require more maintenance in the long run.

• New sprouts around cut tops are weakly attached and prone to breaking off in wind and storms as they get larger—far more so than would occur with the original branch structure.

• Decay invades cut tops, making the thinly attached sprouts even more dangerous as they increase in size.

• Topped trees are more prone to insect and disease problems.

Managing Tree Size Safely

A tree's stability is affected by the strength and condition of the root system and its trunk and scaffold limbs. Wind sail in very dense conifers can be reduced with selective thinning of the crown. Removal of dead or weak limbs will reduce the likelihood of them breaking out in a storm. Tree height and width can be reduced by thinning out and shortening the longest branches to the next largest point of connection.

What to Do with a Tree That Has Already Been Topped

Young trees of some species might be restored with careful selective thinning done over a course of years. For many, the best solution is to remove the tree and start over. Large mature trees which have been topped should be examined by an ISA certified arborist to determine their condition and safety. If a tree has been topped because it is truly too large for the location, it is far better to remove it and start over with a new tree that grows to an appropriate mature size.

Isn't This Just Pollarding?

Pruning well-developed trees back to stubs is just plain topping. Pollarding is a historic technique where young deciduous trees such as **willow** and **plane trees** are trained for annual harvest of shoots for fuel, shelter, fences, basket making, and other uses. The shoots are cut back to the same knobby branch ends each year in a very labor intensive practice that only a few deciduous tree species will tolerate.

FERTILIZING

No routine fertilization this month.

PROBLEMS

Winter storms can take a toll on trees: Snow, ice, and wind can break limbs. Trees in water logged soils may begin to list or fall over. Check on your trees after any severe storm or wind events. Call an ISA certified arborist for assistance with repair and clean up of severely damaged trees or those with large hanging broken limbs that could pose a safety threat (see How to Hire an Arborist, page 241). Stay away from power lines when surveying tree damage after a storm and call your local utility if trees have come in contact with the power lines.

FEBRUARY
TREES

PLANNING

How trees are placed around your property can affect the microclimate of your site. Strategically placed deciduous trees can provide cooling shade in the summer while letting the light and warmth of the sun through in winter months. Shaded buildings have been found to save 20 to 50 percent in summer cooling costs. Planting a long row of evergreen trees perpendicular to prevailing winds will deflect the impact of winter winds, especially in rural open areas, saving up to ⅓ of the heat loss from the building. A windbreak 30 feet tall protects an area extending 300 feet downwind. Shelterbelts of 2 to 5 rows of trees and shrubs offer greater protection, though even a single row of evergreens helps.

Review the seasonal sun and wind patterns around your property to see if additions or changes to tree placement can improve the microclimate. The greatest year-round benefits come with trees placed on the east, northwest, or west sides, keeping more of the south side open. Smaller trees can provide beneficial shade to patios and reflective outdoor surfaces. Be sure to position larger growing trees with enough room to expand without growing too close to roofs or foundations.

PLANTING

Zones 4-6: Not while winter conditions remain below freezing.

Zones 7-9: All types of trees may be planted now. It is a good time to plant bare-root trees. Trees planted now will have time to put on new root growth before shoot growth begins later in spring. They will establish with less drought stress their first summer. Provide a generous ring of coarse organic mulch over bare soil beneath new trees, making sure it doesn't bury the tunk base.

CARE

Zones 7-9: The ground beneath existing trees can be mulched during mild weather when soil conditions are not too soggy. Remember to keep mulch a few inches away from the base of the trunk. Replenish mulch to a total of 2 to 4 inches deep when bare soil shows through. Clear away weeds and thick vegetation from the base of tree trunks so the root flare area is clear and visible.

All zones: Winter storms may still occur throughout the region. Inspect trees for damage after storm events (see January Problems).

PRUNING

Zones 4-6: Evergreens and conifers can be pruned in late winter.

Zones 7-9: Continue dormant season pruning needed for deciduous and evergreen trees. **Maples** and **birches** can "bleed" after pruning. The sap loss itself is not normally harmful, though the continual wetness around larger wounds can damage stem tissue, particularly in milder areas. Pruning at the very end of the dormant season (but before buds begin to swell open) can reduce the amount of time sap flows onto the bark. These trees may also be pruned after new growth has fully expanded, or in summer.

WATERING

Zones 4-6: In high desert country, newly planted shade trees will benefit from an occasional winter watering during periods when the ground is not frozen.

Zones 7-9: Soil moisture is typically ample at this time of year. If temperatures have been warm and rainfall lacking, be sure the rootballs of newly planted trees haven't dried out. The different texture soil on the original soil ball can be prone to drying out, even when the surrounding soil is moist. Keep the soil uniformly

AVOIDING DAMAGE CAUSED BY TREE ROOTS

When large growing tree species are planted too close to sidewalks, sewer lines, and buildings, they contribute to damage as they reach maturity. Planting trees where there is plenty of room for them to grow can help avoid costly future root conflicts. The root flare at the base of tree trunks naturally broadens as large trees age, though some species such as **oaks** and **elms** tend to develop a broader root flare area than other species. Where planting spaces are narrow, the use of smaller growing species can help reduce potential conflicts.

If tree roots are lifting sidewalks, reconfiguring the sidewalk to curve around the tree can be helpful in many locations. Root pruning alone is a temporary solution, as new roots will grow back on healthy trees and root pruning that is too extensive can harm tree health and stability. Check with your municipality for guidelines and requirements on appropriate trees for planting along city streets and sidewalks.

Know where the sewer lines are located on your property and avoid planting tree species known to move into pipes nearby, such as **willow, poplar,** and **birch**. Root entry into sewer lines usually follows an existing break or crack in the line. Roots can usually be routed out of affected pipes by commercial services.

Trees planted too close to buildings can impact foundation walls as they grow larger over time, a problem that is difficult to correct once the trees have grown large. Large growing shade trees and conifers should generally not be planted within 10 feet of buildings. Remember, the crown, trunk, and root flare will continue to broaden in diameter as the tree ages.

moist to support new root growth throughout the planting site.

FERTILIZING

Fertilization is not useful at this time. Nitrogen can be readily leached away by heavy winter rains.

PROBLEMS

Zones 7-9: Dormant oil may be sprayed on deciduous trees which had high populations of aphids, scale, or leaf hoppers the previous year (insects which contribute to excessive dripping of honey dew).

Dormant season copper fungicides applied now will help with leaf and twig fungus diseases on **sycamore, hawthorn,** and **willow** trees.

For large trees, spraying is best done by a professional service.

MARCH

TREES

PLANNING

Early spring blooming trees seem to float like airy clouds in the garden, heralding the close of winter. Most are woodland species of small to medium size, best adapted to grow where they are sheltered from the hot afternoon sun. Look through garden catalogs and local nurseries for trees that greet March and April with cheery blossoms.

The following selections are hardy in zones 5 to 9. **Cornelian cherry dogwood** (*Cornus mas*) is one of the earliest to bloom, with prolific tiny yellow blooms lining its branches. It is a rugged, small, drought tolerant tree and can be grown in sun to light shade. The graceful horizontal stems of **Eastern redbud** (*Cercis canadensis*) are lined with tiny deep pink flowers. **Flowering dogwood** (*Cornus florida*) has large, white leathery bracts cir-

cling its small green flowers, and rose colored bracts on 'Cherokee Chief'. **Carolina silverbell** (*Halesia carolina* and *H. monticola*) is a lovely woodland species with pendulous white blossoms appearing before the leaves. A fine companion tree for **rhododendrons**, it is dramatic with a backdrop of larger conifers.

Beautiful large white blossoms are found on **Merrill magnolia** (*Magnolia x loebneri* 'Merrill'), a sturdy small tree covered in long, waxy, white petals. The smaller 15-foot tall **star magnolia** (*Magnolia stellata*) bears similar flowers. **Yulan magnolia** (*Magnolia denudata*) grows up to 30 feet in height with breathtaking blooms. In colder zones, it requires some protection from winds and frost pockets to prevent damage to the flowers. As a group, magnolias are better planted in spring than fall.

Eastern redbud

PLANTING

This is a good month for planting trees as the weather get warmer and soils are still moist. These trees will establish new root growth earlier than those planted later in the season. Many nurseries ship bare-root trees for planting in March and April, a good planting option for many shade tree species (see Trees Introduction under Planting for details). Companion ground covers can be planted this month (see Chapter Ten).

CARE

Coarse, multi-textured organic mulch under garden trees is like the natural duff layer in forests which replenishes organic matter and nutrients in the soil.

PRUNING

The smell of spring in the air inspires many gardeners to get busy with spring garden clean up. However, trees are vastly different from plants such as **roses, hydrangeas,** and many perennials which benefit from vigorous annual spring pruning. Your trees may be just fine as they are or might be better pruned at a

different time of year with a different technique.

Every spring, many otherwise normal trees of various sizes end up with their limbs lopped off in efforts to "control" their growth. But pruning trees back hard like a rose bush or hedge will permanently damage their structure, strength, appearance, and long-term health.

Never use hedge shears on trees. Lopping or shearing the crowns of small trees into compact shapes not only ruins the natural form but will require more maintenance in the long run. The resulting crop of vigorous new shoots taps stored energy. Insect and disease problems can increase on the extra tender growth. Decay invades the randomly cut tops and branch ends.

Large or small, trees are best pruned using thinning cuts that preserve the natural form of the crown. The best pruning is almost invisible to casual observation. No more than 1/3 of the branch area should be removed at one time. Locate pruning cuts along the branch collar at the point of attachment to the trunk or other branches. Small branches should be kept on the inside of the crown. Over-thinning is harmful. Many trees only need the occasional dead branch removed, and most healthy ornamental trees don't require annual pruning.

DID YOU KNOW?

Tree wound dressings are unnecessary. Tree paints and wound dressings have long been sold to help pruning cuts "heal." The truth is trees don't heal but grow new layers of wood over the damaged wood. The new wood grows from the ring of callus that forms at the edges of a pruning cut. Years of study have found no evidence of benefit from wound dressings. The best protection is to make good clean cuts at the outer edge of the branch collar.

Spring is not the best time to prune trees that are prone to developing basal suckers and water sprouts, such as **hawthorns** (*Crataegus* spp.), **flowering plums** and **cherries** (*Prunus* spp.), **crabapples** (*Malus* spp.), and **birches** (*Betula* spp.). Prune them in early to midsummer to discourage these extra sprouts. Remove dead, broken, or damaged limbs any time of year. Deciduous trees can be pruned in winter when the branch structure is clearly visible. Avoid pruning them in the spring when buds are swelling and new leaves are just emerging, and in the early fall just as they are going dormant.

What if your trees were already topped? Some smaller trees may be restored with careful selective thinning done over a course of years. Often, the best solution is removing the tree and starting over. Large trees which have been topped should be examined by an ISA certified arborist to determine the condition and safety.

WATERING

Zones 4-6: In high desert regions, new trees will benefit from a deep soaking if they have been dry through the winter.

Zones 7-9: Seasonal rains typically provide enough moisture. Check newly planted trees to be sure the original soil ball is as moist as the surrounding soil.

FERTILIZING

Not this month.

PROBLEMS

Zones 4-6: Dormant oil may be applied to deciduous trees to control aphids and scale problems. Dormant season copper fungicides applied now will help with leaf and twig fungus diseases. See April Problems for zones 7 to 9.

APRIL

TREES

PLANNING

Trees are long-lived, enduring inhabitants of our world. Fixed in place, trees must withstand a lot of changes in their environment over their lifetimes—insects, diseases and seasonal weather extremes, not to mention the many insults people can impose on them. Some of these conditions compromise health with serious stresses. And, like all living things, trees can fall to ill health, the vagaries of age, and physical decline. To survive well in our communities, trees need our care and attention. They need regular checkups to stay healthy. They need protection against undue damage. And large trees with physical defects require inspection and attention to reduce potential hazards.

April is Arbor Day month, a time to celebrate trees. This year, honor Arbor Day by seeing to the care and stewardship of valued trees in your landscape and community. If you have very large trees on your property, meet with a professional arborist to review their health and condition.

Make a plan to look at your trees closely each season of the year as a first step to keeping them healthy and safe. Take pictures. Like the relatives in our family photos, it can be amazing

how much even seemingly full-grown trees continue to grow and change.

PLANTING

Zones 4-6: Bare-root trees can be planted this month, as well as container-grown and balled-and-burlapped trees.

Zones 7-9: Finish planting trees before the end of the month to lessen transplant stress in the coming summer.

Planting trees well will ensure their future good growth and development. Plant trees as soon as possible after purchase. Don't keep them confined to containers for too long. See the chapter introduction for more details on tree planting practices.

CARE

If there is bare ground beneath trees, provide a 2- to 4-inch layer of coarse organic mulch. Mulching is one of the best care practices you can provide to young and old trees alike. Always be sure the mulch tapers back to ground level at the base of the trunk.

PRUNING

As spring sap flows rush up from the roots to feed swelling buds and shoots, the bark can be very easily torn during pruning work. It is best not to prune trees during this period when the bark is "slipping." Wait until after the first leaves and shoots have fully expanded.

The growth on young pine trees can be managed with a technique called **candling**. The emerging shoots (candles) can be shortened by up to $1/2$ their length before the needles start to expand. This results in shorter stem length between the whorls of branches, keeping the tree more compact.

WATERING

In desert areas of zones 4-6 and zones 7-9, as temperatures warm and the amount of precipitation decreases, begin monitoring new and established trees for watering.

All zones: Check automatic systems to be sure water spray does not directly wet the lower trunks of trees. When setting up manual sprinklers, position them so the water spray touches ground a few inches away from the base of tree trunks. Bubbler heads are a good option for watering trees under automatic or manual watering. Apply enough water to wet the soil several inches deep, and allow the soil to dry out a bit between watering. Maintaining mulch under trees will reduce the amount of irrigation needed through the season.

Use a trowel to probe into the soil to check soil moisture levels.

FERTILIZING

Established trees do not need to be fertilized every year. Young trees do not need fertilizer at the time of planting.

PROBLEMS

Protect **dogwood** trees against anthracnose with fungicide sprays as buds begin to open and repeated as directed on the label until leaves are fully expanded. This disease is prevalent in moister parts of the region and can be more intense during wetter years. Contact your OSU or WSU Cooperative Extension Office for more information on control methods.

HOW TO HIRE AN ARBORIST

An arborist is a specialist trained in the art and science of tree care. Arborists certified by the International Society of Arboriculture (ISA) must have at least three years of field experience, pass a comprehensive exam, and regularly attend training sessions to keep their certification current. Arborists can help with diagnosis and care for smaller trees and are essential when it comes to large trees. Some firms provide consultation only, and some provide both consultation and tree care services. It can be helpful to get to know an arborist before you have an urgent problem. Among the services provided are:

- Pruning to maintain health, appearance, and safety.
- Cabling and bracing of weak limbs.
- Diagnosis and treatment of insects, disease, and environmental stress.
- Hazard tree evaluation and management.
- Tree preservation during construction.
- Removals
- Emergency tree care.
- Tree value appraisals.
- Tree selection and planting.

The Pacific Northwest Chapter of the International Society of Arboriculture Web page offers these tips for selecting an arborist:

- Hire someone who is bonded, licensed, and insured.
- Ask for references and get more than one bid.
- Ask for an ISA certified arborist.
- Look for membership in professional organizations, such as the ISA, the National Arborists Association, or the American Society of Consulting Arborists.
- Beware of door-knockers. Reputable firms are generally too occupied to solicit work in this manner.
- Avoid tree toppers and workers who use spikes on healthy trees.

For referrals and more information, visit the PNW-ISA at www.pnwisa.org

Oregon celebrates Arbor Week the first full week of April. Arbor Day is the second Wednesday in April in **Washington**.

TREES

PLANNING

Spring blooming trees are a great compliment to the garden. Flowering **crabapples** are an old time favorite, but many of the older cultivars quickly dissolve into a mess of brown leaves as apple scab takes its toll, particularly west of the Cascades. The good news is there are several stellar cultivars which are highly disease resistant. Replace an existing poor performer with one of these for better bloom and summer performance. These small (20 feet or less) trees are a great accent for smaller gardens. All are hardy to zone 4. *Malus domestica* 'Winter Gem' and 'Strawberry Parfait' have a broad upright form. 'Prairifire' blooms deep pink, with maroon leaves for great summer color. 'Louisa' is a broad weeping form. Outstanding for small, narrow spaces is the late blooming columnar 'Adirondack', reaching only about 12 feet in height.

Few tree species tolerate cultivation in patio containers, but the dwarf 'Lancelot' and 'Camelot' crabapples are good considerations for this use. They will need regular water and fertilization and should be taken out of their pots every few years for root pruning and repotting with fresh soil. Containers too large to move into winter protection will need insulation to protect roots during periods of freezing weather. Many of the taller shrub species may also be trained as single trunk specimens in containers, offering seasonal shade for patios and decks.

PLANTING

Complete tree planting before summer temperatures arrive. Trees installed this month will require more watering during warm weather. Check them at least once a week, or when temperatures suddenly soar.

CARE

Trees in grass? Provide a generous ring of mulch around trees growing in turf. Do not use fabric weed barriers. They prevent organic matter from reaching the soil and roots and are not a good choice around trees.

Zones 4-6: Remove tree wrap used for winter protection on young trees. As their bark thickens with age, continued winter protection will not be needed.

PRUNING

Training young trees should take place during the first years after planting, doing a little bit each year. Follow the tree's natural growth habit to make pruning less obvious. Well placed cuts with hand pruners while a tree is young can prevent future structural problems. Many of the limb failures in winter winds occur at double leaders with included bark (where bark becomes imbedded at the branch junction). Limbs tightly clustered at the trunk make for weak structure. And trunks without broader taper at the base are structurally weaker.

1. Use thinning cuts back to the point of attachment on the trunk, cutting at the outer edge of the branch collar.

2. Remove dead, damaged, and broken limbs.

3. Prune out any competing upright shoots and one of the stems in co-dominant leaders so there is one tall central leader.

4. Remove branches with very narrow crotch angles and included bark on trees that aren't of naturally columnar or upright form.

5. If needed, thin out crowded branches along the trunk. The larger the mature size of the tree, the greater the spacing between these limbs, both vertically and around the trunk.

6. Retain lower branches the first few years to develop good trunk taper. As the tree gains height, gradually remove these

lower limbs up to the height of the lowest permanent branch.

WATERING

Water slowly and deeply, wetting the soil at least 8 inches deep. Apply mulch to conserve soil moisture.

FERTILIZING

Young trees, except those planted this past spring, will benefit from an annual application of a slow-release product at 1 to 2 pounds of actual nitrogen per 1000 square feet or about 2 tablespoons granules with 15 percent nitrogen per 3-foot circle. (see General Introduction). Rake granules into mulch and water well. Fertilize young trees during their first three years of establishment.

PROBLEMS

Avoid broadcast weed-and-feed lawn products that contain 2, 4-D, and other broadleaf weed herbicides. Trees are also broadleaf plants and can be harmed by repeated or over-applications of these products.

Flowering cherries (*Prunus* spp.) have long been the mainstay in

Though they do have problems, flowering cherries are magnificent in bloom.

CARING FOR NEWLY PLANTED TREES

The best transplant treatment you can provide is to use good planting techniques, water well through the first growing season, and use mulch to help retain moisture and control weeds.

Special transplant products cannot make up for poor planting practices or lack of water. For example, repeated research has found no added benefits with Vitamin B-1. Many transplant products, such as bone meal, are high in phosphorous. However, these elements are rarely deficient in landscape soils. Raising the level of soil phosphorous can suppress beneficial mycorrhizal fungi that enhance root growth and nutrient uptake. Runoff of excess phosphorous contributes to water pollution in local waters. Mycorrhizae inoculums have begun to show up in some new transplant products, but consistent benefits have not been proven for these applications.

flowering trees, though they suffer many insect and disease problems. Spray flowering cherries for brown rot blossom blight if they were severely affected last year. The cherry bark tortrix trunk borer is a recently arrived pest in Washington and parts of Oregon. To minimize these problems, give these trees good care and plant them in well drained soil and open sunny sites for best health and display. Contact your OSU or WSU Cooperative Extension Office for more information on these *Prunus* problems.

New disease resistant **cherries** that have recently become available are good choices to replace older cherries that may have lost their luster in the garden: *Prunus* 'Cascade Snow', 'Dream Catcher', and 'Royal Burgundy'.

JUNE
TREES

 PLANNING

How can you adjust planting areas to help trees and lawn coexist more effectively? Vigorous turf will stunt the growth of young trees. Lawns thin out under large, established trees. Mowers and string trimmers can seriously damage bark. Roots bulging through the soil surface get scalped and make mowing difficult. What can be done?

Maintain a generous ring of mulch beneath trees to eliminate turf competition and avoid mechanical damage from mowing. Place new trees in large beds and keep lawns in open sunny areas. With care to minimize soil disturbance beneath the canopy, it is also possible to create a planting bed beneath large existing trees. (See page 230 for tips on planting beneath trees.)

Where turf has been shaded out, go with mulch and shade-adapted ground covers. Start with a 2- to 4-inch layer of coarse organic mulch or compost to protect bare ground between protruding roots. It is best not to bury these skinned roots with soil or mulch as it can increase decay problems. Plan to add plants in early fall for easier establishment.

 PLANTING

All zones: This is not an ideal time for planting trees, especially where water is scarce. If you must plant now, do it during cool damp weather, or late in the day. Thoroughly soak rootballs beforehand, and check them daily the first weeks after planting. Don't forget to mulch.

 CARE

Create broad, soil rimmed basins under young trees to aid water penetration over their root zones. Maintain mulch rings around trees in turf areas.

 PRUNING

Summer pruning can begin for many trees this month, including **Japanese maples** (*Acer palmatum* cvs.). Pruning work should follow the tree's natural architecture, leaving it to look as though it were never touched by human hands. Use good sharp tools. Remember to stand back frequently to look at the whole plant. Remove no more than about $1/4$ of the crown area. Remove branches back to the point of origin at the main trunk or larger side branch. Prune at the branch collar, being careful not to cut flush to the trunk.

The first (and sometimes only) task is to remove dead branches. Next, work on any branches that may be growing out of bounds from the rest of the tree or interfering with a walkway or building.

Remove any branches whose leaves don't match with the rest. Prune them cleanly at the trunk or soil.

Some small trees develop a canopy which shades out smaller inside stems. Lightly thin out some of the branches to allow filtered light to the inside and to reveal glimpses of the architecture of the trunk and main branches. Branches of weeping or low growing trees that drag should be lifted by thinning out the longest branches.

Disinfect tools between cuts within a tree and from tree to tree if there has been evidence of diseases such as verticillium wilt or fire blight. Isopropyl alcohol or a 10 percent bleach solution in a hand spray bottle will suffice. Sanitizing tools is not usually necessary unless vascular diseases are suspected.

 WATERING

Check trees planted over the past three years about once per week for water needs.

Use caution when installing new irrigation around large

trees—severe root damage results from trenching too close to trunks. Position lateral lines in a spoke fashion from beyond the drip line to minimize root damage. Heads should be located closer to the drip line, with the spray stopping short of hitting the trunk. Frequent watering to the root flare area may cause root rot and early death.

FERTILIZING

Established trees with good foliage color and mulch usually don't need routine fertilization.

If you haven't already, fertilize young trees with slow-release fertilizer at 1 to 2 pounds of actual nitrogen per 1000 square feet (see page 14). Water thoroughly.

PROBLEMS

Dutch elm disease symptoms appear with the sudden wilting and browning of leaves along a single branch, called "flagging." Contact your OSU or WSU Extension Office or your community forester as soon as you suspect the disease in your trees. Many areas of Oregon and Washington have active monitoring and control programs. Early control helps limit its spread.

Crabapples with apple scab drop leaves as the weather

WEED KILLERS CAN BE HARMFUL TO YOUR TREES AND SHRUBS

Commonly used garden herbicides can damage trees and shrubs. The pre-emergent dichlorbenil (in Casoron) leads to stunted yellow leaves and death if over-applied or used repeatedly. It is harmful to new plants. Weed and feed lawn products containing 2, 4-D and other broadleaf herbicides can reach woody plant roots that migrate under lawns. Trees and shrubs are also broadleaf plants and can suffer symptoms of deformed or discolored foliage.

Spray drift from glyphosate (in Roundup and other products) can cause dieback, stress, or death when it lands on thin bark and leaves. The source of damage can be confusing, as it may not show up until the next year when leaves come out small and twisted.

Use herbicides selectively and only when necessary. Apply them only as directed. Get specific weed problems identified and seek alternative methods of suppression. Overuse of herbicides can harm permanent landscape plants and soil organisms, and they may leach into waterways and aquifers.

warms. Rake up and destroy fallen leaves. Replace the chronically affected trees with a disease-resistant cultivar.

Tent caterpillars, which appear on many trees and shrubs, are most troublesome to smaller trees. Knock nests off with a strong blast of water. Tent caterpillar cycles vary, and some years show more infestation than in others.

Replace your crabapple with a disease-resistant cultivar if it is infected with apple scab.

JULY

TREES

PLANNING

Trees provide a green backdrop in summer and some even offer opportunities for color and fragrance. Look at existing gardens for exciting arboreal blooms. Some may be subtle, like the small flower clusters dangling from pale green bracts on **lindens** (*Tilia* spp.). Robust *Catalpa* trees boast oversized leaves and blooms. The fine features of *Stewartia* bring elegance to the woodland garden with its camellia-like blooms in midsummer. White **lily-of-the-valley**-style flowers appear in August on the small, narrow **sourwood** (*Oxydendrum arboreum*), a tree with outstanding fall color. **Golden raintree** (*Koelreuteria paniculata*) is a fine mid-sized tree for urban yards, with upright yellow flowers clusters followed by pinkish seedpods. It is drought tolerant and hardy to zone 5. **Idaho locust** (*Robinia* x *ambigua* 'Idahoensis') will grow in dry and poor soils, heralding fragrant purple blossoms in June. **Japanese tree lilac** (*Syringa reticulata*) is a 30-foot tree with cherry-like bark. Drought tolerant and suitable as a street tree, it also bears fragrant pale blooms in June.

PLANTING

The peak dry heat periods of summer bring some of the worst conditions for successfully planting trees. It is best to wait until shorter, cooler days return at the start of fall.

CARE

Do not tie ropes or chains around tree trunks. They can cause serious damage by chafing or constricting the trunk. Check staking on young trees and remove it as soon as the support is no longer needed.

Inspect and photograph your trees. Walk all the way around to look at all sides. Look from the tiptop branches to the ground. Are there any dead branches or changes in leaf appearance? Compare with previous photos. Regular inspections help catch problems before they become severe. If you need help, call a professional arborist or contact your OSU or WSU Extension Office.

PRUNING

Remove any sucker growth present at this time. Very small sprouts are easily removed by rubbing them off by hand. Use hand pruners on thicker sprouts.

Low branches that have grown down into walkways can be pruned back to the main trunk.

To reduce crown height and width, remove the longest branches back to the next largest branch within the crown. Trees pruned this way won't need pruning as often to maintain their size or form. Always prune moderately in summer, removing no more than 1/4 of the live branches at this time.

WATERING

Established trees not routinely irrigated benefit from a deep soaking midsummer. Apply water slowly to moisten the area beneath the canopy at least 8 inches deep. Watering now prevents summer drought stress and early leaf drop.

On heavy soils, adjust the rate of water application to complement absorption. Always probe the soil before watering. Trees in waterlogged soil will also wilt, the oxygen deprived roots unable to take in water. If you find waterlogged soil that smells bad, correct soil drainage and/or irrigation applications.

FERTILIZING

The slowly decomposing organic matter from coarse mulches like composted wood chips, leaf mold, or shredded bark replenishes soil nutrients and improves moisture holding capacity.

If no fertilizer has been applied yet this year, give young trees a very light application of a slow-release material early in the month (see June Fertilizing), being sure to water it in thoroughly. Remember soil must be moist for fertilizer to be available to the roots.

PROBLEMS

Zones 4-6: Bronze birch borer occurs in eastern Washington and Oregon. Raised channels and D-shaped exit holes are visible on the trunks of affected trees. Reduce tree stress and susceptibility with mulch and summer water. Choose alternate shade trees where this pest is prevalent. It is difficult to treat.

Port Orford cedar (*Chamaecyparis lawsoniana*), **arbor vitae** (*Thuja* sp.), and evergreens suffering from phytophthora root disease will suddenly turn olive then brown in summer when they can no longer take up enough

water to survive. On **rhododendrons** and other broadleaf evergreens, root rot wilts entire branches and curls leaves. This disease moves in surface water and is more severe on water-logged, poorly drained soils. Once the symptoms appear, the plants are not treatable.

Less common, but affecting trees in Oregon, is another form of phytophthora called sudden oak death for the tree it was first noted to kill. It infects a broad range of trees and shrubs and is fatal to some. Less affected plants display dead lesions on the leaves, and they can serve as an infection source for other vulnerable plants. Nursery growers have developed active programs to limit the spread of sudden oak death.

PROTECTING TREES DURING CONSTRUCTION

Misunderstandings about where and how tree roots grow has led to the untimely demise of many desired old specimens intended for preservation. Trenching and grade cuts too close to trees sever vital roots. Heavy equipment and grading work can cause soil compaction fatal to root health. Even as little as 6 inches of fill soil can smother roots. The effects of construction damage may not be apparent until a few years later, at which time little can be done. Construction damage is far easier to prevent than to cure. Consult with a certified arborist to develop a plan for tree preservation and care during and after construction.

Verticillium wilt shows up through an isolated wilted branch or with leaves that curl up and hang on into winter. It is common on **maples** but may also infect **lilac, privet, sumac,** and **viburnum**. A vigorous tree may survive with it for many years. This soil-borne disease can be spread on bits of soil clinging to tools and shoes. Disinfect tools after each pruning cut on affected (or suspected) trees.

Laboratory tests are required to accurately identify these diseases. Contact your OSU or WSU Cooperative Extension Office for assistance.

AUGUST

TREES

PLANNING

The term "shade tree" elicits thoughts of sultry summer days, soft breezes, and the cool cover of a green rustling canopy overhead. Many of our favorite shade trees shift to lovely hues in fall before the leaves disappear for the winter. If you are longing for better shade by this time of summer, take a look at which kinds of trees in your area are still looking good after weathering summer conditions. Planting deciduous shade trees to the southwest side of a house moderates the exposure to summer heat. The largest of these trees, such as **scarlet oak** (*Quercus coccinea*), **European beech** (*Fagus sylvatica*), or **red maple** (*Acer rubrum*), might shade the whole side of a house, while those reaching 30 feet or less in height can serve as a cool natural umbrella over patios or entry ways. **Eastern redbud** (*Cercis canadensis*), **Himalayan birch** (*Betula utilis* var. *jacquemontii*), and **Japanese snowbell** (*Styrax japonicus*) provide intimate shade for smaller garden spaces.

You can prepare the site now for fall tree planting. Clear away unwanted vegetation, turn the soil (if it's moist enough to dig), and cover a broad area with compost or mulch. After mulching, water thoroughly to support continued mulch decomposition and soil microbe activity. At planting time, rake mulch and compost away to expose the soil before digging the hole. Use the material to keep a large mulch ring around the base of the new tree.

PLANTING

This is the least advisable time for tree planting but a good time to start shopping for fall planting season.

CARE

Look closely at the largest trees on your property to monitor their general health and condition. Take pictures. If you notice unusual changes or problems, have them inspected by a certified arborist (see November).

Do not allow heavy vines to grow high up into trees where they can add weight and shading on tree branches. Always remove invasive species such as **English ivy**, **old man's beard**, and **kudzu** (see Vines Introduction, page 258). Heavier woody garden vines such as *Wisteria* and *Actinidia* should be kept off trees. Also be sure to keep vines from blanketing lower trunks where they can hold in dampness and can conceal any developing problems at the root collar area.

PRUNING

Dead branches are easily spotted for removal in summer. Any branches that droop into walkways can be removed to increase overhead clearance. Prune these lower branches all the way back to the trunk for best effect. Keep pruning light.

WATERING

Trees that have not received water all summer may show drought stress symptoms: Inner leaves yellow and drop as water supply becomes short. Early fall color may appear. Check the soil conditions. Provide mulch for trees surrounded by bare soil, and water slowly and deeply so roots are well hydrated as trees go into dormancy. If you find waterlogged soil that smells bad, soil drainage or irrigation rates probably need correction.

FERTILIZING

Maintain a light layer of coarse compost or organic mulch around trees. Allow mulch to decompose thinly enough for the soil to begin to show through before replenishing to a total 2- to 4-inch depth.

PROBLEMS

Wilt disease problems may continue to show up on deciduous and evergreen trees (see July Problems). Check **camellias, holly,** and **maple** trees for scale insects coating the stems. Honeydew dripping from **birches, oaks, maples,** and other trees reveals healthy aphid populations. Black sooty mold may grow on the honeydew. Scale can be treated with insecticidal soap when the spider-like crawlers are out. (You'll need a magnifier to see them.) Use it also for aphids, coating the undersides of leaves and repeating as needed. A single, dormant season application of horticultural oil between December and March will suppress these pests. Aphids increase on drought stressed trees. Maintain mulch and periodic irrigation for affected trees to improve summer health and vigor. Contact your OSU or WSU Extension Office for information on suspected problems.

SHADE TREES FOR TOUGH SITES

Drought tolerant trees for zones 4-6:
- **American hop hornbeam** (*Ostrya virginiana*), tolerant of dry, rocky, alkaline soils
- **Black maple** (*Acer saccharum* subsp. *nigrum* 'Greencolumn')
- **Blue ash** (*Fraxinus quadrangulata*), grows well on dry alkaline soils
- **Chinese juniper** (*Juniperus chinensis*)
- **Colorado spruce** (*Picea pungens*), for dry sun exposures
- **Crabapples** (*Malus* cultivars)
- **Idaho locust** (*Robinia* x *ambigua* 'Idahoensis')
- **Japanese pagoda tree** (*Sophora japonica*), tolerant of summer heat
- **Limber pine** (*Pinus flexilis*)
- **Marshall's seedless green ash** (*Fraxinus pennsylvanica* 'Marshall Seedless'), tolerant of alkaline soils
- **Silver linden** (*Tilia tomentosa*), tolerant of heat and drought

Shade trees suitable to naturally damp sites:
- **Black gum** (*Nyssa sylvatica*)
- **Dawn redwood** (*Metasequoia glyptostroboides*)
- **Red maple** (*Acer rubrum*)
- **Willow** (*Salix* spp.)

Black gum is a good choice for a damp site.

September

TREES

PLANNING

In arid zones where water for irrigating trees is scarce, it is wise to choose the most drought adapted species for long term health and benefits from tree planting. Look to the predominant native and garden trees which thrive in your area as indicators for choosing species with similar adaptations. Some highly ornamental drought tolerant species hardy to Zone 5 include evergreen **Chinese juniper** (*Juniperus chinensis*), **limber pine** (*Pinus flexilis*), **Idaho locust** (*Robinia x ambigua* 'Idahoensis'), and **Japanese pagoda tree** (*Sophora japonica*) with summer flowers, specimen shade trees **European hornbeam**, (*Carpinus betulus*), **silver linden** (*Tilia*

tomentosa), early blooming **Cornelian cherry dogwood** (*Cornus mas*) for smaller garden spaces, and **Persian parrotia** (*Parrotia persica*) and **sourwood** (*Oxydendrum arboreum*) with brilliant fall color.

Good soil management that improves moisture holding capacity is equally important. Even a drought tolerant species will struggle in heavily compacted soil. Plan to thoroughly prepare problem soils weeks before planting. Till or turn compacted soils and add modest amounts of organic matter to surface layers as needed (see General Introduction for more soil preparation information). At a minimum, maintaining coarse organic mulches over droughty soils will improve the moisture holding capacity.

PLANTING

Fall planting allows time for roots to settle in and begin growth before top growth begins the next season. These plants will establish with lower irrigation requirements during their first summer. Even drought tolerant species need adequate water the first two or three years until they are large enough to withstand longer periods without water.

Sourwood has brilliant fall foliage.

Soils can be at their driest before seasonal rains have returned. Remember to water and mulch at planting time (see planting information in Trees).

This is also an optimal time to add companion ground covers beneath large trees (see Ground Covers October).

CARE

Remove staking from young trees as soon as they can support themselves.

Remove heavy vines near trees (see August Care).

PRUNING

This is not a good time for routine pruning on deciduous trees. Avoid pruning live limbs as they go into dormancy. No new wood forms until spring, and new wounds are open to damp fall weather when fungal spores are more abundant. Do remove dead or broken limbs as needed.

WATERING

Water recently planted trees as needed to prevent their rootballs from drying out. Check the original rootball soil, as nursery soils can dry out more quickly than the surrounding native soil.

Water any trees that have become extremely dry so their roots are recharged with moisture before winter dormancy.

As weather cools and rains return, watering is no longer needed. Established plants that received some irrigation over summer should not need supplemental water unless conditions remain very warm and dry.

FERTILIZING

Apply organic mulch or compost to maintain soil nutrients and replenish organic matter. This also coincides with the natural nutrient cycle in forests as autumn leaves naturally "mulch" the forest floor.

PROBLEMS

Extremely heavy rains that soak deciduous trees still in leaf sometimes add enough weight to severely bend or even break weaker branches. Gently shake bending branches on young trees to release the weight load. Have larger trees with broken limbs inspected and pruned by a certified arborist.

Fall webworm nests stand out now in some trees, though they've been feeding for quite a while. The occasional nest is not too problematic for healthy trees, and at this late point in the season, there is no point to control. This is a native critter, most prevalent on **willow, poplar,** and **alder**. Caterpillars begin feeding in early summer. They seldom do as much damage as do tent caterpillars which appear much earlier in the season.

TREES AND POWER LINES

Tall trees growing close to power lines results in a chronic conflict for space and safety. Tree branches contacting power lines are a major cause of power outages, especially during storm events. Branches growing into power lines can conduct electricity, creating potential electrocution hazards. Utilities periodically prune and remove trees to maintain safety and continuity of service. This routine clearance pruning on large trees typically requires much more drastic pruning than would be done for trees in other locations.

Before you plant a new tree, look up to make sure there will be good overhead clearance. Primary and secondary electric lines run 28 and 25 feet above ground. Trees which mature around 25 feet in height will rarely require clearance pruning. Medium height trees with broad spreading crowns should be set back at least 20 feet from sidewalks and utility lines, columnar trees around 10 feet back, for optimal clearance. Very large trees that have begun to decline are well replaced with more appropriate species planted in optimal positions to avoid future tree and power line conflicts.

Contact your local utility for their guidelines and recommendations for tree planting in and near utility strips.

Some 20- to 35-foot height trees suitable to different sun and soil conditions include:

- **Hedge maple** (*Acer campestre* 'Queen Elizabeth')
- **Amur maple** (*Acer tataricum* subsp. *ginnala*)
- **Japanese maple** (*Acer japonicum* cultivars)
- **Cornelian cherry dogwood** (*Cornus mas*)
- **Crabapples** (*Malus* cultivars)
- **Eastern redbud** (*Cercis canadensis*)
- **Japanese snowbell** (*Styrax japonicus*)
- **Lavalle hawthorn** (*Crataegus lavallei*)
- **Mountain ash** (*Sorbus hupehensis* 'Coral Cascade', 'Pink Pagoda')
- **Sourwood** (*Oxydendrum arboreum*)
- **Japanese tree lilac** (*Syringa reticulata*)

OCTOBER

TREES

PLANNING

This is the month of fall color. The timing will vary by zone and elevation, with trees at higher elevations and cooler areas coloring first. Color intensity depends on the predominant temperature patterns during leaf senescence. Bright sunny days followed by rapidly cooling night temperatures causes greater amounts of sugars to remain in the leaves, which combine with leaf pigments to produce greater colors. Fall seasons with cloudy, rainy days and moderate temperatures between day and night have more subdued colors (typical for areas west of the Cascades). Visit local nurseries now to select shade trees at their best fall color.

Ginkgo (*Ginkgo biloba*) has clear yellow fall color on its small fan shaped leaves. **Red maple** (*Acer rubrum*) is one of the most utilized trees for fall color, and with some aptly named cultivars: 'October Glory', 'Autumn Flame', and 'Red Sunset'. **Japanese maples** come into their own with a range of reds, oranges, and yellows. **Japanese stewartia** (*Stewartia pseudocamellia*) has warm reds and purple. **Katsura** (*Cercidiphyllum japonicum*) has apricot to orange fall color, emit-

ting a sweet cinnamon scent as leaves fall. **Persian parrotia** (*Parrotia persica*) with a continuum of golden yellow to orange to scarlet creates a color show within one specimen. **Scarlet oak** (*Quercus coccinea*) is true to its name, and equally deep scarlet reds appear on **sourwood** (*Oxydendrum arboreum*).

PLANTING

Fall planting can continue throughout the region, although in zones 4 to 6 less hardy species and **magnolias** fare better if planted in spring. See the Introduction to Trees for planting details. Water and mulch after planting.

CARE

Fallen leaves can sometimes feel like a nuisance when they flood the yard, but they are great mulch waiting to happen. Allow smaller leaves to remain on the ground beneath trees and shrubs wherever possible without accumulating against stems or over low plants. Shredded leaves can be spread as a fall mulch to replenish where cover has thinned or to protect bare soil. Well composted leaves (leaf

mold) are attractive mulch and are one of the best materials to use around woody plants. See General Introduction, page 15 for leaf composting techniques.

PRUNING

With the exception of removing dead limbs, this is not the best time for pruning deciduous trees. Wait until later in the dormant season for routine pruning. Conifers may be pruned.

WATERING

Established plants will need no further watering as fall rains return.

FERTILIZING

Discontinue fertilization as heavy rains return to the region. Organic mulches will slowly add nutrients to the soil as they decompose, reducing the need for fertilizers.

PROBLEMS

Too much water or fertilizer during the growing season will delay dormancy. This can reduce cold-hardiness and increase

10 TIPS FOR HEALTHY TREES

Be kind to the roots—digging up or compacting the soil beneath trees, trenching, and raising or lowering the grade can seriously damage roots. Planning a remodel or construction near established trees? Call in an arborist well before you break ground to help determine if and how the tree can be preserved.

Protect the bark—avoid wounding or breaking the bark with nails or equipment. Don't tie ropes or chains around trees that can damage bark or constrict the trunk. These kinds of wounds can invite the start of decay. Painting wounds doesn't help; prevention is the best cure.

Avoid turf vs. trees conflicts—replace turf growing around trees with a broad ring of coarse organic mulch. This prevents bark damage from mowers and string trimmers and reduces turf and tree root competition for nutrients and moisture. Don't use weed-and-feed turf fertilizers near trees; they contain broadleaf weed killers that can be absorbed by tree roots.

Mulch—coarse, multi-textured mulch provides many benefits to root growth and tree health. Apply mulch where the ground is bare and in place of turf around the base of trunks. Don't let mulch contact the bark, but taper it to the soil level next to the trunk.

Prune to natural form and don't top your trees—good pruning preserves the natural branching habit. Get instruction or hire a professional. Topping can permanently disfigure and weaken smaller trees and create future hazards in large trees.

Plant with care—planting a tree correctly will ensure its future health and performance in the landscape. Use the right tree in the right place, plant it well, and provide regular water during the first three years of establishment.

Don't overstake—overstaking can actually impair trunk strength on young trees, and forgotten ties that imbed in the bark cause more damage than not staking at all. If needed at all, stakes should be removed from young trees within the first year of planting.

Water—give your trees an occasional slow, deep soaking if the soil gets extremely dry, especially later in summer. Don't overwater (let soil dry some between times) and don't allow irrigation spray to constantly wet bark, especially on older existing trees in the landscape.

Remove invasive and heavy vines (such as **ivy**, **old man's beard**, **wisteria**, or **kudzu**)—their weight can make trees more vulnerable to wind damage. Cut vines away from the base of the tree.

Know when to call a professional—before construction work near valued trees, for hazard assessment and management, and other problem diagnosis. And any work off the ground is best done by someone trained and equipped to work safely in trees. Visit **www.pnwisa.org** to locate an ISA certified arborist in your area.

freeze damage. If your trees are staying lush longer than others of their kind, moderate watering and eliminate fertilization next season.

Install protective collars around the base of young trees where winter rodent damage is a problem.

NOVEMBER

TREES

PLANNING

As the quality of light shifts and the clutter of foliage lessens, the architecture of large trees comes into focus. The unique structure and beauty of each tree's trunk and limbs are revealed anew. The fine texture and colors of conifer foliage complements the leaf color and emerging bare stems of their deciduous neighbors. Trees preside like silent sentinels over the garden in winter, their forms punctuated with the beauty of a light snow or thick frost. They create a sense of place, of permanence, through the seasons.

At a time when garden interest may seem to be waning, we can look to trees with interesting foliage, bark, and branching patterns to enliven the scene. The almost iridescent pale bark of the **Himalayan birch** (*Betula jacquemontii*) stands out brightly against evergreens in the background. Plant the petite **paperbark maple** (*Acer griseum*) near entries for a close view of its delicate, peeling cinnamon bark. In larger spaces, the wide spreading limbs of *Ginkgo biloba* stand out with deeply furrowed light gray bark. Weeping trees become even more dramatic focal points in winter silhouette.

Review the unique ornamental qualities of winter trees in your garden. It is a good time to assess spaces lacking in trees for potential well placed additions. In zones 7 to 9, trees may still be planted. Plan now for early spring planting in colder areas.

PLANTING

Zones 4-6: Planting stops as deep cold, wind, and snow arrive.

Zones 7-9: Fall planting can continue as weather and soil conditions permit.

CARE

Zones 4-6: Wrap the trunks of young, thin-barked trees with paper tree wrap late in the month to prevent sunscald. Start at the bottom so that the layers overlap like shingles on the side of the building and will shed water well. Tree wrap should be removed in early spring just before new growth begins.

Install a ring of 8-inch tall wire mesh around the base of shrubs vulnerable to winter rodent chewing.

All zones: Check the lower trunks of all trees and clear away any mulch or leaf debris that may be piled up against the

Himalayan birch

bark. This debris can hold harmful moisture against the lower trunk and, in colder areas, provides protective cover for rodents that chew on the bark.

PRUNING

Large conifers with extremely dense canopies may be lightly thinned to reduce wind resistance. Have large dead limbs removed from tall trees before winter winds arrive.

WATERING

November marks the start of heavy rainfall season throughout the region.

Zones 4-6: In arid locations, deeply water conifers and evergreens before winter temperatures set in.

FERTILIZING

Don't apply fertilizers now, as heavy rains will leach away much of the nitrogen before plant roots can absorb it. Organic mulches may still be applied as needed, on dryer days when soil is not soggy wet.

PROBLEMS

While it's impossible to predict what kinds of storm events may arise, taking some time to look at your trees, large and small, will help to prepare them for whatever kind of weather arrives. Most healthy trees withstand the impacts of winter, and many of the common causes of tree failures in storms can be prevented if noted in time. Some are as simple as pruning large dead limbs before they are blown out. Larger trees with structural defects have greater potential to be hazardous than smaller trees.

Here are some common signs, in both evergreens and deciduous trees, of potential problems that merit attention before winter. These are best assessed by a professional arborist.

• Large, dead limbs or hanging branches. Have them pruned now, before they are knocked out in the wind. Dead trees should not be left standing.

• Large conks (shelf-like fungal growths) or mushrooms on the trunk, especially near the base.

• Large open cavities, cracks, or loose bark on trunks and large limbs.

• A new lean in a previously upright tree can mean it has become unstable. Look also for any signs of humps or cracks in the soil at the base the tree.

• Co-dominants or multiple trunks of near equal size with bark pressed between them.

• Recent construction activity near the roots. Grade changes, trenching, or other construction activities can seriously damage supporting roots and leave the tree unstable to strong winds.

• Heavy growth of **English ivy** and other woody vines in the crown can add weight beyond the tree's normal capacity, making it more vulnerable to limb breakage and increasing wind sail.

• Previously topped trees are more vulnerable in storms, especially when several new tops have grown from the cut top.

• Trees near power lines. Contact your local utility if you have any concerns here.

Always check on your trees after any serious storm activity to look for any damage or changes.

Regular tree care can help reduce tree problems and prolong tree life.

255

DECEMBER

TREES

PLANNING

The prospect of saving your **Christmas tree** as a plant for your garden can be very enticing. Practical as it sounds at first glance, it takes serious consideration and special care to make this a successful project. The first step is to make sure you have enough space in your garden for a tall conifer; it will need open sunny exposure and well drained soil.

Nurseries and **Christmas tree** growers stock special selections for living trees, including true **firs** (*Abies* spp.), **Douglas fir** (*Pseudotsuga menziesii*), and **pines** (*Pinus* spp.). Double-check nursery tags and mature sizes for the listed species or cultivar. Trees are sold in large containers or balled and burlapped. The soil ball of a balled-and-burlapped tree will be protected from damage and be easier to handle if it sits in large pot. Smaller-sized trees will be easier to handle and transport.

The next vital step is to have a cool storage area such as an unheated garage to acclimate the tree between outdoors and in. It will need to be kept there for a few days again after the holidays before taking it back outdoors. The rootball needs to be kept moist.

The high temperatures and low humidity inside our homes is stressful to trees. They can't be kept inside any more than a week or they will suffer. Keep it as cool as possible, away from fireplaces and heat vents. Set it in a good size tub as a "drip tray" and keep the rootball moist (but not sopping wet). Coat the needles with an anti-desiccant like Wilt-Pruf to help hold moisture in. Use "cool" lights and modest decorations.

Plant your tree as soon as possible. This is more easily done in the moderate winters of zones 7 to 9. Establishing a living Christmas tree is more difficult with the more adverse winter conditions of zones 5 to 6, where there is a greater temperature extreme between indoors and out and soils are cold or frozen. You'll need to select the site early and mulch it heavily with straw or woodchips.

PLANTING

Zones 4-6: It is typically too cold for planting this month.

Zones 7-9: Planting deciduous and evergreen trees can continue as the weather permits.

CARE

Check trees again after wind- or snowstorms, removing broken or damaged limbs.

PRUNING

Save some of your dormant season pruning tasks to provide interesting branches for holiday decorations. Always use thinning cuts so the pruning looks natural and inconspicuous. Branches from evergreens such as **western red cedar, arbor vitae** (*Thuja* spp.), **pines, Douglas fir,** and **English holly** can be blended for attractive wreaths and arrangements. Deciduous **birch** stems provides interesting contrast against evergreen foliage.

PROBLEMS

Zones 7-9: Apply dormant oil by mid-December to **spruce** trees (*Picea* spp.) that have been heavily afflicted with spruce aphid. This aphid feeds over winter and disappears by the time the older damaged needles fall off the next summer. Trees in shade (and even the shady side of a tree) are more heavily affected. Thorough coverage is essential, and larger trees may need to be done by a spray service. Consider replacing spruce trees growing in too much shade with better adapted plants to avoid the annual burden of spraying. **Colorado spruce** (*Picea abies*) is one of the most susceptible species.

VINES & GROUND COVERS

Vines can add color and drama to the garden, gracefully skirting an arbor, leaving color accents where they mingle among trees and shrubs, or giving the illusion of depth as they fill the narrow vertical of a fence. Garden vines come in a range of habits, from the discreet fine stems of clematis to the robust, muscular woody trunks of wisteria. Most are best trained on supports, such as a fence, trellis, or arbor, or directed along vertical wires beside a wall. If space is tight, try a smaller vine in a large container with a vertical support. This is also a good way to grow more tender vines, which can be moved to shelter over winter.

KEEPING VINES IN CHECK

A word of warning when embarking on adding vines to your garden:

Adding vines to your garden requires a commitment to manage and monitor their growth.

Without regular attention, many species of cultivated vines can quickly outrun their boundaries, wreaking havoc in neighboring cultivated gardens or native woodlands alike. However, with

CAUTION

The following vines are included on Noxious Weed Lists in Washington and Oregon, and every effort should be made to control them from invasion. Do not plant these:

English ivy cultivars—*Hedera helix* 'Baltica', 'Pittsburg', 'Star', and 'Hibernica'

Old man's beard—*Clematis vitalba*

Kudzu—*Pueraria lobata* var. *montana*

well timed pruning throughout the year, the effort is manageable and the results rewarding.

DETERMINING SUPPORT SYSTEMS

It is important to match the strength and type of support system with the growth characteristics of the selected vine. A light wooden trellis ideal for clematis will be quickly overcome by the weight and vigor of wisteria. Annual vines are easily grown on simple, lightweight supports. There are a variety of styles and materials that can be used. Unpainted wood or plastic materials will be easier to maintain. Chain link or large wire mesh fences can also be ideal for growing vines. Or you can display vines in the middle of a garden bed with a freestanding tripod, or teepee, made from metal, wood, or bamboo. From purely functional to truly artistic, you can find ready-made supports at garden centers and nurseries.

Vines that cling by tendrils or twining stems are best grown on supports such as an open lattice, wire mesh, or vertical wires.

Some vines, by contrast, attach themselves to surfaces with suction grips, or by aerial roots. These are good choices for a concrete wall, lattices or broad timbers. Avoid growing vines directly against the side of a building, where they can hold moisture against the exterior or find their way into the structure and cause damage.

Vines with arching and trailing stems will remain prostrate or ascend through larger woody plants. Tie these vines to vertical positions on open supports or posts.

TRAINING

To prevent vines from becoming a massive nest of shoots at the ends of long bare stems, start out with good training on young plants. Choose a set of well spaced stems to develop a framework for future growth. Prune seasonally to stimulate and manage new growth along this framework. Older, overgrown vines can be cut back to the ground in early spring and trained properly as they re-sprout.

PLANTING WOODY VINES

Most woody vines can be planted and handled in the same manner as shrubs. They may be sold bare root or in containers.

Shade and shelter the base of your woody vine with companion shrubs or perennials. When training up supports near a building, position the rootball outside the dry shadow of eaves or overhangs. If a vine has ended up in the wrong spot, it can be dug and transplanted in fall or early spring. Before transplanting, cut the stems back to within two to three feet of the ground and tie them together for easy handling and retraining in the new location.

ANNUAL VINES

Annual vines quickly cover and add color accent for the summer season. Since they don't accumulate much weight or girth, support can be simple, making them ideal for children's gardens.

Red runner beans trained on a teepee of small poles create a

child's hide-a-way. Sweet peas can be grown up garden twine or lightweight wire extended from the ground to the top of a fence or porch rail.

Many annual vines can be started indoors or sowed directly in the garden in early spring. (See Annuals.)

WHEN TO WATER, MULCH, AND FERTILIZE

Keep newly planted vines mulched and watered during their first two to three years of establishment (see page 205 in Shrubs for instructions).

Most woody vines are rampant growers by nature and need little fertilizer. Some vines, such as wisteria, flower less when nitrogen is abundant. On the other hand, vines such as climbing roses may require some added nutrients to grow and bloom well. Annual applications of coarse organic mulch replenishes some soil nutrients.

Annual vines benefit from additional nitrogen at the beginning of the growing season and require more frequent irrigation than woody vines. (See Annuals.)

GROUND COVERS

Often relegated to utilitarian functions needing little attention, ground covers deserve more prominent positions throughout the garden. Consider ground covers as the companion plants that will enhance the appearance, health, and function of the landscape. Just as low-growing shrubs and herbaceous perennials fulfill a vital environmental niche as the understory layer in natural woodlands, so is the case for including ground covers throughout the cultivated garden.

Most ground covers are prostrate or low-growing with spreading growth habits. Some have mounded or clumping growth habits. They may be herbaceous perennials (see Perennials), woody, deciduous or evergreen.

Some types spread above ground with long slender branches, such as kinnikinnick (*Arctostaphylos uva-ursi*), or via runners bearing rosettes, such as beach strawberry. Others spread by underground stems or rhizomes, including Japanese spurge (*Pachysandra terminalis*), and creeping mahonia, *Mahonia repens*.

BENEFITS

Ground covers offer many aesthetic and cultural functions to the landscape. The brilliant autumn hues of a Japanese maple (*Acer japonicum*), or sumac (*Rhus typhina*), are intensified against a lush green expanse of *Rubus pentalobus* (*calycinoides*) or Japanese spurge. The upright blue spikes of carpet bugle, *Ajuga reptans*, join the floral chorus of spring. Low-growing plants along front edges provide a gentle transition from lawn or pathway to taller plants at the interior.

Large expanses of bare ground are an invitation for weeds. Ground covers suppress weed growth and enhance the garden's health acting as living mulch, and sheltering the soil from surface evaporation and erosion.

In water-wise landscapes, ground cover plantings provide green swaths with far less irrigation than turf. And for those areas where turf is difficult to maintain, such as under large trees or in shady corridors, several ground cover selections thrive.

Ground covers also become a temporary filler to provide needed coverage while small young shrubs are growing, easily yielding the space as the shrubs grow larger. It is a good way to avoid the temptation to place young shrubs too close together, only to have to deal with unmanageable pruning and overcrowding as they grow larger.

PLANT SELECTION

Successful selections grow rapidly and maintain good soil cover without overwhelming surrounding plantings. And they

will thrive in the given microclimate without too much attention: kinnikinnick on sunny banks with well drained soil, Japanese spurge in the dappled shade of damp woodland-like soil. Lily of the valley (*Convallaria majalis*), and Oregon oxalis (*Oxalis oregana*) have heavy rhizome systems that keep out most weeds even when they are not in leaf.

Grouping compatible plants will create a tapestry of color and texture, with fewer openings for weeds. Simple groupings of two or three selections can also provide optimal cover as each plant type establishes within the light variations of the planting area. Choose plants with similar growth rates. Use a mix of heights and textures: blue star creeper, *Pratia pedunculata*, beneath carpet bugle, *Ajuga reptans*. Don't be afraid to experiment to achieve the best effects for your garden, especially with herbaceous species which can be easily transplanted.

PLANTING GROUND COVERS

Ground cover plants can be purchased in four- to six-inch pots, one-gallon containers, or in flats. Plant densely enough to have good coverage in two or three years. Using a few more plants at the first installation pays off with quicker coverage and less open ground for weeds.

The number of plants needed depends on the size of plants purchased, their growth habit, and growth rate. Start by measuring the area to be planted. Then calculate the number of plants to fill that area at the desired spacing. One hundred plants 8 inches apart should cover approximately 44 square feet (typical for small spreading herbaceous plants such as ajuga or strawberry), while a spacing of 18 inches covers 225 square feet (as for woody plants such as cotoneaster in gallon containers). Arranging plants in a triangular grid will provide equal spacing in all directions. Making a template of cardboard or bamboo stakes can be helpful for planting large areas. Expect to add some filler plants the second year.

Plant herbaceous ground covers in early spring. With mulch and irrigation, they can be added to the garden throughout the growing season. Plant woody species as described for shrubs (see Shrubs).

Prepare the planting area well ahead of time, removing existing weeds and their roots and mulching thickly with 4 inches of *coarse* organic material. This can be done a few weeks to several months before planting, clearing out any new weeds that may crop up during this time. New ground cover plants can be installed through the existing mulch. Simply scoop away enough mulch to expose a bare patch of soil for each planting spot. The mulch will also help keep the soil damp, a plus for establishing new plants.

ESTABLISHMENT PERIOD

All new ground cover plantings need regular attention while establishing lest weeds overrun them. Expect to weed new ground cover plantings three to four times a month during the first growing season, making sure to remove weeds before they develop flowers and seeds. Coarse mulch allows for less weeding. The overall frequency of weeding will taper off each year as the plants fill in. Smaller sized plants from 4- or 6-inch nursery pots will need more frequent watering at first than larger sized transplants. Light fertilization during the first couple years will boost quick coverage.

PLANTING TO REDUCE EROSION ON SLOPES

Ground cover plants are often used to anchor and retain soil on slopes in order to prevent surface erosion. The best plants for this function will depend on the size of the area involved as well as the climate and microclimate factors. Smaller, gentle slopes might be carpeted with a single low-growing species as a backdrop to other shrubs or trees. Larger, steeper slopes can be challenging sites to plant and maintain, and choosing plants wisely is critical to success here. Look to the predominant regional native species as indicators of the best types of native and cultivated species to choose for your location. For banks, select low shrubs and ground covers that spread by underground stems and are good at "knitting" together the surface layers of soil. **Oregon grape** (*Mahonia* spp.), *Stephanandra incisa* 'Crispa', **creeping St. Johns-wort** (*Hypericum calycinum*), and **snowberry** (*Symphoricarpos* spp.), are strong examples for western and coastal parts of this region. In areas impacted by heavy winter rains, surface erosion will be further reduced by the addition of a mix of plant types of different sizes. A good mix will include deciduous and evergreen plants, including low ground covers, **ferns**, and various sized shrubs and trees. This variety of plant types and sizes covers a greater surface area than a single ground cover type to intercept and absorb rainfall before it reaches the ground. And however the slope is planted, surface erosion risk is greater when the land above the slope is paved or covered in turf. A mixed shrub border placed on the more level ground at the top will intercept and help slow water runoff sheeting towards the slope. Attention to above-slope drainage systems, catch basins, and outlets is also important in reducing water impact on slopes.

In the eastern arid climes of Oregon and Washington, wind and run-off from snow melt are the greater threats to soil surface erosion on slopes. Here, too, a mix of different plant types will provide better year-round protection. Install plantings with a combination of species adapted to withstand long dry summers and cold winters: native **sagebrush** (*Artemisia* spp.) or garden *Artemisia* 'Powis Castle'; native and garden **stonecrop** (*Sedum* spp.); **common snowberry** (*Symphoricarpos* spp.); native **sandwort** (*Arenaria obtusiloba*); and native shrubby *Penstemon fruticosus*. **Antelope bitterbrush** (*Purshia tridentata*), is a rugged plant that performs well in re-vegetating disturbed sites. Woodland choices might include **Douglas-fir** and **pines**, creeping **Oregon grape** (*Mahonia repens*), and **sadler's oak** (*Quercus sadleriana*), as well as native **sword fern**.

PRUNING

Many ground covers perform better with periodic pruning or mowing down in early spring, such as bishop's cap (*Epimedium*), periwinkle (*Vinca minor*), Japanese spurge, creeping St. John's wort (*Hypericum calycinum*), and *Pachysandra terminalis*.

Woody species, such as creeping mahonia (*Mahonia repens*), kinnikinnick (*Arctostaphylos uva-ursi*), or prostrate cotoneaster (*Cotoneaster horizonatalis*) are pruned in the same manner as shrubs (see Shrubs).

JANUARY
VINES & GROUND COVERS

PLANNING

All zones: Review your garden for large bare soil areas that would benefit from added ground cover plantings. Are there areas where the existing ground cover has grown poorly and should be replaced with a better adapted selection? Are there areas with chronic weed problems? Make notes of the soil, light, and weeds present in these spots then look through garden books and catalogs for plant selections that match those growing conditions. In addition to the "standard" ground cover selections, also review low-growing shrub species and cultivars to fill those bare areas. Some hardy selections include the prostrate **Russian cypress** (*Microbiota decussata*); dwarf **Japanese spirea** (*Spiraea japonica* 'Nana''); *Rhododendron* 'Ruby Heart'; and violet *Rhododendron impeditum;* or the many ground cover roses (see Roses). Shrubs that spread by underground stems make a good soil-anchoring cover for banks. These include *Stephanandra incisa* 'Crispa' in Zones 4 to 8 and *Sarcococca hookeriana* var. *humilis* in Zones 7 and 8. **Prostrate junipers** and low-spreading conifer cultivars provide hardy evergreen cover throughout the region.

PLANTING

Zones 4-6: It is typically too cold for planting this month.

Zones 7-9: Woody plants can be planted during warmer weather periods this month, when low temperatures are in the 40s. Avoid digging and planting when soils are very wet. See Shrubs for dormant-season planting of woody plants.

Prostrate junipers provide hardy evergreen cover throughout the region.

 CARE

Winter winds and freezing temperatures can occur in all areas this month. Winter protection is most critical for Eastern Washington and Oregon, and the Columbia Gorge. Check and adjust the attachments of mature vines to their supports. Secure any loose branches being whipped about by the wind. If heavy snows occur, gently shake the snow loose with a soft broom to lighten the load on permanent vine stems.

Zones 7-9: Mulch any exposed, bare ground with coarse organic mulch such as wood chips to protect the soil surface from the destructive effects of hard winter rains.

 PRUNING

Zones 4-6: It's too early for seasonal pruning of vine and ground cover plantings.

Zones 7-9: Thin out rampant branches that jut out of place or crowd neighboring plants on woody ground covers such as **prostrate cotoneaster**, **Point Reyes ceanothus** or *Euonymus fortunei*.

Wintercreeper (*Euonymus fortunei*)

 WATERING

Watering is not typically a winter concern. However, if the weather has been mild and short on rainfall, be sure to check plantings growing near building eaves and beneath dense conifers for dry soil. Water when the ground is very dry and temperatures are well above freezing.

Containerized vines that are being overwintered in a protected area should be checked monthly and watered if the soil becomes dry.

 FERTILIZING

No fertilization this month.

 PROBLEMS

Frost heaving can be a problem during very cold periods punctuated by sunny days. Small plants can be literally thrust out of the ground as soils expand and contract in a cycle of freezing and thawing, especially where exposed to winter sun. Cover roots of heaved plants with a mulch of straw, wood chips, or evergreen boughs until warmer temperatures return and stay.

Zones 4-6: Protect exposed ground covers just after the ground freezes in early winter each year. Remove protection as soils begin to thaw in spring.

Zones 7-9: Protect plants as needed when extended freezing weather is expected.

FEBRUARY
VINES & GROUND COVERS

PLANNING

With the garden at its most skeletal stage at this time of year, it's a good time to review the edges—those places where turf meets shrub bed, perennial border meets sidewalk, garden meets wild slope. The shape and content of these edges holds some of the greatest impact on maintenance requirements.

Are you forever trimming the ivy off the edge of the sidewalk? Replace it with something like **Japanese spurge**, *Pachysandra terminalis*, which spreads by underground stems and won't march across the sidewalk so readily. Tight corners and peninsulas that are tricky to get at with the lawn mower can be smoothed out by reshaping the edges into broad sweeping curves. Add new ground covers or other garden plants to newly opened spaces. Draping a garden hose along the ground is an easy way to shape and visualize the new edge before making the final lawn removal cut.

Browse the colorful seed catalogs that arrive this month for annual vines such as **sweet pea** (*Lathyrus odoratus*); **scarlet runner bean** (*Phaseolus coc-*

Plant pachysandra by a walkway for a low-maintenance ground cover.

cineus); **black-eyed Susan vine** (*Thunbergia alata*); **morning glory** (*Ipomoea* spp.); or **canary creeper** (*Tropaeolum peregrinum*). (See Annuals.) For a headstart on their seasonal display, plan to start seed indoors a few weeks before the last hard frost.

PLANTING

Zones 4-6: It is too soon for planting.

Zones 7-9: You can continue to install woody plants provided the temperatures are moderate and the soil is not waterlogged. Be cautious not to trample or dig garden soil that is soggy wet—a sure way to damage and compact the natural soil structure. **Sweet pea** can be sown outdoors by late February.

CARE

Zones 7-9: Inspect new ground cover plantings for winter weeds. Many of these germinate in fall, patiently awaiting warm enough weather to explode in size. Watch for the small leafy rosettes of shotweed and herb

Robert, as well as grasses, chickweed, and dandelions. Smother large areas of tiny seedlings with coarse mulch. Be sure to pluck these early season offenders from within ground cover plantings. Herb Robert—sometimes known as "Stinky Bob" for its characteristic strong odor when touched—is notorious for its ability to germinate in shady conditions, and its removal before bloom (when seeds set) will help diminish its presence in the garden.

Winter weather can continue to dislodge vines throughout the entire region, so continue to check on them and re-tie any loose stems as needed.

PRUNING

Zones 7-9: Dormant-season pruning of vines can begin. Prune **Japanese wisteria** (*Wisteria floribunda*), and **Purpleleaf grape** vines (*Vitis vinifera* 'Purpurea'), back to a main framework of older, thicker stems, with long thin shoots shortened to spurs with 3 to 5 buds. Thin out alternate stems where shoots are crowded together. This is a good approach for managing these vines growing on pergolas or arbors.

For deciduous vines **Honeysuckle vine** (*Lonicera* spp.), and **Variegated kiwi** (*Actinidia kolo-*

HOW TO PRUNE CLEMATIS

Clematis comes in three basic types based on growth and bloom habits, each type with different pruning needs and timing. Plan the timing of pruning by learning and responding to the time of bloom.

Group I—blooms early in spring on wood produced last season. After it blooms, do light pruning to remove spent blooms and maintain shape and spacing between stems:

Clematis montana and its cultivars; *C. macropetala* cultivars; evergreen *Clematis armandii*.

Group II—large-flowered hybrids blooming in early summer on wood produced last season, then again in late summer on new growth. Prune in late winter to early spring, before new growth emerges. Retain a framework of well-spaced old stems. These may also be cut back hard to the ground periodically, resulting in larger blooms in late summer only:

Clematis 'Nelly Moser' and other larger flowered cultivars

Group III—large-flowered hybrids blooming in summer on the current season's growth. Prune in late winter to early spring. Cut these back to a framework of well spaced stems 6 to 12 inches in height. A taller stem height might also be used as needed to provide good display of new growth and flowers:

Clematis viticella, *C.* 'Jackmanii', *C. texensis* cultivars

---

mikta), with dense stem networks, thin out selected canes at their base and shorten remaining stems as needed to maintain desired size.

The large-flowered deciduous **clematis** hybrids are best pruned in late winter to early spring.

WATERING

Most soils should be at their maximum saturation levels at this point in the season. Continue to check soil moisture in containerized plants under protective cover.

FERTILIZING

All zones: No fertilizers are needed this month.

PROBLEMS

Check for and repair winter damage to woody vines and ground covers. Prune out broken stems. Re-tie loose vine stems. Freeze damage is often not evident until new growth begins later in spring.

MARCH
VINES & GROUND COVERS

PLANNING

Take inventory of the existing and potential vine locations in your garden. This is a good time of year to add architectural details to your garden and entry areas with new arbors or trellises, followed by early spring planting of woody vines.

Inspect existing vine supports for maintenance needs or improvements. Doing the work this month coincides nicely with the timing for pruning and renovation for woody vines.

PLANTING

Zones 4-6: Begin planting woody species in early spring. Start annual vines indoors three to four weeks before the last frost.

Zones 7-9: Ground covers and vines planted this month will have a good period of naturally moist soils for good root establishment before the onset of spring growth. Including 2 to 3 inches of coarse mulch at planting time will increase water retention, saving on the time and water needed for summer irrigation.

Dormant woody species of ground covers and vines such as **clematis, honeysuckle, cotoneaster,** or **Point Reyes ceanothus** can be transplanted throughout the region this month, provided

temperatures are above freezing and soils are not waterlogged.

When positioning vines for planting, space the planting hole far enough from the support to give it room to grow, but close enough for stems to reach the support.

Multiply your herbaceous ground cover plants by digging up divisions of plants such as **ajuga, saxifrage, epimedium,** and **pachysandra**. (See Perennials for dividing techniques.)

CARE

Zones 4-6: Carefully inspect ground cover plantings for weeds that may be creeping in. The adage "a stitch in time saves nine" definitely holds true for this early season effort. Weed removal now allows optimal time for the surrounding ground covers fill in. New plants can also be added this month to fill in larger voids after weeding. Eliminating early weeds before they go to seed also makes for less work later in the season.

Containers holding tender vines can be brought out of winter storage into a sheltered position. Check soil moisture. Top-dress with new soil as needed and reset supports. Prune to thin, shape, and remove dead wood. This is also a good time to repot into larger containers as needed. Do

not set them outside permanently until night temperatures are above freezing.

Zones 7-9: Groom ground covers as the weather warms up, clearing out any matted layers of leaves and debris. Young woody weeds that found their way in last season are easily uprooted from the damp soil.

PRUNING

Zones 4-6: Begin early spring pruning of vines as described for Zones 7 and 8 in February.

Zones 7-9: Continue early season vine pruning. Vines to be rejuvenated may be cut back to the ground or reshaped to a scaffold structure of a few selected larger stems.

Ground covers: Overgrowth of woody ground covers can be pruned out this month. Thin out those longest branches creeping over walkway and lawn, cutting them all the way back to their attachment to other branches or to ground level toward the center. The remaining shorter branches become the new edge, with reduced need for continued pruning compared with trimming branch ends at the bed edge. Also thin out other out-of-place growth such as those growing vertically or tangling into neighboring shrubs. This method is effective for plants such as **kin-**

nikinnick, **Point Reyes ceanothus, creeping rosemary,** or **prostrate cotoneaster**.

Herbaceous ground covers: Refresh the growth of several types of ground covers this month with a good mowing or shearing. Trim the old leaves off **bishop's hat** (*Epimedium* sp.), before new growth appears at the base. A beautiful carpet of flowers will emerge later in spring, followed by a cover of fresh new leaves. This can be done every year, or alternate years. Other ground covers that rejuvenate with periodic mowing—actually using the lawn mower at its tallest setting or with electric hedge trimmers—include **Japanese spurge** (*Pachysandra terminalis*); **carpet bugle** (*Ajuga reptans*); **creeping St. John's wort** (*Hypericum calycinum*); and *Vinca* spp.

Vines: Overgrown vines may be rejuvenated this month, cutting them back to the ground or retaining some existing stems to re-establish a set of scaffold branches.

Prune the Group III, late blooming **clematis** hybrids back to a set of well spaced stems 6 to 8 inches tall. This includes the *Clematis viticella* and *texensis* cultivars.

WATERING

Soils in most areas should be at maximum saturation at this point in the season. Exceptions will be containerized plantings near or under overhangs, or ones that were in winter storage.

Indoors, keep emerging annual vine seedlings moist, but not soggy.

FERTILIZING

Top-dress ground covers with fine compost and wash residue off the leaves. Mulch vines with coarse organic compost. For plants lacking good growth and vigor, a slow-release nitrogen fertilizer can be helpful. It is important to have the cause of poor growth diagnosed and to test soil nutrient levels before applying extensive fertilizer. See Gardening Resources on the Web, page 288, for information on soil testing.

Indoors, fertilize annual vine seedlings weekly with a water-soluble fertilizer, as labeled for annual transplants.

PROBLEMS

Zones 7-9: Start monitoring for slugs as warmer rainy weather returns with night temperatures in the 50s. Check under rocks or larger debris for slugs and slug eggs. Eggs are about $1/16$ to $1/8$ inch, pearly white or yellow, often found in small clusters beneath wood or leaves on the ground. Use a flashlight or headlamp to look for slugs just after dark, when they come out to roam freely through the garden. While they may not feed directly on all ground cover plants, they might take cover there during daylight hours. Eliminate slug eggs and slugs early in the season to reduce damage to tender new spring growth. As you poke about the mulch layer, celebrate the sight of ground beetles. These inch-long shiny black beetles feed on several pest insects.

Carpet bugle (*Ajuga reptans*)

267

APRIL
VINES & GROUND COVERS

PLANNING

The bloom period for vines and ground covers is soon upon all garden areas in the region. Take notes of bloom dates and colors in a garden log, paying attention to compatibility with the colors and bloom periods of adjacent landscape plants. Make notes for future adjustments or additions. Vines and ground covers properly selected and placed will compliment adjacent plantings with color and texture.

Heather 'J. F. Letts'

PLANTING

This is a good month to plant herbaceous ground covers, which will take off quickly in periods of moderately warm and moist weather. Finish up your planting of woody species. Planting work completed this month will make for easier establishment and less potential for drought stress the first season in the ground.

Zones 4-6: **Sweet pea** can be sown outdoors in. Sow other annual vines indoors about three to four weeks before last frost date.

Zones 7-9: Plant out annual vines started indoors as warmer weather predominates. Harden off transplants first by bringing

them outdoors for gradually longer periods over a few days, bringing them back in at night.

When soils have warmed above 55 degrees F. and all danger of frost has passed, sow the following outdoors: **scarlet runner bean** (*Phaseolus coccineus*); **black-eyed Susan vine** (*Thunbergia alata*); **morning glory** (*Ipomoea* spp.); or **canary creeper** (*Tropaeolum peregrinum*).

CARE

This is the month for early season weeding and grooming of ground cover plantings. Stay a step ahead with frequent removal of smaller weeds before they bloom to diminish the work load

for later weeding. Replenish areas where mulch is thin to suppress new weeds.

Check the base of vines and replenish the mulch cover where bare soil is peeking through.

PRUNING

Last year's spent blooms on **heather** (*Calluna vulgaris*), can be cut off. Annual grooming will help keep plants full and prevent them from becoming leggy.

Zones 4-6: Prune woody ground covers such as **kinnikinnick** or **prostrate cotoneaster** following the method described for Zones 7 and 8 in April. Mow or shear back herbaceous ground covers before new growth begins: **Bishop's hat** (*Epimedium* spp.); **Japanese spurge** (*Pachysandra terminalis*); **carpet bugle** (*Ajuga reptans*); **creeping St. John's wort** (*Hypericum calycinum*); and *Vinca* spp.

Zones 7-9: Prune early-flowering vines as their blooms fade. Evergreen *Clematis armandii* can be pruned this month, needing little more than the removal of spent blooms and selective thinning to keep it trained to its support system. Ground covers spurt into growth this month, and pruning should have been completed in March.

WATERING

Start inspecting plants and soil for watering needs, especially on newly planted or transplanted material.

FERTILIZING

Zones 4-6: To maintain good soil fertility and structure, lightly top-dress ground covers with fine compost, brushing or rinsing it off the leaves, and mulch vines with a coarse organic material. For plants lacking good growth and vigor, a slow-release nitrogen fertilizer can be helpful. It is important have the cause of poor growth diagnosed and to test soil nutrient levels before applying extensive fertilizer. See Gardening Resources on the Web, page 288, for information on soil testing.

PROBLEMS

Fungal diseases can develop in herbaceous ground covers growing in very damp, shady conditions. Patches of browned then rotting leaves and stems of **pachysandra**, **ajuga**, and **vinca** can signal a disease problem. Stem cankers, black root rot, botrytis, and other disease fungi are favored by warm, humid weather and are encouraged by overhead irrigation and waterlogged soils.

To discourage fungal diseases in ground cover plantings, water early in the day, with time for leaves to dry before evening. Apply water and fertilizers modestly, especially in shadier locations. Periodically thin out overly dense plantings. Clean off any fallen leaves and organic debris that accumulate on top of plants. If you suspect disease in your plants, take a sample to your local WSU or OSU Master Gardener Extension clinic for diagnosis and specific control recommendations (see Gardening Resources on the Web, page 288, for contact information).

TREAD ON ME!

Creeping thyme (*Thymus* spp.); **blue star creeper** (*Pratia pedunculata*); and **New Zealand brass buttons** (*Leptinella squalida*), are some ground covers that quickly come to mind when looking for traffic-tolerant plants to use between pavers and around patios. These plants carry color and texture across a variety of otherwise barren patches in the landscape. Use these prostrate selections for pathways, bed edges, under bulbs, and even beneath other plants in containers. Creeping **sedums** are a plant of choice for cover in rock gardens and other dry sunny patches. For a turf substitute in small areas of partial shade and occasional foot traffic, try **Irish** or **Scotch moss** (*Sagina* spp.), or **mountain sandwort** (*Arenaria montana*). **Carpet bugle** (*Ajuga reptans*), and **Roman chamomile** (*Chamaemelum nobile*), are commonly known to tolerate foot traffic. In the continued hunt for more ground covers that can be routinely walked upon, Under A Foot Plant Company has tested and marketed a broad selection of such plants under the STEPABLES® name. *Leptinella minor* and *Pratia pedunculata* 'County Park' are two suggested as lawn substitutes.

MAY
VINES & GROUND COVERS

PLANNING

Spring colors are coming into full swing this month throughout the region. Pause to take in garden views from inside your home and outdoors. Enjoy the colors and smell the flowers. Take photos of what pleases you most in your garden, or of what you'd like to improve upon for next year.

PLANTING

Choose cooler, overcast days to complete planting. The sunny warm days of this month can impose heavy stress on newly planted material, especially in exposed areas. Give extra attention to regular watering, and monitor for first signs of wilting.

Zones 4-6: After the last frost, seeds and transplants for many annual vines can be planted outdoors. These include **scarlet runner bean** (*Phaseolus coccineus*); **black-eyed Susan vine** (*Thunbergia alata*); **morning glory** (*Ipomoea* spp.); and **canary creeper** (*Tropaeolum peregrinum*).

Zones 7-9: Take divisions early in the month from very dense ground cover plantings to use in other areas of the garden. **Pachysandra, ajuga, vinca, sedum,** and **saxifrage** are among those that can be divided now. Softwood cuttings can be taken on **climbing hydrangea**. (See the General Introduction.)

CARE

Tie in long, rambling vine shoots or prune them off as needed. Check old ties on vines and remove those that have become tight or are beginning to strangle the stems. If neglected, they can become tight enough to damage and kill stems. Avoid using wire or nylon cord for woody vines; they are the worst offenders at becoming embedded and damaging stems. Position ties with a loose figure-eight loop to provide support with room for stem growth. Sisal garden twine and adjustable rubber or plastic plant ties can also be found in garden centers.

Zones 4-6: Potted vines may be brought back outdoors toward the end of the month. Check supports and prune vines to prepare them for a new season's growth. Water, replenish soil, and re-pot as needed.

Continued spot weeding of new sprouts in ground covers will keep this repetitive task easy and manageable.

Mulch the soil around annual vines with compost to conserve moisture and maintain soil nutrients.

Scarlet runner bean

 PRUNING

Prune spring blooming vines after bloom. **Five-leaf akebia** can be kept in scale with selective thinning of weaker or excess shoots and shortening the remaining shoots by one-third. Similarly, thin and shorten stems of **honeysuckle** and others. See February for tips on pruning **clematis**.

Begin a monthly schedule for **wisteria** after it blooms, routinely cutting out the long, trailing, non-blooming whips. This will encourage more blooms, keep the vine contained and attractive, and can take less work over the entire season.

As blooms fade out on **heath** (*Erica carnea*), lightly shear them to keep new growth strong over the whole plant. Take care not to cut back into bare wood, which will not re-sprout well.

 WATERING

Keep actively growing ground covers and annual vines well watered this month. For woody vines and woody ground covers, allow the soil to dry between applications. To decrease fungal problems, water ground covers early enough in the day for leaves to be dry by nightfall.

USING DWARF SHRUBS AS GROUND COVERS

Dwarf versions of many favorite garden shrubs serve well in ground cover positions in the landscape. Plant them toward the front of shrub borders or as low cover in small beds. Look for selections that mature at 18 to 20 inches in height. *Sarcococca hookeriana* var. *humilis* and dwarf *Nandina domestica* 'Nana Purpurea' and 'Harbor Dwarf' all spread by underground stems and are good choices for slopes. **Rhododendrons** offer the low growing 'Ruby Heart', 'Carmen', and 'Ginny Gee'. *Rhododendron impeditum* is a dependable low-grower hardy in Zones 4 to 8. In roses, there are the Flower Carpet™ and Pavement™ series. Also hardy to Zone 4, *Spiraea japonica* 'Nana' and 'Little Princess' contrast nicely against evergreens with early summer blooms and fall color. Countless dwarf and prostrate forms can be found among the conifer species of **juniper**, **spruce**, **pine**, **hemlock**, and **cypress**.

 FERTILIZING

Continue to fertilize annual vines with a of water-soluble fertilizer, weekly or bi-weekly, as needed.

If slow-release fertilizers were used in April, none should be needed this month. To keep garden maintenance low, avoid too much nitrogen fertilization that might push extra growth that will need to be trimmed and pruned back. Using fertilizers too often causes or worsens many garden maladies, including aphids and some fungal diseases. See General Introduction for more information on fertilizer use.

 PROBLEMS

Bloom failure on **wisteria** can occur where fertilizer and water have been generous and pruning has been modest. To encourage bloom, prune smaller stems back to strong laterals in early spring, and continue to prune out long, wild growth through the growing season. Withhold fertilizers, and allow soil to dry out between watering.

Black sooty mold may appear on some ground covers, thriving on aphid secretions (called "honey dew") dripping from plants overhead. Sooty mold doesn't kill plants. Reduce sooty mold by managing aphids.

JUNE
VINES & GROUND COVERS

PLANNING

Many nurseries and garden centers begin having special sales this month. It's a good time to stock up on extra ground cover plants to embellish thin plantings or to have on hand to fill in gaps as weeds are pulled out.

Take a good look at the turf in your garden. Areas that are difficult to mow or keep watered might be better converted to ground cover plantings in fall when weather moderates. Keeping grass green can place huge demands on water during the driest months of the year, particularly in the desert regions of Eastern Oregon and Washington. Replacing some of the grass area with well chosen ground covers is a great step toward water conservation while keeping green cover (see Lawns). Look at other gardens and in nurseries to choose ground covers suited to your planting site and prepare those areas for planting in September.

PLANTING

Zones 4-6: Early in the month, divide very dense ground cover plantings to get more plants to use in other areas of the garden. **Pachysandra, ajuga, vinca, sedum,** and **saxifrage** are among those that can be divided now. Softwood cuttings can be taken on **climbing hydrangea**.

Zones 7-9: As temperatures rise and rainfall diminishes, avoid summer planting where irrigation water is limited.

Western Oregon and Washington: This is the most challenging point in the growing season to install woody plants, especially in dryer, exposed sites. Plants installed this month will require greater attention for watering and suffer greater transplant stress than those installed in early spring.

With adequate watering, herbaceous ground covers can still be planted, particularly in areas that are shaded during the hottest times of day. If you must add plants now, plant in cooler hours later in the day, or on cooler days.

Take softwood cuttings of **variegated kiwi, clematis, cotoneaster,** and **climbing hydrangea**.

CARE

Continue to monitor vine growth, check supports and ties, replenish mulch where it has gone thin, and prune back growth that is heading out of bounds.

Watch out for weeds that have made their way to flowering this month, and pluck them from ground covers before they have the chance to drop their seeds.

PRUNING

Continue pruning for vines that have completed flowering this month. Keep up with removal of long whips on **wisteria**. All vines will be actively growing this month and may need some thinning and shortening of selected stems.

VINES FOR CONTAINERS

Annual and perennial vines make wonderful displays in containers. Add them in combination with other plants or as a solo feature. Display less hardy types such as **cup and saucer vine** (*Cobaea scandens*), **white jasmine** (*Jasminum officinale*), and **passion flower** (*Passiflora caerulea*), in large deep containers that can be stored under shelter for winter months. Add variety to hanging containers with *Rhodochiton atrosanguineum*, **sweet potato vine** (*Ipomoea batatas*), variegated *Vinca major*, **nasturtium**, and almost any of the array of annual vines available.

Thin out the oldest stems on **creeping rosemary** to encourage new growth and prevent the center from becoming too woody and bare.

WATERING

Keep plants that are actively growing this month well watered. Be sure to check that the water has soaked several inches into the soil and not just dampened the surface. It is equally important to allow the soil to dry between watering. Some mulches can appear dry on the surface, with moist conditions below. To water correctly, it's very useful to take a trowel and probe the soil first.

FERTILIZING

Hold back fertilization on woody plants at the warmest point in the growing season.

PROBLEMS

Clematis wilt can take you by surprise as beautiful strong vines suddenly wilt and fail after blooming. This fungal disease, *Ascochyta clematidina*, invades stems near the ground level, stopping the movement of water up the stems. Damp weather and

NECTAR FOR HUMMINGBIRDS

You can use vines for special locations and reasons, such as in a container or for nectar sources for hummingbirds. The blooms of these vines and ground covers are nectar sources for hummingbirds. Position them in view from windows and outdoor seating areas.

Annuals:
- **Cardinal climber** (*Ipomoea quamoclit*)
- **Scarlet runner bean** (*Phaseolus coccineus*)
- **Sweet pea** (*Lathyrus* spp.)

Woody:
- **Clematis** (*Clematis* x *jackmanii* and other species)
- **Honeysuckle** (*Lonicera* spp.)
- **Kinnikinnick** (*Arctostaphylos uva-ursi*)
- **Oregon grape** (*Mahonia* spp.)
- **Point Reyes Creeper** (*Ceanothus gloriosus*)
- **Trumpet vine** (*Campsis radicans*)

active plant growth are ideal conditions for this fungus. The good news is that most vines will eventually replace the damaged stems with new growth, even in following years, so don't be too hasty to dig up roots on affected plants. Sanitation is important, so prune out infected stems at ground level and clear out dead leaves in the fall. The larger flowering cultivars are most vulnerable. To have **clematis** free of fungal problems, you can choose from several possibilities. *Clematis montana* (pink), *Clematis macropetala* (blue, early spring), and *Clematis alpina* and *Clematis viticella* are reported to be resistant as are some of their cultivars, though they all bear much smaller flowers.

Annual vines, such as mandevilla, are great container plants.

JULY
VINES & GROUND COVERS

PLANNING

This is truly the month to be outdoors and experience the unique atmosphere of your garden. Take more pictures and make notes in your garden log. Where do you spend most of your time outdoors? Are there threadbare areas through turf or ground cover areas that would function better with pavers or stepping stones? What are the sun and shade patterns this month? Are vines and arbors well-placed, or are adjustments needed to add or diminish shade and screening? Collect these notes for changes that can be done now, such as installing pavers, or planting and transplanting that will be done in other seasons.

PLANTING

This month begins the quietest time for planting throughout much of the region with the arrival of the year's warmest temperatures coupled with lowest rainfall and humidity. If you must plant now, choose the cooler evening hours, mulch well, provide vigilant care for watering the rest of the season, and provide temporary shade from direct sun to lesson water stress.

Softwood cuttings of several vines and ground covers can be done at this time of year, including **variegated kiwi, five-leaf akebia, kinnikinnick, ceanothus, clematis, roses,** and **wisteria**.

CARE

Check ties and supports on vines to make sure rapidly growing stems aren't becoming too tight. Watch for any new weeds cropping up in new plantings. Check for weeds weekly, as many are quickly going to seed this month. Herb Robert foliage will turn a pale red as summer heat peaks, poised to shoot its maturing seeds to cling to overhead foliage until fall rains wash them to the ground. Top-dress ground covers with fine compost. Use a gentle water spray to wash down any bits of mulch sticking to leaves.

PRUNING

Continue with selective thinning and shortening to manage summer vine growth. With its compact habit and modest growth rate, **climbing hydrangea** (*Hydrangea anomala* ssp. *petiolaris*), has fewer pruning needs than other vines. Provide light pruning to shape and thin as needed immediately after bloom.

Fading blooms can be cut back on **carpet bugle** (*Ajuga reptans*), to encourage new leaves and keep the plants tidy.

WATERING

This is typically the warmest month throughout the region. As some soils dry out, water may roll off the surface before soaking in. This is common in ground covers growing on slopes. Check the soil to be sure the water is going where you want it. If run-off is a problem, apply the water at a slower rate. One method is to run the water just to the point before it starts to run off. Wait a short while for the water to soak in, and then run the water again. Many automatic systems and timers have a "Repeat" cycle option for this purpose. Where soil has dried with a hard crusty surface and become 'hydrophobic'—water just beads up and rolls off—try dampening the surface first with a wetting agent. This will reduce the surface tension, allowing the water to break through the dry surface. Commercial garden products are available, or try a dish soap solution for a similar effect.

FERTILIZING

Look at the growth produced by your vines and ground covers this season. Are vines growing before your eyes and lacking bloom? This is a common symptom of excess nutrients. Back off fertilizing this season and next for those plants. Has the growth been stunted, with leaves small and yellow? Fertilizer may help, but make sure there isn't another condition causing this stress, such as excess shade or waterlogged soil that may be leading to root rots.

PROBLEMS

Scout for aphids feeding on tender vine shoots and for slugs among ground covers.

Climbing hydrangea

VINES AND GROUND COVERS THAT OFFER TASTY TREATS

Even if your yard is too small for a dedicated food garden, you can include vines and ground covers with the bonus of some delectable fruits and berries to graze on. Position **edible grapes** (*Vitis* spp.), and **kiwi** (*Actinidia chinensis*), on sturdy arbors as ornamental features. They will need good exposure to summer sun and adequate water to provide fruit. Check with OSU and WSU Extension for recommended selection for your growing zone. Edible **strawberries** can be incorporated as a ground cover on a gentle sunny bank, providing enough berries for summer tasting and maybe even breakfast if they make it all the way to the kitchen uneaten! The native strawberry species of this region are great garden ground covers and also bear small but very tasty berries. Experience the original wintergreen taste in the bright red berries of *Gaultheria procumbens*. It grows best in partial shade and soils rich in humus. Another woodland ground cover, low-growing **lingonberry** (*Vaccinium vitis-idaea*), is hardy in Zones 5 to 8, tastes similar to cranberries, and is best after the first frost.

275

AUGUST
VINES & GROUND COVERS

 PLANNING

This is the month that the wear and tear of the growing season shows up on many garden plants when heat, drought, and other environmental stresses take their toll. Review plantings for the best and worst of your garden plants. Those plantings that repeatedly show drought stress this month might be best replaced with more drought tolerant selections. Smaller specimens might be transplanted to a shadier location with damper soil. Review where irrigation schedules and system design were inadequate and plan for improvements to implement for the next growing season. Disease-prone plants can be replaced by more resistant varieties or with different plant selections. This is a good time of year to examine how well matched plants are to their planting sites and to determine if they might fare better in a different position in the garden. Get prepared for fall planting season. Choose new homes for those that will be transplanted in fall. Remove failed plants now and mulch the bare ground in preparation for fall planting season in mid-September and October.

 PLANTING

This is the least optimal time to install new plants in the landscape. Save any specials you have purchased over the summer for September, keeping them in a shaded location. Check them daily for watering needs. Surround pots with mulch to help keep roots cool and damp. Direct sunlight on black nursery pots can raise soil temperatures to root-killing levels.

 CARE

Tie up any vines that may have worked loose during summer rain squalls or windy times. Clean up dead and damaged leaves from disease or drought. Don't put diseased plant parts in your home compost.

 PRUNING

Prune ground covers and vines as needed to keep them in bounds and groomed. Continue with monthly removal of long shoots on **wisteria**. Keep pruning light this month so as not to stimulate extra growth as plants should be hardening off for the dormant season.

Softwood cuttings can be taken of **kinnikinnick**, **sarcococca**, **ceanothus**, **jasmine**, and **grape**.

 WATERING

This is the month that symptoms of drought stress show up, particularly in areas that are not regularly irrigated. Common symptoms are scorched leaf edges, yellowing and dropping of inner leaves, and drooping of all the leaves. If you discover plants have completely wilted, water the soil immediately. Because dry soils can become "hydrophobic" and repel water, apply the water slowly. Pre-wetting the surface with a weak dish soap solution will help break the surface tension and allow water to soak in more readily. Don't forget to add some mulch to bare soils that have dried out. Coarse-textured mulches will help hold in moisture and improve water penetration when irrigation is applied.

 FERTILIZING

This is not the time for fertilizing vine and ground cover species.

PROBLEMS

Inspect plantings for general health. Many insect and disease problems will have taken their toll by this time—leaf damage and loss due to aphids and other insects as well as some blight diseases and plant death from root rot diseases. Get problems you don't recognize diagnosed through your local WSU or OSU Extension Master Gardener clinic. See Gardening Resources on the Web, page 288. Many local nurseries may also be of help. Frequently, the controls will occur at different time of year. With good diagnosis, you will be ready to follow up during the next growing season with cultural care and controls to reduce the problems. Collect a large enough sample, including healthy portions of the stems.

Leaves of **Oregon grape** (*Mahonia* sp.), commonly display dry curled edges of leaf scorch or whitish patches of powdery mildew at this later part of the growing season. It is not usually extensive enough to cause serious damage. Mildew can be reduced by pruning earlier in the growing season to thin plants and improve air circulation. Wash down leaves in the early part of the day before mildew has spread heavily throughout the plants. Leaf scorch is more common where plants are growing on droughty soils with exposure to sun.

Oregon grape

MYTH: PLANT GROUND COVERS FOR A MAINTENANCE-FREE GARDEN SOLUTION

While planting ground covers is a great improvement over dealing with the repeated work of weeding or mowing a difficult garden area, ground cover plants still require good cultural care to perform well. Ground cover plants are especially vulnerable during their first few years of establishment, when they can quickly be overcome by fast growing weeds or succumb to drying out in summer heat before their root systems have fully spread through the soil. Once established, ground covers do provide the benefits of reduced weeding, mulching, or mowing requirements. But just like other plants of the garden, they require routine well-timed cultural care for soil cultivation, weeding, fertilization, watering, and even periodic pruning to maintain their vigor and growth. Left unattended, even dense, established ground covers can have invasive species such as **English ivy**, **Scotch broom**, or **blackberry** creep in and overtake their space.

September
VINES & GROUND COVERS

PLANNING

Vivid seasonal color returns with the hues of fall color. Pause to take in the splendor, as viewed from indoors and out. This is a good month to see how the garden looks from inside views and outdoor approaches. Look to see where vines and ground covers will dress up high traffic entries and areas. Garden specimens with beautiful colors will be enhanced by companion evergreen ground covers. Traceries of delicate vines through trees and shrubs accent the tapestry of fall color and texture. Look for places to add fall blooming crocus to provide seasonal accent to ground cover beds.

PLANTING

This is a great time of year to get spreading ground covers planted. With moderate temperatures and warm soils, roots will continue to grow as top growth has slowed down. Returning seasonal rains also help new plantings at this time of year.

Containerized woody plants can also be planted this month. If you have stored plants over the summer, be sure to shake the container soil from the roots to break up any matted roots. Prune out woody roots that are kinked or circling. Pre-soak the roots thirty to sixty minutes before planting. (See Shrubs for planting details.)

CARE

Zones 4-6: This is a good time to prepare tender potted vines for over-wintering. Water about half as often now to encourage hardening off to dormancy. Remove dead leaves. Tie stems together for easier handling and storage.

Zones 7-9: Replenish mulch on bare ground at the base of vines. Coarse organic mulches such as wood chips and shredded leaves are good choices.

PRUNING

Prune vines lightly this month, clipping only broken or dead branches. No further pruning should be necessary until late winter or early spring.

WATERING

Taper off regular watering, but be sure to water anything that has become excessively dry. Winter injury can be more severe on plants that go into winter drought stressed.

FERTILIZING

Ground covers that spread by underground stems will benefit from a light application of nitrogen fertilizer the first half of this month (no more than two pounds actual nitrogen per 1000 square feet). Light applications benefit fall root growth and are absorbed for improved top growth in spring.

PROBLEMS

Plants which have suffered prolonged drought stress during the growing season will be more vulnerable to winter stress injuries. They may display premature fall color and leaf drop, or scorched and shriveled leaves which hang on to stems. Water these plants deeply now, as it can still take some time fall rains to penetrate dry soils. Where soils are bare, apply coarse organic mulch to improve moisture retention.

Before continued wet weather returns, clean up and remove leaves and plant debris where leaf spot and other blights have been present. Burn or otherwise dispose of this debris; never add it to home compost piles.

ENGLISH IVY CAN BE A REAL NUISANCE

Once touted as one of the best all-purpose vines and ground covers for the Pacific Northwest, English ivy has recently been included on the State Noxious Weed Lists in Washington and Oregon. The Washington list specifies four **English ivy** cultivars—*Hedera helix* 'Baltica', 'Pittsburg', 'Star', and *Hedera helix* 'Hibernica', while Oregon lists English ivy singly. 'Hibernica' has been found to be the most active invader of Western Washington woodlands. Ivy's rampant growth is suppressed in colder Zones 4 to 6.

Poor Soil Stabilizer: Many slope failures have occured on ivy-covered slopes after very heavy rain storms.

High Maintenance: With its rapid growth for extended periods of the year, frequent pruning and edging are required to keep it in bounds.

Plant Damage: The unchecked vigor can quickly smother low plantings and engulf taller shrubs and trees. Accumulated growth in trees can add weight and wind sail, contributing to increased tree failures in winter storm events. It can also smother out leaf area in the crown, further weakening tree health.

Invasiveness: English ivy's invasive habits are destructive to wild and cultivated plantings alike, smothering out valued plants as it quickly spreads across the ground or seeds into adjacent areas. On slopes and vertical positions, it will reach mature, flowering form, producing dark fruit which is spread by birds. Ivy seeds are capable of germinating in dry shade, a common condition beneath large trees.

Harbors Rodents: If its other habits aren't enough to dissuade its use, large expanses of ivy have also proven to be ideal havens for rats and other vermin.

What to Do: Choose alternate plants when seeking vines and ground covers for new plantings. Many nurseries now offer good "ivy alternatives."

The smaller-leafed, more timid growing ivies such as 'Glacier' are manageable in mixed container plantings.

Wherever possible, replace existing ivy with alternative plants.

Keep the edges of existing garden ivy trimmed and contained.

Slow seed dispersal by pruning out flower heads in the fall, before the seeds mature in early spring, or by removing ivy plants that have reached flowering stage.

MORE INFORMATION:
Washington State Noxious Weed Board—
www.wa.gov/agr/weedboard
Ivy OUT—http://ivyout.org
Oregon Department of Agriculture Noxious Weed Control—
http://egov.oregon.gov/ODA/PLANT
No Ivy League www.noivyleague.com

Be aware of the invasiveness of English ivy.

OCTOBER
VINES & GROUND COVERS

PLANNING

Enjoy the character of color and light that comes to the fall garden. Many nurseries have sales this month. Visit gardens and nurseries to see plants with great fall color. Make note of striking plant combinations, such as blue-leaved conifers alongside vines with deep hued autumn leaves. **Wisteria** colors to a warm yellow, while ornamental and fruiting grape range from yellows to purple. Carpets of evergreen ground covers provide lush contrast for a dramatic display of fall foliage changing above them. Choose plants that will add dramatic, late season color and prepare them for planting by the months end.

PLANTING

October is a great month for planting woody plants throughout the region (see Shrubs). Ground covers with spreading root systems can be divided now. Roots will put on continued growth after planting, while autumn soils are still warm and moist. These plants will have a great jump start on the next growing season. Remember to mulch around all new plants at planting time, and water if conditions are dry.

CARE

Autumn leaves are falling throughout the region this month, nature's season for replenishing the organic layer on the soil. Keep thick layers of leaves raked up where they accumulate on top of ground covers, lest they smother out the plants. Allow smaller bits of leaves that reach soil level without burying desired plants to remain. Shredded leaves are great mulch when tucked under ground covers.

Zones 4-6: Organize care for tender plants that need protection over winter. Move containers under cover in frost free storage such as a garage or heated shed. Choose a place with reasonable access to keep an eye on them over winter. Clean up dead leaves and water thoroughly before moving them into storage. Keep them moist throughout winter.

PRUNING

Most vines and ground covers do not require general pruning now, and none should be hard pruned at this time. However, masses of wild stems can be partially trimmed back for neater appearance and to reduce their being pulled about in the wind

all winter. This can be helpful for some of the Group III **clematis**, or **wisteria** that has grown into a tangle. Do not remove too much wood, and follow up in early spring with routine pruning and training.

WATERING

Landscape irrigation is rarely necessary this month as seasonal rainfall returns and increases throughout the region. Continue to check on and water containers.

FERTILIZING

This is a month off from applying fertilizers for vines and ground covers.

PROBLEMS

The effects of compacted and infertile soils often show up as bare areas. Such barren areas can be improved at this time of year with a generous layer of mulch. Where they are available, wood chips are an excellent choice, as are chopped leaves and very coarse compost. Crumble hard crusted surfaces first with a spade fork or hard rake. Don't work or tromp on wet soil, lest you cause more compaction. For severe areas that

GROUND COVERS UNDER LARGE TREES

The shady, root laden area under large trees can tend to become barren zones as lawn grasses and other plants fail to thrive under the shade and root competition. Attempts to encourage better growth of lawns and other plants by pruning the trees and adding more water are rarely effective solutions for the long term. The good news is that there are several types of ground covers adapted for use in these situations. Drought tolerant **sword fern** (*Polystichum munitum*), **wood rush** (*Luzula* sp.), and *Vancouveria hexandra*, are rugged choices that can be grown in combination under conifers or deciduous trees with heavy autumn leaf fall. Compliment them with naturalizing bulbs such as **snowdrops**, **daffodils**, or **scilla**. To mimic the profile of a lawn, plant low spreading ground covers such as *Euonymus fortunei* 'Kewensis', **Japanese spurge**, or **Oregon wood sorrel** (*Oxalis oregana*).

PLANTING TIPS:

• Fall planting will allow optimal time for roots to settle in before the flush of spring growth.

• Avoid damage to important small feeder roots as you prepare the site for planting: Do not dig up or rototill large areas of ground near trees.

• Apply coarse organic mulch such as wood chips or shredded leaves.

• Use plants from 6-inch or smaller containers to minimize tree root disturbance.

• Do not try to plant too close to tree trunks, especially where larger surface roots are present. Instead, plant a foot or more away with spreading plants that will fill in on their own.

• When watering newly planted ground covers under trees, be careful not to over-saturate the ground, and keep sprinkler sprays from direct contact with tree trunks.

SELECTIONS:
• **Carpet bugle** (*Ajuga reptans*)
• **Indian strawberry** (*Duchesnea indica*)
• *Epimedium perralderianum*
• **Ferns** (*Polystichum munitum* and other drought tolerant species)
• **Alpine strawberry** (*Fragaria vesca*)
• **Lily turf** (*Liriope spicata*)
• **Sorrel** (*Oxalis* sp.)
• **Japanese spurge** (*Pachysandra terminalis*)
• *Vancouveria hexandra*
• *Vinca minor*
• **Labrador violet** (*Viola labradorica*)
• **Barren strawberry** (*Waldsteinia fragarioides*)
See also Trees

Vinca minor (periwinkle)

are void of trees, shrubs, or other valued plants, mulch can be layered 8 inches deep. Go no deeper than 6 inches where trees and shrubs are growing and be sure to keep the mulch away from contact with their trunks. With the moisture from autumn rains and the action of soil insects and microbes encouraged by the organic mulches, compacted and infertile soils will show improvements in tilth, fertility, and moisture retention by the next spring.

NOVEMBER
VINES & GROUND COVERS

PLANNING

This is probably the least active month in the garden throughout the region, delivering the highest precipitation rates of the year, along with cooler and freezing temperatures. Thoughts and activities for vines and ground covers can be set aside this month.

PLANTING

Zones 4-6: For most areas in these zones, fall planting season ends as freezing temperatures return. New plants should all be watered in and mulched before winter conditions settle in.

Zones 7-9: Dormant-season planting of woody plants can continue while temperatures remain above freezing.

CARE

Zones 7-9: Bring in tender containerized vines early this month. Clean up dead leaves and tie stems together for easier handling and storage. Make a final pass at cleaning up accumulated leaves from ground covers toward the end of the month as leaf drop ends for the season.

Check hardy vines for secure attachment to their supports. Trim back any unnecessarily long stems that might catch in the wind.

PRUNING

This is a time off from pruning vines and ground covers, which will respond better with new growth when pruned in late winter and early spring. With routine pruning and grooming provided earlier in the year, robust woody vines can lend a beautiful form to the garden in their dormant state. Accentuate the pattern of a **wisteria, grape,** or **kiwi** by adding a winter string of lights to the arbor.

WATERING

Be sure containers have been well watered before they are put into storage.

Zones 4-6: Thoroughly water ground cover plantings before the ground freezes to reduce the incidence of cold injury in the coming winter. This is especially important for evergreen plants, which will continue to lose moisture when exposed to sun and wind, as well as all plants in "dry shadows" near building eaves or overhangs.

Zones 7-9: Irrigation is no longer a concern for landscape plants as we enter the coolest, wettest months of the year.

FERTILIZING

No landscape fertilization should occur this month. The onslaught of heavy rains can quickly wash away applied nutrients, dumping them into nearby waterways where they can add to pollution problems.

PROBLEMS

Zones 4-6: Be sure that ground covers and vines planted the previous year have been well mulched before the ground freezes. Covering plants for winter protection is helpful in areas where extremely cold temperatures persist while snow cover is sparse. Evergreen boughs and burlap can be used. Be sure the materials are secured tightly against being loosened by the wind.

Zones 7-9: Temperatures may remain frost free, or rapidly plunge from the 40s to below freezing in a sudden early cold snap. Have materials ready to provide hasty cover for plants vulnerable to freeze damage, such as new transplants or plants whose growth has not yet completely hardened off. Old lightweight blankets, sheets, tarps, or burlap are good quick cover for vulnerable new ground covers. Be sure to remove them as soon as temperatures return to above freezing.

VINES GROWING ON TREES

The heavy growth of English ivy over the entirety of a tree can become a maintenance nightmare.

Trees are often considered a great ready-made support for planting garden vines. In many garden situations, vines can be complimentary companions: a **climbing hydrangea** against a tall expanse of bare trunk on a **Douglas fir** or the surprise of blooms in a shade tree where delicate **clematis** has woven through the crown. At other times, vines can spell doom (or a maintenance nightmare) when heavy growth makes its way over the entirety of a tree. The extreme example is found in the invasive **English ivy** (*Hedera helix* 'Hibernica' and others) and **old man's beard** (*Clematis vitalba*) which can smother and break up larger trees as they grow to dense, heavy dimensions in their crowns. Vigorous garden vines can also cause similar trouble: **Wisteria, kiwi, honeysuckle,** and **grape** are some that should be kept away from trees. Less rampant growers such as hybrid **clematis** and some **climbing roses** are more easily grown in balance with a sturdy tree.

The dormant season is a good time of year to look closely at any vines growing on trees. If you find your trees are being overcome by invasive or planted vines, cut them away at the base of the tree along the soil line. It is not always necessary to remove the entire vine from the upper portions of the tree. In some cases, you may need the help of an ISA certified arborist to release a large tree that is being smothered or to remove excessive vine branches caught up in high branches. Uproot as much of invasive vines as you can from all around the trunk, and follow up on any new sprouts that might make their way back to the trunk.

If it is a garden vine that has gotten out of hand, cut it back near the base and begin a regular annual schedule of pruning to keep it in scale with the tree. Vines on trees should be pruned as routinely as those grown on a built support. And finally, keep an eye out for any vines that may have quietly slipped away from a support structure and made their way into nearby tree crowns.

DECEMBER
VINES & GROUND COVERS

PLANNING

The areas closest to the entrances to your home tend to have the most visibility of anywhere in the garden at this time of year. Do you like what you see as you come and go? Have planting areas become dull and barren at this point in the season? Bring colorful, bold textured plants with winter interest closer to the areas you frequent at this time of year. Liven up expanses of bare ground and stems with a bold textured evergreen ground cover such as low **Oregon grape** (*Mahonia repens* and *M. nervosa*), or with the brightly colored berries of **prostrate cotoneaster**.

PLANTING

Zones 4-6: It is typically too cold for planting this month.

Zones 7-9: Dormant-season planting of woody plants can continue, provided temperatures are above freezing and soils are not waterlogged. See Shrubs, page 203, for information on dormant season planting.

CARE

Zones 4-6: Gardening tasks are coming to a close this wintry month. Save evergreen boughs

to provide winter protection for vines and ground covers.

Zones 7-9: It is still a good time to complete any leaf clean up left over from last month and even to get some more mulch down on any remaining bare soil in the garden.

PRUNING

There are no routine pruning requirements for vines and ground covers this month.

WATERING

Remember to check on container plants in winter storage at least once a month, adding water if soil is very dry.

FERTILIZING

All zones: No landscape fertilization should occur this month.

The onslaught of heavy rains can quickly wash away applied nutrients, dumping them into nearby waterways.

PROBLEMS

Zones 4-6: When colder weather sets in and food sources diminish, deer browsing intensifies in gardens throughout the region. Protect any vines which have been targeted in previous years with wire fencing. To protect from the cold, light layers of evergreen boughs can protect newly planted and other vulnerable ground covers from both freeze and browse damage.

Zones 7-9: Keep materials such as light-weight blankets or burlap sheeting ready to provide hasty cover for vulnerable plants in case extended freezing weather descends.

WHAT DEER DON'T LIKE

These vines and ground covers are *least* favored by deer:
- *Clematis* spp.
- *Cotoneaster* spp.
- **Creeping rosemary** (*Rosmarinus officinalis* 'Prostratus')
- **Dwarf bamboo** (*Pleioblastsus pygmaeus* and *P. variegatus*)
- **Heath** (*Erica* spp.)
- **Kinnikinnick** (*Arctostaphylos uva-ursi*)
- *Lonicera* spp.
- **Native strawberry** (*Fragaria* spp.)
- *Wisteria* spp.
- **Wood sorrel** (*Oxalis oregana*)

PLANT HEALTH CARE & IPM

Integrated Pest Management (IPM) and Plant Health Care are current terms used to describe the holistic approach to reducing pests and improving plant health in the garden. It is a multi-faceted approach that takes into consideration the garden ecosystem and its influences on both plants and pests. The old stance of "see the pest, kill the pest" may seem to offer instant results, but isn't usually effective in the long run.

CONSIDER THAT:

• The time when the pest or its damage is first noticed may not be the best time for control applications. Spruce aphids feed in winter, but are no longer on the branches in late spring when damaged needles turn brown. Attempting control when the damage is present but the insect is not is a waste of time and resources.

• Broad-spectrum insecticides also kill beneficial predator insects, giving many pest insect populations the opportunity to spike to damaging levels.

• Leaf spot diseases may persist in spite of applied fungicides if the effects of frequent overhead irrigation are overlooked.

• The focus of pest control on a single plant type or pest can lead to a dependence on pesticide applications with marginal improvements to overall garden health and appearance.

• Insects and diseases may develop resistance to the products. Needlessly applied pesticides can create further pest and health problems as they accumulate in our gardens and the surrounding environment. In addition, the noticed pest may be a secondary symptom of plant stress from other causes.

IPM utilizes a combination of strategies to reduce pest damage.

1. **Identify the plant and pest.** When a plant health problem arises, the first step is accurate identification of the host plant and the pest problem. Contact your State Extension or a landscape professional for diagnostic assistance (See Gardening Resources on the Web). Some problems are host-specific and without plant identification, it's impossible to diagnose the problem accurately. Good identification of the pest along with data on its life cycle is essential in determining effective solutions.

2. **Collect a sample:** When collecting a sample for diagnosis, choose pieces with different stages of damage, as well as a piece that looks normal. Include suspected insects if they are present. Observe the plant and gather information. **When did the problem begin? Has this happened in previous years? What parts of the plant are most affected? Is it on a single plant or several? What else has happened nearby?** Take pictures and keep track of changes. This information will be valuable to those assisting you with diagnosis.

3. **Evaluate the threat:** After the problem has been identified, an evaluation of the problem in the context of the landscape is needed to determine the next step of action. **What is the potential impact of the damage—aesthetic or life threatening?** Be willing to accept some damage and imperfections as part of the life cycle of the garden. Manage only those pests which are truly life-threatening to valuable plants. **How important is the specimen to the landscape? Is the plant still**

IPM & PLANT HEALTH CARE

healthy enough to recover if the pest problem is brought under control?

Many gardeners feel they must try to save their ailing plants at all costs, yet removal may be the most effective long-term solution. A severely infested plant that continues to decline can harbor a pest or disease that may spread to other plants, and in the case of large trees, may also become unsafe. Replacement of pest prone plants with more resistant species or cultivars is an effective way to reduce garden pest problems, especially with plants such as roses, crabapples, and flowering cherries. On the other hand, a plant's pest problems may be due to being placed in the wrong site: sun-loving spruce will remain aphid-ridden in shady conditions; shade-loving *Skimmia* will accumulate mites in sunny exposures. In these cases, transplanting and selective removal of overcrowded plants become pest management tools.

4. Monitor the plant and pest throughout the growing season: Many plant problems can be successfully addressed with early identification and evaluation in the context of the larger landscape. Look for signs of emerging pest activity based upon the life cycle information gathered earlier. Assess the level of damage routinely. Many problems are cyclic, and may not need aggressive attention. Resident insect predators or seasonal weather changes may naturally suppress many pests.

There are, of course, some problems which are so life-threatening to valuable plants that pro-active management efforts are essential—such as the imported pest problems of Dutch elm disease and gypsy moth. In either case, monitoring of the plants and pests throughout their life cycle provides vital information for accurate timing of control measures. Professionals may use sticky traps with pheromone lures as a tool to track the emergence and population levels of some insect pests.

IPM brings into play **well timed control measures** at critical points in the pest life cycle. It combines cultural practices with least toxic materials and methods. This might include avoiding overhead irrigation and raking up fallen leaves on plants with leaf diseases, or providing supplemental irrigation to conifers vulnerable to bark beetles attracted to drought stressed trees.

This integrated approach can also be applied to many weed problems. Pulling or cutting weeds before seeds develop, applying coarse mulch to bare soil, spot treating the most serious weed threats and shading open ground with desirable landscape plants are examples of IPM strategies. The timing and selection of techniques will vary for different weed species, so, again, correct identification of the pest species and its life cycle is critical for effective management.

Many gardeners are surprised to find out that most common plant maladies are more due to environmental and cultural problems than directly from insects or diseases. Poor soils, too little or too much water, over crowding, the wrong amount of light, and too much or too little fertilizer are all cultural factors that can lead to a variety of plant problems.

Plant health care takes on a broader proactive approach to managing the health and appearance of the entire landscape, with IPM as a component. It assesses the garden environment as a whole and includes routine preventive tasks from putting the right plants in the right place, to seasonal pruning and mulching. The emphasis is on long-term landscape development rather than quick fixes.

Many plant problems can be minimized or avoided by choosing gardening practices that promote plant health and that complement the local soil and environmental conditions. Encourage natural suppression of pest problems by avoiding broad routine applications of pesti-

cides, herbicides, and fertilizers. It may take a few seasons for predators and beneficial organisms to return after scaling back on these materials. Take care of the soil—protect it from compaction and replenish organic matter with compost and mulch. Choose plants well adapted to the growing conditions of the site, and select resistant cultivars of pest-prone plant species. Include native species in your garden to support pest predators such as birds, spiders, and wasps. Use proper planting practices and continue aftercare during the first three years when adding new plants. Manage irrigation to avoid drought stress and promote soil water retention. Provide moderate seasonal pruning as needed to maintain good vigor and air circulation. Prevent mechanical injury to the trunks of trees and shrubs. Remove diseased plants and plant parts to reduce their spread.

While these techniques are generally beneficial, it is possible to have too much of a good thing. Excess watering, mulching, pruning and fertilization can all lead to plant health problems. As emphasized throughout this book, moderation is the key. It is a mistaken assumption that very vigorous plants will be more resistant to pest problems. These plants can be more inviting to some diseases and sucking insects. Woody plants with extremely rapid new growth may end up structurally weak, with flopping branches or more brittle stems. At the other extreme, drought stress and nutrient deficiencies which severely weaken plants will leave them more vulnerable to secondary pests such as borers and some root diseases. Good gardening practices will promote healthy plant growth that lies between these two extremes.

As an added caution, it is best to determine the source of plant symptoms before stepping up care. It is tempting to supply more water or to fertilize when leaves look stunted or droopy. However, if waterlogged soil, compaction, or root diseases are the culprits, these actions may not offer any help, and may make existing problems worse.

These and other plant health care techniques are described within the monthly chapter entries of this book. Gardening with an approach to plant health in the context of the larger landscape can lead to greater pleasure as you get acquainted with the seasonal rhythms and life cycles of your garden, with less focus on battling enemies. Remember that landscapes are dynamic—they grow and change over time. We need to expect that some plants may be lost, and that opportunities for new plants will follow in their place.

GARDENING RESOURCES ON THE WEB

You have the wide world of gardening at your fingertips when you log on to a computer and type in a few key words.

Here are some great reference websites for Northwest gardeners:

MASTER GARDENER SITES

Oregon:
http://extension.oregonstate.edu/mg/
Links to each county's Master Gardener program and clinic locations. You'll also find information about becoming a Master Gardener.

Washington:
http://mastergardener.wsu.edu/
A statewide site for Washington's Master Gardener program, with links to WSU Extension, each county's Master Gardener program and clinic locations, and the Master Gardener Foundation. You'll also find information about becoming a Master Gardener.

COOPERATIVE EXTENSION PUBLICATIONS

Oregon State University:
http://extension.oregonstate.edu/gardening/
Garden news, articles, calendars, weekly garden tips, and pest management information.

OSU Extension Publications:
http://eesc.oregonstate.edu/agcomwebfile/ EdMat/edmatindexgar.html

Washington State University:
http://gardening.wsu.edu
Read monthly gardening information for your region, do a "key word" search for plants or subjects, submit a question to "ask an expert," and follow links to specialty nurseries and native plant sources.

WSU Extension Publications:
http://pubs.wsu.edu/cgi-bin/pubs/index.html

PLANT DIAGNOSTICS

WSU Plant Health Care Website:
http://pep.wsu.edu/hortsense/
WSU's site devoted to Integrated Pest Management. Search the site by common cultural problems, diseases, and insects.

OSU Extension Page:
http://extension.oregonstate.edu/gardening/
This page has links to OSU's Urban Entomology site with bulletins, fact sheets and images of common insects and insect pests, and to OSU's Extension guide for plant disease control site with photos and management information.

University of California Statewide Integrated Pest Management Program:
http://www.ipm.ucdavis.edu/index.html
This site covers how to identify and manage pests, publications, and links with information useful to many common problems throughout the Northwest.

GARDENING RESOURCES ON THE WEB

WEEDS

Washington State Noxious Weed Board:
http://www.nwcb.wa.gov

Oregon Department of Agriculture: Plant Division, Oregon Invasive Species Council:
http://egov.oregon.gov/OISC/

The Invasive Species Initiative:
http://tncweeds.ucdavis.edu/esadocs.html has photos and weed management information for problem plants throughout the United States, including many for the Pacific Northwest.

PLANTS, ORGANIZATIONS AND SOCIETIES

Miller Horticultural Library:
www.millerlibrary.org is a reference website at the University of Washington Botanic Gardens in Seattle. See the "Plant Answer Line" to email a question to reference librarians (or call Monday through Friday, 9 a.m. to 5 p.m., 206-897-5268 (206-U W-PLANT).

Great Plant Picks:
www.greatplantpicks.org features more than 200 superior plants for gardens west of the Cascades.

Oregon State University Landscape Plants:
http://oregonstate.edu/dept/ldplants/index.htm is an online reference with plant photos and information sheets.

Native Plant Society of Oregon:
www.npsoregon.org has information on gardening with natives and a variety of programs and activities.

Washington Native Plant Society:
www.wnps.org has educational information and a Native Plant Stewardship volunteer program.

International Society of Arboriculture:
www.treesaregood.com is a consumer information web page covering a range of tree care topics and certified arborists links.

Pacific Northwest Chapter—International Society of Arboriculture:
www.pnwisa.org homepage has consumer information links: Certified Arborist lists; tree care information; hazard tree prevention.

Oregon Department of Forestry:
Urban and Community Forestry
http://www.Oregon.gov/ODF/URBAN_FOREST/urban_forests.shtml

Washington State Department of Natural Resources:
Washington Community Forestry Program
http://www.dnr.wa.gov/wcfc/

Plant Amnesty:
www.plantamnesty.org offers consumer information on plants and pruning; arborist and garden services referrals.

DID YOU KNOW?

MAKING SENSE OF PLANT NAMES

We know many of our favorite garden plants by their common names. Like nicknames, they are useful, and easy to remember. Lilacs are unmistakable by their common name. "*Hydrangea*" is both a botanical and common name. And some plants have so many common names it can be confusing. The botanical name belongs to the same plant the world over, and can be most useful in helping you locate the correct plant in a nursery or garden reference book.

Common name: European highbush cranberry

Botanical (species) name: *Viburnum opulus*

Genus—there may be many different species in a genus group.

Specific name—listed after genus, a single plant in the genus group.

Cultivar and **variety** names are listed next. They differ from the basic species by some quality of leaf color, fruit color or size, height, or form. They may also have a common name.

Cultivar—*Viburnum opulus* **'Nanum'**, dwarf European highbush cranberry

Variety—*Viburnum opulus* **var. *americanum*,** American highbush cranberry

Hybrids—*Viburnum* x *burkwoodii*, Burkwood's viburnum

NEW WOODY PLANTS FROM SOFTWOOD CUTTINGS

It can be fun to grow new vines, shrubs, or trees using softwood cuttings. Cuttings are best taken in cool weather conditions. Collect them in plastic bags to keep them from wilting. Look for long, healthy new shoots with several leaf nodes that have just begun to firm up. Prepare cuttings in the shade.

• Trim cuttings to 4 to 6 inches in length and remove leaves from the lower 2 to 3 inches of stem. Remove flower buds if they are present.

• Dip the stem ends in a rooting hormone powder or gel.

• Use a well drained potting soil mix containing extra perlite or pumice.

• Moisten the soil and use an old pencil as a dibble stick to make a hole in the soil for each cutting. Firm the soil around the cuttings as you set them in.

• Cover securely with plastic and set outdoors in a sheltered location out of direct sun.

Check the soil every few days to make sure it stays moist, not soggy, and doesn't dry out.

A super simple technique is to place a couple inches of moist soil mix and cuttings directly into a zip-lock bag, which can be easily opened and resealed as needed to vent excess moisture. Transfer the cuttings to individual containers when roots are visible through the plastic. Keep transplants in light shade. Some plants may grow large enough to plant out in fall; others may need another season's growth before they are large enough.

PUBLIC GARDENS

Here is a selected list of public gardens to visit in Oregon and Washington. Be sure to contact the garden before you visit to confirm days and times they are open to the public. Many have very informative web pages. More information on local gardens can be found in *The Northwest Gardeners' Resource Directory*, 9th ed., Debra Prinzing, Editor (Sasquatch Books, 2002).

WASHINGTON

Bellevue Botanic Garden
www.bellevuebotanical.org
12001 Main Street
Bellevue, WA 98005
425-452-2750

Bloedel Reserve
www.bloedelreserve.org
7571 N.E. Dolphin Drive
Bainbridge Island, WA 97110
206-842-7631

Carl S. English Jr. Botanical Garden at the Hiram M. Chittenden Locks
3015 N.W. 54th Street
Seattle, WA 98107
206-783-7059

Discovery Garden
http://skagit.wsu.edu/mg/discovery-gardens.htm
Mt. Vernon—WSU Research & Extension Unit
16602 State Route 536 (Memorial Highway)
Mt. Vernon, WA 98273
360-428-4270

Evergreen Arboretum & Gardens
www.evergreenarboretum.com
Legion Memorial Park
Alverson Avenue & West Marine View Drive
Everett, WA 98201
425-257-8300

Finch Arboretum
3404 W. Woodland Boulevard
Spokane, WA
509-624-4832

Kruckeberg Botanic Garden
www.kruckeberg.org
20312 15th Ave. N.W.
Shoreline, WA 98177
206-542-4777

Manito Park
www.thefriendsofmanito.org
S. Grand at 18th Avenue
Spokane, WA
509-625-6622

Meerkerk Rhododendron Gardens
www.meerkerkgardens.org
3531 Meerkerk Lane
Whidbey Island, WA 98253
360-678-1912

Ohme Gardens
www.ohmegardens.com
3327 Ohme Road
Wenatchee, WA 98801
509-662-5785

PUBLIC GARDENS

Point Defiance Park - Gardens
www.Metroparkstacoma.org
5400 N. Pearl Street
Tacoma, WA 98405
253-305-1070

Rhododendron Species Botanical Garden
www.rhodygarden.org
2525 S. 336th Street
Federal Way, WA 98003
253-838-4646

University of Washington Botanic Gardens
www.Metroparkstacoma.org
- Center for Urban Horticulture - Miller Library -
  Hyde Herbarium - Union Bay Natural Area
  3501 N.E. 41st Street
  Seattle, WA 98105
  206-523-8616

- Washington Park Arboretum
  2300 Arboretum Drive E.
  Seattle, WA 98115
  206-543-8800

Washington Park Arboretum
2300 Arboretum Center for Urban Horticulture
Elisabeth C. Miller Library
Union Bay Natural Drive E.
Seattle, WA 98112
206-543-8800

Yakima Area Arboretum & Botanical Garden
www.ahtrees.org
1401 Arboretum Drive
Yakima, WA 98901
509-248-7337

Seattle Parks & Recreation - Gardens
www.seattle.gov/parkspaces/gardens.htm
- Japanese Garden
- Kubota Garden
- Volunteer Park Conservatory
- Woodland Park Rose Garden

OREGON

Berry Botanic Garden
www.berrybot.org
11505 S.W. Summerville Avenue
Portland, OR 97219
503-636-4112

Crystal Springs Rhododendron Garden
www.parks.ci.portland.or.us/Gardens/
publicgardens.htm
S.E. 28th and S.E. Woodstock Boulevard
Portland, OR 97286
503-771-8386

Hoyt Arboretum
www.hoytarboretum.org
4000 S.W. Fairview Boulevard
Portland, OR 97221
503-228-TREE (8733)

Leach Botanical Garden
www.parks.ci.portland.or.us/Gardens/
publicgardens.htm
6704 S.E. 122nd Avenue
Portland, OR 97236
503-823-9503

Mount Pisgah Arboretum
www.efn.org/~mtpisgah
34901 Frank Parish Road
Eugene, OR 97405
541-741-4110

Portland International Rose Test Garden
www.parks.ci.portland.or.us/Gardens/
publicgardens.htm
400 S.W. Kingston Avenue
Portland, OR 97201
503-823-3636

Classical Chinese Garden
www.portlandchinesegarden.org
N.W. 3rd and Everett
Portland, OR 97208
503-228-8131

BIBLIOGRAPHY

Allen, Chrisstine. *Growing up: a gardener's guide to climbing plants for the Pacific Northwest.* Vancouver, Stellar Press, 2002.

Armitage, Allan. *Armitage's Manual of Annuals, Biennials, and Half-Hardy Perennials.* Timber Press, Portland, 2001.

Armitage, Allan M. *Herbaceous Perennial Plants.* Varsity Press, Athens, Georgia, 1989.

Brenzel, Kathleen Norris, editor. *Sunset Western Garden Book.* Sunset Publishing Corp., Menlo Park, 2001.

Brickell, Christopher. *The American Horticultural Society Pruning and Training.* New York, NY: DK Publishing, Inc., 1996

Brooklyn Botanic Garden. *Shrubs: the new glamour plants.* Bob Hyland, guest editor. Brooklyn, NY: Brooklyn Botanic Garden, Inc. 1994.

Cook, Dr. Tom. "Maintaining a Healthy Lawn in Western Oregon," EC1521, OSU Extension, 2000.

Dirr, Michael A. *Manual of Woody Landscape Plants.* Stipes Publishing, 1998.

DiSabato-Aust, Tracy. *The Well-Tended Perennial Garden.* Timber Press, Portland, Oregon, 1998.

Dunn, Teri and Morris, Ciscoe. *Beautiful Roses Made Easy.* Cool Springs Press, 2003.

Fitzgerald, Tonie. "Landscaping with Native Plants in the Inland Northwest", MISC 0267, WSU Extension, 2000.

Fitzgerald, Tonie. "Lawn Care for the Inland Northwest," Spokane Extension, WSU.

Fitzgerald, Tonie. "Gardening in the Inland Northwest", MISC0304. WSU Extension 2001.

Grant, John A. and Carol L. *Trees and Shrubs for Pacific Northwest Gardens, 2nd Ed.* Portland, OR: Timber Press, 1990.

Grissell, Eric. *Insects and Gardens.* Portland, OR: Timber Press, 2001.

Hansen, Richard, and Stahl, Friedrich. *Perennials and Their Garden Habitats.* Timber Press, Portland, Oregon, 1993.

Harris, Richard W., James R. Clark, and Nelda P. Matheny. *Arboriculture, 4th ed.: Integrated Management of Landscape Trees, Shrubs, and Vines.* Upper Saddle River, New Jersey: Prentice Hall. 2004.

Heath, Brent and Becky. *Daffodils for American Gardens.* Elliott and Clark Publishing, Washington, D.C., 1995.

Heath, Brent and Becky. *Tulips for North American Gardens.* Bright Sky Press, Albany, Texas, 2001.

Hume, Ed. *Gardening With Ed Hume.* Sasquatch Books, Seattle, 2003.

Hunter, Raymond. "Establishing a Lawn in Eastern Washington," EB1153, WSU Extension, 2000.

Huxley, Anthony ed. *Success with House Plants.* Reader's Digest Association, 1981.

BIBLIOGRAPHY

Jalbert, Brad and Peters, Laura. *Roses for Washington and Oregon*. Lone Pine Publishing, 2003.

Kruckeberg, Arthur R. *Gardening with Native Plants of the Pacific Northwest*. Seattle, WA: University of Washington Press, 1982.

Link, Russell. *Landscaping for Wildlife in the Pacific Northwest*. Seattle, WA: University of Washington Press, 1999.

Lovejoy, Ann. *Seasonal Bulbs*. Cascadia Gardening Series, Sasquatch Books, Seattle, 1995.

McHoy, Peter. *The Complete Houseplant Bible*. Lorenz Books, 2004.

Olkowski, William, Sheila Daar, and Helga Oklowski. *Common-Sense Pest Control*. Newtown, CT: The Taunton Press, 1991.

Pinyuh, George and E. Blair Adams. "Houseplants," EB 1354, Washington State University Extension, rev. 1993.

Souders, Cindy and Susan Oliver. *Olympic Peninsula Gardening Book*. PenPrint Inc., Port Angeles, Washington, 2002.

Spurr, Joy, editor. *Cuttings Through the Year, 5th ed.* Seattle, WA: Arboretum Foundation, 2003

Stahnke, Dr. Gwen. "Home Lawns," EB 0482, WSU Extension, rev. 2004.

Stell, Elizabeth. *Secrets to great soil : a grower's guide to composting, mulching, and creating healthy, fertile soil for your garden and lawn*. Pownal, Vt.: Storey Pub., 1998

VanMiert, John and Cheryll Kingsley. *Garden Sense: A Book of Common Wisdom*. Self-published, 2003.

Wasson, Ernie, Chief Consultant. *The Complete Encyclopedia of Trees and Shrubs*. San Diego, CA: Thunder Bay Press, 2003.

WSU Master Gardeners, Spokane. "Roses for the Inland Northwest," MISC0251, Washington State University Extension.

Zucker, Isabel. *Flowering shrubs and small trees. Revised and expanded by Derek Fell*. New York, NY:Friedman/Fairfax Publishers, 1995.

PHOTOGRAPHY CREDITS

Liz Ball and Rick Ray: Pages 73, 137, 140, 228, 229 (bottom), 243, 249, 254, 275

Tom Eltzroth: Pages 33, 45, 48, 63, 70, 77-79, 87, 88, 90, 97, 98, 100, 103-107, 118, 126, 184, 131-133, 145, 157, 159, 163, 164, 175-177 (top), 201-205 (top), 223, 229-233 (top), 237, 245, 263, 264, 267, 268, 270, 277, 281

Pam Harper: Page 201

Charles Mann: Page 173

Netherland Flower Bulb Assoc.: Page 60

Jerry Pavia: Pages 7-22 (top), 34, 37, 46, 51-53 (top), 64, 149-151, 175 (bottom), 218, 221, 234, 238

Ralph Snodsmith: Page 279

Neil Soderstrom: Pages 40, 43, 54, 56, 59, 66, 74, 84, 152, 161, 169, 170, 191, 211, 215

Mark Turner: Page 7

Andre Viette: Pages 95, 257-261, 273

PLANT INDEX
BY COMMON NAME

PLANT INDEX

PLANT INDEX

PLANT INDEX

PLANT INDEX

PLANT INDEX

PLANT INDEX

PLANT INDEX

MEET THE AUTHORS

MARY ROBSON has been dedicated to the green world since she helped move threatened trilliums from the Ohio woods to a wildflower preserve at age 9, helping her gardening mother. She worked for Washington State University Extension for 17 years, 8 years as coordinator for the Master Gardeners of King County, and 9 years as faculty Horticulture Extension agent. She's known for her skill in speaking, writing, and educating. She's trained over 2000 WSU Master Gardeners in King and Pierce Counties, and received a Community Leadership Award in 2004 from the Seattle Garden Club for her contribution to educating Northwest gardeners.

She has steady experience in answering gardening questions as writer of 'The Practical Gardener' for *The Seattle Times* since 1992. Mary wrote the *Washington and Oregon Gardener's Guide* with co-author, Debra Prinzing (2005). Her education includes a B.A from Middlebury College, Vermont, and an M.A from The Johns Hopkins University, Baltimore.

CHRISTINA PFEIFFER is a Seattle area horticulture consultant, garden writer and instructor who has worked with landscape plants all of her adult life. Previously, she led horticultural care and renovation for the plant collections at The Washington Park Arboretum in Seattle, and at the Holden Arboretum in Ohio. Christina did her undergraduate training in horticulture at Michigan State University and completed an M.S. in urban horticulture from the University of Washington. She is an ISA Certified Arborist and a member of the Washington Park Arboretum Bulletin Editorial Board. She gardens for pleasure at home with her husband and son, and also volunteers with children's gardening activities at the Magnuson Children's Garden and at her son's elementary school.

ENJOY THESE OTHER HELPFUL BOOKS FROM COOL SPRINGS PRESS

Cool Springs Press is devoted to state and regional gardening and offers a selection of books to help you enjoy gardening where you live. Choose Cool Springs Press books with confidence.

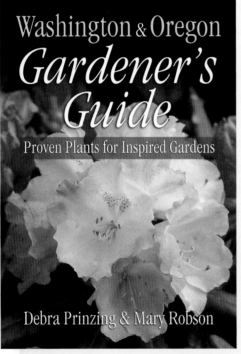

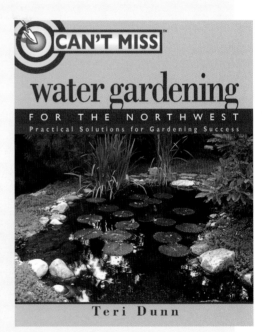

Washington & Oregon Gardener's Guide
ISBN# 1-59186-112-8 • $24.99

Can't Miss Water Gardening for the Northwest
ISBN# 1-59186-152-7 • $18.99

COOL SPRINGS PRESS
A Division of Thomas Nelson Publishers
Since 1798

www.coolspringspress.net

See your garden center, bookseller, or home improvement center for these Cool Springs Press titles. Also, be sure to visit www.coolspringspress.net for more great titles from Cool Springs Press.